W9-BAW-901

DATE DUE			

FIVE GREAT PLAYS
FROM THE GERMAN THEATRE

NATHAN THE WISE The spirited drama in which Lessing gave direct and elevated expression to the ideals of religious tolerance

EGMONT Goethe's splendid depiction of a noble revolutionary whose unworldliness frustrates his lofty dreams of freedom

MARY STUART Schiller's dramatization of the historic clash of two strong-willed women—Elizabeth I and Mary Queen of Scots

THE PRINCE OF HOMBURG The shattering effect of a decreed execution upon a brave young Prussian officer

DANTON'S DEATH The breathless pace of the French Revolution and its hero-victims, Danton and Robespierre, caught in the swirl of unleashed revolution

The Library of World Drama presents these outstanding dramatic works in vivid new translations.

THE LIBRARY OF WORLD DRAMA

JOHN GASSNER

*Sterling Professor of
Dramatic Literature
Yale University*

GENERAL EDITOR

CLASSICAL GERMAN DRAMA

TRANSLATED BY
THEODORE H. LUSTIG

WITH AN INTRODUCTION
AND PREFACES BY
VICTOR LANGE
PRINCETON UNIVERSITY

BANTAM BOOKS / NEW YORK

CLASSICAL GERMAN DRAMA

Published as a Bantam Classic / January 1963

Library of Congress Catalog Card Number: 63-8352
All rights reserved.
© Copyright, 1963, by Bantam Books, Inc.
Published simultaneously in the
United States and Canada.

CONTENTS

Classical German Drama

The German Classical Theatre

BY

JOHN GASSNER

In the history of the theatre, as well as in the world's dramatic literature, the German classical drama holds a unique place. It arrives late in the development of the national culture of which it is a part, having been retarded twice, once by the Protestant Reformation and the ensuing religious conflicts culminating in the Thirty Years War that ravaged Central Europe from 1618 to 1648, and later, but less seriously, by the rigidity of French neo-classicism imposed on the eighteenth-century German stage. German drama, moreover, developed under conditions unfavorable to strict classicism. If the individual works are to be called classical, they are, more often than not, *unclassically* classical. They are classical in the loose sense that they are the classics of German literature, and in the particular sense that they represent efforts to establish the drama on the most austere intellectual and artistic levels compatible with the individual taste and talent of each author.

This is evident enough in the most distinguished work of the period under consideration, which extends roughly from the last quarter of the eighteenth to the first third of the nineteenth century. To this period belong the nation's leading dramatists before the advent of late nineteenth-century naturalism which brought Gerhart Hauptmann into the theatre in 1890; and several of these dramatists—Lessing, Goethe, and Schiller—also happen to be among Germany's most celebrated authors of non-dramatic literature. All of them, moreover, enjoined upon themselves and the German theatre an obligation to attain the "high-seriousness" in art that we associate with the idea of classicism. Universality, or the search for universal principle, is their aim, but hardly less earnest is their striving for relatedness to individual and social reality, which is in their case only another aspect of their desire ("idealistic" in Schiller's case, "materialistic" in Büchner's) to find universal law operative in the world.

A considerable degree of "toughmindedness" can indeed be

located in the midst of the superficially romantic matter of the dramatists represented in the present volume. It appears in numerous instances such as Goethe's well-known conclusion (after much personal experience) that classicism is health whereas romanticism is disease, not to mention the very demonstration of the need to see things in perspective and to resist extreme subjectivity or the morbid inclinations of egocentricity as in his famous play about a poet, *Torquato Tasso*; as well as in the conclusion of the second part of *Faust* in which the ever-questing hero translates his "Faustian" spirit into the limited practical activity of building dams and draining swamps in the small sector of the world on which he endeavors to establish a sound and prosperous society. This after illimitable aims!—or, as Faust himself puts it so well in the last act of the play, *erst gross und mächtig;/ Nun aber geht es weise, geht bedächtig*. Even in so early a work as *Egmont,* he takes a great step forward beyond the Storm and Stress fervor of his *Götz von Berlichingen,* as Ronald Peacock has observed, because he "creates in the person of Egmont a symbol for himself and for an attitude toward life, and therewith becomes apparent an early form of a profound Goethean problem, namely the conflict between personal romanticism and social or moral realities" (*Goethe's Major Plays,* pp. 4–5). Egmont, as Peacock says, "cannot fulfil his ideal of his personal genius and its way of life and at the same time, by political realism and skill, be the benefactor of his people" (p. 10). A sense of limit, along with a hard-won realization of the need for *Entsagung,* renunciation, in life, lies at the heart of Goethean classicism. One may be reminded here of T. E. Hulme's statements that "in the classical attitude you never seem to swing along to infinite nothing" and that "you are always faithful to the conception of a limit" (*Speculations,* p. 120). In various ways, it is possible to discover the crystallization of a similar attitude in such "romantic" figures as Schiller and Kleist. And, finally, we arrive at such a strong fibre in the heartbreakingly young and idealistic Georg Büchner that "classicism" passes over into "naturalism," a territory not usually considered adjacent to it. "God," wrote Büchner in justifying *Danton's Death,* "didn't create history to provide reading matter for young females"; and in his novel *Lenz,* he declared that he demanded in all things "life, the possibility of existence," and that it was not the artist's business to ask whether the work of art is beautiful or ugly: "The feeling that there's life in the thing created is much more important than considerations of beauty and ugliness." Goethe and Schiller would not have gone along with him, of course, and in such statements, as well as in Büchner's great fragment *Woyzeck* and some portions of *Danton's Death,* we are well past the Weimar friends' idealistic formulation for writing and performing plays.

The dramatists are not content with the flux of experience or with the incidence of mere accident in life. In one way or another, whether they draw promissory notes on future human enlightenment (as in *Nathan the Wise*) or predicate tragic fatality in their work, they manifest a sense of destiny in the affairs of men. They tend to observe humanity, moreover, in a historical or quasi-historical matrix, thereby giving further significance to a character's endeavors, errors, and circumstances. We can observe the connection between individual fate and history in three of the five plays of the present volume: *Egmont, Mary Stuart,* and *Danton's Death.* And it is not by accident that Lessing set the philosophical drama of *Nathan the Wise* in the Holy Land during the time of the Crusades, involving the three principal religions of Europe and the Middle East in Nathan's story, or that Kleist associated the psychological drama of *The Prince of Homburg* with the historical role and disciplinary ideal of eighteenth- and nineteenth-century Prussia. A sense of period and place appears, in fact, in a large number of the authors' other plays, such as Lessing's *Minna von Barnhelm* and *Emilia Galotti,* Goethe's romantic *Götz von Berlichingen* and anti-romantic *Torquato Tasso,* and Schiller's numerous historical dramas from the early *Fiesco* and *Love and Intrigue* (*Kabale und Liebe*) to the *Wallenstein* trilogy and *Wilhelm Tell,* written toward the close of his life.

One might conclude from the historical backgrounds of many of the plays that when German culture arrived at a national drama it did so with an international or universal as well as with a national orientation. And it is significant that its "classicism" is more or less blended with the romantic afflatus and outlook to which classicism theoretically represents an absolute opposite. In this matter it is possible indeed to be at odds with categorizing criticism and literary historiography, but this is too large a subject to be dealt with here. It is more important to observe that it is precisely to the fact that no absolute classicism was attained that many of the plays owe their dramatic vitality and literary value.

If *Nathan the Wise,* for example, can be set down as neoclassical in its verbal texture and in the rationalism of its argument, the complicated plot and liberal sentiments can be de-

scribed as somewhat "romantic." (The doctrine could certainly
be so designated—and probably also *derogated*—by foes of the
perfectibility-of-man, idea-of-progress, and trust-in-nature Rous-
seauist cult such as Irving Babbitt, T. E. Hulme, Wyndham
Lewis, and, during at least a part of his career, T. S. Eliot.) Yet
there is nothing so appealing in *Nathan the Wise* as Lessing's
blending of "head" and "heart"—his being, so to speak, cool
with argument and warm with sentiment in the same work,
dedicated to a blending of rationalism and religion that some of
their strict proponents would regard as contradictory. Both
Goethe and Schiller struggled hard to achieve a victory over
much ingrained romanticism when they aimed at the classical
in their work. Goethe surmounted the *Götz von Berlichingen*
and *The Sorrows of Young Werther* element in his later work,
and resolved the conflict between sentiment and the sense of
reality in his *Iphigenia in Tauris* and *Torquato Tasso*. He accomplished this to some degree, also, in his study of character
as destiny in *Egmont,* while Schiller subdued the inchoate youthful idealism of *The Robbers* and other early work when he arrived at his mature work. Kleist mastered excessive individualism
and *morbidezza* in *The Prince of Homburg,* and Büchner gave
attention to historical necessity and expressed disillusion with
the glowing, romantic promises of revolution in *Danton's Death*.
In every instance it is the combination of disparate elements and
the conflict or tension between them that constitute the life of
the work. Whatever classicism there is in it—and this is most
manifest as a quality of balance or control that constitutes the
intelligence and artistry of the work—is not at all anachronistic
or "academic."

Such classicism made its appearance in anything but a calm
and orderly "classical" period; the historical background of the
authors comprises the French (and, let us not forget, the American) Revolution, the Napoleonic era of wars and invasions,
and, in the case of Büchner, the struggle against the political
reaction ushered in by the final defeat of Napoleon, and against
the suppression of liberalism. Büchner was a radical pamphlet-
eer and political fugitive during his all-too-brief career. Kleist
was fired for a while by the struggle against Napoleon and by a
flaring up of nationalist sentiment in politically divided Germany.
Goethe was disturbed by the French Revolution and Schiller
became disillusioned in it, although his own work was associated
with the passion for liberty to such an extent that the Assembly
in Paris made him an honorary citizen of the French Republic.
Lessing experienced the Seven Years War at close hand as secre-

tary to General Taudenzien, the governor of Breslau, and was in his last years notably involved in the conflict between partisans of liberal and orthodox theology. *Nathan the Wise* was written during the revolutionary struggle of the American colonies against British rule, and was published in 1779, less than three years after their Declaration of Independence.

The classical German drama was not, then, created on a foundation of social and political stability, and there was also considerably more flux than fixity in the labors of its authors. Goethe's entire life and his poetic masterpiece *Faust,* which occupied him for more than half a century, testify to a long career of experiment and adventure on constantly changing ground. Lessing's work runs the gamut of eighteenth-century dramatic style, including romantically colored comedy-of-manners (*Minna von Barnhelm*), middle-class or bourgeois tragedy (*Miss Sara Sampson* and *Emilia Galotti*), and rationalist philosophical drama (*Nathan the Wise*). Schiller undertook experiments in classical choral tragedy in *The Birds of Messina,* tragedy of fate in *Wallenstein,* lyrical drama in *Wilhelm Tell,* political drama in *Don Carlos,* and "bourgeois tragedy" or "social drama" in *Kabale und Liebe.* In the course of a pathologically abbreviated career, Kleist moved restlessly from one type of drama to another (comedy, tragedy, historical and psychological drama) before killing himself at the age of 34 in a double suicide compact. In writing *Danton's Death* and *Woyzeck* in the years 1835–36, Büchner anticipated both late nineteenth-century naturalism and twentieth-century expressionism.

The theatre of the period covered in the present volume manifests the same flux of styles as the dramatic literature and a similar quest for a species of art at once elevated and natural. During Lessing's youth, the leading actress-manager, Caroline Neuber (1692–1760), adopts and later partly drops neo-classic style, "blending French stateliness with German emotion," as the *Oxford Companion to the Theatre* puts it. In the theatre, too, Lessing, functioning as drama critic between 1767 and 1768, wages war on French neo-classicism and deplores the example of Corneille while extolling that of Shakespeare, and he advocates an acting style midway between marmoreal formalism and casual naturalism. The prominent actor Konrad Ekhof (1720–78), whose art exemplified Lessing's specifications, establishes a German academy of acting as early as 1757; and in 1765, Konrad Ackerman (1710–71) endeavors to create a national theatre at Hamburg, which was then becoming the intellectual center of Germany. Ackerman's intentions miss realization

despite the support of Lessing as critic and publicist, but efforts
to create the kind of theatre he had in view are continued in
other cultural centers such as Gotha, Mannheim, and Vienna
by the celebrated Wilhelm Iffland (1759–1814) and others.
Another distinguished actor-manager, Friedrich Ludwig Schröder
(1744–1816), undertakes to play Richard III, Othello and Lear,
and secures the success of Shakespearean drama and its influence
on the German stage with his productions. A suitably named
"Storm and Stress" romanticism, extravagant and violent, cap-
tures the German theatre for a while, giving rise to the early
plays of Goethe and Schiller, *Götz von Berlichingen* (1773)
and *The Robbers* (1781) respectively. Thereafter, the old, un-
naturally restrictive neo-classicism having been driven out of the
theatre, efforts are made to restore the balance and reintroduce
order and dignity. An extreme approach to idealizing, anti-
naturalistic stage production is followed by Goethe as director
of the theatre at Weimar when he turns to classicism in the
1790's and proceeds to stamp out emotional and realistic acting.

Goethe, as he told his admirer Eckermann, wanted the actor
to go to school to a sculptor or painter to acquire that natural
grace in sitting, standing and walking which he would need in
playing classic characters. At the same time, the actor should
cultivate his mind with diligent study of classic and modern
writers—so that he might add "a higher tone to his entire personality and deportment." To the ideality of performance the
actor should bring, moreover, great purity of speech, which
culminated, both at its best and its worst, in a style of de-
livery that approximated operatic recitative and was properly
criticized and later banished from realistic acting. (Hauptmann satirized it in *The Rats* in 1911 as a vestige of artificial
acting style.) Goethe, in his capacity of stage director, made
every effort to ensure a classically pure production even for
plays we should be inclined to designate as romantic rather
than classical, and to this end he gave thought to every detail of
production and performance. Notes kept by two actors of the
Weimar company to whom he gave some close instruction in
the year 1802 were assembled for publication in 1824 by Eckermann under the title of *Rules for Actors*. These "rules" require
the actor to use his limbs easily and harmoniously, to refrain
from turning his back to the audience, and to speak toward
the audience, keeping at least three quarters of his face toward
the spectators; further, he should forget neither the character
he addresses on the stage nor the public; and finally, he
should realize that he is obliged to present reality *ideally* rather

than literally and that he is to combine ease with formality, truth with beauty, in his performance. On his part, Goethe ensured ideality in staging the play; he tried to have as little traffic as possible with detailed, strictly illusionistic, settings and rejected the use of the box-set that was coming into vogue because it took the action into a confining realistic environment. For Goethe, the "truth of nature" was one thing and the "truth of beauty" another. For Schiller, too, mere theatrical illusion was contemptible deception. Schiller believed that the playgoer's mind should be able to detach itself from the emotions and should not be overwhelmed by the passions. The true artist disdains to excite "the blind force of the affections" and attains the perspective on things, the sense of propriety, proportion and order, that we often call "esthetic distance."

Goethe and Schiller, once joined in abiding friendship at Weimar, promulgated the idea of a theatre dedicated to effectuating ideal representations of life by means of dignified phrasing and gesturing as well as carefully maintained groupings. Their "clinical" principles reached well beyond the little duchy of Weimar, as far as Berlin. And while the Weimar style became deplorably artificial, German stagecraft was revitalized by a succession of gifted actors and directors such as Ludwig Devrient (1784–1832), Karl Immermann (1796–1840), and (in Vienna) Josef Schreyvogel (1766–1832). At the same time, while German drama deteriorated on the whole under the extravagances of the Romantic School after 1800, the sober, comparatively classical modes of drama represented in the present volume became a national heritage. It even found a gifted immediate successor in the Austrian dramatist Franz Grillparzer (1791–1872), the author of beautifully written semi-classical plays such as *Sappho* (1819) and *The Golden Fleece* (1822). And in entering into the national stream (constituting a large portion of it, indeed) the plays of Lessing, Goethe, and Schiller entered into the stream of Western theatre as a whole in the nineteenth century, while the plays of Kleist and Büchner began to flow into it in the twentieth.

To the theatre of the English-speaking world, the main classical German contribution was Goethe's *Faust,* and next to it, it would appear, Schiller's, *Mary Stuart,* although the latter's most impressive dramatic work, the *Wallenstein* trilogy, was translated by Samuel Taylor Coleridge as early as 1799. *Nathan the Wise* had two productions in New York City during the World War II period in the early 1940's, and *Mary Stuart* had successful American and British productions in the 1950's.

Earlier, Schiller was represented in the Helena Modjeska
repertoire (February-March, 1900) at the Fifth Avenue Theatre
in New York, with *Mary Stuart;* and in Richard Mansfield's
repertoire at the New Amsterdam Theatre in New York (March-
April, 1906), with *Don Carlos,* revived in New York for the first
time in 56 years in 1962 in an off-Broadway production that
could scarcely be described as successful. (This does not, of
course, take into account German-language productions in the
United States, such as those given in New York City at the Irving Place Theatre at the beginning of our century in a note-
worthy repertory—"certainly," as Lee Simonson was to recall in
1943, "the most extraordinary repertory theatre this city has had
in the last fifty years and one whose history has been almost
entirely neglected." Schiller was represented here with *Die
Jungfrau von Orleans, Don Carlos,* and *Wallensteins Tod.*) Goethe
fared less well in the American theatre, although Sir Henry
Irving brought a production of *Faust* with him on one of his
successful American tours, and the young Theatre Guild made a
valiant but unsuccessful attempt to put *Faust* into its New York
repertory with a production in the fall of 1928 that included such
outstanding actors as Dudley Digges, George Gaul, and Gale
Sondergaard.

In inviting the eminent scholar-critic Victor Lange to edit the
present volume of new translations for the World Drama series,
Bantam Books has endeavored to give some representation to an
important body of dramatic literature.

Introduction

BY

VICTOR LANGE

Drama is at its best the product not merely of private inspiration nor public pathos but of judicious social and intellectual criticism; it can be truly achieved only by an artist who commands a mature and comprehensive view of the issues that shape his age and who is determined, above all, to assert the power as well as the frailty of the human judgment. G. E. Lessing, the most admirable German critic of the eighteenth century, is also the first German dramatist of such universal stature; for in that astonishing efflorescence of the European drama in the seventeenth century, Germany had almost no share. Physically ravaged by the Thirty Years' War and socially divided by dynastic and religious allegiances, it could offer neither an audience nor the kind of intellectual curiosity and vitality that made the French, Spanish, and English theatre so effective and articulate. The capricious patronage of countless petty courts and the prevailing academic notions of dramatic form and subject matter limited the scope of the stage and the drama to ecclesiastical and humanistic circles.

Only one distinguished playwright, Andreas Gryphius (1616–64), produced in Germany a body of drama comparable in vision to the achievements of his contemporaries and masters Vondel, Corneille, and Molière. Gryphius' travels in Holland, Italy, and France revealed to him an interest abroad in dramatic and theatrical art such as his own country could not provide, and in his large, violent, and flamboyant plays (*Leo Armenius,* 1650; *Carolus Stuardus,* 1659) he attempted to write tragic spectacles in the neoclassical manner, historical in subject, essentially rhetorical, and preoccupied with the dependence of even the great upon the inexorable workings of fate and retribution. Gryphius' somewhat stilted pathos and his early delight in an exuberant display of language gave way to a more intricate and conscientious dramatic design in his best tragedy, *Cardenio und Celinde* (1657); but he is most effective and most influen-

9

tial in his comedies, *Absurda Comica oder Herr Peter Squentz* (1658) and *Horribilicribrifax* (1663). In these he seems entirely independent of any compelling models: in a series of grotesque situations, and through absurd characters and a deliberately precious or bombastic provincial speech, he exposes the inanities and pretensions of men and women in all strata of society.

Gryphius is the first German playwright to bridge the gulf that existed between the academic principles of classicist dramaturgy and the interests of a heterogeneous audience that was all too seldom given an opportunity to recognize itself in the performances, either stilted or burlesque, on the contemporary stage. His contributions to the German theatre were nevertheless largely determined by the convictions and conventions of European humanism; his successors, especially Daniel Caspar von Lohenstein (1635–83), developed the resources of the fashionable baroque imagination: the brilliant effervescence of decorative language in the manner of the Spanish and Italian writers, and the predilection for plots of extreme passion, sensuality, and cruelty.

It was the literary and theatrical reform movement initiated by J. G. Gottsched (1700–66) that brought about an increasing self-confidence and effectiveness in the German drama of the eighteenth century. Gottsched was committed to the new philosophy of rationalism with which Leibnitz and Wolff had established a foundation for all forms of intellectual and ethical judgments: moral as well as aesthetic criteria were derived from a faith in the power of logic; clarity and distinctness of perception were the presuppositions of reliable and communicable concepts, and language became the witness and the instrument of this belief in a rational structure of all being.

Gottsched's work in Leipzig as a university teacher and as the author of handbooks of social and literary criticism is without parallel in German intellectual history: his *Versuch einer Kritischen Dichtkunst vor die Deutschen* (1730) remained canonical throughout the century. Indebted to Boileau and French poetics rather than to the English, he was, of course, concerned more with the efficacy of ideas and the discipline of mind than with the passionate or imaginative resources of man, more with the possible conflict between impulse and duty than with the inescapable power of God. The theme and purpose of all his work is *moral* and in this sense he continued to provide the central impetus for dramatic literature in Germany until long after Goethe and Schiller.

As a dramatist Gottsched wished above all to supply the

practical examples for his campaign as preceptor of a new bourgeois culture; *The Dying Cato* (1732) is in the main an adaptation of scenes from Addison and Deschamps, a stoic biography in the manner of French classicism, which was often reprinted and widely performed, but which Gottsched himself did not overrate as a work of art. His rational view of the human being tended to favor the form of comedy with its opportunities for the representation of remediable character weaknesses and absurdities rather than any inescapable involvement in tragic situations. Comedy is for Gottsched the imitation of a depraved action which by its laughable eccentricity amuses but also elevates the spectators. The Italian *commedia dell' arte*, the celebrated French playwright Destouches and the Danish dramatist Holberg were his models: stock figures, a simple and realistic plot, the unity of time, place, and action, and an uncomplicated contemporary speech were for him the essential prerequisites of a comedy that was to entertain as well as to move.

Gottsched's most striking efforts were directed toward the reform of the stage; he knew that without a serious professional theatre, a serious German drama could not be expected to develop. In the company of Johann and Caroline Neuber he formed a troupe such as he had in mind: it required of the actors a strict faithfulness to the literary text, and a serious devotion to the craft of acting—particularly in comedy, where burlesque and gross clowning had hitherto been the rule and for which Gottsched's own translations of the French and English repertoire were to provide fresh material.

If Gottsched confined himself to being the advocate of the new German drama and of a theatre that was to serve as a compelling element in the social and intellectual maturing of the German eighteenth century middle class, Johann Elias Schlegel (1719–49) supplied the first body of original drama in the new key. It is true that his tragedies (*Orest und Pylades, Die Trojanerinnen, Dido,* etc.) obey the "French" rules: his themes are taken from the Greek dramatists, and by affinity of temperament he manages to project in his heroic figures that ample and expressive intensity which he had come to admire in Racine. But it was Schlegel, too, who in an important essay (1741) was the first German critic to draw attention to the exemplary character of Shakespeare's work. Schlegel's sense of the specific nature of aesthetic values enabled him to write comedies of remarkable elegance and naturalness: his *Die Stumme Schönheit* (1747) is the best German comedy before

Lessing's *Minna von Barnhelm,* and a superb illustration of Schlegel's conviction that the purely theatrical and inventive play of the comic imagination, as Shakespeare or Molière had made it familiar, should henceforth be given still more of human sympathy, compassion, and understanding.

II

In G. E. Lessing (1729–81), one of the greatest European critics and dramatists of the Enlightenment, the qualities of his two distinguished predecessors, Gottsched and J. E. Schlegel, were superbly united. He shared their passion for the theatre as an instrument of individual and social persuasion, their interest in dramaturgical issues, their skill in adapting classical poetics to contemporary views of man, and their faith in the efficacy of language.

He is above all intensely curious about the psychological and moral structure of the human being. Like the contemporary English novelists he tests the spiritual resources of the individual under the pressure either of strict conventions or of private impulses, and, in the give and take of dramatic argument and challenge, he asserts the ultimate validity of a sensible, humane, and altogether pragmatic rationalism. His dramatic work and his theoretical writings are the reflection of his own essentially discursive, argumentative, and forensic temperament. Far from pursuing merely academic or aesthetic predilections, Lessing aimed at the widest public effectiveness in the service of an ideal of truth in which faith and modern skepticism were equally present, and which rested on a profound respect for the living continuity of the classical as well as the Christian tradition.

Miss Sara Sampson (1755), Lessing's first major play, was an attempt to introduce a dramatic form new to German audiences, a middle-class tragedy in the manner of Lillo's *Merchant of London,* "English" in its social setting and its figures as well as the "sentimental" course and motivation of its plot. Pity and fear, the Aristotelian attributes of the tragic action, were here evoked in a series of pathetic involvements of characters who are neither heroic in the Corneillian sense nor mere puppets of an inexorable fate: their humanity is their undoing. The types which Lessing here created—the noble and sensitive heroine, the fascinating seducer, the abandoned mistress, the avenging father—come from the tradition of English Restoration tragedy and can be found again and again in subsequent German drama; Lessing's originality and genius lay in the skillful management of the plot and in the precision of his dialogue. In *Emilia Galotti* (1772), he develops this sense of theatrical craftsmanship still further: the superb handling of an intricate action and the completely successful rendering of a variety of characters through their speech makes *Emilia Galotti* one of the most accomplished German dramas.

What Lessing wished above all to achieve was a "tragic" mode compatible with an essentially rational view of life. Whether he managed to write a genuine tragedy or only a pathetic spectacle, whether he produced genuine tragic conflicts or merely a network of appalling intrigues has often been debated. Lessing's profound admiration for Aristotle led him again and again to re-examine this central question as to the feasibility of tragedy in an enlightened age. To what extent, he asked, can pity and fear, those two cardinal experiences in Aristotle's concept of tragedy, be evoked in a modern, emancipated mind, and in what sense can the categorical postulate of spiritual freedom from which any rational philosophy must evolve, be brought in harmony with obedience to a transcending order?

If this order was to be defined as essentially social, then comedy and not tragedy could best illuminate its power and scope. In *Minna von Barnhelm* (1763) Lessing had produced a brilliant example of a realistic comedy that was contemporary and appealing in its subject matter and free of the absurd clichés of the fashionable French or English comedy of manners. To the topic of comedy, Lessing returned in a remarkably perceptive series of essays on the craft of the theatre which he published a few years later, in 1767–69, under the title of *Hamburg Dramaturgy*. Few European works of dramatic criticism have had greater impact upon subsequent playwrights. Lessing here examines Aristotle's theory of tragedy, finds it, properly understood, more applicable to Shakespeare than to Corneille, and warns at the same time against the blind use of this or any other set of precepts for a judgment of the dramatic intentions and achievements of a particular society that must rather be understood in terms of its own historical situation.

For Lessing this situation was determined by the conflict between absolutism and the growing self-confidence of the middle class; its intellectual creed was humane, compassionate, and idealistic. In *Nathan the Wise* (1779) the supreme faith of the Enlightenment in the single but many-faceted presence of truth is most movingly elaborated; it is a dramatic poem that once more demonstrates all of Lessing's virtues and talents: his sense of theatrical effectiveness in the development of characters as the vehicles of attitudes and ideas, his wonderful command of a language that had seldom before proved so persuasive, and his belief in the ultimate integrity of man.

III

If Lessing remained to the end an eloquent fighter against obscurantism and bigotry, if his chief passion was to be articulate in thought and speech, he did not easily accept the radicalism of mind and manners with which the younger writers proclaimed against the ever more intolerable social abuses and obsolescent conventions of the age. The young Goethe (1749–1832) was of this "Storm and Stress" group the most gifted and the most civilized; yet his first play, *Götz von Berlichingen* (1773) seemed to Lessing, for all its energy of language and its sweep of historical characterization, a lapse into primitive effusiveness. But what Lessing regarded as a loss of artistic discipline was to Goethe's own generation the very evidence of genius. *Götz* was to be a picture, more epic than dramatic, of the early sixteenth century, an age, like Goethe's, of crisis and revolution, in which the great charismatic individual attempts to maintain a vision of truth against the politics of power and the claims of ideologies. The conflict in this colorful play was between freedom and law, or between individualism and obedience, or, indeed, between nature and culture. With varying emphasis and subtlety this same issue is reiterated in much of Goethe's later work. That he could project this conflict not only in the dithyrambic manner of *Götz* but equally well in the form of Lessing's middle-class tragedy he proved in two other early plays, *Clavigo* (1774) and *Stella* (1775). But Goethe's interests were never primarily technical; indeed, they were seldom directed toward the specific resources of dramatic or theatrical craftsmanship. In *Egmont* (1775/1787), *Iphigenie* (1779/1786) and *Torquato Tasso* (1789) he developed a form of poetic portraiture that corresponded to his predilection for a careful exploration of the human being, and to his interest in the interplay of a "natural" individual endowment and the moral or cultural claims of society. When he recast *Iphigenie* from prose to magnificent poetry, Goethe achieved one of the most disciplined pieces of neoclassicist writing: the familiar plot of Euripides' play, with its tensions of guilt and inexorable retribution, is transformed into a psychologically consistent account of exemplary humaneness in which the tragic conflicts are eventually resolved.

The art of Goethe's *Torquato Tasso* lies similarly in the fusion of poetic language and characterological exploration: Tasso is the prototype of the modern artist—romantic, egotistical, and convinced of his eccentric prerogatives; in the play his special claims are tested against the civilized conventions of the court and the evidence of self-denying maturity in Tasso's antagonist. If Tasso appears to the end to assert the incompatibility of the artist and society, his attitude and that of his opponent together indicate that measure of conflict between two poles of existence which Goethe, however conciliatory his temperament, would regard as tragic. *Faust* (1808/1832), too, is of course, and not merely by Goethe's own specific designation, a tragedy. But in that most ample of Goethe's dramatic poems the complex and wide-ranging account, not simply of a human being but of a total vision of culture, is evolved in an open and entirely unconventional design. *Faust* evolves from the chronicle, in the first part, of a superhuman representative of feeling and knowledge, to scenes, in Part II, of symbolic discourse and spectacles of vast metaphorical intricacy. In the manner of modern poetry, paradoxical spiritual positions rather than merely the psychological orbit of a single character are in *Faust* explored and rendered intelligible. The work was not in its entirety known or appreciated during Goethe's lifetime; the large fragments of the Second Part which he published at the height of his career were rightly judged and admired more for their mastery of every conceivable poetic idiom than for their dramatic coherence.

Only Schiller (1759–1805), for a time Goethe's closest associate, recognized in these sketches the appropriateness of Goethe's "open" form for a rendering of the modern critical or experimental intelligence. Of the two, Schiller was perhaps the less sovereign poet, but he was undoubtedly the greater dramatic genius: he was unremittingly preoccupied with the possibility of justifying life, which in its natural state seemed chaotic and meaningless, by transforming it into an achievement of ideal coherence. Schiller's idealism, induced by his pietistic upbringing and his reading of Kant, and sustained by a fanatical willpower, differed profoundly from Goethe's far more realistic and pragmatic philosophy. And it produced a very different kind of drama. Ever since in his first play *Die Räuber* (1781) Schiller had attacked social abuses with a shrill and melodra-

matic violence, his purpose, no different from Lessing's, was to
illuminate the range of human capacities for good and evil.
Like Lessing, he believed in the essentially dialectical nature of
judgment and, like many of his contemporaries, he regarded
history as the sphere of action in which the great issues of
human self-definition, of freedom and of truth were decided. For
a time he was a lecturer on history and aesthetics: in his
dramas he explored and defined the interdependence of character, idea, and historical setting; to be free, he reiterated, is
to pursue to the end the supreme postulate of human dignity.
Don Carlos (1787), a drama of ideas, written in the elevated
iambic pentameters that were henceforth to be used as the
"classical" meter of German drama, proclaims the universality
of human rights; in the *Wallenstein* trilogy (1798/1799), the two
chief figures, Wallenstein the realist and Max Picolomini the
idealist, together form the totality of experience; their aspira-
tions revolve around power and freedom, those "grand issues of
mankind." *Maria Stuart* (1800) and *Die Jungfrau von Orleans*
(1801) resolve the conflict between these two "political" alternatives in favor of self-mastery and self-denial; and *Wilhelm
Tell* (1804), Schiller's last play, extends the plea for freedom
and dignity beyond the private sphere to the community.

In craftsmanship and intellectual consequence, Schiller has
few rivals among modern European dramatists; his form is related to his conviction that the idea itself is a structure of de-
monstrable dramatic tensions and that the movement of a
dramatic action provides in turn the palpable model of that
achievement of ideal and moral "logic" which is, for Schiller,
the ultimate human opportunity. It was his hope that the
emerging German stage should be fascinating by the seriousness
of its message as well as the spectacular power of its theatrical
illusions, and that it should serve as a "moral" institution—a
notion which, even today, long after Schiller's peremptory idealism has lost much of its force, justifies and sustains in Germany
a remarkably lively respect for the theater as a public concern.

IV

When Schiller died in 1805, still feverishly occupied with
plans for a classical tragedy that was to employ some of the
musical and picturesque devices which the romantic drama
had begun to develop, he was in Germany by far the most re-

spected dramatist and critic. No subsequent German dramatist has been able to disregard his example. But the climate of opinion tended at the turn of the century increasingly to question the validity of Schiller's theory of tragedy, which rested on the assumption that the evidence of tragic antinomies could only be reconciled intellectually by asserting a speculative and dualistic order of values. The achievement of German idealism was still to reach its perfection in the philosophy of Hegel; but the work of Heinrich von Kleist (1777–1811) demonstrates that a dramatist who had experienced the full consequence of Kant's proposition that truth is elusive and cannot be grasped in even the most exacting philosophical procedures, must seek forms and themes adequate to this radical denial of the autonomy of mind.

In his plays, Kleist represents the modern issue of man without certitude in as precise and disciplined a dramatic form as possible. He is one of subtlest masters of the kind of dialogue that suggests the ambiguity of all communication. Misunderstanding, that most pervasive theme of his work, is the corollary of his view of truth. In a tragic as well as a comic mode, his characters seem forever to talk past one another: two comedies, *Der Zerbrochene Krug* (1802/3) and *Amphitryon* (1807), render the equivocal nature of reality with superb charm and transparency. *Penthesilea* (1808) and *Käthchen von Heilbronn* (1808) state the theme of error and confusion in a more complicated context: they are concerned with the exclusive and fatal demands of passion—one retells the tragedy of Penthesilea's violent desire for domination over Achilles, her equal in rank and heroism, the other is a "grand mediaeval spectacle" of somewhat melodramatic romanticism in which love and tenderness are asserted to the point of complete submission. Kleist's last two plays, *Die Hermannsschlacht* (1808) and *Prinz Friedrich von Homburg* (1810) have sometimes been taken as documents of patriotic fanaticism. They echo, in fact, his elemental hatred of Napoleon; but their validity for us rests on Kleist's accomplishments as a dramatic artist of uncompromising logic, emotional intensity, and a magnificent Shakespearean feeling for theatrical effects. He sought in all his plays to set forth something of the absolute experience of truth, of love or of justice, without recourse to idealistic reassurances or any prospects of spiritual comfort. This is indeed the peculiarly modern mainspring of Kleist's work, and in keeping with it he transcended as well the formal conventions of classical dramaturgy. Goethe's and Schiller's open dislike of his hectic and uncompromising manner has in part been responsible for the slow growth of Kleist's fame. We think of him today as one of the most stirring and profound of German dramatists.

The generation that came to maturity between Kleist's suicide in 1811 and the appearance of Georg Büchner's *Dantons Tod* in 1835 was often painfully aware of standing, as it were, in the shadow of those formidable figures who had brought about the maturing of German intellectual life during the classical and romantic periods. Kleist, even though he was scarcely read and seldom performed, had in his plays shown the insufficiency of an idealistic philosophy; Büchner himself was to demonstrate that life must be lived in desperate recognition of its inherently amoral and overwhelming character. Although he died at the early age of twenty-four, his work— three plays and a short story—suggests astonishing perception and an entirely independent talent. He was a characteristic representative of a new rationalism: man as a physiological phenomenon and as a social animal was the object of his scientific and political studies. Like Schiller, but without any idealistic presuppositions, he was intensely conscious of history as the matrix of all judgment. In *Dantons Tod* he focuses upon the events and figures of the French Revolution and gives a large panoramic chronicle of the motives that make history and that plunge the great to destruction. But Büchner's heroic characters are without the tragic pathos of Schiller's protagonists: "The individual," he insisted, "is merely foam on the crest of the wave; greatness is but an accident; and the assertion of genius is merely a laughable struggle against an iron law." *Woyzeck* (published 1879) is a balladlike and fragmentary account of a profoundly pathetic creature, a miserable object of life, who can only kill himself in utter solitude and despair when the love that has given his life its only meaning proves faithless.

No other German dramatist of the early nineteenth century has, through his existential radicalism and his Shakespearean technique of loosely connected but highly charged and intensely atmospheric scenes, so strongly influenced the naturalistic and expressionist theatre of our own time. Whatever such poets as Grillparzer, the greatest Austrian dramatist, or Hebbel added in a pessimistic key to the grand tradition that was begun by Lessing and consummately fulfilled by Goethe and Schiller, the faith in human freedom through idealisms or ideologies was no longer effective: in Büchner's dramas, the heroic if tragic self-assertion of the individual ceased to be a valid form of protest against the natural insufficiency of man. Henceforth, under the pressure of social, political and psychological determinism, the drama of action tended in Germany and elsewhere to become increasingly static; relationships between characters gave way to an exploration of the motives of a single mind, and reflective monologue replaced the give-and-take of dialogue. The classical drama had with Büchner come to an impressive but irrevocable end.

Nathan the Wise

A DRAMATIC POEM IN FIVE ACTS

by
G. E. LESSING

❖ ❖ ❖

Nathan the Wise, written in 1779 and unenthusiastically received at its first performance in Berlin four years later, is the last of Lessing's plays—a "dramatic poem," yet a work specifically designed to reinforce his position in a theological controversy in which he had become involved. Representatives of a strict Lutheran orthodoxy, attacked by the spokesmen of an "enlightened" theology who insisted on the "natural" and historical foundations of Christian faith as against any form of *revealed* religion, had in turn sought to justify revelation by various rational arguments. Lessing opposed both views and was denied the right to publish his refutation of a member of the Hamburg clergy. "I must see," he said, "whether they will not let me preach undisturbed from my old pulpit, the stage."

To attack intolerance is, therefore, the most urgent purpose of the play, and respect for the various religions in which the one central truth appears, is the plea which culminates in the retelling of Boccaccio's famous parable of the three rings. A magic ring with the power to make its possessor "please God and man" is handed down from one generation to the next until the father of three sons cannot decide to which of them he is to leave it. He has two more rings made, identical with the first, and now leaves one to each son. Which is genuine? The sons appear before a judge who cannot make a decision, but suggests that whoever believes he has the genuine ring will have its power. Love, understanding, and intelligent compassion free of prejudice, this is to say, are the ingredients of that humane idealism which Lessing here proclaims and which becomes the central creed of Goethe and Schiller, the chief representatives of German neoclassical thought.

In *Nathan* these sentiments are given remarkably sharp relief through precisely delineated characters and a plot of slightly artificial ingredients but deliberate complexity. Two actions, both set in Jerusalem "in the late middle ages," are skillfully intertwined: one concerns Nathan's adopted daughter, Rebecca, a Christian whom the Jew took into his house when his own six sons were murdered during a pogrom. A young Templar, who rescues Rebecca from a fire and who falls in love with her, turns out to be her brother: his passion for the girl proves to be a dangerous aberration of brotherly affection—a motif common in the dramatic literature of the time from Voltaire's *Zaïre* to Diderot's *Fils Naturel,* and which here seemed to Lessing appropriate to his intention. The other strand of the plot brings the Sultan and Nathan together: the Jew is called to lend money to the Mohammedan, and their early aloofness turns into friendship and a common belief in the equal value of all forms of religious feeling. As if to affirm this natural affinity between Christianity, Jewry, and Islam, Rebecca and the Templar are in the end revealed to be the children of the Sultan's brother.

The play must be read with Lessing's rationalistic assumptions in mind: to prove the effectiveness of the "true" ring is the task of the kind of ethical humanism which he wished to proclaim; all theoretical distinctions between the religions, he argues, must remain tentative and premature until reason has grasped the indubitable character of divine providence. The search for the truth, the definition of identity, the slow revelation of puzzling or unsuspected relationships, these determine in turn every phase of the plot and justify the swift and incisive flow of the dialogue.

The double purpose of intellectual persuasion and emotional involvement suggested to Lessing the use of the Shakespearean blank verse. This loose metric form of iambic pentameters enabled him to achieve an easy and realistic dialogue, and at the same time a poetic tone compatible with the ideal propositions of the play. After the terse style of *Minna von Barnhelm* and the "laconic" technique of *Emilia Galotti,* he returned in *Nathan* to what Goethe described as the "serene and naïve manner so becoming to him."

Nathan the Wise

❖

CHARACTERS

SULTAN SALADIN
SITTAH, his sister
NATHAN, a rich Jew in Jerusalem
REBECCA, his adopted daughter
DAJA, a Christian woman serving in Nathan's
    house as Rebecca's companion
A YOUNG TEMPLAR
AL HAFI, a dervish
THE PATRIARCH OF JERUSALEM
A FRIAR
AN EMIR and several Mamelukes, in Saladin's service

Scene: Jerusalem.

❖

ACT I

SCENE 1. *The entrance hall in Nathan's house in Jerusalem. Nathan has just returned from a journey; Daja comes
to meet him.*

DAJA. Oh, Nathan! It is you! May God be thanked
That you are home at last!

NATHAN. May God be thanked, indeed. But why "at last"?
Did you have reason to expect me sooner?
How could I have returned from Babylon
Much earlier? You know how far it is
When one is forced to pick one's way, now right,
Then turning left. Collecting debts, at best,
Is slow and tedious business.

DAJA. Oh Nathan, when I think how miserable
You might have been on your return—your house—

25

NATHAN. I know. There was a fire. I surely hope
That I have heard the worst.

DAJA. It might have burned to its foundations.

NATHAN. We would have built another house,
More beautiful than this, more comfortable.

DAJA. Another house—oh yes, but by a hair
Your daughter would have perished in the fire.

NATHAN. Rebecca burned? No one has told me that.
If she had died, we would indeed not need
A house at all. She almost burned, you say?
Tell me the truth! She did not die? Tell me
The worst! Kill me, but do not torture me!
Oh yes, I'm sure she died.

DAJA. No, Nathan, if she had been killed,
Would you not long ago have heard of it?

NATHAN. Then why do you not answer me? Why keep
Me in suspense and frighten me? My child!

DAJA. *Your* child? Do you pretend that she is yours?

NATHAN. She has been mine for many years
And I shall always think of her as mine.

DAJA. Is that enough? Do you not have a better title
To all your other property?

NATHAN. I have no better right to anything I own.
All my possessions but this one mere chance
Or nature granted me; this one possession
I own because I merit it.

DAJA. Your kindness, Nathan, has its price! But can
One call a kindness kind that rests
On your intentions?

NATHAN. And what are those?

DAJA. My conscience—

NATHAN. Let me first tell you, Daja—

DAJA. I said, my conscience—

NATHAN. Wait till you see the beautiful material
I bought for you in Babylon! It is so rich
And elegant, it seems to me that even
What I have brought Rebecca is not more exquisite.

DAJA. What good are presents if I cannot stifle
The screaming of my conscience?

NATHAN. And how you will adore the clips, the ring,

The necklace and the earrings which I carefully
Selected for you at the market of Damascus!
I long to see if they will please you.

DAJA. Oh Nathan, this is how you always are!
If only you can give!

NATHAN. Accept as gladly as I give—and say no more!

DAJA. And say no more! Who doubts that you are nothing
If not generous and honest? Yet—

NATHAN. Yet I am but a Jew. Is that
What you had in your mind, but did not say?

DAJA. You must know better what I meant to say.

NATHAN. Say nothing, then!

DAJA. I shall say nothing. Very well! But if
I thus abet what surely before God is criminal,
If I do nothing to prevent or change it,
You will be held responsible.

NATHAN. Yes, I shall be responsible. —Where is Rebecca?
If you deceived me, Daja! Does she know
That I am here?

DAJA. You may well ask! Her nerves are still atremble
With terror; her fantasies still add a fire
To every image that they paint. Her mind
Is sleeping when her body wakes and is awake
When she is sleeping; sometimes she is less
Than any animal, at times she rises higher than an angel.

NATHAN. Poor child! How helpless are we human beings!

DAJA. This morning she was lying in her bed,
Her eyes still closed, as if dead, when suddenly
She started up and shouted: "Listen, listen!
I hear my father's camels come! I even hear
His voice!" Then she fell back again
And closed her eyes. But I rushed out to see,
And there—behold!—I saw you coming!
Small wonder. During all the time you were away,
Her soul was traveling with you—and him.

NATHAN. With him? Who is this "he"?

DAJA. The man who rescued her.

NATHAN. Who is he? And where is he now? Who saved
Rebecca? Where can he be found?

DAJA. A Templar who not many days before
Had been brought to Jerusalem as prisoner

And had been pardoned by the Sultan.

NATHAN. A Templar spared by Saladin? Oh God!
How many miracles were necessary
To save my daughter from the flames?

DAJA. He did not hesitate a moment, risked
Anew the life which Saladin had only recently
Restored to him as unexpected gift.
Had it not been for him, she would have died.

NATHAN. Where is he now? Take me to him. I must
Express my gratitude to him on bended knees.
You gave him all the gold I left with you,
I hope, and promised him that I would add
To his reward as soon as I returned?

DAJA. How could we?

NATHAN. You did not?

DAJA. He came from nowhere, and he disappeared
Without a trace as quickly as he came.
He did not know the house, the rooms, the doors,
And thus with nothing but his ears to guide him
Through flames and smoke, he searched the voice
That cried for help, the cape he held in outstretched arms
His only shield. We thought him lost,
When suddenly he stood before us, carrying
Rebecca in his arms. He paid no heed
To our outcry of joy and gratitude,
Deposited his booty, mingled with
The crowd and disappeared.

NATHAN. I hope he did not disappear forever!

DAJA. After some days we saw him walking
Among the palms that shade the tomb of Christ.
Delighted, I approached, thanked and implored him
To come and see once more the pious girl
Who could not rest until her tears of gratitude
Had washed his feet.

NATHAN. And then?

DAJA. It was in vain. He had no ear for all
My supplications; instead he scorned me bitterly,
Until at last—

NATHAN. You were discouraged and abandoned—

DAJA. Oh no! I went to see him every day,
I let him mock me every time I went.

How he humiliated me! Oh, how I suffered!
And yet, I would have gladly suffered more,
But now for many days he has not come
To walk among the palms that shade our Master's Tomb,
And no one knows where he has gone.
You are amazed? You ponder?

NATHAN. I am reflecting on the influence
Which such events must have upon Rebecca's mind.
To be despised by someone whom one holds
In high regard, repulsed and yet attracted—
Her heart and reason will engage
In long disputes until at last
Sadness or hate will be victorious.
And often neither wins the battle.
When fantasy joins in the fray,
We lose ourselves in reveries, and then
Sometimes we use our heads to feel, sometimes
Our hearts to reason; that's a poor exchange!
But if I know Rebecca well, that is
Her case—she dreams, awake or sleeping.

DAJA. But she is such a lovable and pious dreamer.

NATHAN. A dreamer, nonetheless.

DAJA. Especially there is—what shall I call it—
A fanciful invention which she dearly loves.
The Templar is, she fancies, not a mortal man;
An angel, she imagines, has watched over her
Since early childhood as her guardian, but always
Had remained behind a nearby cloud until,
Now, at this moment of her mortal danger,
Emerging from his cloud he took the Templar's shape
And suddenly thus stood before her.
You smile? Who knows! Let her indulge
In this one dream which Christians, Jews, and Muslims share!
And what a lovely dream it is!

NATHAN. A dream which I too cherish. Go now, Daja!
See where she is, if I can talk to her.
Then I shall go at once and find her wild
And willful guardian angel; I'll track him down
And bring him here, if he still condescends
To walk among us—even if he should
Turn out to be a strange, ill-mannered knight!

DAJA. That will be difficult.

NATHAN. If I succeed in bringing her, instead

Of lovely dreams, an even sweeter truth—
And, Daja, being human, all of us prefer
A human being to an angel—would
You really be angry with me, angry
If she is cured of her angelic dreams?

DAJA. You are so good, but also very wicked!
I'll go and look for her. But here she comes.

SCENE 2. *Rebecca enters.*

REBECCA. Oh, Father! It was you, then! And I thought
You only sent your voice ahead! At last,
We are no longer kept apart by mountains,
By foaming rivers and the parched desert.
You finally are here, you breathe the air
Which I am breathing, and you do not rush
To take into your arms your only daughter
Who meanwhile almost burned to death? Almost!
To burn alive is such a fearful death!

NATHAN. Rebecca! Oh, my dearest child!

REBECCA. You had to cross the Euphrates and Tigris,
The Jordan and who knows how many other rivers!
How often did I tremble for your safety
Before I came so close to dying in the flames!
But since that moment, when I was engulfed
By fire, to drown seemed almost like deliverance,
Like a refreshing, soothing death.
But you escaped the treacherous currents
And I was rescued from a flaming death.
Let us rejoice and let us praise the Lord!
He brought you back. Unseen, his angels carried you
Across the waters; but I saw the angel
Who on white wings brought me through smoke and flames.

NATHAN (*aside*). On his white wings! Of course! The Tem-
      plar spread
His cloak and held it high to shield himself!

REBECCA. I saw the angel and his shining wings,
I saw an angel face to face, I saw—*my* angel!

NATHAN. Who would begrudge you this angelic vision!
And I am certain that the angel
Was even more enchanted with the sight *he* saw.

REBECCA (*smiling*). Oh, Father! Do you want to flatter me,

The angel, or perhaps yourself?

NATHAN. But even if whoever saved you was
An ordinary man, a man just as we see
Around us every day, you still would look,
Yes, you would have to look upon him as an angel.

REBECCA. No, he was not an angel of that kind.
He was one of those real angels who,
You always said yourself, might well exist.
You also taught me that God could, if He
Desired to favor those who love Him most,
Work miracles. I do love God—
And I did see a miracle!

NATHAN. And God loves you, I know. Nor do I doubt
That every hour of every day He does
Perform for you and others, who like you
Believe in Him, such miracles as He
Has worked since time began.

REBECCA. You say yourself—you do agree—

NATHAN. Agree? Would it be natural and commonplace
If not an angel but a real Templar
Had rescued you? Would that be less miraculous?
The greatest miracle, I think, is this:
That what, indeed, is most miraculous
Appears to us as ordinary, that we seem
To see a real marvel only in
Those extraordinary, strange events
Which even children, who gape only at the most
Unusual sight or sound, would recognize
As miracles.

DAJA. Oh Nathan! With your subtleties you will
Completely shatter her poor brain,
Already strained enough by her attempts
To solve the puzzle of her rescue.

NATHAN. No, let me tell her this! Is it not marvelous
That she was rescued by a man who had
Just days before been saved from death himself
Most wondrously? Can anything be stranger
Than Saladin sparing a Templar's life?
Did any Templar ever ask or even hope for mercy?
Did any Templar ever offer more to buy
His freedom than his chains or else his dagger?

REBECCA. Oh, Father, now I am convinced! That's why

It only seemed but could not be a Templar.
If not one Templar, taken prisoner,
Has ever come here but to face his death,
If none has ever freely walked our streets,
How could a Templar, then, appear and rescue me?

NATHAN. How cleverly you reason! Tell me, Daja—
You mentioned that this man came to Jerusalem
As prisoner. Don't you know more about him?

DAJA. That is what I've been told. But there's a rumor
That he was pardoned for his most remarkable
Resemblance to the Sultan's younger brother
Of whom he had been very fond, but who
Has now been dead for more than twenty years.
I do not know this brother's name, nor how
Or where he died. But this seems so incredible
That it is probably not true at all.

NATHAN. Unlikely, yes. But may we not believe it
If otherwise we must believe something
Still less believable? Why should not Saladin
Have lost one of his brothers? And why could
This brother not have been his favorite?
Is it so rare that we see faces
That strongly bring to mind another face?
Are old impressions always lost?
Don't equal causes have the same results?
Why, then, incredible? My clever Daja,
For you, of course, it would no longer be
A miracle! For only what *you* call
A miracle deserves to be believed!

DAJA. You're mocking me!

NATHAN. Because you laugh at *me*. (*To* REBECCA.) And yet
    it's still
Miraculous enough that you were saved,
And only He could work the miracle
Who guides the fate and the design of kings
With silken threads—to Him a game, perhaps a jest.

REBECCA. I may have been mistaken, but you know
That I don't like to be.

NATHAN. No, for you like to learn. You see:
A forehead curved in this way or in that,
A nose shaped thus or so, the eyebrows arched
In certain fashion, a line, an angle

Or a mark, a wrinkle of the skin—a trifle—
That is what Saladin saw in a Frankish face,
And that is why you are alive today.
Do you need still more miracles to satisfy
Your craving for the supernatural?
Do you need angels, too?

DAJA. If I may speak my mind, what harm is there
In thinking that her rescuer was not
A human being but an angel?
Does one not feel much closer to the real cause
Of her salvation, to that unknown force
That governs life, if angels intervened?

NATHAN. Pride! Nothing but the arrant pride that makes
An iron pot wish ardently to be
Raised off the fire with tongs of purest silver,
Believing that it thus will turn to silver, too.
What harm is there in thinking as you do?
I ask, what good can come of it!
For saying that it makes you feel so close
To God, is either foolishness or blasphemy.
And even worse. Is it not true
That you were anxious to reciprocate
And show the rescuer your gratitude,
Be he an angel or a man?
Can you do anything for angels?
Yes, you can thank him, you can sigh and pray,
You can dissolve in blissful ecstasy,
Fast on his feast day, in his name be charitable.
All that does nothing for an angel.
For you and those who may receive your alms
Gain far more by your actions than the angel.
You do not fatten him with food
That you refrained from eating, he does not
Get richer from the gold you give away,
His glory is no brighter for your praises,
His might no greater for your trust in him.
Is that not true? But, oh, if he were human!

DAJA. Of course, a man would certainly have given us
More opportunities to do something for him.
God knows how much we wanted that!
But he refused, he needed nothing, content
Within himself, as only angels are.

REBECCA. And when he disappeared—

NATHAN. He disappeared? How did he disappear?
Did he not show himself among the palms?
And you? Did you attempt to find him elsewhere?

DAJA. No, not exactly.

NATHAN. No? You did not? Now you can see what harm
It does to dream, you cruel dreamers!
Suppose your angel now had fallen ill!

REBECCA. Ill!

DAJA. Oh no, not ill!

REBECCA. Oh, Daja, I am terrified to think—
I shudder—feel my forehead—is it cold?

NATHAN. He is a European and hardly used
To our more torrid climate, he is young
And unaccustomed to the rigors
Of his profession, to hunger, lack of sleep—

REBECCA. Oh no, not ill!

DAJA. But Nathan only said he might—

NATHAN. There he now lies alone, with neither friends
Nor money, neither help nor medicine!

REBECCA. No, Father, no!

NATHAN. Without a soul to help or to advise him,
Deserted, wracked by pain and close to death—

REBECCA. But where? Where is he, Father?

NATHAN. The man who did not hesitate to risk
His life for someone he had never seen,
For whom it was enough that someone needed help—

DAJA. Do not be cruel, Nathan!

NATHAN. A man who did not ask to see again
The girl he saved because he wished to spare
Her the embarrassment of thanking him—

DAJA. Enough!

NATHAN. And who was deaf to all her pleas to come again,
Unless she needed help a second time—

DAJA. Have pity, Nathan!

NATHAN. May well lie on his death bed in despair,
The knowledge that he saved a life—
Your life—his only consolation.

DAJA. Stop, Nathan! You will kill her.

NATHAN. And you killed him—or might have killed him.
My only wish, Rebecca, is to cure

And not to poison you. Compose yourself!
I'm sure he is alive.

REBECCA. He is not ill, or even dead?

NATHAN. I'm certain that he is alive, for God
Rewards good deeds where they were done—on earth.
But do you see now that it is much easier
To dream in pious innocence
Than acting as you should? Do you now see
That dreaming is a weakling's substitute
For action, although he may be unaware of it?

REBECCA. Oh, Father, promise me that you will never
Leave me alone again! Is it not possible
That he went only on a journey?

NATHAN. Could be. But now leave me alone. I see
A Muslim there who curiously stares
At all my camels and their burden. Who is he?

DAJA. Your friend, the dervish.

NATHAN. Who?

DAJA. The dervish, your old friend and chess companion.

NATHAN. Al Hafi? That, Al Hafi?

DAJA. He has become the Sultan's treasurer.

NATHAN. Is this another dream? Al Hafi? Yes,
By God, it is Al Hafi! Here he comes.
Quick to your rooms now!   (REBECCA and DAJA leave.)

SCENE 3. *Nathan and Al Hafi.*

AL HAFI. You may well stare at me!

NATHAN. Al Hafi! Is it really you? A dervish in such splendor?

AL HAFI. Why not? Do you believe a dervish
Is useless, never can amount to anything?

NATHAN. Of course not. But I always thought a dervish,
That is, a real dervish, would refuse
To have himself turned into something else.

AL HAFI. Yes, by the Prophet's beard, it may well be
That I am not a real dervish! But then,
I was compelled—

NATHAN. Compelled? Who can compel a dervish?
No man can ever be compelled, and yet
A dervish was? What then were you compelled to do?

AL HAFI. When someone urges him and he himself
Believes that it is good, a dervish must agree.

NATHAN. Yes, that is true. Let me embrace you, friend!
For you are still my friend.

AL HAFI. You do not ask what I've become?

NATHAN. In spite of what you have become!

AL HAFI. Could I not have become a man of state
Whose friendship would be inconvenient?

NATHAN. If you have still a dervish's heart,
I'll take that risk. The man of state
Is nothing but your garment.

AL HAFI. Which also merits your respect!—
What would I be at court, if you were Sultan?

NATHAN. A dervish. Nothing more or less, except
That I would possibly appoint you cook.

AL HAFI. So that I would forget all I have learned
Of cookery? A cook! Not waiter, too?
Admit that Saladin knows me much better!
He made me treasurer.

NATHAN. You—his treasurer?

AL HAFI. Of course, I only keep the household money.
His father is still master of the treasury
In which the fortune of the family is kept.

NATHAN. His household, though, is large.

AL HAFI. And larger even than you think.
For there's no beggar who does not belong to it.

NATHAN. But Saladin, I thought, despises beggars.

AL HAFI. He hates them so that he has sworn
Extermination to the last of them,
Should he himself become a beggar over it.

NATHAN. Exactly. That is what I meant.

AL HAFI. In fact, he is a beggar now, despite
All I have tried to do. For even though
The tide may swell the coffers in the morning,
At noon it has receded and at sundown
The chests are once more emptier than empty.

NATHAN. Because they have been drained through ditches
Which one can neither fill nor plug.

AL HAFI. Precisely.

NATHAN. How well I know!

AL HAFI. It's bad enough when princes act like vultures
That prey upon their carrion subjects;
But ten times worse if they're the carrion
On which the greedy vultures prey.

NATHAN. Oh no, it cannot be as bad as that.

AL HAFI. That's what you think! —What do you offer me?
I'll gladly cede you my position.

NATHAN. What do you gain from all your labors?

AL HAFI. Not much. But you, in my place, might well make
A fortune. For when it's ebb tide in his treasure,
You raise the flood gates of your own,
Advance the money that he needs and take
As much in interest as you desire.

NATHAN. And interest on interest's interest?

AL HAFI. Of course.

NATHAN. Until my capital consists of interest only!

AL HAFI. That does not tempt you? Well, in that event
Consider our old friendship ended.
I really had counted on your help.

NATHAN. How so?

AL HAFI. By helping me to be an honest treasurer,
By giving me the credit that I need.
You shake your head?

NATHAN. Now, let us understand each other.
We must make a distinction; for Al Hafi,
The dervish, will be always welcome
To anything he needs and I can do for him.
The Sultan's treasurer, however, who—

AL HAFI. I thought so. You are always kind, as kind
As you are circumspect, as circumspect
As you are wise. Be patient! Soon the two
Al Hafis which you see in me will split again.
Look at this dress of honor given me
By Saladin! Before its colors fade,
Before it is so ragged that it suits
A dervish, you'll see it hang upon a peg,
And I shall once again be at the Ganges
Where, barefoot and at ease, I'll walk
Upon the burning sand with my old teachers.

NATHAN. That is more like yourself again.

AL HAFI. And play at chess with them.

NATHAN. Your favorite pastime.

AL HAFI. Do you know what persuaded me?
That I myself would have to beg no longer?
That I could play the rich man with the other beggars?
Or that I would be able to transform
The richest beggar quickly into a poor Croesus?

NATHAN. No, hardly that.

AL HAFI. No, something far more stupid turned my head.
It was the first time in my life that I felt flattered.
Imagine! I felt flattered by Saladin's
Well-meaning fantasies.

NATHAN. What fantasies?

AL HAFI. "Only a beggar knows," he said, "how beggars feel.
Only a beggar knows to give in such a way
That other beggars are not hurt.
Your predecessor was too cold and rough
And too ill-humored when he gave his alms.
Never content with knowing that there was
A need, he also had to know its cause,
So that he stingily could measure
His gifts accordingly. You would be different.
You would not make me seem unkind
In all my kindness, would not be a dirt-clogged pipe
From which the purest water it receives
Emerges as a foul and filthy stream.
We think and feel alike, Al Hafi!"
The fowler's luring whistle sounded sweet,
And soon the bird was in his net.
Oh, what a hypocrite and fool I was!

NATHAN. Come now, Al Hafi!

AL HAFI. Of course! Is it not pure hypocrisy
For someone to oppress humanity,
To rob, to starve, to choke and to torment
Them by the hundred thousands but to vaunt
His love of Man because he helps a few?
Is it not pure hypocrisy to imitate
The ways of God, who spreads his gifts among
The good and bad, the deserts and the fields,
By rain or sunshine? But without possessing
God's ever overflowing hands, is it—

NATHAN. Enough!

AL HAFI. But I must also mention my hypocrisy.

Is it not hypocritical to search
For one redeeming feature in all this,
And having found it to take part in staging
The hypocritical performance?

NATHAN. Al Hafi, you must leave as soon as possible.
Your desert waits for you. I fear that here
If you stay longer among other men,
You'll cease to be a man yourself.

AL HAFI. That is what I, too, fear! Farewell!

NATHAN. Al Hafi, wait! Don't rush away!
Are you afraid your desert will not wait?
He does not hear me. And I meant to ask him
About the Templar! I am sure he knows him.

SCENE 4. *Nathan. Daja enters hurriedly.*

DAJA. Oh Nathan, Nathan!

NATHAN. Well? What is it?

DAJA. He has appeared again! He has been seen!

NATHAN. Who, Daja? Who?

DAJA. He! He!

NATHAN. He? Well, whenever could you not see him?
Oh yes, your "he" alone is "he."
He should not do that, even if he were an angel!

DAJA. He walks again among the palms
And from their branches picks dates from time to time.

NATHAN. And does he eat them, as a Templar would?

DAJA. Do not torment me! With her avid eyes
She guessed his presence in the thickest clump of trees,
And she implores you that you speak to him.
Oh hurry! From her window she will wave
To show you the direction which he takes.
Oh hurry, please!

NATHAN. But not dust-covered as I've just come home!
Would that be proper? Run and tell him
That I've returned. You'll see, the honest man
Only refused to come while I was absent.
Now that her father asks, he will not hesitate.
Tell him that I invite him cordially—

DAJA. It is no use, he will not come! Because—
He will not come to see a Jew.

NATHAN. Go nonetheless! At least you can delay him.
See where he goes, and I shall follow you at once.

(NATHAN *goes into house,* DAJA *leaves.*)

SCENE 5. *A square with palm trees. The Templar walks
up and down, followed by the Friar who keeps a little to
the side and seems on the verge of addressing the Templar.*

TEMPLAR. He does not follow me to while away
The time! And how he eyes my hands! Good Friar!
Or may I call you Father?

FRIAR. No, I'm a friar only, sir, and at your service.

TEMPLAR. Well, my good Friar, then, I only wish
That I had something for you, but I've nothing.

FRIAR. No matter, sir, I thank you all the same.
May God repay you thousandfold the gift
You would have given me if you were able to.
What counts is the intention, not the alm.
And, anyway, I was not sent to beg from you.

TEMPLAR. But sent you were.

FRIAR. Yes, from the monastery.

TEMPLAR. Where I had hoped to find at least a small
Repast fit for a pilgrim?

FRIAR. The tables are already crowded; still,
Come with me, sir! We shall go back.

TEMPLAR. Why should we? True, I have not tasted meat
For quite some time, but does that matter
While dates are ripe and plentiful?

FRIAR. Oh, my good sir! Be careful with these dates!
Too many of them are not good for you.
They clog the spleen and give you melancholic blood.

TEMPLAR. But if I like to feel a little melancholic?
Now, I am sure you were not sent to me
So you could warn me of the dates.

FRIAR. Oh no, indeed! I am supposed to snoop
A little and to find out what you are like.

TEMPLAR. And that you tell me—just like that?

FRIAR. Why not?

TEMPLAR (*aside*). A cunning friar! (*To the* FRIAR.) Are there
others like you

In your monastery?

FRIAR. That I don't know, kind sir. I just obey.

TEMPLAR. And you obey without much questioning?

FRIAR. Would it be called obedience if I did?

TEMPLAR (*aside*). Simplicity is always right!
                                        (*To the* FRIAR.) You are
Perhaps at liberty to tell me who
Has such a great desire to know me better?
I'm sure it is not you.

FRIAR. That hardly would be fitting for a friar.

TEMPLAR. For whom, then, is it fitting to be curious?

FRIAR. I must believe it is the Patriarch.
For it was he who sent me on your trail.

TEMPLAR. The Patriarch? Does he not know the cross
In red on a white mantle?

FRIAR. Of course he does! Why, even I know that.

TEMPLAR. Well then? All right: I am a Templar and I am
The Sultan's prisoner. Add that it was
At Tebnin I was taken, in an attempt
To scale the castle's walls and thus to open
The way to Sidon in the hour before
The armistice; add that I was the only one
Of twenty prisoners who was not killed—
Then I believe the Patriarch knows all
He needs to know, and even more.

FRIAR. But hardly more than he already knows.
He certainly would like to know what made
The Sultan let you go, and you alone.

TEMPLAR. I wish I knew myself! My neck already bared
And kneeling on my mantle, I waited for the blow,
When Saladin looked at me closer, gazed,
Stepped up and waved his hand to stop the sword,
Had me untied and ordered me to rise.
Turning to thank him, I saw him in tears.
I did not speak, nor he; he left, I stayed.
What all this means the Patriarch himself
Will have to figure out.

FRIAR. He thinks, I think, that God has chosen you
For more important things. That's why He saved you.

TEMPLAR. Important things, indeed! Such as to pull
A Jewish girl out of a burning house,

To guide the craning pilgrims to Mount Sinai
And other noble deeds like these!

FRIAR. A little patience, sir! Meanwhile, that's not
Too bad, and possibly our Patriarch
Already has some more important work
In mind for you.

TEMPLAR. Oh, Friar? Do you think so? Has the Patriarch
Already given you a hint?

FRIAR. Perhaps. But first he wanted me to see
If you would be the man for it.

TEMPLAR. Well, go ahead and see. (*Aside.*) I'm curious
How this good friar will find out.
                    (*To the* FRIAR.) Well, Friar?

FRIAR. The quickest way would be, perhaps,
If I would simply tell you what he wants.

TEMPLAR. Go on.

FRIAR. The Patriarch would like you, sir, to take
A little letter for him somewhere.

TEMPLAR. A letter? I am not a messenger!
Is that what you've described as much more glorious
Than rescuing a Jewish girl?

FRIAR. It must be so! For, says the Patriarch, all Christendom
Is very much concerned about this letter.
For forwarding the letter, says the Patriarch,
To its address, God will some day reward you
In heaven with a special crown.
And no one, says the Patriarch, deserves
This crown, sir, more than you.

TEMPLAR. Than I?

FRIAR. For no one, says the Patriarch, could be
More suited, sir, to gain this crown than you.

TEMPLAR. Than I?

FRIAR. For, says the Patriarch, you are at liberty
To come and go—and look, as you desire;
You know, he says, how to attack and to defend
A city; hence, so says the Patriarch,
You would be able to assess the strength
Of the interior, second wall which Saladin
Has recently constructed and to give
A clear description of it to God's soldiers.

TEMPLAR. Now, my good Friar, if I only knew

Exactly what this little letter says.

FRIAR. The letter? Why—I hardly know myself.
He wants to send it to King Philip, that I know.
The Patriarch—I often wonder how
A saintly man like he, who seems so much
At home in heaven, can condescend to be
So knowledgeable in the business of the world.
It must be difficult for him!

TEMPLAR. Well then? You said, "The Patriarch"—

FRIAR. Oh yes! He knows exactly and reliably
Just how and where, from which direction Saladin
Would open his campaign, if it should start again.

TEMPLAR. He knows all that?

FRIAR. Oh yes! And he is anxious to inform
King Philip of it, so that he can judge
How dangerous it is and if he should,
No matter what the cost, seek to renew
The armistice with Saladin,
Now broken by your upright Order.

TEMPLAR. Your Patriarch is quite a man! I see!
This dear, courageous clergyman wants me,
Not as an ordinary messenger,
But as a spy! Good Friar, go and tell
Your Patriarch that this, as far as you
Can see, is not a task for me.
Tell him that I am still a prisoner
And that a Templar is a soldier, not a spy!

FRIAR. Just as I thought. I cannot blame you, sir.
But wait, the best is yet to come.
The Patriarch has recently found out
Where in the hills of Lebanon the castle is,
And what its name, which hides the untold treasure
Amassed by Saladin's precautious father
To pay his army and its stores in case of war.
From time to time now, Saladin discreetly,
With scanty escort and on rarely traveled roads,
Betakes himself there. Do you understand?

TEMPLAR. Never!

FRIAR. What could be easier than to abduct him,
To do away with Saladin? You shudder?
Well, some God-fearing Maronites
Have volunteered already for the coup;

They still need a courageous leader.

TEMPLAR. And your good Patriarch believes that I
Would be agreeable to be their leader?

FRIAR. He deems it likely that King Philip
Would gladly lend a hand from Ptolemais.

TEMPLAR. To me? Lend me a hand? Have you forgotten
How much I am obliged to Saladin?

FRIAR. Oh no. I do remember what you told me.

TEMPLAR. And still—

FRIAR. Yes, says the Patriarch, that may well be,
But then your Order and the Lord—

TEMPLAR. Will make no difference.
They do not order me to be a knave.

FRIAR. Of course not! Still, so says the Patriarch,
What men consider knavery may not
Be knavery before the eyes of God.

TEMPLAR. I owe my life to Saladin and should take his?

FRIAR. It's a revolting thought! But, says the Patriarch,
The Sultan still is Christendom's arch-foe
And therefore cannot claim your friendship.

TEMPLAR. Who speaks of friendship? I will not become
A knave, a most ungrateful scoundrel!

FRIAR. Perish the thought! But, says the Patriarch,
You owe no thanks, before the eyes of God
Or man, for anything that was not done
For your sake; also, says the Patriarch,
Since rumor has it that the Sultan showed you mercy
Only because your face, your bearing
Recalled to him his long-lost brother—

TEMPLAR. So that the Patriarch knows, too! And still?
If I were only sure of that! Oh, Saladin,
If Nature gave me but a single trait
That's in your brother's image, would not then
My soul bear some resemblance to his, too?
Could I suppress whatever does resemble him
To please a Patriarch? No, Nature does not lie.
God does not contradict Himself in His
Creations. Go, Friar! Go before my fury rises!

FRIAR. I'll go. And I leave happier than I arrived.
Forgive me, sir; you know I am a friar,
I must obey superior orders.

SCENE 6. *The Templar. Daja has observed the Templar from a distance for some time and now approaches him.*

DAJA (*aside*). The Friar did not put him, it would seem,
Into a very pleasant frame of mind.
Still, I must talk to him.

TEMPLAR (*aside*). Oh, this is excellent! The saying must be
    true
That monk and woman are the devil's claws.
Today he's after me with both of them.

DAJA. What do I see? Thank God! Oh, noble knight,
A thousand thanks to God! Where have you been
This endless time? You were not ill, I hope?

TEMPLAR. No, I was not.

DAJA. You are in perfect health?

TEMPLAR. I am.

DAJA. We have been greatly worried for your sake.

TEMPLAR. You have?

DAJA. You have been traveling, perhaps?

TEMPLAR. You guessed it.

DAJA. And you returned today?

TEMPLAR. No, yesterday.

DAJA. Rebecca's father, too, arrived today.
May she now hope to see her wish come true?

TEMPLAR. What wish?

DAJA. The wish she asked me to express to you
So many times before. Her father now adds his
Most fervent invitation. He has come
From Babylon with twenty camels, laden
With all the spices, precious stones, and fabrics
Which India, Persia, Syria, and even China
Offer the world as their most valuable gifts.

TEMPLAR. I am not buying.

DAJA. His people honor him as one of their
Great princes, but I've often wondered why
They usually call him Nathan the Wise
And not Nathan the Rich.

TEMPLAR. To them wisdom and wealth is probably the same.

DAJA. Above all else, they ought to call him "Good."

You do not know how good a man he is.
The moment he was told how much Rebecca
Is obliged to you, what would he not have done
For you or given you.

TEMPLAR. Indeed!

DAJA. See for yourself! Come with me!

TEMPLAR. See what? How quickly such a moment fades?

DAJA. If he were not so good, would I have stayed
With him all these long years? Do you believe
That I don't pride myself on being Christian?
When I was born, no one foresaw that I
Would with my husband go to Palestine
And educate a Jewish girl. My husband
Was one of Emperor Frederick's noble servants—

TEMPLAR. Who, born in Switzerland, had the great honor
Of drowning in the same rapacious river
As His Imperial Majesty! Good God,
How many times have you already told
This story, woman? Must you keep on pursuing me?

DAJA. Pursuing you! Oh no!

TEMPLAR. Yes, yes! Pursuing me! I do not want
To see you, ever hear from you again!
I do not wish to be reminded
Again and yet again of what I did
Without a thought, of what, when I reflect,
I do not understand myself. I hope
That I will not regret what I have done.
But should I ever find myself again
In such a situation, it will be
Your fault if I do not act fast, delay
And make inquiries first, and meanwhile—
Let burn what's burning.

DAJA. Heaven forbid!

TEMPLAR. At least, from now on, please, do me a favor:
Ignore me! Do not see me! Above all,
Please keep her father off my back! A Jew
Will always be a Jew—and I'm a Swabian oaf.
The picture of the girl has vanished
From my heart if ever it was there.

DAJA. But yours is still in hers.

TEMPLAR. Why should it be? What good is it to her?

DAJA. Who knows! Man is not always what he seems to be.

TEMPLAR. But rarely something better. (*He turns to leave.*)

DAJA. Don't go! Why do you rush away?

TEMPLAR. Oh, woman, do not make me hate these palms
I used to like so much! (*He leaves.*)

DAJA. Go then, you German bear! Be on your way!
But I'll stay on your trail, wild animal!

ACT II

SCENE I. *The palace of the Sultan. Saladin and Sittah are
seated at a chess table.*

SITTAH. Where do you have your mind? How are you playing?

SALADIN. Am I not playing well? I thought I was.

SITTAH. You play my game, and not too well at that.
Take back that move and make another one.

SALADIN. Why should I?

SITTAH. You left your knight without protection.

SALADIN. You're right. Well, this way, then.

SITTAH. And I move here and threaten both your king and
queen.

SALADIN. You're right again. Check, then!

SITTAH. That move won't save you, for I interpose
And you are still exactly where you were.

SALADIN. I cannot extricate myself, I realize,
From this predicament without a penalty.
Go on and take the knight, then!

SITTAH. No, I don't want him. I shall go around.

SALADIN. You are not giving anything away!
The knight means less to you than your position.

SITTAH. Perhaps.

SALADIN. But do not count your chickens yet! You see?
That move was unexpected, eh?

SITTAH. It surely was. For how could I suspect
That you were tired of your good queen?

SALADIN. My queen?

SITTAH. I see! You simply will not let me win
More than my thousand dinars!

SALADIN. How so?

SITTAH. You ask? You try with all your might to lose,
And I can never get my due that way.
A game played as you play it is no fun;
Besides, do I not always win much more
When I'm the loser? You always give me twice the stake
As consolation when I lose.

SALADIN. I see! So when you lose, you lose
Intentionally, little sister?

SITTAH. Your generosity quite possibly
Is no incentive to improve my game.

SALADIN. Back to our game! Give me the *coup de grâce!*

SITTAH. You leave your men, then, as they are? All right!
Check to the king, check to the queen!

SALADIN. Indeed! I did not see this double check
Which threatens to undo my queen.

SITTAH. Let's see if there was anything
You might have done to counter the attack.

SALADIN. Go on and take the queen! I never was
Too fond of her.

SITTAH. Just this particular queen?

SALADIN. Take her! Her loss won't hurt me, for my men
Will once again be well-protected.

SITTAH. You always taught me that one has to be
Considerate and civil toward queens.
(*She leaves the queen on the board.*)

SALADIN. Take her or leave her on the board—I shall
No longer count her mine.

SITTAH. Why take her? Check! And check again!

SALADIN. Go on!

SITTAH. Check to the king—and check—and check!

SALADIN. Checkmate!

SITTAH. Not quite. You still can move your knight
Or make whatever other move you care to make.
However—

SALADIN. You're right. You win, Al Hafi pays!
Ask him to come at once. It's true that I
Have been distracted, Sittah; no, I didn't pay
Too much attention to the game.
But who insists on always giving us
These vapid chess men which have no appeal?
They might serve well enough for playing chess
With someone like the Imam. But—
A lost game always calls for explanations.
No, Sittah, not the chess men were at fault
If I was beaten. It was you, your skill,
Your calm and quick perception—

SITTAH. No, no. That still is only an attempt
To soothe your pain of losing. Quite enough,
You were distracted, and more so than I.

SALADIN. You were distracted? Why?
Your absent-mindedness was not the cause.

SITTAH. Oh Saladin, when will the time arrive
When we can play again so often?

SALADIN. If not so often, we shall relish all the more
The few occasions that present themselves.
You mean—because the war may start again?
All right! Let it begin! I did not draw
The sword, I wanted to renew the armistice.
This, too: I wanted very much to see
You married to a worthy man. That man
Is Richard's brother—because he is his brother.

SITTAH. If you can only praise your Richard!

SALADIN. If then our brother, Melek, could have won
The hand of Richard's sister—what a family!
One of the greatest families on earth!
You see, I do not hesitate to praise
Myself as well. I feel that I deserve my friends.
What children would have sprung from such a union!

SITTAH. Have I not always laughed at this fantastic dream?
You never did and do not want to know the Christians.
They pride themselves on being Christian, not
On being human. Even where some kindness,
A memory of what their founder taught,
Tempers their superstitions, they don't prize it
As proof of their humanity, but only
Because it was the Christ who taught and practiced it.

How fortunate for them that Christ was good!
How fortunate that they are able to accept
On faith his virtue! Yet what they propagate
Around the world is not His virtue but His name.
They use His name to soil and to stamp out
All virtue that may go by other names—
His *name* alone they cherish.

SALADIN. You mean, why else would they insist that you
And Melek be converted to their faith
Before you are allowed to love
A Christian as your spouse?

SITTAH. Precisely. They believe that love, which God
Has put into the heart of every man
And woman, lives in Christians only,
That love itself is Christian.

SALADIN. The Christians do believe in so much that is petty,
It's not surprising they believe this, too.
And yet you're wrong. The Templars are the culprits,
Because they're Templars, not because they're Christians.
Because of them nothing will come of it.
They will not yield us Acca which they would be forced
To give to Richard's sister as a dowry.
To safeguard their advantages as knights
They act like silly monks. Relying on
One clever, quickly executed stroke,
They were impatient for our truce to end.
Go to it, Knights! It's all the same to me.
If only everything were ready!

SITTAH. What else is there to worry you? What else
Disturbs your peace of mind?

SALADIN. The very thing that always haunts me.
I went to Lebanon to see our father;
He is concerned—

SITTAH. Oh no!

SALADIN. He twists and turns, but cannot find a way,
Something is missing everywhere—

SITTAH. A way to where? And what is missing?

SALADIN. The thing I never deign to mention, that
Which seems superfluous when it is handy
And indispensable when it is not.
Where is Al Hafi? Did you send for him?
The cursed, miserable gold! At last, you're here.

SCENE 2. *Al Hafi enters. Saladin and Sittah.*

AL HAFI. I hope that the Egyptian money has arrived,
And that there's plenty of it.

SALADIN. Do you have any news?

AL HAFI. I? No, indeed. I thought that I would get
Some news from you.

SALADIN. Pay Sittah a thousand dinars.
(*He paces up and down, lost in thought.*)

AL HAFI. Instead of getting money, "pay"! How charming!
When there is nothing anyway! Again
To Sittah? Did you lose again? One more
Game lost? Is this the game you played?

SITTAH. Do you begrudge me my success?

AL HAFI (*studying the chess board*).
Begrudge you what? If— Oh, you know quite well!

SITTAH (*gesturing to* AL HAFI). Al Hafi! Psht!

AL HAFI (*still contemplating the game of chess*).
I hope you are content yourself.

SITTAH (*as before*). Psht, Al Hafi, psht!

AL HAFI (*to* SITTAH). You had the white men? You gave
check?

SITTAH. A good thing that he did not hear.

AL HAFI. Is it his move?

SITTAH (*stepping closer to him*). Just say that I can have my
gold.

AL HAFI (*his eyes still on the game*). Of course, you can, as
always.

SITTAH. What? Are you mad?

AL HAFI. This game was never finished, Saladin,
And what is more, you did not lose.

SALADIN (*absent-mindedly*). Of course, I lost. Just pay her!
Pay!

AL HAFI. Pay, pay! And you still have your queen.

SALADIN (*as before*). The queen no longer counts.

SITTAH. Come on, Al Hafi. Say that I can send
Someone to get the money.

AL HAFI (*still lost in contemplation of the game*).

Of course, as always. Even so, although
The queen no longer counts, you're still not checkmate.

SALADIN (*steps up and throws the chess men over*).
I am checkmate. I want to be.

AL HAFI. Oh well! Then let the prize be equal to the game!
As it was won it will be paid.

SALADIN (*to* SITTAH). What does he say?

SITTAH (*repeatedly gesturing to* AL HAFI).
You know him. He just loves to make a fuss.
He likes one to ask nicely and repeatedly
And even is perhaps a little envious.

SALADIN. Of you, my sister? Is that true, Al Hafi?
Can you be envious of her?

AL HAFI. Quite possible! I would not be averse
To having brains like hers, and I would love
To be as good as she.

SITTAH. But all the same he's always paid the right amount
And he will doubtless pay today. Don't mind him.
That's all, Al Hafi, you may go. I'll send
For what you owe me later.

AL HAFI. Enough! I can no longer play my part
As a comedian. Some day he must find out.

SALADIN. Who must find out? And what?

SITTAH. Is this how you keep promises, Al Hafi?
I have your word!

AL HAFI. How could I know that it would go this far?

SALADIN. Well? Will you tell me?

SITTAH. Al Hafi, please, no more!

SALADIN. How odd! What could it be that Sittah asks
A stranger solemnly and urgently
To hide from me, her brother? Why does she
Prefer a dervish as a confidant to me?
Al Hafi, I now do command you: speak!

SITTAH. Oh, do not take our harmless, little secret
More seriously than it deserves.
You know that I won more than once from you
The same amount of money playing chess.
Since I did not have any need for all this gold,
And since Al Hafi's coffers are these days
Not often overflowing, I simply trusted him
With it. But have no fear. I shall collect

The debt. I do not mean to make a gift of it
To you, Al Hafi or the treasury.

AL HAFI. If this were all!

SITTAH. And other things like that. I also left
The money which not long ago you gave me
With him just for a little while.

AL HAFI. And that's not all!

SALADIN. What else is there? Now out with it!

AL HAFI. All this long time that we have been awaiting
The gold from Egypt, she—

SITTAH. Don't listen to him.

AL HAFI. Not only did not draw—

SALADIN. Kind-hearted girl! She also loaned me money, eh?

AL HAFI. She has maintained your court and, all alone,
Paid every bit of your expenses.

SALADIN. How like my sister! Ah! (*He embraces her.*)

SITTAH. No one but you made me so rich
That I could do what I have done.

AL HAFI. And he will make you just as poor as he
Is now himself.

SALADIN. You call me poor? When have I ever been
A richer man than now? I have a sword,
A dress, a horse—I have *one* God!
Do I need more? What do I lack if I have that?
And yet, Al Hafi, I should scold you.

SITTAH. Don't scold him, brother. If I only could
As easily make our dear father's burden lighter!

SALADIN. And so you kill again the happiness
I felt. No, I lack nothing for myself,
And never will, but he lacks many things
And with him so do we. What can I do?
We may still have to wait a long, long time
Until the gold from Egypt will arrive.
God knows what causes the delay since everything
Is quiet there. For my part, I will gladly
Hold back and skimp and save. I do not mind,
As long as I'm the only one concerned
And no one else must suffer. But what good is that?
I need a sword, a garment and a horse,
Nor can I bargain with my God, who is in any case
Content with very little, with my heart.

I counted on the surplus from your coffers, Hafi.

AL HAFI. The surplus? You would have me speared or
    throttled
If ever you found out that I had hidden
A surplus in the treasure chest.
I would much rather take the risk of stealing!

SALADIN. What, then, is there to do? Could you not have,
At least, found someone else to borrow from?

SITTAH. I would not cede this privilege to anyone
And I insist on exercising it.
I'm not quite bankrupt yet.

SALADIN. Not bankrupt! No, indeed! Al Hafi, go
And see from whom and how you can arrange
A loan. Go, borrow, promise anything!
But do not go to those whom I made rich.
For borrowing from them might look as if
I asked them to return a gift. Go to
The stingiest, most avaricious men
You know; they won't mind lending, for they realize
That their investment will be profitable.

AL HAFI. That kind of man I do not know.

SITTAH. I just remember having heard, Al Hafi,
That your good friend has recently returned.

AL HAFI (disconcerted). My friend? Who might that be?

SITTAH. The Jew whom you have always praised so highly.

AL HAFI. I? Did I praise a Jew?

SITTAH. A Jew—I still recall your very words—
On whom God has bestowed the fullest measure
Of His gifts, the least and the most valuable.

AL HAFI. Did I say that? I wonder what I meant!

SITTAH. The smallest gift—his wealth, the greatest—wisdom.

AL HAFI. I said that of a Jew?

SITTAH. Did you not say that about Nathan?

AL HAFI. Oh, Nathan! Now you mention it, I do
Remember. Is it true? Has he at last returned?
Well, things must have gone well for him. Oh yes,
The people call him wise, and also rich.

SITTAH. It seems that he is even richer now
Than formerly. The town is full of talk
About the treasures he brought home.

AL HAFI. If he is richer than he used to be,

He's wiser, too, perhaps.

SITTAH. What do you think, Al Hafi? If you went to him?

AL HAFI. To him? To ask for money? You don't know
The man! Borrow from him? His wisdom's essence is
Never to give a loan to anybody.

SITTAH. You used to paint his picture rather differently.

AL HAFI. At best, he might consider giving you
Some credit when you buy from him. But lending?
No! Never! But apart from that, he is
Exceptional among the Jews. He is
Intelligent, knows how to live and plays
A splendid game of chess. But in his faults
He is just as exceptional as in his virtues.
Don't count on him! He makes enormous gifts,
Of course, to help the poor—and that, perhaps,
To spite you, Saladin—and gives as gladly,
If he does not give quite as much as you,
To anyone in need, without concern
If he be Christian, Muslim, Parsee, or a Jew.

SITTAH. And such a man—

SALADIN. How is it possible that I have never heard
His name before?

SITTAH. Could he refuse a loan to Saladin
Who needs so little for himself, so much for others?

AL HAFI. That is where you can recognize the Jew
In him again, a common, ordinary Jew.
Believe me, he is jealous of your charity.
He wants to be the only one to whom
A "thank you" is addressed in all the world.
He does not lend in order to be sure
That he will always have enough to give:
Because the law ordains that he be charitable,
But does not order him to be obliging,
He is the least obliging man in all the world.
Our friendship has been somewhat strained of late,
But don't think that for that I judge unjustly.
He's good for many things, but not for this.
For this he is no good at all. I'll go
And knock at other doors—I just remembered,
I know a Moor who is both rich and stingy.
I'm off at once.

SITTAH. What is your hurry, Hafi?

SALADIN. Let him! He's on his way.

SCENE 3. *Sittah and Saladin.*

SITTAH. He's rushing off as if he were most anxious
To get away from me. I wonder if
He really was fooled by Nathan—
Or is he trying to make fools of us?

SALADIN. Do not ask me! I hardly know
About whom you were talking, I had never heard
His name until you mentioned it.

SITTAH. It's hard to think that you have never heard
Of such a man. They say he has explored
The tombs of Solomon and David
And knows a secret, mighty word with which
He can unlock their seals. From them he draws
From time to time those untold treasures
Which could not come from any other source.

SALADIN. If there are graves which hold so many treasures
That they could be the source of Nathan's wealth,
They surely are not Solomon's or David's tomb.
Fools must be buried there.

SITTAH. Or scoundrels. And, at any rate, he must
Have found a more abundant well than graves
Could ever be, were they filled with gold,
For wealth to flow in such unending stream.

SALADIN. Is he a merchant, then?

SITTAH. His camels and his mules are seen on all
The roads and desert trails, his sailing ships
In all the ports, Al Hafi says, admiringly.
He's also taken with the noble way
In which his friend disposes of the fruits
Of the prodigious and sagacious work
Which he does not disdain to take upon himself.
And he admires Nathan's mind,
Free of all prejudice, and how his heart,
A fount of virtue, is attuned to beauty.

SALADIN. And yet, a while ago, Al Hafi spoke of him
So coldly and so full of doubt.

SITTAH. Not coldly, I believe; perhaps embarrassed.
He thought it might be risky now to praise him

But did not want to be unjustly critical.
Or is it true that Nathan, though the best
Of all his people, is still one of them?
Or could Al Hafi really have cause
To be ashamed of him in this respect?
Well, be that as it may. Enough for us
That he is rich, and let him be a little more
Or else a little less like other Jews.

SALADIN. But surely you do not intend to take
His wealth by force?

SITTAH. What do you call "by force"? With fire and sword?
Of course not. Their own weakness is the force,
The only force one needs to fight the weak.
For now, come with me to my harem and admire
A little singer whom I purchased yesterday.
Meanwhile, perhaps a plan I have to catch
This Nathan will mature. Come on.

SCENE 4. *In front of Nathan's house, where it adjoins the grove of palm trees. Rebecca and Nathan come out. Daja joins them later.*

REBECCA. Oh, Father, you are here at last! But surely he
Has left by now.

NATHAN. Now, now. If he has left the grove, we shall
Look elsewhere and, no doubt, shall find him.
Be calm and patient. Look, is that not Daja
Running toward us?

REBECCA. I'm sure she must have lost him from her sight.

NATHAN. I hardly think so.

REBECCA. Oh, she would run much faster otherwise.

NATHAN. She probably has not yet seen us.

REBECCA. Now she has!

NATHAN. And now she's running. Let us wait for her,
And calm yourself.

REBECCA. You would not want your daughter to be calm
At such a time and unconcerned about
The man who saved her life, the life she loves
Because from you she first received it.

NATHAN. I do not want you to be different
From what you are, not even if I knew

That gratitude is not the only thing you feel.

REBECCA. What other feelings could there be?

NATHAN. You ask *me,* timidly, what other feelings?
Whatever moves you, it is innocence
And—nature. Don't let it worry you,
It does not worry me. But one thing promise me:
That you will not conceal your heart from me
When you begin to understand yourself
The meaning of its pounding.

REBECCA. I tremble at the thought, the possibility
That I would ever wish to hide my heart from you.

NATHAN. Enough of that. It's settled once and for all time.
Now here is Daja. Well?

DAJA. He's still continuing his promenade
And in a moment will come round that wall.
Look, there he comes!

REBECCA. He looks around, seems undecided what to do,
Debating if he should continue on,
Turn back, go to the right or left.

DAJA. No, no. He certainly will walk some more
Around the monastery. If he does,
I'll wager he will pass right here.

REBECCA. That's right. But did you talk to him?
How does he feel today?

DAJA. He is the same as always.

NATHAN. Now off with you! He must not see you here.
Step back or, better still, into the house.

REBECCA. Just one more glance at him! Oh no!
That beastly hedge still hides him from my view.

DAJA. Come on. Your father's right. He might turn back
If ever he perceived you here.

REBECCA. That beastly hedge!

NATHAN. And if he suddenly comes from behind the hedge,
He cannot help but see you. Hurry on!

DAJA. Come on! I know a window on the upper floor
From which the view is excellent.

REBECCA. You do?

(REBECCA *and* DAJA *leave.*)

Scene 5. *Nathan alone. Then the Templar.*

NATHAN. I almost shrink from meeting this peculiar man.
His prickly rectitude perplexes me.
How strange that one man has the power
To make another feel so shy and ill at ease.
Here he is now. He's young, indeed, and yet
He is a man. I like his good, defiant eyes,
His firm, determined step. However hard
The shell, I doubt the meat it hides is bitter.
He looks familiar— Pardon me, my noble sir—

TEMPLAR. What do you want?

NATHAN. Permit me, sir—

TEMPLAR. Permit you what? What is it, Jew?

NATHAN. Forgive my boldness in addressing you.

TEMPLAR. I can't prevent you, but be brief.

NATHAN. Do not so proudly and so full of scorn
Rush past a man who is obliged to you forever.

TEMPLAR. How so? Oh, I believe I know—you are—

NATHAN. My name is Nathan, and my daughter is the girl
Who lives because you risked your life. I've come—

TEMPLAR. To thank me? Save yourself the trouble.
For I've been importuned enough by gratitude.
Besides, you owe me nothing, certainly not you.
I did not even know she was your daughter.
We Templars are obliged to give our hand
To anyone who may require our help.
What's more, just then I did not care much for
My life and, therefore, welcomed any chance
To risk it—even though the life I saved
Might be as unimportant as a Jewish girl.

NATHAN. Magnificent! How great—and utterly
Abominable! But I think I understand.
You hide your generosity behind
Those awful words in order to evade
Our admiration. Now, if you despise
Our praise, is there not something we can do
That would seem less despicable to you?
If you were not a stranger here, a prisoner,
I would not be so bold as to inquire of you:

What can we do for you? Give me your orders.

TEMPLAR. There's nothing you can do for me.

NATHAN. I'm rich—

TEMPLAR. I never thought that wealth improved a Jew.

NATHAN. But even so, could you not use his wealth,
Not use the things he has, the things you lack?

TEMPLAR. Now that I won't deny, if for no other reason
Than that my cloak some day may need your help.
As soon as it is quite beyond repair,
When cloth and thread no longer hold together,
I'll gladly come and ask you for a loan
Of cloth or money. But, for now,
You need not look so worried, you're still safe.
As you can see, it is still serviceable.
This corner only has been badly stained;
The fire scorched it when I carried
Your daughter from the burning house.

NATHAN (*lifts up the corner of the cloak and looks at it*).
Is it not strange that such a spot describes
A man far better, does more justice to him
Than his words? Oh, I would like to kiss this spot!
Ah, pardon me! It was an accident.

TEMPLAR. What was?

NATHAN. A tear dropped on your cloak.

TEMPLAR. No matter. You have more of them, I'm sure.
(*Aside.*) This Jew begins to puzzle me.

NATHAN. I wonder if you would be kind enough
To let my daughter see and touch your cloak?

TEMPLAR. Why that?

NATHAN. So she may press her lips upon this spot.
For I am certain now that all her hopes
Of thanking you in person, on her knees, are vain.

TEMPLAR. Now, Jew—your name is Nathan? Nathan, then,
You turn a clever phrase—you're shrewd—
You are a clever man—I am embarrassed—
Yes, in fact—I would—

NATHAN. Go on! Keep on pretending if you must.
I know. You were too decent and too good
To be polite. The girl was overwhelmed
By her emotions, Daja overanxious
To be of help and I, her father, far away.

So you took it upon yourself to see
That her good name should not be tarnished.
You did not want to put her to an unfair test
Nor win an easy victory—and kept away.
For that I thank you, too.

TEMPLAR. You know how Templars are supposed to think.

NATHAN. Why Templars only? Why *supposed* to think?
And only in obedience to their Order's rules?
I know how good men think. I also know
That good men walk upon the soil of every country.

TEMPLAR. I hope you recognize some differences, though!

NATHAN. I do. They differ in the color of their skin
And in their build and dress.

TEMPLAR. And more good men are found in one
Than in another country.

NATHAN. I have my doubts about that difference.
Great men, like trees, wherever they may live,
Need space. If they are bunched, they stunt each other's growth.
But ordinary men, not excellent but good,
Like we, grow in profusion everywhere.
They should not criticize each other; trees
Can grow beside each other whether they
Are gnarled or straight, and none of them pretends
That he alone did not grow from a seed.

TEMPLAR. Well spoken! But you also know, of course,
Which people were the first to practice
This carping criticism of their fellow men?
You know which people was the first
To call itself the chosen people, Nathan?
How can I help despising, if not hating,
A people so inordinately proud?
They have bequeathed on Christians and on Muslims
Their arrogant insistence that their God
Is *the* true God. You are surprised to hear
A Christian and a Templar talk like this?
For where and when has pious frenzy clamored
More stridently that one God is the only one,
More ruthlessly attempted to coerce the world
Into accepting one God as the best?
If anyone is blind to this—let him be blind!
Forget what I just said—and let me go. (*He turns to leave.*)

NATHAN. No, on the contrary! Now I shall try

To hold you even closer. Come, we must be friends!
Despise my people if you wish; we did not choose
Our race when we were born. Are we our race?
What is a race? Are people Jews and Christians more
Than they are human? Oh, if I had found
In you another being who prefers
And is content to be a human being!

TEMPLAR. You have, Nathan! Give me your hand. I am
Ashamed! I should have recognized you sooner.

NATHAN. And I am proud that you did not,
For only common things are obvious.

TEMPLAR. And what is rare one does not easily forget.
Yes, Nathan, friends we must become!

NATHAN. We're friends already; oh, how glad
Rebecca now will be! And what delicious,
Distant views begin to open up!
Oh, if you only knew her!

TEMPLAR. I cannot wait to see her. Who is that
Approaching from your house? Is it not Daja?

NATHAN. It is, and she looks frightened.

TEMPLAR. I hope that nothing has happened to Rebecca!

SCENE 6. *Daja enters hurriedly.*

DAJA. Oh, Nathan! Nathan!

NATHAN. What happened?

DAJA. Forgive me, noble Knight, for interrupting you.

NATHAN. Well? What has happened?

TEMPLAR. What is troubling you?

DAJA. There is a messenger from Saladin!
He wants to talk with you. My God, the Sultan!

NATHAN. The Sultan wants to talk to me? He must
Be curious to see what I have brought.
Tell him that nothing, hardly anything
At least, has been unpacked.

DAJA. No, no. He does not want to see your goods,
He wants to talk to you as soon as possible.

NATHAN. All right, I'll go. Go on ahead.

DAJA. Please, don't be cross with me, good sir—
My God, we are so worried about what the Sultan wants!

NATHAN. That we shall soon find out. Go on, I'm coming.

SCENE 7. *Nathan and the Templar.*

TEMPLAR. But don't you know him? I mean, personally?

NATHAN. The Sultan? No, not yet. I never tried
To meet nor to avoid him. So it went.
His reputation is so good that I preferred
Believing what the people say to meeting him.
But now that he has saved your life—provided
What I heard is true—

TEMPLAR. Yes, it is true. The life I live
I have received as a gift from him.

NATHAN. A gift with which he gave a double, more,
A triple life to me, and thus I feel
No longer as I did. This changes everything.
He's thrown a rope around me, and I'm tied
Forever after to his service.
Now I can hardly wait to hear his first
Command. Now I'm prepared for anything,
Prepared to tell him that it is because of you.

TEMPLAR. I have myself had no occasion yet
To thank him, though I often stepped into his path.
The feelings I aroused in him
Came suddenly and were as soon forgotten.
I doubt that he remembers me at all.
Yet he will have to think of me at least
Once more, for he must still decide my fate.
He spoke the word that saved my life,
He ordered *that* I am to live;
He now must tell me *how.*

NATHAN. Exactly; one more reason that I hurry.
A chance remark perhaps will give me the occasion
To speak of you. Permit me—pardon me—
I·hasten to him. But—when will you come
To see us?

TEMPLAR. As soon as you give me permission.

NATHAN. As soon as you may wish.

TEMPLAR. Today!

NATHAN. Now—may I ask your name?

TEMPLAR. My name is Curd von Stauffen.

NATHAN. Von Stauffen? Stauffen? Stauffen?

TEMPLAR. Why is that so remarkable?

NATHAN. Von Stauffen? There have perhaps been several—
Some other members of your family?

TEMPLAR. Oh yes, there have been several whose bones
Are mouldering here. My uncle even—no,
That is to say, my father—but why are
Your eyes becoming more and more suspicious?

NATHAN. But not at all! No, no. How could I ever tire
Of looking at your face?

TEMPLAR. Let me, then, be the first to take my leave.
Quite often an explorer's eye sees more
Than he had wished to find. I am afraid
Of too much searching. Let time bring knowledge,
Step by step, and not our curiosity.   (*He leaves.*)

NATHAN (*amazed, follows him with his eyes*).
"Quite often an explorer's eye sees more
Than he had wished to find." As if he read
My mind! That is, indeed, exactly what might happen.
Not only that he has Wolf's build, his bearing, no,
He has his voice! He throws his head back—
Just like Wolf! That's how he used to hold his sword,
And just like that he used to pass his hand
Across his eyes, as if to hide their fire.
How deeply etched some pictures are in us,
Asleep but quickly wakened by a word,
A sound, a gesture, anything. Von Stauffen!
Right! Of course! Filneck and Stauffen!
It won't be long before I know much more
About it. Well? What is it, Daja? Come!

SCENE 8. *Nathan and Daja.*

NATHAN. Oh yes, I understand. You both are anxious
About something quite different than why
The Sultan wants to speak to me.

DAJA. You cannot blame her! You had just begun
To talk more intimately with the knight
When we were driven from the window
By the arrival of the messenger.

NATHAN. Tell her that she may now expect him here
At any moment.

DAJA. No! Are you sure? Quite sure?

NATHAN. I hope I can rely upon you, Daja.
Be careful, please! You won't regret it,
Your conscience will approve of it
If you do nothing to disrupt my plan.
Be sure to speak and ask your questions
With modesty and with restraint—

DAJA. There is no need to tell me that. I'm going;
You, too, must leave, for here already is
A second messenger from Saladin,
Your friend, Al Hafi. *(She leaves.)*

SCENE 9. *Nathan and Al Hafi.*

AL HAFI. You are the man I've come to see.

NATHAN. His business must be pressing, but what does he want?

AL HAFI. Who?

NATHAN. Why, Saladin, of course! I'm on my way.

AL HAFI. You're on your way—to Saladin?

NATHAN. Did he not send you?

AL HAFI. Me? No, no. Has he already sent for you?

NATHAN. Indeed, he has.

AL HAFI. It's true, then.

NATHAN. What is true?

AL HAFI. That— Oh, it's not my fault! God knows how hard
I tried, it's not my fault. The tales I told
About you! How I lied!

NATHAN. What did you try? And what is true?

AL HAFI. That you are now his treasurer.
I sympathize with you, but I won't stay
To watch. I'm on my way within the hour,
You know where to and know the way.
If there is any errand I can do
For you along the way, I'm at your service.
But it must not be more than I can carry.

NATHAN. Now wait and catch your breath; remember
That you have told me nothing yet.
What is this all about?

AL HAFI. The bags, of course, you'll take along with you?

NATHAN. What bags?

AL HAFI. The gold, of course, which Saladin
Expects you to advance him.

NATHAN. And that is all he wants?

AL HAFI. Do you expect me to stand by and watch
When he proceeds to use you like a mine,
Until your toes are hollow? How can I
Stand idly by while he keeps borrowing
From you and wastes what he has borrowed?
Until the bins which you have patiently
And wisely stocked are empty, swept so clean
That even mice would starve to death in them?
I hope you don't believe that he, although
He needs your money, would accept advice from you?
He, take advice! Has Saladin at any time
Accepted counsel? Hear what happened
Just now when I was with him.

NATHAN. Well?

AL HAFI. I came just as he finished playing chess
With Sittah, who plays quite a decent game.
The game which they had played and Saladin
Thought lost was undisturbed. I looked at it
And saw that he had not yet lost at all.

NATHAN. Oh, what a find for you!

AL HAFI. Responding to her check, he only had to move
A pawn a little closer to the king.
I wish I had the board to show you!

NATHAN. I trust your judgment.

AL HAFI. That done, his castle had the room to move,
And she was lost. I meant to show him that,
I called him over, but—

NATHAN. He disagreed with you?

AL HAFI. He did not even listen! Deprecatingly,
He overturned the game.

NATHAN. Not possible!

AL HAFI. He said he wanted to be checkmate.
Do you hear? He wanted! Is that playing chess?

NATHAN. Hardly. That I call toying with a game.

AL HAFI. And yet the stakes were not exactly small!

NATHAN. The money does not matter, that is nothing.
But to refuse to listen to you,

Not to consult you on this most important point,
Not to admire your eagle eye—oh yes,
That fairly screams for vengeance, eh?

AL HAFI. Bah! Nonsense! I just told you that to prove
What kind of man he is. In short,
I can no longer bear to stay with him.
Here I am chasing round and call on all
The dirty Moors in town to find just one
Who might give him a loan—I never begged
A penny for myself and here I am,
Begging for others! For borrowing
And begging is about the same, just as
A lender who takes interest is not
Much better than a thief. When I'm among
My teachers by the river Ganges,
I won't be forced to beg or lend,
Nor to be become an instrument for either.
There, only there, are human beings; here
You are the only one who merits
Living there. Come with me now! Give up
This trash, give it to him—it will
Be his eventually in any case.
Thus you'll have finished with your worries. Come,
I'll get you what you need. Come on!

NATHAN. I think this step could always be the last
Resort, but I shall think about it. Wait—

AL HAFI. You want to think about it? There is nothing
To think about.

NATHAN. Only until I've seen the Sultan, only
Until I've said good-bye—

AL HAFI. To think about it means to find a reason
For doing nothing. One who can't decide
Right on the spot to live the way he pleases
Will always be a slave to others. Suit
Yourself. Arrange your life as you see fit.
I'll go my way, and you go yours. Good-bye!

NATHAN. Al Hafi, you will surely put
All your affairs in order first?

AL HAFI. Bah, nonsense. What is in my treasury
Is hardly worth the counting. My accounts
Are guaranteed by either you or Sittah.
Farewell!   (He leaves.)

NATHAN (*following him with his eyes*).
I'll guarantee them. Wild, good, noble—
What can one call a man like him?
True beggars only are true kings.

> (*He leaves in the opposite direction.*)

ACT III

SCENE 1. *Nathan's house. Rebecca and Daja.*

REBECCA. Just what did Father say? "You can expect him here
At any moment?" Does that not sound as if
He should be here by now? How many moments have
Already passed? But then, why think of those
That went? From now on I shall live each minute
For the next, and one of them will surely bring him.

DAJA. Oh, cursed be the Sultan's messenger!
If he had not arrived just then, your father
Would certainly have brought him here at once.

REBECCA. But when that moment comes, when finally
My ardent wish has been fulfilled, what then?

DAJA. Then—I shall hope that *my* most ardent wish
Will also be fulfilled.

REBECCA. What will replace in me this overpowering yearning?
How can I live without an all-commanding wish?
Will there be nothing? Ah, it frightens me.

DAJA. My wish will take the place of yours, once that
Is satisfied, to see you in the hands
Of someone who deserves you—and in Europe.

REBECCA. How wrong you are! What makes this thought so dear
To you, I find abhorrent. For if you
Feel Europe's pull so powerfully, why
Should not my country hold me with an equal force?
Why should the picture of your people,
Indelible to you, pull me more strongly
Than people whom I daily see and hear,

Whom I can touch—who are my people?

DAJA. Protest against it as you will, the ways
Of Heaven are immutable. Suppose
The man who saved you is the instrument
By which his God, for whom he fought, intends
To lead you to the country and the people
For whom He destined you when you were born?

REBECCA. Oh, Daja! How you talk, my dearest Daja!
You do sometimes have strange ideas.
"His God, for whom he fought!" Does God belong
To any man? What kind of God is this
Whom men can own? Who lets men go to war
In His behalf and in His name?
And how can any mortal know *for* which
Especial piece of soil he has been born
If not for that *on* which he saw the light of day?
If Father heard you talk! What has he done
To you that you always describe my happiness
As founded on my being far away from him?
What has he done to you that you insist on mingling
Your country's weeds and flowers with the seed
Of reason which he planted in my soul?
Your many-colored flowers cannot grow
Upon my soil. I even feel that they destroy
The soil in which I'm rooted even though
They may well be a pretty decoration.
Their perfume, their sweet-sour aroma stifles me.
I do not criticize those who, like you,
Are used to it, are strong enough to bear
And even to enjoy this powerful attack
On all the senses. I cannot.
Your story of the angel even—
Did it not almost make a fool of me?
The farce I played for Father makes me blush.

DAJA. The farce? As if the only power in the world
Were reason! If only I could speak!

REBECCA. Are you not free to speak? When did I ever
Refuse to let you entertain me with the pious tales
Of your religious heroes? Did I ever fail
To show my admiration for their deeds,
To shed my tears about their suffering?
Their faith, it's true, did never seem to me
Their most heroic trait, but I was all the more

Attracted by the comforting belief
That we can well accept God's will as guide,
No matter what we think God is.
My Daja, Father often told us that,
And you were always in accord with him.
Why do you now tear down what you and he
Have built together? —But how we are talking!
This is no way to put ourselves
Into the proper mood to meet our friend.
And yet, for me it is, for I want very much
To know if he, too, thinks—but listen, Daja!
Someone is at the door! It must be he!

SCENE 2. *Rebecca, Daja, and the Templar, for whom someone off-stage opens the door with the words:* Come this
way, please.

REBECCA (*starts, then composes herself; she is about to fall
on her knees before the Templar*). My savior!

TEMPLAR. This is why I refused to come before!

REBECCA. Proud man! Kneeling before you I desire
To thank once more, not you, but God.
You do not want my gratitude, want it
As little as a water pail wants thanks
For having helped in putting out a fire,
For being ready to be filled and emptied.
Thus you were somehow pushed into the flames,
And I, somehow, fell into your strong arms,
Just as a spark might fall upon your mantle,
Until at last something—I don't know what—
Propelled us out into the open air.
Why should I thank you, then? What did *you* do?
In Europe, wine spurs men to even greater feats.
A Templar acts like any well-trained dog,
Retrieving on command, from fire or water.

TEMPLAR (*has, during the foregoing, looked at* REBECCA *in
surprise and with increasing alarm*).
Oh Daja, why did you repeat to her
Each foolish word that I let slip
When in a sad and ugly mood I made you suffer?
I hope that in the future you will speak
To her about me in a kinder voice.

DAJA. I don't believe, sir, that those little barbs
Have pricked her heart and hurt your cause.

REBECCA. So you were sad? Then you have been more nig-
gardly
With your unhappiness than with your life.

TEMPLAR. Dear child! My eyes and ears are fighting
For the possession of my soul. This cannot be
The girl I carried from the flames,
For seeing you, who could have hesitated?
How could the others wait until I came?
Of course—great fear—distorts the features.

(*A pause, during which the* TEMPLAR *is steadily gazing at*
REBECCA.)

REBECCA. For my part, I don't think that you have changed.

(*The* TEMPLAR *continues staring at her, until she finally
continues in order to interrupt the long silence.*)
Please, tell us first where you have been,
And, I might add, where you are now!

TEMPLAR. I am—where I ought not to be, perhaps.

REBECCA. And where were you before? Again perhaps
Where you should not have been? That would be bad.

TEMPLAR. I was—what is the mountain's name? I was—
Oh yes—Mount Sinai! That's where I have been.

REBECCA. Mount Sinai? Oh, how wonderful! At last
I can make sure if what I heard is true—

TEMPLAR. If what is true? If you can still inspect
The spot where Moses stood before the Lord—

REBECCA. No, no. Not that. For where he stood, he stood
Before the Lord. All that I know.
But what I want to learn from you
Is whether it is really more tiresome
To climb the mountain than descend it.
With all the mountains I have climbed
It always was the opposite. What is it, sir?
Why do you turn your face? Why do you suddenly
Not want to look at me?

TEMPLAR. Because I want to hear you speak.

REBECCA. You do not want to let me see that you
Are smiling at me, simple-minded girl,
Who does not have a single worthwhile thing
To say about the holiest of holy mountains.

TEMPLAR. Then I shall look at you again. But now

I cannot read what you are saying with your eyes,
Because now you look down to hide a smile;
Not read the words which I believe I hear
You speak, but which you do not say. How right
He was to tell me, "If you knew her!"

REBECCA. Who told you that? And about whom?

TEMPLAR. "Oh, if you knew her," said your father—and
He spoke of you.

DAJA. And I told you the same.

TEMPLAR. Where is he? Is he still with Saladin?

REBECCA. He must be.

TEMPLAR. Still? But no, I had forgotten—no!
He must be waiting for me at the monastery,
Where we agreed to meet—I think.
Excuse me, please! I'll run and bring him here.

DAJA. No, you stay here. This is an errand I can do.
I'll bring him back at once.

TEMPLAR. No, no. He is expecting me, not you.
He also might—who knows—he easily
Might at the palace—you don't know Saladin—
Perhaps he found himself in difficulties.
Unless I go myself it may be dangerous for him.

REBECCA. What danger could there be?

TEMPLAR. Danger—for me—for you—for him, unless
I quickly go myself, unless I hurry.   (*He leaves.*)

SCENE 3. *Rebecca and Daja.*

REBECCA. What do you make of this? What was his hurry?
Did he see ghosts? Is someone after him?

DAJA. Oh, never mind. What it portends I don't believe
Is bad at all.

REBECCA. And what does it portend?

DAJA. That something's happening to him. It's boiling,
And he is trying to prevent the pot
From boiling over. Now it is your turn!

REBECCA. My turn for what? You're as mysterious as he.

DAJA. Now you'll be able to take your revenge
For all the grief he's caused you in the past.
But don't be too vindictive, not too harsh.

REBECCA. I hope that *you* know what you mean.

DAJA. Have you calmed down so much already?

REBECCA. I have—yes, I'm quite calm.

DAJA. Be honest! You are glad to see him restive,
You are composed because it now is he who suffers.

REBECCA. I don't feel anything like that. At most,
I can admit that I'm surprised about myself,
To see how quickly calm has been restored,
How suddenly the storm that raged within my heart
Has died. To see him, hear him talk, has been—

DAJA. Enough?

REBECCA. No, that I would not say! No, far from that—

DAJA. But it has stilled your hunger for the moment.

REBECCA. Perhaps, you could say that.

DAJA. No, I would not say that at all.

REBECCA. I will forever treasure him
And hold him dearer than my life,
Although my pulse does not beat faster any more
At the mere mention of his name,
Although my heart does not begin to pound
Each time I think of him. —What silly babble!
Dear Daja, come—come to our favorite window
That gives upon the grove of palms.

DAJA. Perhaps the hunger, after all, is not yet stilled.

REBECCA. Now I shall see the trees again,
And not alone the man who walks beneath them.

DAJA. This coolness presages, I fear,
A new attack of fever.

REBECCA. What coolness? No, I am not cool.
But watching calmly does not make the sights
One sees less pleasant to observe.

SCENE 4. *A large reception room in Saladin's palace.
Saladin and Sittah.*

SALADIN (*entering, speaks toward the door*).
Bring in the Jew as soon as he arrives.
He does not seem to be in any hurry.

SITTAH. Perhaps they could not find him right away.

SALADIN. Oh, Sittah!

SITTAH. You act as if you were before a battle.

SALADIN. A battle which I am to fight with arms
I never learned to handle: feinting,
Pretending, tempting, setting traps.
I never learned to do these things and cannot do them well.
And to what end? To hunt for gold! For gold!
To scare a Jew and make him give me money!
For that I'm to resort to petty tricks,
For the most trivial of trivialities.

SITTAH. A triviality which, not attended to,
Is apt to take revenge, dear brother.

SALADIN. Regrettable, but true. Now if this Jew
Turns out to be a reasonable man,
Just as the dervish once described him to you,
What then am I to do?

SITTAH. In that case, nothing will be lost.
The trap is baited only for an avaricious,
A frightened, hesitating Jew. If he is good
And wise it will not spring. A man like that
Is one of us and there's no need for trapping him.
Meanwhile, you watch him at your leisure
And smilingly observe if he is strong enough
To cut the ropes with one quick stroke, or if
He sidesteps gingerly and twists himself
Until he's passed the snare.

SALADIN. That's true. I'll relish watching him.

SITTAH. So there is nothing which conceivably
Could be embarrassing. If he is but a Jew
Like all the others, a Jew and nothing else,
You need not be ashamed of acting
As he expects all men to act. The man
He sees in better light would be, to him,
A most pretentious fool.

SALADIN. In order not to be despised by one
Whom I despise, I thus must act despicably.

SITTAH. Provided that it is despicable
To use a thing the way it should be used.

SALADIN. You women know so well to prettify
The schemes that you invent.

SITTAH. Well! Prettify, indeed!

SALADIN. My clumsy hands, I fear, may well destroy
So delicate an instrument, a tool

That must be handled as it was designed:
With skill and cunning. However that may be—
I'll execute the dance as best I can,
But I would rather be an awkward
Than a skillful dancer.

SITTAH. Do not belittle your abilities!
I warrant the success of your performance.
But you must *want* to win. Men of your ilk
Are always trying to persuade us
That all their victories were won with arms.
Of course, the lion hunting with the fox
Resents the fox, but not his slyness.

SALADIN. And women always try to drag a man
Down to a level where they feel at home.
Leave me alone now. I have learned my lesson.

SITTAH. Am I supposed to go and leave you?

SALADIN. Did you intend to stay?

SITTAH. Not so that you would see me, but—I thought
I might stay there, in the adjoining room.

SALADIN. To listen? No, not even that!
Not if I am to win. Please, hurry now.
I hear the curtains rustle— He is here—
Don't tarry, I shall check!

(SITTAH *leaves by one door, as* NATHAN *enters by another.*
SALADIN *sits down.*)

SCENE 5. *Saladin and Nathan.*

SALADIN. Come in, come closer, Jew! No need to be afraid.

NATHAN. To fear you, one would have to be your enemy.

SALADIN. Nathan—you call yourself?

NATHAN. I do.

SALADIN. Nathan the Wise?

NATHAN. That I do not.

SALADIN. If you do not, the people do.

NATHAN. The people—that may be.

SALADIN. I hope you don't believe that I despise
The people's voice? For some time now I've wished
To meet the man whom people call "the Wise."

NATHAN. Perhaps they praise me but to mock me better.

To many people wisdom is the same
As prudence, and prudence is to know
One's own advantage.

SALADIN. You mean, of course, one's true advantage?

NATHAN. In that case, selfishness and prudence would
Be one, prudence and wisdom be the same.

SALADIN. You prove what you intended to refute.
You know, as few men do, what true advantage means.
At least, you have explored, have thought about
Its meaning, and that alone would make you wise.

NATHAN. As wise as everyone believes to be.

SALADIN. Enough of modesty! I hate to hear
The voice of modesty each time
I hope to hear the voice of reason.
    (*He jumps to his feet.*)
Let us get down to business now. Be sure
That you are truthful, Jew!

NATHAN. I shall attempt to serve you, Sultan,
That you will think me worthy of your patronage.

SALADIN. How do you mean to serve me?

NATHAN. By selling you the best at lowest cost.

SALADIN. What do you think you'll sell me? Merchandise?
My sister, I am sure, will love to bargain with you.
(*Aside.*) I hope the eavesdropper has heard. (*Aloud.*) I did not
call you as a merchant.

NATHAN. In that case, you would like to know perhaps
What I have learned about the enemy;
It's true, they are about to move,
And to be frank—

SALADIN. No, that is not why I have called you here.
I've heard all that I need know about their plans.
To put it briefly—

NATHAN. I am at your disposal, Sultan.

SALADIN. I'm anxious to have your advice on quite
A different subject. Since everyone agrees
That you are wise, tell me which is the best religion,
Which set of laws you've found most reasonable.

NATHAN. I am a Jew.

SALADIN. And I a Muslim. The Christian is the third religion.
Of these religions only one can, after all,
Be true. A man like you will not, I'm sure,

Be satisfied with what the accident of birth
Has given him. Or if he is content with that,
Would be so only for good reason, having learned
And understood and made his choice. Well then!
Share your enlightened judgment, tell me how
You have arrived at your conclusions.
I never had the time to think about
The reasons you, I'm sure, have weighed before
You made your choice. Give me—in confidence,
Of course—your reasons and I'll make your choice
My own. You are surprised? You are suspicious?
It may well be no other Sultan ever made
Such crotchety inquiry of a man,
But it is not unworthy of a Sultan, I believe.
What is your answer? Would you like
To think about it for a while? You may.
(*Aside.*) I wonder if she's listening. (*Aloud.*) I'll soon be back.
  (*He leaves by the same door through which* SITTAH *went
  earlier.*)

SCENE 6. *Nathan alone.*

NATHAN. Hm. Strange. What does he want? I was prepared
To talk of money, and he wants—the truth!
He wants the truth, as shiny and as pure
As newly minted gold! Perhaps, if truth
Were like a coin of yore which one must weigh;
It's surely not like modern coins,
Struck with a die and counted on a board.
Can truth be put into a head
Like money into bags? Which one of us
Is acting like a Jew? And does he really
Want truth? It would be petty to suspect a trap.
But is there anything too petty for the great?
And how he rushes in, without permission,
Not even knocking at the door, not asking first
If he is welcome, or whether I am friend or foe!
I must be on my guard, must neither play
The arch-Jew nor appear no Jew at all.
For if I'm not a Jew he might well ask
Why I am not a Muslim. That is it!
I have the answer. Not only children love
A fairy tale. I am prepared.

SCENE 7. *Saladin and Nathan.*

SALADIN (*aside*). The coast is clear. (*To* NATHAN.)
Have I returned too soon?
Have you made up your mind? Tell me your thoughts.
We are alone, no one will hear us here.

NATHAN. I wish that the whole world could hear us.

SALADIN. Are you so sure of your opinions, Nathan?
You must be wise, indeed, if you will not allow
The truth to hide, if you dare risk your wealth,
Your life to make it known.

NATHAN. If necessary, yes.

SALADIN. Perhaps, at last, I will deserve the title,
"Improver of the World and of the Law."

NATHAN. That is, indeed, an admirable title.
Before confiding in you, Saladin,
May I begin by telling you a story?

SALADIN. Why not? I'm very fond of well-told tales.

NATHAN. For telling stories well I have,
I am afraid, no talent.

SALADIN. Again so proudly modest? Tell your tale.

NATHAN. Long, long ago, there lived in Eastern lands
A man who owned a ring of untold worth,
A gift received from loving hands. Its stone,
An opal which returned each ray of light
In a hundred colors, possessed a magic power:
Whoever wore the ring and trusted it,
Gained favor in the eyes of God and Man.
Is it surprising that this man
Would never be without his ring?
And that he made provision that the ring
Would stay forever in his family?
This was his plan. He left the ring
To that one of his sons whom he loved most,
Providing that this son, in turn, bequeath
The ring upon his most beloved son.
Thus handed down from son to favorite son,
The ring was to confer upon its owner,
Be he the first-born son or not, the right to be
The head and guardian of the family.

SALADIN. I understand. Go on.

NATHAN. Passed down from son to son, the ring at last
Came into the possession of a man
Who had three sons whom he loved equally,
Each one as loving and obedient as the others,
Although from time to time now this, now that
And now the third appeared to him
The most deserving of the three,
As each in turn had for a while his sole
Attention and his undivided love.
In loving weakness now the father promised
Them all the ring's exclusive ownership.
Thus all went well until the father,
Well knowing that his death was near,
Became aware of his predicament.
It caused him pain to think that he must break
The promise he had given two of his dear sons.
What now? In greatest secrecy, at last,
He called an artisan whom he enjoined
To make two copies of his ring.
Without regard to the expense or difficulty
Which fashioning the duplicates might cause,
They were to be like the original
In every detail. The artisan
Succeeded in his task and when he brought
The rings, the father could not tell himself
The duplicates from the original.
Relieved, he summoned joyfully his sons
And, separately, gave each one his blessing,
Gave each his ring—and died.

SALADIN (*confused, turns his back to* NATHAN).
Yes, yes. I understand. But is your story
Finished soon? Continue.

NATHAN. It almost is, for it is clear what happened next.
No sooner had the father died than each
Of his three sons came forward with his ring
To claim his place as head of all the family.
They scrutinized, they quarreled and, at last,
Brought suit. But all to no avail. No one
Could prove that he possessed the genuine ring.

(*He pauses, waiting for* SALADIN *to speak, and then continues.*)
Almost as now; no one can prove
That his religion only is authentic.

SALADIN. Is that your answer to my question?

NATHAN. It is intended only as apology
For not deciding which of the three rings
Was genuine. For had the father not
Intended them to be alike
And absolutely undistinguishable?

SALADIN. You talk of rings! Do not play games with me!
I think that the religions I have named
Can be distinguished easily enough,
Down to their laws on dress and food and drink.

NATHAN. Down to the last detail—except their origin.
Are not all three of them based on tradition,
May it be writ in books or word of mouth?
And must we not accept on faith their teaching?
Whose faith and which tradition now
Are we most likely to accept? Of course,
The faith of those who have since childhood given us
Proof of their love, who are our blood, our kind,
The faith of those who never have deceived us,
Or only then at least when it was good for us.
Why should I trust my father less than you
Trust yours? Or, turned around, can I demand
Of you to give your ancestors the lie
In order not to contradict my ancestors?
The same is true for you and for a Christian.

SALADIN (aside). By God, the man is right! I have no answer.

NATHAN. But let me finish with my tale of the three rings.
I told you that the sons took their dispute
To court. Each of the three affirmed and swore
He had his ring directly from his father—
Which was quite true—and that before his death
He'd promised him possession of the ring
With the attending rights—and that was also true.
His venerated father, each declared,
Could not have broken faith with him, and so,
Refusing to suspect his father,
He had to charge his brothers with foul play,
Although he was most willing to believe
The best of them in every other way.
Each vowed that he would find the means to prove
The traitors guilty and take his revenge.

SALADIN. And what about the judge? I am most anxious
To hear how he decided the dispute.

NATHAN. The judge spoke thus: unless you quickly bring

Your father here to testify,
I shall dismiss the case. Do you believe
That I am here to solve your riddles?
Or are you waiting for the genuine ring to speak?
But wait! I hear that the authentic ring
Has magic powers, that its wearer
Gains favor in the eyes of God and man.
That will decide the issue, for the copies
Will surely not possess this magic force.
Do any two of you love one the most?
Speak up! You have no answer? Do the rings
Work only inwards and have no effect
On others? Do you love yourselves the most?
Oh, you are all deceivers, all deceived!
All three rings must be imitations,
The genuine ring must have been lost;
To hide the loss, your father surely had
Three new rings made to take the place of one.

   SALADIN. Magnificent!

   NATHAN. And so, the judge continued, if you want
A verdict—leave. If you want my advice,
Accept the situation as it is.
Your father gave his ring to each of you;
Let each assume, then, that his ring is genuine.
Perhaps your father meant to free his family
From the tyrannical authority
The ring had exercised for generations.
It's certain that he loved all three of you,
And that he loved you equally, for he refused
To favor one and to aggrieve the others.
It's up to you. Let each strive zealously
To prove his love and lack of prejudice;
Let each attempt to prove the power of the ring
He wears and aid that power with his own resolve
To do good works, his understanding kindness,
His whole-hearted trust in God and his humility.
And when the magic which these rings possess
Has proven its continued power in your children's
And children's children's lives—
Then I invite them to appear again
Before this court. When a thousand years have passed
A wiser man will sit upon this chair
And render justice. Thus the modest judge.

SALADIN. My God!

NATHAN. If you believe that you're this wiser man
Of whom I spoke—

SALADIN (*quickly rises, steps close to* NATHAN *and takes his hand, keeping it in his during the remainder of this scene*).
I who am merely dust? I who am nothing? God!

NATHAN. What troubles you?

SALADIN. Oh Nathan! No, the thousand years have not yet
    passed,
The judge's chair is not for me.
Go, Nathan; leave me now—but be my friend.

NATHAN. But—have you nothing else to tell me?

SALADIN. No, nothing.

NATHAN. Nothing at all?

SALADIN. Nothing at all. Why do you ask?

NATHAN. I should have liked to have the opportunity
Of putting a request before you.

SALADIN. You'll always have that opportunity.
What is it, Nathan?

NATHAN. I've just returned; I've traveled far and wide
Collecting debts and find myself embarrassed
By the amount of money I have on my hands.
Now, since the future once again looks dark,
I wonder where it would be safe,
And it occurs to me that you—since wars
Are always costly—might have use for it.

SALADIN (*looking steadily into his eyes*).
I shall not ask you, Nathan, if Al Hafi
Has come to talk to you since you've been back,
Nor question if you made this offer on your own
Or only to forestall what you suspected I—

NATHAN. Suspected?

SALADIN. You would be right! Forgive me—I could see
No other way—I must confess—I was about—

NATHAN. To ask for what I offered you?

SALADIN. Precisely.

NATHAN. Well, all the better. We have found a way
To help each other. I will not be able, though,
To send you all I have at once because
I first must pay a debt, a large amount,

To a young Templar whom I think you know.

SALADIN. A Templar? Does your gold support
The worst of all my enemies?

NATHAN. I speak of only one—the one whose life you spared.

SALADIN. Oh yes. I do remember now.
I had forgotten him completely. Yes—
Do you know him? Do you know where he is?

NATHAN. But don't you know how great a blessing
The mercy that you showed him proved for me?
He risked his life, but recently regained,
To save my daughter from a fiery death.

SALADIN. He did? He looked the man to do such things.
My brother would have done the same.
They're very much alike. Go, Nathan—find the youth,
Bring him to me. My sister never knew
My brother. Now at last she'll see the likeness
Of Assad, about whom she's heard so much from me.
How strange! How one good deed, although the fruit
Of but one moment's fleeting passion,
Gives birth to other noble deeds! Quick, bring him here.

NATHAN (*lets go of* SALADIN'S *hand*). I will. As for the
    rest, we are agreed.   (*He leaves.*)

SALADIN. I should have let my sister listen.
How can I ever tell her all that's happened?
                        (*He leaves by the other door.*)

SCENE 8. *The grove of palm trees near the monastery. The
Templar is waiting for Nathan.*

TEMPLAR (*walks up and down, silently arguing with himself;
finally he blurts out*):
Here, tired out, the sacrificial lamb must rest.
All right—I do no longer ask myself
What happens in my soul, nor do I try
To get the scent of what the future holds.
I fled in vain. And yet—what else was there to do?
I had to flee, and now—now come what may.
The blow I had so long and strenuously
Avoided fell—and hit me like a thunderbolt.
To see her, whom I had no wish to see,
And to decide that I could never take
My eyes from her again, was one. Decide?

Deciding is to have a purpose and to act;
I let things happen to me and did nothing.
To see her meant to feel that I was snared,
Enmeshed with her. That's how it will remain.
To live without her is unthinkable,
It would be death, death even where we may
Go after death. If this is love,
A Christian and a Templar loves a Jewish girl.
What of it? I have buried many prejudices.
In this, the Praised and Promised Land,
Which I, too, shall now praise forever.
What can my Order ask of me,
Now that the Templar I once was is dead?
He died the moment he was taken prisoner
By Saladin. And is this head, a gift
From Saladin, the same head that I used to have?
This head is new, knows nothing of the foolish thoughts
Which kept that other, older head enslaved.
This is a better head and better suited
To understand God's laws. This much I know.
With this new head, I can begin to think
The way my father must have thought,
Unless they told me lying fairy tales
About him. Fairy tales? Perhaps,
But now that I risk stumbling over the very stones
Which made him fall, they seem more credible than ever.
And I would rather fall where other men
Have fallen than walk on unscathed
On roads that only weaklings choose.
He set me an example and of his
Approval I am sure. Why look to others, then?
To Nathan? He is sure not only to applaud,
But spur me on. Oh, what a Jew is Nathan!
He wants to look like nothing but a Jew.
And here he comes, he runs! His face aglow
With happiness. Who ever came from Saladin
Unhappy? Nathan! Hey!

SCENE 9. *Nathan and the Templar.*

NATHAN. Thank God, I've found you!
TEMPLAR. You stayed a long time with the Sultan.
NATHAN. It did not seem so long. I was delayed

Before I went to him. Oh, Curd! That man
Deserves his fame. And yet his fame
Is but a shadow of the man.
Now I must tell you first—

TEMPLAR. What?

NATHAN. He wants to see you, wants you just as soon
As you can come. But first come home with me;
There's something I must do for him before I go.
And then we shall be on our way.

TEMPLAR. I cannot set a foot into your house again
Before—

NATHAN. You went, then. Good! And have you talked to her?
Well? Tell me, did you like Rebecca?

TEMPLAR. I like her more than I can say. But I—
I won't see her again—unless you promise,
Promise now, that I can see her always and forever.

NATHAN. What do you mean?

TEMPLAR (*after a short pause, suddenly embraces* NATHAN).
My father!

NATHAN. Young man!

TEMPLAR (*just as quickly lets go of him*).
Young man? Not son? Please, Nathan! I implore you!
Do not think less of nature's bonds
Because they are the first, do not think more
Of others that may follow later. Be content
With being human. Do not push me back.

NATHAN. My dear, dear friend!

TEMPLAR. Not son? Not even if her gratitude
Already had prepared the way for love?
Not even if the merest hint from you
Were all that both of us awaited
To sink into each other's arms?
Why don't you speak?

NATHAN. You take me by surprise, young Knight.

TEMPLAR. Surprise? Am I surprising you perhaps
With your own thoughts? Do they seem strange
When I express them? No, you cannot be surprised.

NATHAN. I shall first have to know your father's place
Among the Stauffen family.

TEMPLAR. What, Nathan? At this moment you feel nothing
But idle curiosity?

NATHAN. You see, I knew a Stauffen once whose name
Was also Conrad.

TEMPLAR. What of it if my father had that name?

NATHAN. Is that the truth?

TEMPLAR. I am called after him; for Curd is Conrad.

NATHAN. And still—the Conrad I once knew
Could not have been your father, for he was, like you,
A Templar, and he never married.

TEMPLAR. Oh that!

NATHAN. I beg your pardon?

TEMPLAR. He could have been my father all the same.

NATHAN. You must be joking.

TEMPLAR. And you are so particular! Suppose
I were his bastard. I don't mind.
That's not a bad breed, either. But enough
Of this investigation of my pedigree.
I shall dispense with questions about yours.
Not that I have the slightest doubt
About your genealogy. Oh no!
I'm sure that you can trace it, branch by branch,
To Abraham, and back from there I know
The family so well myself
That I would certify it under oath.

NATHAN. Do not be bitter. I do not deserve it.
As yet I have refused you nothing.
But I don't want to rush
What must be well considered. That is all.

TEMPLAR. You are quite sure that there is nothing else?
In that case, please forgive me.

NATHAN. Come with me, then.

TEMPLAR. Not to your house! No, no. There is a fire!
Go by yourself, I shall await you here.
If ever I see her again, I'll see her always.
If I do not, I have already seen her once too often.

NATHAN. I shall be back as soon as possible.

SCENE 10. *The Templar alone; later Daja.*

TEMPLAR. Enough! More than enough! The human brain
Can hold so much and yet, at times,
It suddenly is filled, unable

To grasp another thing, be it the merest trifle.
No matter, let the brain be brimful
With whatever it may be. Just patience!
The soul will knead the bloated matter,
Will sort it out and thus make room for more,
Let light and order reappear.
Is this the first time that I've been in love?
Was what I know as love, not love at all?
Is only what I now feel real love?

DAJA (*has stealthily come up from the side*).
Psht! Sir! My lord!

TEMPLAR. Who calls? Oh, Daja, it is you.

DAJA. I have crept past him, but where you are standing
He can still see us. Quick, come over here
Behind this tree.

TEMPLAR. What is it? Why so secretive?

DAJA. It is, indeed, a secret I must tell you;
In fact, a double secret. One of them
I know, the other one is yours.
Shall we exchange our secrets? You tell yours,
And then I'll tell you mine.

TEMPLAR. I gladly would if only I had some idea
What you consider my great secret.
However, when you tell me yours, no doubt,
I'll understand. So—go ahead.

DAJA. What do you think? Oh no, sir, you come first.
Believe me, what I know would be useless to you
If I don't know your secret. Quick now, tell me!
If I must ask a lot of questions first,
You would not prove your confidence in me,
I would not tell my secret while you would
Have squandered yours. Poor Knight! Poor men
Who even think that they can keep a secret
That one of us would like to know!

TEMPLAR. A secret which we do not even know we have.

DAJA. Perhaps. In that case I shall prove my friendship
By showing you just what your secret is.
Now tell me this: why did you leave the house
In such unseemly haste? Why did you leave
Rebecca high and dry? Why did you not come back
With Nathan? Were you then not impressed at all?
Or else so much? That must be it. That's it!

Yes, I can always tell when a poor bird
Is stuck upon the lime and beats his wings.
Why not confess? You are in love with her!
You love her madly! Let me tell you something—

TEMPLAR. I love her madly—yes! You understand
These things extremely well.

DAJA. Admitting that you are in love with her
Will do. The madness is not necessary.

TEMPLAR. Because it's obvious. A Templar must be mad
To love a Jewish girl.

DAJA. Quite true, that does not make much sense, but sense
Appears sometimes where we would least suspect it.
Would it be really so strange if Christ
Showed us a way to Him which prudent men,
Left to themselves, would never choose?

TEMPLAR. So solemn? (*Aside.*) If I put "circumspection"
Instead of "Christ," she may be right.
(*Aloud.*) You now have made me much more curious
Than I am used to being.

DAJA. This is the land of wonders!

TEMPLAR (*aside*). Of wonderful events, at least.
Could it be otherwise when all the world
Crowds into this one, little spot?
(*To* DAJA.) I have admitted what you wanted, Daja:
I am in love with her and cannot live without her.

DAJA. You're certain? Promise me, then, on your oath
That you will marry her, that you will save
Her life on earth—her soul for all eternity.

TEMPLAR. How can I swear that I will do
What is not in my power to accomplish?

DAJA. You have the power. With a single word
I give you all the power you will need.

TEMPLAR. A power which would even overcome
Her father?

DAJA. Her father! He will have to give his blessing.

TEMPLAR. Will have to, Daja? No, he has not fallen
Among robbers yet! He can't be forced.

DAJA. All right. He will be forced to want it, then.
And in the end he may be glad of it.

TEMPLAR. Will have to want it? Will be glad of it?
Then let me tell you, Daja, that I've tried

Already once to sound him out.

DAJA. And he did not agree?

TEMPLAR. His answer was a dissonance, and I felt hurt.

DAJA. What do you say? He did not jump with joy
At the mere hint that you might want to marry her?
Did he retreat into his shell, shrink back
In icy silence and make difficulties?

TEMPLAR. About like that.

DAJA. Well then! I shall not hesitate another moment.
(*Pause.*)

TEMPLAR. But—you still hesitate?

DAJA. He's such a good man otherwise. I owe
So much to him. Why can he not see reason?
God knows, I hate to force his hand.

TEMPLAR. Please, Daja, make it short and quick!
Dispel this terrible uncertainty.
But if you are not sure yourself
If what you are about to do is good or bad—
Be silent. I shall soon forget
That you have kept a secret from me.

DAJA. You do not hold me back—you spur me on!
This is the secret: Rebecca is not Jewish,
She is a Christian.

TEMPLAR (*coldly*). Is that right? My congratulations!
Has it been difficult? The trouble is well worth it.
Continue to increase the heaven's populace
If you cannot achieve the same on earth.

DAJA. Does what I told you merit this derision?
Does it mean nothing to a Christian knight
That his beloved is a Christian, not a Jewess?

TEMPLAR. I'm all the more impressed since it is you
Who made her Christian.

DAJA. Oh, that is what you thought? Oh no!
I want to see the one who could convert
That girl. No, fortunately she has always been
What to become would be impossible for her.

TEMPLAR. Explain yourself—or go.

DAJA. She is the child of Christian parents, baptized—

TEMPLAR (*quickly*). And Nathan?

DAJA. He is not her father.

TEMPLAR. Nathan is not her father? Do you know
What you are saying, Daja?

DAJA. I speak the truth, and it has often made me weep
The bloody tears of outraged innocence.

TEMPLAR. He brought her up as if she were his daughter
And thus transformed a Christian child into a Jewish girl?

DAJA. That is exactly what he did.

TEMPLAR. She does not know the circumstances of her birth?
He never told her anything about all this?

DAJA. He never did.

TEMPLAR. Not only did he raise the child in this delusion,
He let the girl, as she grew up,
Continue in her childish error?

DAJA. Unfortunately, that is true.

TEMPLAR. How is it possible? How could a man,
As good and wise as Nathan, dare to falsify
The voice of nature, to misguide her heart
Which, left alone, would take a different course?
Indeed, you have confided to me, Daja,
A secret—which has great importance—
Which may have consequences—which confuses me—
To which I have no ready answer.
Give me some time to think. Go—leave me now.
He will come back and may surprise us here.

DAJA. My God!

TEMPLAR. I cannot talk to him just now.
If you should see him, tell him please
That I will meet him later at the Sultan's palace.

DAJA. Be careful that he does not notice anything.
It's only meant to give the final push,
And to remove all scruples you may have
About Rebecca. When you take her with you
To Europe—you will not leave me behind?

TEMPLAR. That—we shall see about. Now hurry back.

ACT IV

Scene 1. *The cloisters of the monastery. The Friar; later the Templar.*

Friar. Yes, yes. He must be right, the Patriarch.
Although, to tell the truth, I have not had
Much luck in doing all these chores for him.
Why does he always give me things like this to do?
I do not like to act so primly,
I don't enjoy persuading people what to do
Or sticking my big nose into affairs
That are of no concern to me.
I have my fingers in too many pies.
Did I retire, all by myself, from the big world,
Only to get involved with everyone
To suit the whim of others?

   Templar (*hurries toward him*). Oh, here you are, good
      Friar. I have looked for you
In every corner of the town.

   Friar. You've looked for me, sir?

   Templar. But don't you recognize me, Friar?

   Friar. Of course, I do. But I had hoped
That I would never in this life see you again.
I have been hoping that, because—God knows—
I hated making that proposal
That I was forced to put before you, sir.
And secretly I hoped that you would turn it down.
How glad I was—just privately, of course—
About your quick and firm refusal.
That job was nothing that a knight
Had any right to do. But now—you're here.
The poison slowly took effect.

   Templar. How do you know what brought me here?
I hardly know myself.

   Friar. You must have thought it over and, at last,
You came to the conclusion that, perhaps,
The Patriarch was right; that if you went

Along with him, his schemes would bring you gold
And honors; and, to clinch the matter,
You thought a foe remains a foe,
May he have proved a hundred times to be your friend.
You must have weighed all that and now you're here
To offer him your services. Good God!

    TEMPLAR. You are a good and pious man. Don't worry!
That's not the reason why I want to see
The Patriarch. I have not changed my mind,
And would not want to spoil for anything
The good opinion which a decent, honest man
Has thought I merited. No, it's not that.
I've come in order to consult the Patriarch—

    FRIAR. Consult the Patriarch? A knight consult
The clergy? (*He glances timidly in all directions.*)

    TEMPLAR. Quite right. The point I have in mind
Is rather—clerical.

    FRIAR. But even so, a cleric never asks a knight's advice,
In questions that concern the knighthood.

    TEMPLAR. A cleric has the right to make mistakes,
A right which knights don't envy him.
In my case, if what I must do concerned
Myself alone, if I had to account
For what I do to no one but myself,
I would not need your Patriarch at all.
But sometimes I would rather do what's wrong,
Although the experts think it's right,
Than what in my opinion is correct.
And then, religion, too, is partisan;
No matter how objective we may think to be,
And without realizing it,
We only counterbalance what religion says.
Since that's the way it is, it probably is well.

    FRIAR. Now there—I just don't know. Quite frankly, sir,
I am not sure I understand all that.

    TEMPLAR. And yet—(*Aside.*) What do I want, in fact? Let's
      see.
Do I want dictum or advice? And if advice,
The common sense or the profound variety?
(*To the* FRIAR.) Thank you, good Friar. Thank you for the hint.
Why ask the Patriarch? You be my Patriarch!
For, after all, I want to put my question

Not to a Patriarch who may or may not be
A Christian, but to a Christian who just happens
To be a Patriarch. My question, then, is this—

FRIAR. Oh no, sir! Please, no more! You are forgetting
Who I am. To know a lot brings lots of worries.
I vowed that I would care for one thing only.
Thank God, here comes the Patriarch.
Stay here. He has already seen you.

SCENE 2. *The Patriarch approaches through the cloisters
with all the pomp of his clerical office; the Templar and
the Friar.*

TEMPLAR. I wish I could avoid him. That is not the man for
    me.
A red-faced, fat, and friendly prelate. And—
What splendor!

FRIAR. Oh that! Why, you should see him when he goes
To court! Now he has only visited the sick.

TEMPLAR. He must put Saladin himself to shame.

PATRIARCH (*comes closer and signals to the* FRIAR).
Come here! That is the Templar, is it not?
What does he want?

FRIAR. I do not know, your Eminence.

PATRIARCH (*approaches the* TEMPLAR, *while the* FRIAR *and the*
PATRIARCH's *retinue retire to the background*).
Well, sir. I am delighted at having finally
The pleasure! So brave and still so young!
God willing, something may become of you.

TEMPLAR. But hardly more than I am now, your Eminence.
Quite likely even less.

PATRIARCH. I surely hope, my pious Knight, that you will live
And flourish in the service of Christianity.
And for the greater glory of our Lord.
I'm certain that you will succeed
If only you will let your youthful courage
Be guided by mature advice.
What can I do for you?

TEMPLAR. Give me what you just said a young man needs
The most: mature advice.

PATRIARCH. Delighted. But I hope that you will follow it.

TEMPLAR. Not blindly, though?

PATRIARCH. Of course not. God intended Man to think,
And Man should use his reason where appropriate.
Yet, can our reason be—or should it be—
Applied to every question? Not at all.
Let us assume, for instance, that the Lord,
In His great wisdom, deems one worthy
Of being shown by one of His angelic servants—
That is to say, by one who serves His church—
A very special way in which he could
Advance the welfare of all Christendom
And help the church to prosper—would he
Be bold enough to question, in a case like that,
The reasonableness of the demand
Which God, creator of all reason, makes of him?
And would he dare to measure the eternal laws
Of the resplendent Heavens with the puny yardstick
Of little vanities and honor? Enough.
What is the question, sir, on which you seek advice?

TEMPLAR. Suppose, your Eminence, there were a Jew
Who had an only child—let us assume,
A girl—whom he had carefully brought up
And whom he loved more than his life.
The girl, in turn, loved him with filial
Devotion. Now, if I were told that she
Was not, in fact, the Jew's own daughter,
But that she had been found as child, or bought
Or stolen; if it were further known
That she was born of Christian parents,
Was baptized but had been brought up
In the belief that she was Jewish,
And that our Jew, who never told her who she was,
Was really not her father—in that case,
Your Eminence, what should be done?

PATRIARCH. I shudder! First, however, tell me, sir,
If this is a fictitious case or fact?
I mean to say, did you invent this story
Or did it happen, happen still, perhaps?

TEMPLAR. I thought, your Eminence, that your reply
Would be the same in either case.

PATRIARCH. The same? There you can see, dear sir, how wrong
Our reasoning can be in matters of the church.
No, not at all the same! If you thought up

This story just to play a game of wits,
It certainly does not deserve our serious
Attention. In that case, it is more suitable
For presentation on the stage
Where questions of this kind are frequently discussed
Amid the public's generous applause.
But if it's not a droll, dramatic tale,
Invented to make fun of me, if it is fact,
If furthermore the case concerns our diocese,
Our much beloved city of Jerusalem,
Why, then of course—

TEMPLAR. What then?

PATRIARCH. The Jew would expeditiously be punished
As both the papal and imperial laws provide
For such a vile and criminal offense.

TEMPLAR. I see.

PATRIARCH. These laws provide that any Jew who may seduce
A Christian to commit apostasy
Be burned—burned at the stake—

TEMPLAR. I see.

PATRIARCH. And all the more, in case the Jew is guilty
Of breaking forcibly the holy bond
Of baptism, by which a poor, defenseless child
Is tied to his Eternal Mother.
And is not everything we do to children force,
Except, of course, that which our church sees fit
To do to them?

TEMPLAR. But if the child may easily have died
In misery unless the Jew had taken pity?

PATRIARCH. That makes no difference. The Jew must burn.
Far better for the child to die in misery
Than to be saved and be forever damned.
And furthermore, what right has any Jew
To outwit God? For God can save without his help
Whomever He decides to save.

TEMPLAR. But He could also, I should think, admit
To heaven anyone He likes, despite the Jew.

PATRIARCH. That makes no difference. The Jew must burn.

TEMPLAR. That saddens me. Particularly since I'm told
That he did not bring up the girl in his religion,
But rather without any special faith,
And that he taught her about God no more,

Nor less than what is reasonable.

PATRIARCH. That makes no difference. The Jew must burn.
If that is true, he ought to burn, in fact,
Three times. To let a child grow up without religion!
And not to teach a child the duties of his faith!
That's terrible! And I must say, dear sir,
That I am quite surprised—

TEMPLAR. Your Eminence, the rest, God willing, at confession.
(*He turns to leave.*)

PATRIARCH. What's that? Do you refuse to tell the rest?
You do not name the scoundrel? You refuse
To bring the Jew before me? Oh, I know
What I shall do. I shall immediately
Go to the Sultan. He has signed and sealed
Capitulations under which he grants
Assistance in enforcing our prerogatives.
He must protect all doctrines which we count
As sacrosanct in our religion.
Thank God, we still have the original
Which bears his signature and seal.
I shall explain to him, and he will understand
How great a danger even for the state
Lies in a lack of faith. No faith—
And all the bonds of civil life are loosened,
If not torn to shreds. Such villainy must perish.

TEMPLAR. I very much regret that I have not the time
To savor this most exemplary sermon
More leisurely. I'm on my way to Saladin.

PATRIARCH. You are? Well, in that case—indeed—

TEMPLAR. I shall announce your visit to the Sultan
If that is what your Eminence desires.

PATRIARCH. Yes, yes. Of course. Yes, I have heard
That Saladin has shown you mercy.
I would be grateful, sir—indeed, most grateful—
If you were to remember me most kindly to His Highness.
My zeal to serve the Lord inspires me,
And if perchance I go too far, it is
To serve Him all the better. Please, keep that in mind.
That story of the Jew, of course, was just—
A point of disputation, shall we say?
And nothing else? That is to say—

TEMPLAR. Indeed, a point of disputation. (*He leaves.*)

PATRIARCH (*aside*). Which I am going to explore most thoroughly.
That might well be another little job
For Brother Bonafides. (*To the* FRIAR.) Psst, come here, my son.
(*He leaves, talking to the* FRIAR.)

SCENE 3. *A room in Saladin's palace. Slaves are bringing in bags which they arrange in rows on the floor. Saladin; later, Sittah.*

SALADIN (*enters*). Are there still more! Are many left?

A SLAVE. As many as we've brought.

SALADIN. Take what is left to Sittah. Where's Al Hafi?
He shall take all that we have here.
Or should I send it to my father?
If I keep it, it will again slip through my fingers.
I must be hard this time. It will take crafty beggars
To pry the money loose. Until the gold
From Egypt comes at last, the poor will have to see
How they get on. But we must still keep up
The custom of distributing our alms
At the Sepulchre. The Christian pilgrims must not leave
With empty hands. If only—

SITTAH (*enters*). Why do you send the gold to me?

SALADIN. To pay my debts. If there is more, put it aside.

SITTAH. Has Nathan not yet come? Where is the Templar?

SALADIN. We're searching for him everywhere.

SITTAH. Look what I found in glancing through a box
Of jewelry. (*She shows him a small painting.*)

SALADIN. My brother! There he is! Or rather—was.
Oh, that I had to lose you at such tender age!
What could I not have done with you as my
Companion! Let me have the picture, please.
Yes, I remember well. One morning,
He gave it to your older sister, Lilla,
When she refused to let him go.
That was the last time he rode out—
And I just let him go—alone. It broke her heart.
She never did forgive me; soon she died.
I should have held him back. No one has seen him since.

SITTAH. Poor brother.

SALADIN. Poor brother, yes. But some day all of us will go
And not return. And then—who knows?
Not only death can bring a youth of his kind down.
Some dangers are as fatal to the strong
As to the weak. Now, let me keep the picture.
When I compare it with the man
We are about to see, I wonder—
Is there a real similarity between the two
Or has my fantasy created it?

SITTAH. Exactly. But give me the picture.
Let me compare. A woman's eye sees more.

SALADIN (*to a guard who enters*). Is it the Templar? Send
    him in.

SITTAH. I do not want to interrupt your conversation,
Nor irritate him with my curiosity.
    (*Off to one side, she sits down on a sofa and drops her veil.*)

SALADIN. Yes, you are doing well to sit aside.
(*To himself.*) I wonder! Will his tone of voice remind me
Of Assad? The memory of Assad's voice
Must still be somewhere, sleeping in my soul.

SCENE 4. *Saladin and the Templar.*

TEMPLAR. I am your prisoner—

SALADIN. My prisoner? I granted you your life,
Would I not also grant you liberty?

TEMPLAR. You must decide, and I shall listen.
It is not fitting for a prisoner
To take his captor's generosity
For granted. But don't expect effusive thanks
For having spared my life. That would not be
In keeping with my knighthood and my character.
In any case, my life belongs to you.

SALADIN. My only wish is that you never use
Your life to help my enemies.
I'd gladly grant them one more pair of hands,
But I would envy them possession of your heart.
You are a brave young man. You did not disappoint me.
In body and in soul, you are like Assad.
So much so that I feel like asking you,
Where have you hibernated? Where's the Jinnistan
In which this flower was so well preserved?

I feel like asking, do you still remember
The time when we did this or that together?
I feel like scolding you for going out alone
On one adventure which I could not share,
For having this one secret which is yours alone.
Yes, I would say these things to you
If I saw only you; but looking at myself,
I know that I am dreaming. Dreams or not,
This much is true: some Assad has returned
To brighten with his bloom my autumn.
Are you content to play that part?

TEMPLAR. Whatever you may wish I've always wanted.

SALADIN. Let's see if that is true. Would you consent
To stay with me, as Christian or as Muslim?
Stay as you like, a helmet on your head
Or else a turban. Choose. I never asked
That all the trees must grow the self-same bark.

TEMPLAR. No, if you did, you would not be the man
You are: a hero who would rather be
A gardener in Paradise.

SALADIN. Your high opinion of me gives me hope
That we are half-agreed.

TEMPLAR. Not only half, we *are* agreed.

SALADIN (*extending his hand to the* TEMPLAR). Your word?

TEMPLAR (*taking his hand*). My bond. And so I give you more
Than you could ever take. Now I am yours.

SALADIN. How many gifts a single day can bring!
You did not bring him with you?

TEMPLAR. Whom?

SALADIN. Nathan, of course.

TEMPLAR (*coldly*). I came alone.

SALADIN. How brave a deed! How wise the fortune
Which let it benefit so good a man!

TEMPLAR. Yes, yes.

SALADIN. But why so cold? No one whom God has chosen
As instrument of His designs should be so cold,
Not even for the sake of modesty.

TEMPLAR. There are so many sides to everything
That it is often difficult to see
How they can fit together.

SALADIN. Consider only those which are the best,

And praise the Lord. He knows how all the parts
Will fit to make a whole. But if you are
So difficult, I must be on my guard.
I, too, have many sides which may be hard to fit.

TEMPLAR. Your disapproval hurts, especially
Since usually suspicion
Is not one of my graver faults.

SALADIN. Of whom are you suspicious, then? Of Nathan?
Why should you be suspicious of him? Tell me.
Give me the first proof of your confidence.

TEMPLAR. I do not blame him. I'm angry with myself—

SALADIN. And why?

TEMPLAR. For dreaming that a Jew could ever stop—
Being a Jew. That was the daydream which I had.

SALADIN. Tell me about your dream.

TEMPLAR. You know of Nathan's daughter, Sultan,
And what I did for her, I did—because I did it.
I was too proud to harvest what I had not sown,
I did not want her gratitude.
Thus I refused to see her while her father
Was far away. As soon as he returned
And heard the story, he was quick to come,
He thanked me, said he hoped that I might like
His daughter, spoke of prospects and of pleasant vistas.
At last, I was persuaded and agreed to visit her.
I found, indeed, a girl—I am ashamed
To tell you, Sultan—

SALADIN. Ashamed? Because a Jewish girl
Made such a deep impression on you? No,
That cannot be!

TEMPLAR. Not that. Ashamed because my heart,
Still giddy with the father's amiable babbling,
Did not resist. Thus, like a fool,
I jumped into the fire a second time.
Now I was pleading—and I was refused.

SALADIN. Refused?

TEMPLAR. The prudent father did not turn me down
With just so many words, of course.
He needed time to think, he said.
He had to make inquiries! Certainly!
Just as I did! Did I not make inquiries
And carefully consider all the pros and cons,

While she was screaming in the burning house?
By God, it must be wonderful to be
So wise, so prudent and deliberate!

SALADIN. Now, now. Make some allowance for his age.
How long can he resist? Does he demand
That you become a Jew before agreeing?

TEMPLAR. Who knows?

SALADIN. Who knows? A man who knows him better.

TEMPLAR. The superstitions which we learn as children
Do not relax their grip on us,
Not even when we know them just for what they are.
Not all are free who mock their chains.

SALADIN. Yes, very well observed. But Nathan—

TEMPLAR. The worst of superstitions is to think
One's own the only tolerable superstition.

SALADIN. That may well be, but Nathan—

TEMPLAR. To think the superstitions which one has oneself
To be the one which men, in their stupidity,
May well accept until, some day, they may be wiser.
To think—

SALADIN. All very well. But Nathan does not have
That weakness.

TEMPLAR. Exactly what I thought. But if this paragon
Of virtue should turn out to be
So common and so mean a Jew that he would try
To get his hands on Christian children
And bring them up as Jews? What then?

SALADIN. Who's saying that about him?

TEMPLAR. The very girl he used as bait for me,
Whom he paraded as the prize with which
He would reward what I was quite content
To do for him without a payment—
That girl is not his daughter, she's a Christian child!

SALADIN. And yet he would not give her to you?

TEMPLAR (*violently*). No matter if he wants or not. He is
    exposed,
His talk of tolerance—hypocrisy;
And I shall set the dogs upon his trail
Who soon will catch this Jewish wolf,
Dressed in his sheep's coat of philosophy.

SALADIN (*sternly*). Be quiet, Christian!

TEMPLAR. What? Quiet, Christian? When Jews and Muslims
    may insist
On being Jews and Muslims, why not give
A Christian, too, the right of being Christian?

    SALADIN (*still more sternly*). Be quiet, Christian!

    TEMPLAR (*with equanimity*). I feel the full weight of the
    accusation
Which you compress into this word
Ah, if I only knew how Assad, in my place, would act!

    SALADIN. Oh, not much better. Just as furiously, probably.
But how have you already learned
To charm me, just as Assad, with a single word?
Of course, if everything is as you say,
I do not recognize myself
The Nathan whom I thought I knew.
He is my friend, however, and my friends
Must never quarrel with each other.
Let me advise you. Do not go too far too quickly.
Don't throw him to the rabble, the fanatics,
Without a further thought. Keep quiet;
Your clergy would demand at once that I avenge them.
Don't be a Christian just to spite a Jew or Muslim.

    TEMPLAR. It almost would have been too late for your advice.
Had not the Patriarch been quite so thirsty
For Jewish blood, I might well have become his tool.

    SALADIN. You went to see the Patriarch before
You came to me?

    TEMPLAR. I did. Yes, in the storm of passion,
The maelstrom of my doubts, I went. Forgive me.
You will, I fear, no longer recognize
In me the traits of your beloved Assad.

    SALADIN. No, even in your doubts and fears you are like him.
I think I know the faults from which our virtues spring.
Develop them—and I shall never blame
You for your faults. Go now and look for Nathan,
As he searched you before, and bring him here.
I must and will succeed in reconciling you.
If you are serious about the girl,
Be without fear. She will be yours.
And Nathan will be taught a lesson
About his bringing up a Christian girl
Without the benefit of pork!

(*The* TEMPLAR *leaves.* SITTAH *rises from the sofa.*)

SCENE 5. *Saladin and Sittah.*

SITTAH. How strange!

SALADIN. Now, after seeing him, would you not say
That Assad must have been a good and handsome youth?

SITTAH. Yes, if he was like him—unless the Templar served
As model for this picture. You forgot
To ask about his parents.

SALADIN. And especially about his mother, eh?
To see if not his mother lived, perhaps,
Once in our country? Is that it?

SITTAH. Not bad.

SALADIN. That's not impossible at all.
Assad was always welcome to the company
Of pretty, Christian ladies and himself
So fond of them that there was even talk—
Enough. One does not like to talk about it.
Suffice that he is back, with all his faults
And all his moods, and with his tender heart.
Oh, Nathan must give him the girl.

SITTAH. Not give him—leave her to him.

SALADIN. Quite true. For where are Nathan's rights
If he is not her father? Raising her
Meant only taking her own father's place,
Not being in reality her father.

SITTAH. Well, then, why could you not at once
Remove her from the tutelage of her illegal owner
And bring her here?

SALADIN. Do you think there is need for that?

SITTAH. Not really—but I am curious.
That's why I asked. With certain men,
I simply have to know as soon as possible
What kind of girl they love.

SALADIN. Well, let us send for her, then.

SITTAH. Do I have your permission, Brother?

SALADIN. You have, but watch that it will not appear
To Nathan that we wish to separate
The girl from him by force.

SITTAH. I shall keep that in mind.

SALADIN. And I must see what happened to Al Hafi.

SCENE 6. *The open hallway in Nathan's house, looking out toward the grove of palm trees; this is the same setting as that of the opening scene in Act I. Some of the goods and valuables which Nathan has brought back have meanwhile been unpacked. Nathan and Daja are discussing them.*

DAJA. Oh, how exquisite! How magnificent!
No one but you can choose such gifts.
Where did you get the gold-stitched silver fabric?
Was it expensive? What a bridal gown!
Fit for a queen.

NATHAN. Why bridal gown?

DAJA. Of course, you did not think of that the day
You bought it; now, however, nothing else
Will do. It must have been designed for brides:
The background white, the symbol of her innocence,
The golden rivers which run here and there—
The symbol of her wealth. You see? How lovely!

NATHAN. What is all this? About whose bridal gown
Was this most erudite, symbolic lecture?
Are you by any chance the bride?

DAJA. What? I?

NATHAN. Well, who then is the bride?

DAJA. I! Oh, dear God!

NATHAN. Well, who? Whose bridal gown then could it be?
All this is yours, these are your presents.

DAJA. This is for me? Not for Rebecca?

NATHAN. What I brought for Rebecca is in other bales;
Now take your things and hurry; take your plunder.

DAJA. You're tempting me! But if you offered me
The wealth of all the world, I would not touch
A single thing until you swear to use
This golden opportunity
Which heaven will not grant a second time.

NATHAN. What opportunity am I to use?

DAJA. Do not pretend you do not understand.
In brief: the Templar loves Rebecca,

And you must give her to him. Thus, at last,
Your sin, about which I can keep
No longer silent, will be ended.
Rebecca will be once more with her Christian friends,
Will once again become what she has been;
And you, our benefactor who deserves
Our gratitude, will not instead reap hate.

NATHAN. So it is still the same old melody?
You've added only one new string
To the old instrument; and that, I fear,
Is neither tuned, nor will it last.

DAJA. And why?

NATHAN. I don't have anything against the Templar;
Him less than anyone would I begrudge
Rebecca, but—you must be patient.

DAJA. Be patient? Is that not the same old tune
That you have always played?

NATHAN. A few more days; that's all I ask.
Who's coming over there? A friar.
Go, ask him what he wants.

DAJA. What do you think?
(*She walks toward the friar and talks to him.*)

NATHAN. Well? Give him something. Do not make him ask.
(*Aside.*) If only I could see a way to broach
The subject to the Templar, yet to hide
The reason for my curiosity!
For if I tell him why, and my suspicion proves
Without foundation, I will have needlessly
Divulged the father's secret. (*To* DAJA.) Well?

DAJA. He wants to talk to you.

NATHAN. Then bring him in and let us talk alone.

SCENE 7. *Nathan and the Friar.*

NATHAN (*aside*). I wish I could remain her father!
If not in name, I still could be her father.
And she would even call me Father,
Once she discovers what that means to me.
(*To the* FRIAR.) What can I do for you, my pious Friar?

FRIAR. Not much. I'm glad to see you well, kind sir.

NATHAN. You seem to know me.

FRIAR. Why, of course. Who has not heard of Nathan?
You have impressed your name on many hands,
It's been on mine for many years.

NATHAN (*reaches for his purse*). Come, Friar, let me then
    refresh the imprint.

FRIAR. No, thank you. I don't want to steal
From poorer men than I. But I would like,
On my part, to refresh your memory a little,
Your recollection of my name. I, too,
Take pride in having given you a little something
Which you did not despise.

NATHAN. Forgive me. I'm ashamed. What is your name?
What did you give me? Take its value sevenfold
As penalty for my forgetfulness.

FRIAR. First let me tell you how, and just today,
I was reminded of the token
With which I once entrusted you.

NATHAN. A token?

FRIAR. Not long ago I was still living
As hermit at Quarantana, near Jericho.
One day I was attacked, a band of Arab robbers
Burned down my chapel and destroyed my cell.
They dragged me with them. Luckily, I got away
And reached Jerusalem. I asked the Patriarch
For just a little place where I would have
An opportunity to serve my Lord
In solitude until I died in peace.

NATHAN. I'm burning with curiosity, good Friar.
Be brief. The token! How about the token?

FRIAR. I'm coming to it, Mr. Nathan. Well,
The Patriarch was kind enough to promise me
A hermitage, as soon as one be empty, on Mount Tabor.
Meanwhile he asked me to remain as friar
Here in the monastery. That is where I am.
But many hundred times a day, I wish
I were on Tabor in my hermitage,
For many of the things the Patriarch
Asks me to do are most distasteful to me.
For instance—

NATHAN. Please, good Friar!

FRIAR. I'm coming to it now. Someone has told

The Patriarch today a tale about a Jew
Who—so it seems—lives hereabouts
And raises—so he says—a Christian child
As his own daughter.

NATHAN (*taken aback*). What?

FRIAR. Allow me, Nathan. Let me finish. Now—
He ordered me to snoop around and find
This Jew as soon as possible,
And all the while he greatly fumed and raged
About this misdeed, which he calls a sin
Against the Holy Ghost, a sin that is to us
The sin of sins, except that fortunately
We do not know ourselves too well
In what it really consists—now then,
When I heard that, my conscience suddenly
Awoke and I remembered that, quite possibly,
I might myself have been a helper long ago
In the commission of this monstrous,
Unpardonable sin. Now tell me this:
Did, eighteen years ago, a groom bring you
A little girl, a few weeks old?

NATHAN. Why—yes—indeed—of course—

FRIAR. Then look at me! I am that groom.

NATHAN. You—are—

FRIAR. The knight who had me take the girl to you
Was—if my memory is right—a gentleman
Called Filneck—Wolf von Filneck.

NATHAN. That's right!

FRIAR. Because her mother recently had died,
And since he was to join the siege, I think,
Of Gaza—where, of course, he could not take
The girl—he sent the little one to you.
Did I not meet you with her in Darun?

NATHAN. Exactly.

FRIAR. It would not be surprising if my memory
Played tricks on me. I served so many gentlemen,
And this one only for the shortest time.
Soon after, he was killed near Askalon.
And he was such a good and kindly gentleman!

NATHAN. Yes, yes—a man who did so much for me.
He saved me more than once from dying by the sword.

FRIAR. Oh, good! You must have taken all the better care
Of your friend's little daughter.

NATHAN. Indeed, I have.

FRIAR. Where is the child? I hope she did not die?
Oh God, I hope she is alive! For then,
If no one else knows anything about
This story, all is well.

NATHAN. You're sure?

FRIAR. Oh, you can trust me, Nathan. Don't you see,
The way I feel is this: when I believe
That what I am about to do is good,
But it is very, very close
To being very, very bad—then I prefer
Not doing anything at all.
We usually are pretty clear about what's bad,
But never know too well just what is good.
It was quite natural that you would raise
This Christian child as your own daughter,
If you really meant to raise her well.
If that is what you did, with love and conscience,
I would not want to see you ill-rewarded.
I don't want that. Of course, it might have been
More prudent to have had another person raise
The girl as Christian, but then you certainly
Would not have loved this child as much.
And children do need love at such a tender age—
And be it love from a wild animal—
Far more than Christianity.
There's always time for that. If she grew up
A pious, healthy girl before your eyes,
She stayed just what she was before the eyes of God.
And is not all of our religion built
On Judaism? I have often stormed and wept
When Christians kept forgetting that our Lord,
That Christ himself was, after all, a Jew.

NATHAN. You, my good Friar, must step up and speak for me,
In the event that hate and bigotry
Should rise against me. Why?
Because of something—something— You shall know
The story, you alone, and take it to your grave.
My vanity has never tempted me
To tell the tale to anyone, but you

Shall be my confidant. Your heart is innocent.
And innocence alone can understand
What man, when he submits to God, can do.

FRIAR. You're moved to tears! What is it, Nathan?

NATHAN. When you found me in Darun with the child,
You did not know that only days before
The Christians in the town of Gath had killed
All Jews. Among them were my wife and sons—
My seven sons for whom I had great hopes.
They had found refuge in my brother's house,
And there they burned to death—

FRIAR. Good Lord!

NATHAN. When you arrived, I had been on my knees
Before my God for three whole days,
In sackcloth and in ashes, weeping bitter tears.
I wept, I also argued with the Lord;
I raved and ranted, cursed myself
And all the world—and swore undying hatred
To all Christianity.

FRIAR. I well believe it.

NATHAN. Yet, slowly reason did return.
With gentle voice it spoke: "There is a God
Despite all this; this, too, is God's design.
Arise and act the way you've always known
You should. It surely is not harder now to *act*
Than it has been to *understand*,
If only you are resolute; arise!"
I rose and called to God: "I have the will.
It's up to you. Will that my will persists."
That very moment you dismounted from your horse
And handed me the child, wrapped in your cloak.
I have forgotten what I said to you
And what you said to me, but this I know:
I took the child, I put her on my bed
And kissed her, fell on my knees and sobbed,
"My God, the first of seven has come back to me!"

FRIAR. Oh Nathan! Nathan, you're a Christian!
By God, a better Christian I have never seen.

NATHAN. So much the better—what makes me a Christian
In your eyes, makes you a Jew in mine.
But let's be done with all this sentiment.

Now we must act. Although the bonds of love
Which tie me to this one, strange girl are sevenfold;
Although the thought of losing seven sons again
By losing her is deadly, still—if Providence
Demands that I surrender her, I shall obey.

FRIAR. That is exactly what I meant to ask you.
But now your better self has given you
The same advice.

NATHAN. But I will not let anyone who comes along
Take her away from me by force.

FRIAR. Of course not.

NATHAN. Whoever wants her has to prove his prior right,
If not a better right than mine.

FRIAR. Why, certainly.

NATHAN. His right must be the right of blood and nature.

FRIAR. That's what I mean.

NATHAN. Well, then. Do you know any of her relatives?
A brother, uncle, cousin—anyone?
To him I shall surrender her, this girl,
Born and brought up to be the pride of any faith,
Of any family. I hope that you know more than I
About the family of your late master.

FRIAR. Unfortunately, Nathan, I do not.
I served him only briefly, as I told you.

NATHAN. But do you know her mother's family
At least? Was she not a von Stauffen?

FRIAR. That's possible. In fact, I think she was.

NATHAN. Was not her brother called Conrad von Stauffen?
A Templar?

FRIAR. Yes, if my memory is right, he was.
But wait! I just remember that I have
A little book that was my master's.
I took it from his cloak, next to his heart,
Before we buried him at Askalon.

NATHAN. Well?

FRIAR. It is a prayer book—we call it breviary—
A book, I thought, that might be useful yet
To someone—who can read. For I, of course, cannot.

NATHAN. That does not worry me. But what about the book?

FRIAR. This little book has, front and back, so I've been told,
Some notes which are—so I've been told—in his,
That is, my blessed master's hand. It is,
It seems, a list of all their relatives.

NATHAN. Oh, what a find! Run, hurry, bring the book.
I'll pay its weight in gold and a thousand thanks
For it! Please, hurry! I must have it.

FRIAR. With pleasure. But the writing is, I'm told,
In Arabic.   (*He leaves.*)

NATHAN. No matter. Bring it! God! If I could keep
The girl a little longer and thus get
A son-in-law like him! But that's not likely.
Well—come what may. But who could have
Been telling stories to the Patriarch?
I must find out. I wonder—Daja, maybe?

SCENE 8. *Nathan and Daja.*

DAJA (*hurries in, embarrassed*). Imagine, Nathan!

NATHAN. Imagine what?

DAJA. The poor child was quite terrified.
A messenger arrived just now from—

NATHAN. The Patriarch?

DAJA. No, from the Sultan's sister, Princess Sittah—

NATHAN. You're sure? Not from the Patriarch?

DAJA. Now will you listen? Princess Sittah sent
A messenger with orders to return
Immediately and—bring Rebecca.

NATHAN. To bring Rebecca? Sittah sent for her?
Well, if it's Sittah's messenger and not
The Patriarch's—

DAJA. What has the Patriarch to do with this?

NATHAN. You did not recently have word from him?
You're sure? And did not send him anything?

DAJA. I? To the Patriarch?

NATHAN. Where is the messenger?

DAJA. He's in the hall.

NATHAN. Better be careful. I shall talk to him

Myself. I hope there is no hidden Patriarch!   (*He leaves.*)

DAJA. And I have other fears. Why not?
The only daughter of a wealthy Jew,
As he must think, would not be bad for any Muslim!
Ha, that would be the end of our good Templar.
Unless, that is, I take the second step,
Unless I tell her, too, the truth about herself.
I have to talk to her alone; I'll use
The first occasion—which is now,
When I go with her to the palace.
A little hint, to start with, will be good
For her. It's now or never.   (*She follows* NATHAN.)

ACT V

SCENE 1. *A room in Saladin's palace; the bags of money
brought in earlier are still lined up on the floor. Saladin;
shortly, several Mamelukes.*

SALADIN (*enters*). The money is still here and no one yet
Has seen the dervish. He has most likely found
A chess board somewhere and is stuck to it.
He probably forgot himself—so why not me?
I must have patience with him. Yes? What is it?

MAMELUKE. I bring you welcome news. Rejoice, O Sultan!
A caravan approaches from Kahira;
It brings the tribute from the wealthy Nile
For seven years. It's here!

SALADIN. Good Ibrahim! You are, indeed,
A welcome messenger. At last, at last!
My thanks for your good news.

MAMELUKE (*does not move and waits, aside*).
Well? Is that all I get?

SALADIN. Why are you standing there?

MAMELUKE. My message pleased you; nothing else?

SALADIN. What else?

MAMELUKE. The man who brings good news gets no reward?
Oh—Saladin has learned at last to pay
With words, and I'm the first—that, too, is fame—
The first to meet a stingy Saladin.

SALADIN. Well, take a bag, then.

MAMELUKE. No, now I won't. Not if you gave them all to me.

SALADIN. Defiance! Come, take two!

(*The* MAMELUKE *leaves.*)
He was in earnest?

He wants to be more generous than I,
Although for him it's harder to refuse
A present than for me to give. Come back!
And what came over me that I could try
To change so late in life? Does Saladin
Refuse to die as Saladin? Then he
Should not have lived so long as Saladin.

SECOND MAMELUKE. My greetings, Sultan!

SALADIN. If you have come to tell me that—

SECOND MAMELUKE. The caravan from Egypt has arrived.

SALADIN. Yes, I have heard.

SECOND MAMELUKE. Then I have come too late!

SALADIN. And why too late? Here—take a bag or two.
I shall reward your good intentions.

SECOND MAMELUKE. Not three?

SALADIN. Oh, you can count? Take three, then.

SECOND MAMELUKE. A third one will most likely come—
That is, if he is able to.

SALADIN. How so?

SECOND MAMELUKE. He probably has broken all his bones.
As soon as we, the three of us, were sure
The caravan was near, we galloped off
To bring the news to you. One was ahead,
But he fell off his horse; then I became
The leader and I kept in front
Until we passed the gate. Then Ibrahim,
Who knows the streets much better, overtook me.

SALADIN. What happened to the man who fell?
You must ride out again and look for him.

SECOND MAMELUKE. I shall, indeed! And if he is alive,
I'll give him half of what is in these bags.   (*He leaves.*)

SALADIN. A noble fellow! Who can pride himself
On having finer Mamelukes?
And may I not believe that my example
Helped form them into what they are?
How could I teach them, after all these years,
A different way of thinking?

THIRD MAMELUKE. Great Sultan—

SALADIN. Are you the one who fell?

THIRD MAMELUKE. No, Sultan. I am to announce
That Emir Mansor who has brought the caravan
Is even now dismounting from his horse.

SALADIN. Quick! Bring him here. —Ah, there he is.

SCENE 2. *Saladin and Emir Mansor.*

SALADIN. You are most welcome, Emir. Well,
How was your journey? You have made us wait.

MANSOR. This letter will inform you. It explains
How Abul Kassem first had to suppress
Rebellions in Thebais, that only then
We dared to leave. I've forced our journey
As much as ever possible.

SALADIN. I do believe you, my good Mansor.
But now you must at once—I hope that you won't mind—
Select another escort; you must leave
Again immediately and take the greater part
Of what you've brought to Lebanon, to Father.

MANSOR. I gladly will.

SALADIN. Be careful, Mansor. Make the escort strong.
It is no longer safe in Lebanon.
The Templars once again are restive.
But now I want to see the caravan.
I want to see it and take care of everything.
Where did it stop?
(*To the doorkeeper.*) You! I shall be with Sittah later.

SCENE 3. *The grove of palm trees in front of Nathan's house. The Templar.*

TEMPLAR (*walking back and forth*). I won't set foot into this
  house.
He must come out eventually. How quick
They used to be! How eagerly they used
To notice me before! And now I risk
Being requested not to be a quite
So frequent visitor to his domain.
Hm. I was stupid, that is true. Why should I feel
So bitter toward him? He said himself
That he did not refuse me, and now Saladin
Has promised to persuade him. Is it possible?
Is then the Christian in me really be more powerful
Than is the Jew in Nathan? But—who knows himself!
Why should I otherwise begrudge him the small loot
Of which to rob the Christians he made such a point?
Of course, to steal a creature like this girl
Is not exactly petty larceny!
A creature—yes—but whose? She's surely not
The creature of a slave who left a block of marble
At the deserted beach of life—and then ran off.
The sculptor who discovered in this raw,
Abandoned block the form divine
And then created it is her creator!
Despite the Christian who begot Rebecca,
A Jew will always be her real father.
If I imagine her as nothing more
Than just an ordinary, Christian girl,
Without the things that but a Jew could give her,
What would I see in her? Not much—and maybe nothing.
Her smile? If it were but a pretty, sweet grimace,
If what provokes her smile were never worthy
Of all the charm it radiates?
I would not like that empty smile!
I've seen a more attractive smile on other faces,
On faces that belonged to fools and fops,
Wasted on flattery, on lust and mockery.
Was I enchanted by those smiles? Did they inflame
My heart with the desire to bask

In their bewitching rays forever? No!
And still I rage against the man
Whom I should thank for giving meaning to her smile!
Perhaps I do deserve the taunt
With which the Sultan sent me on my way.
It's bad enough that he could even think
That I deserved it. Oh, how small
And how despicable I must have looked to him!
And all this for a girl! Curd, Curd,
It is high time you took yourself in hand.
Give in. Moreover, Daja may have told
A fairy tale that would be hard to prove.
At last! He comes and—is that not the Friar
With whom he is engrossed in conversation?
Does he already know? Or worse, perhaps
The Patriarch already knows his name.
What a fool I've been! How can one single spark
Of passion burn away all our intelligence?
Decide what you must do, and do it quickly.
I'll step aside and wait for them. Perhaps
The Friar will be on his way.

SCENE 4. *Nathan and the Friar.*

NATHAN. Again, my thanks, good Friar.

FRIAR. I thank you, too.

NATHAN. Thank me? For what? For stubbornly
Insisting that you take what you don't need?
I wish I had succeeded, but you did not want
To be the richer of the two of us.

FRIAR. The book was never mine in any case.
By rights it is his daughter's, for it's all
Her father left her. However—she has you.
May God grant that the day will never come
When you regret what you have done for her.

NATHAN. Regret? How could I! Have no fear.

FRIAR. Who knows! Between the Templars and the Patriarchs—

NATHAN. Nothing that they can do would be so bad
That I would have regrets for what I did.
But are you sure that it's a Templar who incites
The Patriarch against me?

FRIAR. It could hardly be someone else.
He had just finished speaking with a Templar,
And what I heard did sound like that.

NATHAN. But there is only one of them
In all Jerusalem, and I know him.
He is my friend, a frank and noble man.

FRIAR. That is the one! But what one is
And what one has to be is often not the same.

NATHAN. Unfortunately true. But let him do,
Whoever he may be, his worst—or else
His best. The book you gave me is my shield,
And I shall take it straight to Saladin.

FRIAR. I wish you luck. Now I must go.

NATHAN. You have not even seen her! You must come
Again and often. Meanwhile let us hope
The Patriarch will not learn anything today.
But then, why not? You tell him anything you want.

FRIAR. I'll tell him nothing. Now—good-bye.   (*He leaves.*)

NATHAN. Do not forget us, Friar! God, I wish
That I could sink upon my knees right here
Where Heaven seems so close!
The web that frightened me so long begins
Miraculously to unravel by itself.
How light I feel now that I need no longer hide
A single secret! How relieved I am,
Oh God, that I stand once again before the world
As free as I have always stood before your eyes!
Oh Lord, you do not judge us by appearances
That rarely are the same as our accomplishments.

SCENE 5. *Nathan and the Templar, who comes toward him from the side.*

TEMPLAR. Wait, Nathan! Wait, take me along.

NATHAN. Who's calling? Oh, it's you? Where have you been?
I thought that I would see you at the palace.

TEMPLAR. We must have missed each other. Don't be angry.

NATHAN. I won't, but Saladin—

TEMPLAR. You had just left—

NATHAN. So you have talked to him? I'm glad.

TEMPLAR. He wants to talk to both of us together.

NATHAN. So much the better. Come with me,
I'm on my way to see him now.

TEMPLAR. Would it be forward if I asked a question?
Who was the friar who just left you?

NATHAN. I don't believe you know him—or—

TEMPLAR. I wondered. Is that not the estimable fellow
Whom our most worthy Patriarch prefers
To use as snooper?

NATHAN. Maybe. He's in his service, that is true.

TEMPLAR. A clever trick: to let the innocent prepare
The way for villainy.

NATHAN. If they are simple-minded, not if they are honest.

TEMPLAR. A Patriarch does not believe in honesty.

NATHAN. This man is honest, I am sure. He would not help
His Patriarch with any wickedness.

TEMPLAR. That is how he presents himself, at least.
Did he not tell you anything concerning me?

NATHAN. Concerning you? He did not mention you
By name; but then, how would he know your name?

TEMPLAR. No, that is hardly possible.

NATHAN. Of course, he did say that a Templar—

TEMPLAR. Said that a Templar—what?

NATHAN. I'm sure it was not you he had in mind.

TEMPLAR. Who knows? What did he say?

NATHAN. He said that someone whom he did not know,
A Templar, had denounced me to the Patriarch—

TEMPLAR. Denounced you? No! That is, if he will pardon me,
A lie. But listen to me, Nathan.
I'm not a man who can deny the truth.
What I have done is done. Nor do I claim
That everything I ever did was right.
Why should I be ashamed when I do wrong
If I'm resolved not to repeat my error?
I know that that's the way for men to get ahead.
Yes, I'm the Templar whom the friar had in mind,
Who has denounced you, as he says. You know
The reason why my temper was aroused
And why my blood was boiling in my veins.

I was a fool. I came to you with open arms,
With heart and soul, and you received me icily—
No, worse yet, tepidly; and you avoided
An outright answer with the greatest care.
The questions which you put to me instead
Were so irrelevant, so meaningless
That even now I find it difficult
To keep my head when I think back.
When I was in this ferment, Daja stealthily
Crept up and threw your secret in my face.
That seemed to be the explanation
Of your mysterious behavior.

NATHAN. How so?

TEMPLAR. I thought that you refused to lose your prey,
So cleverly snatched from the Christians' grasp,
And leave it to another Christian. So—
I thought it might be well to point a knife at you.

NATHAN. It might be well? What good is there about it?

TEMPLAR. Oh, listen, Nathan. It is true, I was
Completely wrong, and probably it's all a lie.
Most likely Daja is a fool who does not know
Whereof she speaks, and vicious—out to cause
You trouble where she can. I'm young, I'm stupid,
I am a dreamer through and through
Who either does too much or else too little.
All that is very possible. Forgive me, Nathan.

NATHAN. Now, if you come at me like that—

TEMPLAR. In short, I went to see the Patriarch.
I did not name you, though—that is a lie.
I only put your case before him,
As a hypothesis, to hear what he would say.
Of course, I should not have done even that.
I knew quite well the Patriarch was evil.
Why did I not ask you, instead? Why risk
This poor girl's losing you, a man like you
As father? Be that as it may.
The Patriarch, as villainous as usual,
Soon brought me to my senses. Let me finish, Nathan.
Suppose he knew your name, what could he do?
If there is no one else to claim her, only you—
And only then could he attempt to take her—
A nunnery would be the only place

Where he could drag the girl. The answer is:
Give her to me! Then let him come. He would not dare
To take my wife. Let her be mine this minute,
No matter whether she's your daughter or a waif,
A Christian or a Jewess, or neither of the two.
No matter. I'm no longer curious.
I won't ask any questions, now or ever.

NATHAN. Do you imagine that I have to hide the truth?

TEMPLAR. What do I care?

NATHAN. I never have and never would deny
That she is Christian, not to you or anyone
Who has a right to know. She is my foster-child.
If I have not yet told her, I don't owe
Apologies to anyone but her.

TEMPLAR. I did not ask you to apologize.
Why spoil her happiness? Remain her father.
Spare her the painful disappointment.
You are still master of her destiny.
Give her to me. Please, Nathan—I'm the one
Who now can save the girl a second time—and that I will.

NATHAN. You might have saved her. Now it is too late.

TEMPLAR. Too late?

NATHAN. Thanks to the Patriarch—

TEMPLAR. The Patriarch? Thank him? For what?
Does he deserve our gratitude? For what?

NATHAN. That now we know to whom she is related,
For knowing in whose hands she will be safe.

TEMPLAR. For that may thank him who'll have more
To thank him for.

NATHAN. You will have to receive her from those hands,
And not from mine.

TEMPLAR. Ah, poor Rebecca, you're pursued by fate.
What happiness this would have been
For any other waif. For you it's misery.
Where are these relatives?

NATHAN. Where are they?

TEMPLAR. And who?

NATHAN. There is a brother, above all, from whom
You now must ask her hand.

TEMPLAR. A brother? And who is this brother?

Is he a soldier? Or a clergyman?
Tell me for what I must prepare myself.

NATHAN. I think that he is neither—or is both.
I don't know him too well as yet.

TEMPLAR. What else?

NATHAN. He is a good man in whose care she will be safe.

TEMPLAR. But he's a Christian. I no longer know
What I should think of you. Do not be angry.
But will she not, among these Christians, have to play
The Christian? Will she not, while she is *playing* one,
Become a Christian in the end?
Will not eventually the seed of pure
And fertile wheat that you have sown
Be suffocated by the weeds? Is that
Of no concern to you? And still you say
That she'll be safe when she is in her brother's care?

NATHAN. I hope so—yes, I think so. And—she still
Has you and me, if ever she should be in need.

TEMPLAR. Oh, she won't lack a thing with him. He'll lavish
Upon his little sister all the food
And clothes and jewels she could want.
What more could Little Sister ask? Oh yes—
A husband. Well, in time, he'll find her one,
The best, and the more Christian he will be,
The better. Nathan! You have made an angel!
And you'll let others spoil your work of art?

NATHAN. You need not fear. He will prove worthy of our
love.

TEMPLAR. Do not include *my* love! There is no room
For bargaining where my love is concerned,
It will not do without the smallest thing
To which it clings, and be it but a name.
But have you told Rebecca what you're planning?

NATHAN. No, I have not. I doubt she knows.

TEMPLAR. Then I will tell her. I will be the first
To tell her what her fate would be—in either case.
I was determined not to see her, not
To speak to her again until she could be mine—
That does not matter now. I'll hurry—

NATHAN. Where to? Stay here.

TEMPLAR. To her! I must find out if she is strong enough

To do the only thing that's worthy of her.

NATHAN. And what is that?

TEMPLAR. To ask no longer what her brother thinks,
What you might say—

NATHAN. And?

TEMPLAR. Follow me. To come with me, although—
By doing so she might become a Muslim's wife.

NATHAN. Stay here. You will not find her home.
She is with Sittah.

TEMPLAR. What? Since when? And why?

NATHAN. If you would like to meet her brother there,
Please, come with me.

TEMPLAR. Whose brother? Sittah's or Rebecca's?

NATHAN. Both, I think. Please, come with me.   (*Both leave.*)

SCENE 6. *Sittah's harem. Sittah and Rebecca in conversation.*

SITTAH. Sweet girl, I am so glad to have you here.
There is no need to be so shy and frightened.
Be gay, have confidence and talk to me.

REBECCA. Oh, Princess—

SITTAH. You must not call me Princess. Call me Sittah.
I am your friend—your sister—and could almost be
Your mother. You are young—and yet so wise.
You know so much and must have read so much.

REBECCA. Read? Sittah, you are mocking me.
Your silly little sister cannot read.

SITTAH. You are a little liar. Surely you can read.

REBECCA. A little maybe of what my father writes.
I thought you meant that I read books.

SITTAH. Of course, that's what I meant.

REBECCA. Well, I find books most difficult to read.

SITTAH. You can't be serious.

REBECCA. I am. My father does not like the knowledge
Impressed upon the brain by cold, dead characters
In books.

SITTAH. How strange! He may be right, of course. But how

Did you then learn all that you know?

REBECCA. All that I know I learned from him.
I still remember when and where and why
He taught me many of the lessons.

SITTAH. That is the way to learn and to remember!
In that way your whole being understands.

REBECCA. I am quite sure you have not read much, either.

SITTAH. I am not proud of it, but you are wrong.
How curious that you should say that. Why?

REBECCA. You are so frank and natural, you are—
Yourself, without pretense.

SITTAH. And so?

REBECCA. My father says that reading books
Makes people different.

SITTAH. Oh, what a man your father is!

REBECCA. I know.

SITTAH. He never seems to hit far from the mark.

REBECCA. I know. And now—they want—my father—

SITTAH. What is the matter, dear?

REBECCA. My father—

SITTAH. My God! What is it? You are crying.

REBECCA. My father— Ah, I have to speak about it.
My heart is bursting, I must talk.
(*Dissolved in tears, she sinks down at* SITTAH's *feet.*)

SITTAH. What is the matter, child? Rebecca!

REBECCA. I am to lose my father!

SITTAH. You are to lose your father? How?
Now, calm yourself; get up. You will not lose him.

REBECCA. You offered to become my sister and my friend,
So I will now—

SITTAH. Of course, I am. But now you must get up,
Or I shall have to call for help.

REBECCA (*collects herself and arises*).
Forgive me, please. My fear made me forget
With whom I am; for Sittah does not like
Despair and moaning. Reason, cold and calm—
That is the language one must use with her,
If one intends to win her mind and heart.

SITTAH. Well?

...ou—my sister and my friend—will not allow
...appen, will not let them force
...upon me as my father.

123

Another man as father? But who could

Or ...ld do that? No one can force you.

REBECCA. Oh yes—my good and wicked Daja can.
She wants to—and she can. But you, of course,
Have never heard of her. May God forgive
Her sins—may He reward her also
For all the good things she has done for me.

SITTAH. If she did wicked things, she is not good.

REBECCA. Oh yes, she is. In many ways, she's very good.

SITTAH. Who is this Daja?

REBECCA. A Christian woman who, when I was small,
Took care of me. You can't imagine how
She pampered me, so I would never miss my mother.
But—how she frightened and tormented me!

SITTAH. But why? What did she do?

REBECCA. Ah, the poor woman is a Christian, as I said,
And so her love made her torment me.
She's one of those fanatic dreamers who believe
That they have found the only true
And certain way to God.

SITTAH. I see.

REBECCA. One of those people who feel forced to guide
All those who, as they see it, missed the way,
Until they find it. How can they act otherwise?
For if it's true that only one way leads to God,
How could they patiently stand by and watch
Their friends walk down another road, a road
That leads inevitably to perdition?
I wish one could adore and hate
A person simultaneously.
But that is not why now, at last, I cannot help
Accusing her. I would have gladly kept on listening
To her unending sighs and warnings,
And to her threats and prayers. Gladly!
They always gave me cause for thoughts
Which do no harm—and maybe serve a purpose.
And who would not feel flattered, in the end,
When someone—anyone—holds him so dear
That the mere thought of losing us forever

Seems utterly unbearable to him?

SITTAH. Yes, that is true.

REBECCA. But—no, this is too much! I cannot meet
This new attack with patience and forebearance.

SITTAH. But what has happened now?

REBECCA. What she has just revealed to me—she says—

SITTAH. Revealed to you? Just now?

REBECCA. When we approached, on our way to the palace,
A ruined Christian temple, suddenly
She stopped; she seemed to fight a battle with herself
And looked, her eyes in tears, now to the heavens, now
At me. At last she said, we might as well
Walk through the temple, and she led the way.
I followed, and my glances roamed
With horror over the decaying ruins.
Then she stood still again. I saw that we had come
Upon the sunken steps below a crumbling altar.
You can imagine how I felt when suddenly
She threw herself down at my feet,
Her face in tears, her hands entwined.

SITTAH. Poor child!

REBECCA. Invoking the divine Madonna,
Who must have listened there to many prayers
And worked Her miracles in days gone by,
She pleaded with me to take pity on myself;
With genuine compassion in her eyes,
She asked that I at least forgive her
If she now told me that her church
Had claims on me—but that she must.

SITTAH (*aside*). Oh, my poor child! I thought as much.

REBECCA. She told me of my Christian parents, said
That I was baptized and was not—
My father's daughter. Oh, my God! My God,
If he is not my father— Let me embrace your feet!

SITTAH. Rebecca, no! Get up! Here comes my brother.

SCENE 7. *Saladin, Sittah, and Rebecca.*

SALADIN. What does this mean? What happened, Sittah?

SITTAH. My God, the girl is quite beside herself.

SALADIN. Who is she?

SITTAH. But you know—

SALADIN. Our Nathan's daughter? What is wrong?

SITTAH. Compose yourself, my child. The Sultan—

REBECCA (*drags herself on her knees toward* SALADIN, *without looking up*).
I shall not rise before—I do not want to see
The Sultan's face before—not to admire
The gleam of justice and of goodness in his eyes,
Nor see upon his face—

SALADIN. Arise, my child.

REBECCA. Before I have his promise—

SALADIN. Arise. I promise you whatever you may wish.

REBECCA. All that I ask is that you let me keep
My father, and let him keep me.
I do not know who else demands the right
To be my father. I don't want to know.
Can only blood create a bond
Between a daughter and her father?

SALADIN (*lifts her up*). I see. I understand. But who has been
So cruel as to put such thoughts into your head?
Has it been proven beyond doubt?

REBECCA. It must be. Daja says—she claims
To have been told the story by my nurse.

SALADIN. Your nurse?

REBECCA. She thought that she ought to confide in someone
When she lay on her deathbed; Daja thus
Became her confidant.

SALADIN. When she lay on her deathbed—and, perhaps,
No longer knew exactly what she said!
But even if the tale were true,
Begetting children is not all a man must do
To be a father. Yes, for animals that is enough.
A man acquires nothing but the right
To earn the title. Have no fear.
But should there ever be two men
Who claim the right to be your father, leave them both—
And take a third. Give me the privilege!

REBECCA. Accept, Rebecca! Please!

SALADIN. I promise you that I shall be a good
And loyal father. But—it just occurs to me,

There's something even better. Why a father?
Fathers die. Far better, it would seem to me,
To look around for someone who will march
Along the road of life in step with you.
Don't you know someone?

SITTAH. Don't make her blush.

SALADIN. That is exactly what I want to do.
If blushing makes an ugly girl look beautiful,
How much more beautiful will blushing make
A pretty girl? I have asked Nathan and—
Another man to join us here. I wonder,
Can you guess who that man is?

SITTAH. Please, Saladin!

SALADIN. Make sure to blush your best, my lovely girl.

REBECCA. Why should I blush? Because of whom?

SALADIN. Do not pretend! If you would rather blanch,
However—blanch! Do as you like.
(*A slave girl enters and approaches* SITTAH.)
Have they arrived?

SITTAH. Good. Let them enter.

LAST SCENE. *Saladin, Sittah, Rebecca, Nathan and the
Templar.*

SALADIN. Be welcome, friends! Be welcome, all of you!
You, Nathan—let me say this first—
Can have your money back at any time.

NATHAN. But Sultan, why—

SALADIN. Now I'm at your disposal if you should—

NATHAN. But Sultan—

SALADIN. The caravan is here, and I am rich again,
Far richer than I've been for many years.
Tell me how much you need, for something big,
Some worthwhile enterprise. For even merchants,
I am told, have never too much cash on hand.

NATHAN. Let's leave these trifles for some other time.
I see a face in tears, and that, I think,
Is more important. (*He steps closer to* REBECCA.)
Why these tears?
What happened? Are you still my daughter?

REBECCA. Oh, Father!

NATHAN. We understand each other. Do not weep.
Compose yourself. Be happy. If no other loss
Is threatening your heart, and if you have not lost
Your heart to anyone, you have lost nothing—
Your father is still yours.

REBECCA. I fear no other loss.

TEMPLAR. You don't? Then I have been mistaken.
What one is not afraid to lose,
One never has possessed or wanted. Nathan,
That changes everything. You, Sultan, asked
To speak to both of us. There is no need
For further efforts now.

SALADIN. Again so rash, young man! Must all the world
Accede to your first wish, or even guess
What you desire?

TEMPLAR. But you have heard and seen what happened,
Saladin.

SALADIN. Indeed, I have. It's bad enough
That you were not more certain of your cause.

TEMPLAR. I'm certain now.

SALADIN. Insisting on the prize of virtue means
Reclaiming what one gave as present.
Because you saved a life, it is not yours.
For otherwise a robber, spurred by greed
And nothing else to rush into a burning house,
Would be a hero, too. (*He steps close to* REBECCA, *intending to
lead her to the* TEMPLAR.) Come, my dear girl.
You must not take this man too seriously.
If he were not so proud and so impulsive,
He never would have rescued you. Take that
Into account. And now, put him to shame.
You do what he should have done long ago.
Confess your love, propose to him.
If he refuses you, or if in future he forgets
That you have done much more for him
By your confession than he ever did for you—
What did he do? Inhale a little smoke?
That's nothing to make such a fuss about—
If he forgets, he's not one bit like Assad.
Then he may have his face, but not his heart.

SITTAH. Go on, dear girl. That is the least that you
Can do for him to show your gratitude.

NATHAN. Wait, Saladin! Allow me, Sittah!

SALADIN. You, too?

NATHAN. There's someone else who has a right to speak.

SALADIN. No one denies it. As her foster father,
You have a right to speak, indeed, a better right
Than others. I am well aware of your
Position, as you see.

NATHAN. Of mine, perhaps; but I meant someone else.
He must be heard before you venture further.

SALADIN. And who is that?

NATHAN. Her brother.

SALADIN. Rebecca's brother?

NATHAN. Yes.

REBECCA. My brother? Do I have a brother?

TEMPLAR (*rises from his silent, furious brooding*).
Where is this brother? Is he late?
You said I was to meet him here.

NATHAN. Have patience, sir!

TEMPLAR (*bitterly*). He faked a father for the girl,
How could he fail to find a brother, too?

SALADIN. That is too much! So low an accusation
Would never have come over Assad's lips.
All right, continue, Christian!

NATHAN. Forgive him; I forgive him gladly, Saladin.
Who knows what we in his place, at his age,
Might do. (*He approaches the* TEMPLAR *with a friendly gesture.*)
Suspicion and distrust are brothers.
If you had thought me worthy, Templar,
Of knowing your true name—

TEMPLAR. What?

NATHAN. Your name is not von Stauffen.

TEMPLAR. What is it, then?

NATHAN. You are not Curd von Stauffen.

TEMPLAR. Who am I, then?

NATHAN. Your name is Leu von Filneck.

TEMPLAR. What's that?

NATHAN. Does that surprise you?

TEMPLAR. It does, indeed. Who has discovered that?

NATHAN. I have—and I could tell you more.
But I am not accusing you of lying.

TEMPLAR. You're not?

NATHAN. Perhaps both names are yours.

TEMPLAR. Well, that is better! (*Aside.*) God made him say
   that!

NATHAN. Your mother was a Stauffen; you were raised,
However, by her brother from the time
When both your parents, fleeing from its windy skies,
Left Germany and came, to find a gentler clime,
Back to this country. Now, your uncle's name
Was Curd von Stauffen; he adopted you, perhaps.
How long is it since you came here with him?
Is he still living?

TEMPLAR. I cannot argue. It is true. My uncle died.
I only came here with my Order's
Last reinforcement. But Rebecca's brother—
What has all this to do with him?

NATHAN. Your father—

TEMPLAR. My father? Did you know him, too?

NATHAN. He was my friend.

TEMPLAR. Your friend? How is that possible?

NATHAN. He called himself von Filneck, Wolf von Filneck,
   but
He was not German—

TEMPLAR. You know that, too?

NATHAN. But he was married to a German lady,
Had followed her to Germany, if not for long—

TEMPLAR. That is enough! Please, Nathan—what about
   Rebecca's brother?

NATHAN. You are her brother.

TEMPLAR. I?

REBECCA. Is he my brother?

SITTAH. They are brother and sister!

SALADIN. Brother and sister!

REBECCA (*turns to the* TEMPLAR). My brother!

TEMPLAR (*steps back*). Her brother!

REBECCA (*stops and turns to* NATHAN).
It can't be true. His heart is silent.
He looks on me as an imposter. God!

SALADIN (*to the* TEMPLAR). Imposter? Is that what you think?
You are yourself the worst imposter.
You are a living lie! Your face, your voice,
Your bearing—everything a lie!
If you refuse to recognize a girl
Like this as sister—

TEMPLAR (*humbly approaches* SALADIN).
No, Saladin, you misinterpret my surprise.
Perhaps you never saw your brother, Assad,
In such a moment of bewilderment.
Do not misjudge both him and me.
(*He quickly steps close to* NATHAN.)
What you so generously offer me
Is both a loss and gain. But you are giving me
Far more than you are taking, Nathan.
(*He embraces* REBECCA.)
My sister! Oh, my sister!

NATHAN. Blanda von Filneck.

TEMPLAR. Her name is Blanda? Not Rebecca?
Not your Rebecca any more?
Do you reject her by bestowing
This Christian name on her again?
Do not reject your daughter for my sake!
Why take revenge on her?

NATHAN. Oh no. You're both my children now. What could
My daughter's brother be, if not my son?
Provided that he wants to be—my son.
(*While* NATHAN, REBECCA *and the* TEMPLAR *embrace each other,* SALADIN, *perplexed and uneasy, steps to his sister.*)

SALADIN. What do you think, my sister?

SITTAH. I am moved—

SALADIN. I almost shrink from what I vaguely feel
Is yet to come. Prepare yourself
For even more profound emotions!

SITTAH. What do you mean?

SALADIN. Please, Nathan! I must talk to you.
(*While* SALADIN *and* NATHAN *are engaged in conversation,* SITTAH *joins* REBECCA *and the* TEMPLAR *to express her happiness to them.* SALADIN *and* NATHAN *drop their voices.*)

Did you not say just now—

NATHAN. Say what?

SALADIN. —their father did not come from Germany,
And was not born a German? Then, where was he born?
Who was their father?

NATHAN. That I don't know. He never told me anything
About his origin.

SALADIN. He was not Frankish? Not a European?

NATHAN. No, he was not. Of that he never made
A secret. The language he preferred
To speak was Persian.

SALADIN. Was—Persian? Are you sure? What else is there
That I must know! It must be he!

NATHAN. It must be—who?

SALADIN. My brother! Assad! I am certain.

NATHAN. Now that you've had that thought yourself,
Accept its confirmation from this little book.
(*He hands him the breviary.*)

SALADIN (*eagerly leafing through it*).
His writing! Yes, I recognize his hand.

NATHAN. They still don't know. It is still up to you
How much they are to know.

SALADIN (*still turning the pages of the breviary*).
Would I refuse to recognize my brother's children,
My nephew and my niece? Would I leave them to you?
(*Aloud.*) It's they! They are our brother's children, Sittah!
(*He rushes to* REBECCA *and the* TEMPLAR *and embraces them.*)

SITTAH. How could it have been otherwise!

SALADIN (*to the* TEMPLAR). Now you will have to love me,
      stubborn man!
(*To* REBECCA.) Like it or not, I'm now what I proposed to be.

SITTAH. And I shall be your mother.

SALADIN (*again to the* TEMPLAR). My son! My Assad's son!

TEMPLAR. I am of your blood, after all. The dreams
Which I have had since childhood, then, were more than dreams.
(*He drops on his knees before* SALADIN.)

SALADIN (*raising him*). Look at this wicked man! He knew
      about it,
Or at least suspected something,

But would have let me murder him. Just wait!

*While all are embracing each other silently,
the* CURTAIN *falls.*

Egmont

by

JOHANN WOLFGANG VON GOETHE

❖ ❖ ❖

EDITOR'S PREFACE

The theme of the great individual paralyzed by the petty but irresistible claims of social convention and political power which Goethe first struck in *Götz von Berlichingen* (1773) is the theme also of *Egmont* (1787). It was a conflict felt intensely by many of the young German men of letters who in the seventeen-sixties began to represent the emerging clash between obsolete convictions and the sense of power which the newly asserted energies of reason or inspiration gave them. Among the poets and critics, the discrepancy between traditional forms and the fresh claims of the imagination was most intensely argued; in political thought, the debate revolved around the postulate of natural rights over obedience to established authority.

The topic of Egmont's rebellion against the tyranny of Spanish rule in the Netherlands seems to have occupied Goethe as early as 1774, at the time, indeed, of his work on *The Sorrows of Young Werther*. He found the facts in F. Strada's *De bello Belgico* (1651) and, without much concern for dramatic continuity, at once wrote a series of colorful scenes: Egmont's arrest, the decisive conversation between Egmont and Orange, and some of the lively portraits of Dutch citizens were undoubtedly sketched first. From time to time, he returned to the manuscript, finished several scenes and rewrote the early draft as his own political and social philosophy matured. It was in Rome, in the fall of 1787 during the Italian journey which contributed so much to his personal and artistic development, that he completed the play as we now have it.

It is clear from Goethe's revisions that the simple-minded and petty grievances of personal discomfort and suspended privileges by which he had first planned to characterize the society that Egmont was to lead to freedom, soon struck him as unsatisfactory for a sustained drama. He came to see that the success of any revolution must rest on an ideal: only the all-consuming desire for liberty and decency and not merely private advantage can justify and carry a popular uprising. As the scheme of the play developed, Goethe concluded that Egmont must be made the embodiment of integrity and visionary faith, and that his fight for victory could only in this spirit be justified. In the figure of Vansen we feel the irony with which the selfish insistence on personal comfort was to be represented. More important still, it became obvious to Goethe that if the play was to gain in dramatic contrast, the counterpositions of the Spanish powers must be delineated more carefully and more sympathetically than he had originally planned.

In its final form, then, Egmont is not so much a historical drama as a study in character and human conflicts. "The unity of the play," Schiller said in a famous review, "lies neither in the situation nor in any dominant passion but simply in Egmont the man." To give life and color to this central human being and to make his power over others plausible is therefore Goethe's primary intention. The historical Egmont, a man of forty-five, husband and father, is in Goethe's play transformed into a radiantly self-confident character, a youthful hero and lover who is, above all, faithful to his own being. Goethe speaks of the "demonic" energies which determine Egmont's actions, and these seem indeed to compel, not only Egmont himself but, in one way or another, every figure in the play, to act according to the law of his own character. This interest in the power of personality is best exemplified in the great discourse between Egmont and Alba, in which each reveals his strength and his weakness, in which each offered proposition seems to increase the antagonists' comprehension of the other, and in which each character equally enlists our sympathy.

Among the citizens who surround Egmont, it is Claire who in her integrity and devotion is closest to Egmont's own character; her love for him is absolute and as she dies in the knowledge of Egmont's certain arrest and defeat, she transcends the cowardice and fear of the world for which Egmont to the end upholds the ideals of freedom. The magic of Egmont's person affects even his enemies. In his last hour in prison Alba's natural son, Ferdinand, confesses his admiration and love for "the star of his youth."

It must be clear that Goethe's play is not in any serious sense concerned with stating an articulate social philosophy; his preoccupation with a human being who contained in himself the pathos as well as the strength of an almost somnambulist self-assurance left little room for an exploration of political alternatives. Egmont's final vision of Claire suggests the promise of eventual liberation which his death may bring about: it is the apotheosis of Egmont's being rather than a satisfying summary of the issues to which his life was devoted.

Goethe's fascination with the "demonic" figure of Egmont is appropriately conveyed in a dramatic style which is not so much argumentative as musical and "open": Shakespeare's influence is clearly present in the structure of the plot as well as in the finely differentiated portraiture of a remarkably rich group of characters. Theatrical, lyrical, and reflective scenes alternate, and it is in keeping with the more and more rarefied idealism of Egmont's last insights that speech and discourse should in the end give way to the language of music, and that the drama should culminate in an operatic tableau which has often been deplored but which Goethe thought an appropriate allegory of Egmont's spectacular character.

Goethe hoped that his friend J. C. Kayser might compose the "symphony, the entr'acte pieces, the songs and a few parts of the final act." But this was not realized. It was not until 1810 that Beethoven provided what Goethe had envisaged; with his music *Egmont* was first performed in Weimar in 1814. It has remained one of the most popular plays on the German stage.

Egmont

❖

CHARACTERS

MARGARET OF PARMA, daughter of Charles V, Regent of the
  Netherlands
COUNT EGMONT, Prince of Gaure
WILLIAM OF ORANGE
DUKE OF ALBA
FERDINAND, Alba's natural son
MACHIAVELL, secretary to the Regent
RICHARD, Egmont's secretary
SILVA ⎫
GOMEZ ⎭ officers in Alba's service
CLAIRE, Egmont's sweetheart
CLAIRE'S MOTHER
BRACKENBURG, son of a citizen of Brussels
SOEST, shopkeeper ⎫
JETTER, tailor ⎪
CARPENTER ⎬ citizens of Brussels
SOAPMAKER ⎭
BUYCK, a soldier serving under Egmont
RUYSUM, an invalid veteran
VANSEN, a clerk
MEN and WOMEN of the people, COURTIERS, GUARDS, etc.

Scene: Brussels in the year 1568.

❖

ACT I

SCENE 1. *A crossbow shoot. Soldiers and citizens with
crossbows. Jetter, a Brussels tailor, steps up and draws his
crossbow. Soest, a shopkeeper from Brussels.*

SOEST. Go on and shoot! Let us be done with it. You cannot
beat me anyway. Three black rings—you never shot so well in
all your life. And so, I am the master shot for this year.

141

JETTER. Master and king. Who begrudges you the prize? But in return, you have to treat us, matching what we pay. You'll have to pay for your skill, as it is custom.

(BUYCK, *a Dutchman serving under* EGMONT, *enters.*)

BUYCK. Jetter, I'll make a bargain with you, just one shot. I'll share the winnings and I'll treat these gentlemen. I have been here for quite a while and am indebted for many a courtesy. If I miss, let us pretend that you have shot.

SOEST. I really shouldn't agree, for when you get down to it, I am the loser. However, Buyck, go ahead.

BUYCK (*shoots*). Now, my dear sir, your compliments are due! One—two—three—four!

SOEST. Four rings? So be it!

ALL. Long live the King! Hurrah! Hurrah!

BUYCK. I thank you, gentlemen! Even Master would be too much! Thank you for the honor!

JETTER. Thank yourself! It's you who won it.

(RUYSUM, *a Frisian invalid and hard-of-hearing, enters.*)

RUYSUM. Let me tell you!

SOEST. What is it, Old Man?

RUYSUM. Let me tell you! He shoots like his master, shoots like Egmont.

BUYCK. Compared to him, I never even hit the target! And with a musket he shoots like no one in the world. Not only when he's lucky or in the mood for it. Oh no, he just takes aim and shoots a bull's-eye. I've learned from him! —That would be something, to serve under him and not learn anything from him! —But let us not forget, gentlemen, a king looks after his subjects; and so, bring on the wine! The King will pay!

JETTER. It's been the custom with us that everyone . . .

BUYCK. I am a stranger here, and I am King. I don't recognize your laws and customs.

JETTER. You're worse than the Spaniard; even he felt compelled to leave us those.

RUYSUM. What's that?

SOEST (*loud*). He wants to treat us, he doesn't want that we pay each his share and the King only matches the total.

RUYSUM. Let him! But that's no precedent! That's his master's way of doing things, too; open-handed, and let it go where it does some good. (*Wine is brought.*)

ALL. Long live His Majesty! Hurrah!

JETTER (*to* BUYCK). *Your* Majesty, that is of course!

BUYCK. Thank you, if this is how you do it!

SOEST. It is! Because a Netherlander does not gladly drink to the health of His Spanish Majesty.

RUYSUM. Who?

SOEST (*loud*). Philip the Second, King of Spain.

RUYSUM. Our most gracious King and Master! May God grant him a long life!

SOEST. Didnt you like his Father, Charles the Fifth, much better?

RUYSUM. May God have mercy on his soul! That was a master for you! His hand spread over the entire globe, and yet, with all that, when he met you he'd greet you like a neighbor; and when that frightened you, he'd be so polite—yes, you know, he went out walking or on horseback, just as the fancy struck him, with hardly any men. Didn't we all weep when he let his son take over the government here! Yes, yes! This one's different, more majestic.

JETTER. When he was here, you never saw him but in all his pomp and royal splendor. He doesn't talk much, people say.

SOEST. That's not a master for us Netherlanders. With us, a prince has to be as free and merry as we are ourselves, he must live and let live. We may be good-natured fools, but we don't like to be despised or oppressed.

JETTER. The King would be a gracious master, I would think, if only he had better counselors.

SOEST. No, no! He has no feeling for us Netherlanders, and in his heart he does not like the people; he does not love us. How, then, could we love him? Why is everybody so fond of Count Egmont? Why do we carry him on our hands? Because you can see that he likes us; because his eyes shine with gaiety, with carefree friendliness and good intentions; because he shares all he owns not only with the needy but even with those who need nothing. Long live Count Egmont! Buyck, it's up to you, you be the first to drink his health! Drink to your Master's health!

BUYCK. With all my heart: long live Count Egmont!

RUYSUM. The victor of St. Quentin!

BUYCK. The hero of Gravelingen!

ALL. Hurrah!

RUYSUM. St. Quentin was my last battle. I could hardly walk any more, hardly carry that heavy musket any more, but I still fired at the Frenchman, and then, as a farewell, I got a grazing shot in my right leg.

BUYCK. Gravelingen! Friends, that was a feast! That victory we won all by ourselves. Didn't those French dogs burn and singe their way all over Flanders? But we met them, I'll say that! Their old stalwarts stood their ground for a long time, and we pushed and shot and swung at them until they twisted their faces and their lines trembled. Then Egmont had his horse shot out from under him, and we fought back and forth for a long time, man against man, horse against horse, platoon against platoon, on that white flat strip of sand by the sea. And then, all of a sudden, it came from the mouth of the river, like thunder from heaven, bang and hrumpph! The cannons shooting into the thick of the French. That was the English who happened to be sailing by, down from Dunkirk under Admiral Malin. It's true, they didn't help us much; only their smallest ships could come close enough, and their shots fell among us, too. But anyway, it did our hearts good to see them! It broke the spirit of the French and lifted our courage. And then it went bang and boom, back and forth! We killed them and we scattered them all over the water, and the rascals drowned as soon as they tasted the water. But we Dutchmen were always close behind them. We can live both ways and really felt in our element only when we got into the water, like frogs. And we always kept bashing at them in the river and picked them off like sitting ducks. And those that got away and broke through were killed by the peasant women with their hoes and pitchforks. And that was enough for them! The King of France had to stretch out his hand and make peace. For that peace we deserve the credit, we and the great Egmont!

ALL. Long live the great Egmont! Hurrah! Hurrah! Hurrah!

JETTER. If only they had made him regent instead of Margaret of Parma!

SOEST. No, no! What's true is true. I won't let you talk badly of Margaret. Now it's my turn. Long live our gracious Lady!

ALL. Long may she live!

SOEST. Truly, they have splendid women in that family. Long live our Lady Regent!

JETTERS. Yes, she is wise and moderate in everything she does; if only she were not so thick with the clergy and wouldn't always stick up for them. She shares the blame that we have fourteen new bishops' hats in the country. What are they good for? It's to push foreigners into these nice seats, to which they used to elect abbots from the chapters, isn't it? And they want to make us believe that it's good for the religion! Ha, sure enough! Three bishops were just right for us, everything was honest and proper. Now everyone has to pretend and prove that he is needed, and squabbles and unpleasantness hit every minute.

The more you shake and stir the thing the muddier it looks. (*They drink.*)

SOEST. That was the King. He ordered it and she could neither add nor take away.

JETTER. So now they don't want us to sing the new psalms, but roguish songs we may sing as much as we like. And why? Because the psalms are full of heresies, they say, and things—God knows! I, too, have sung them, they're something new, and I could see no harm in them.

BUYCK. I should ask them? In our province, we sing exactly what we like. That is because Count Egmont is our governor. He does not bother about things like that. In Ghent, in Ypres, in all Flanders anyone can sing them if he likes. (*Loud.*) There's nothing more innocent than a religious song, it seems to me. Right, Father?

RUYSUM. To be sure! For that is like attending service, it lifts up the soul.

JETTER. But they say it is not the right kind, not their kind of service; and dangerous it is, so better keep away from it. The Inquisition's snoopers slink around and watch. Many an honest man has been made miserable. Suppressing our consciences, that's more than we need! If I can't do what I want, they might at least let me think and sing what I want.

SOEST. The Inquisition won't take hold. We are not made like Spaniards and won't permit them to tyrannize our conscience. And the nobility had better try to clip their wings while there is time.

JETTER. It's really bad. If these good people take it into their minds to storm into my house, and I sit there working away and happen to hum a French psalm, thinking of nothing, neither good nor bad, but humming it because it happens to sit in my throat—I'm a heretic right away and am put in jail. Or I travel across country and stop somewhere because there's a crowd of people listening to a new preacher, one of those who come from Germany, right away I'm a rebel and risk losing my head. Did you ever hear one preach?

SOEST. Good men. I heard one not long ago who was preaching in a field to thousands and thousands of people. That was a different kettle of fish compared with ours who bang around on the pulpit and choke the people with bits of Latin. He was very frank and told how they had led us by the nose until now, and how we could have more enlightenment. And all this he proved to you from the Bible.

JETTER. There may be something to that. I've often said so to myself, and I've thought a lot about this thing. I've often turned it around in my head.

Buyck. And everybody runs after them.

Soest. Why, I should say so! If one can hear something that's good and new.

Jetter. And what about it? Why not let everyone preach according to his own lights!

Buyck. Come on, gentlemen! With all your chattering you are forgetting the wine—and Orange.

Jetter. Let's not forget him! That is a real wall: just think of him and you get the feeling you could hide behind him and the devil himself couldn't get you out. Long live William of Orange!

All. Hurrah! Hurrah!

Soest. Now, Old Man, it's your turn to toast.

Ruysum. To the old soldiers! To all soldiers! Long live the war!

Buyck. Bravo, Old Man! To all the soldiers! Long live the war!

Jetter. War! War! Do you know what you're shouting? That it flows easily from your lips is natural enough. But I can't tell you how awful a man like myself feels when he hears that. To hear that drumming all year long; and to hear nothing but how this troop marched up here and that one there, how here they came across a hill and there stopped near a mill, how many were left behind here and how many there, and how they pushed on and how one wins, the other loses, and you can't for the world find out who wins or loses what! How a town is taken, the citizens killed and how the poor women and innocent children fare. All that fear and anxiety, and one thinks all the time: "There they come! It's our turn now!"

Soest. That's why a citizen should know how to handle arms.

Jetter. Yes, if one has a wife and children one learns. But still I would rather hear about soldiers than see them.

Buyck. I should take offense at that!

Jetter. It wasn't meant against you, friend. When we got rid of the Spanish occupation we started to breathe again.

Soest. That was the worst of them, wasn't it?

Jetter. Don't tease!

Soest. That was a pretty rough crowd you had to billet in your house!

Jetter. Shut up!

Soest. They drove him from the kitchen, the cellar, the living room—and then his bed. (*They laugh.*)

Jetter. You are an idiot.

Buyck. Peace, gentlemen! Does the soldier have to call for peace? Well, since you don't want to know us, give us a toast to your own health, a citizen's health!

Jetter. We'll gladly do that! Safety and peace!

Soest. Order and liberty!

Buyck. Good! We'll be content with that. (*They clink their glasses and gaily repeat the words, but now in such a way that everyone calls another word and it becomes a kind of canon. The Old Man listens and, finally, joins in.*)

All. Safety and peace! Order and liberty!

Scene 2. *The Palace of the Regent. Margaret of Parma in hunting attire; courtiers, page boys and servants.*

Margaret. There will be no hunting today; I shall not ride out. Tell Machiavell to come. (*The entire retinue leaves.*) The thought of these terrible events is with me constantly. Nothing pleases me, nothing diverts me. These specters and these worries blot out every other view. The King will say that this is the result of my kindness and leniency, yet my conscience tells me that I have always done what was best and most advisable at any given moment. Should I have fanned the flames with the high wind of anger and made this fire spread? I had hoped to be able to contain it until it burned out. Yes, I tell myself these things I know so well, and in my own eyes they excuse me; but how will my brother judge them? For I cannot deny that the impertinence of the foreign teachers increases every day. They blaspheme what we hold sacred, they unhinge the dull senses of the rabble and disseminate lies. Dirty minds have mingled with the rebels and terrible things have happened, gruesome to contemplate. Those I now must report to the Court, one by one—and I must do it quickly, so that rumor will not precede the facts, so that the King will not think that I am holding back more than I report. How can I dam this evil flood, by either severe or mild means? Oh, what are the mighty on the waves of humanity? We like to think that we dominate them, but they carry us up and down, hither and thither. (Machiavell *enters.*) Are the letters to the King drafted?

MACHIAVELL. They will be ready for your signature within the hour.

MARGARET. Is the report sufficiently detailed?

MACHIAVELL. Minutely detailed, the way the King likes it. I report how the iconoclastic fury showed itself first at St. Omer; how a raving mob, with sticks, hatchets, hammers, ladders and ropes, accompanied by just a few armed men, attacked chapels, churches, and monasteries and chased away the devout, how they broke open locked doors, turned everything upside down, tore down the altars, smashed the statues of the saints and destroyed the pictures, and how they battered, lacerated and stepped on every consecrated and sacred object they encountered. I describe how the mob grew as it advanced, and how the population of Ypres opened their doors to them, how they laid waste the cathedral with incredible speed and burned the bishop's library, how huge masses of people, gripped by the same madness, spread to Menin, Comines, Verwich, and Lille, encountering no resistance anywhere, and how the enormous conspiracy was executed and became visible all over Flanders at the same time.

MARGARET. Oh, the pain grips me with renewed strength at your retelling the story! And now there is the greater fear that the evil will grow and grow. What do you think about it, Machiavell?

MACHIAVELL. Excuse me, your Highness, my thoughts seem very much like whims. Although you have always been content with my services, you rarely have seen fit to follow my advice. Jokingly you often said: "You look too far ahead, Machiavell! You should be a historian: the one who wants to act must think about immediate necessities." But did I not predict this story? Did I not foresee it all?

MARGARET. I, too, foresee many things, without being able to change them.

MACHIAVELL. I will speak briefly, then: You will not suppress the new doctrine. Let it exist, then, mark it off from the true faith, give them churches, bring them back into civil obedience and thus you dam the tide and pacify the rebels all at once. All other means are useless and you will lay the country waste.

MARGARET. Did you forget with what revulsion my brother refused even to consider the question if we should tolerate the new doctrine? Don't you know how vigorously he admonished me in every letter to defend the true faith; that he does not want unity and peace restored at the cost of our religion, that he himself has sent spies into the provinces whom we don't know, so that he may learn the names of those who incline to the new faith? Were we not taken by surprise when he mentioned the names of this one or that one who right under our noses had secretly committed heresies? Does he not command us to act with rigorous severity? And I am to be lenient? I am to propose that he forget and forgive? Would I not lose his confidence and trust completely?

MACHIAVELL. Indeed, I know. The King gives orders and lets you know what he intends. You are to rebuild peace and order by means which will embitter the minds even more, which will inevitably fan the war on all sides. Consider well what you must do. The greatest merchants, the nobility, the people and the soldiers have been infected. What good is it to persist in our ideas while everything around us changes? Would that a good spirit whispered into Philip's ear that it is more fitting for a king to let two faiths exist among his subjects than to let them grind each other into dust.

MARGARET. No more of that! I know myself that politics does not encourage keeping faith, and that it bans from our hearts frankness, goodness and leniency. In the business of this world that unfortunately is only too true; but can we deal with God as we deal with each other? Can we be unconcerned about our doctrine for which so many have sacrificed their lives? Are we to surrender it for any novelty, uncertain and self-contradictory, that comes along?

MACHIAVELL. Do not think badly of me for what I said!

MARGARET. I know you, know your loyalty and know that one can be an honest, reasonable man even though he has missed the best and straightest road to the salvation of his soul. And there are others, Machiavell, men whom I must both value and reprove.

MACHIAVELL. Whom do you have in mind?

MARGARET. I must confess that earlier today Egmont annoyed me very much and hurt me deeply.

MACHIAVELL. By doing what?

MARGARET. By his usual behavior, his indifference and frivolity. I heard the terrible news just as I left church, accompanied by him and many others. I did not hide my sorrow, I complained loudly and, turning to him, called out: "Look what is happening in your province! And you, Count, let it happen? You of whom the King expected everything?"

MACHIAVELL. And what did he reply?

MARGARET. As if it were a mere nothing, a matter of no

consequence at all, he said: "If the Netherlanders were only reassured about their constitution, the rest would follow."

MACHIAVELL. That may have been closer to the truth than to prudence and piety. How can we create confidence and how can it last, as long as the Netherlander sees that there is more greed for his possessions than concern about his interests and the salvation of his soul? Did the new bishops save more souls than they consumed fat benefices, and are not most of them foreigners? Netherlanders still serve as governors, but are not the Spaniards all too obvious in their well-nigh irresistible cupidity for these positions? These people, any people would much rather be governed by their own in their own manner than by foreigners who, once arrived, will first attempt to line their pockets to the detriment of all, will bring a foreign yardstick and govern without kindness or understanding.

MARGARET. You're taking the part of our adversary.

MACHIAVELL. Certainly not with my heart! And I wish my mind could be completely on our side.

MARGARET. In that case, I ought to cede the regency which I administer to them. Egmont and Orange had great hopes that they would occupy my place. Then they were adversaries, now they have allied themselves against me and are friends, inseparable friends.

MACHIAVELL. A dangerous pair!

MARGARET. To be quite frank, I am afraid of Orange and afraid of Egmont. What Orange hatches is not good, his thoughts roam far and wide, he's secretive, appears to accept anything, never contradicts, and very deferentially and carefully does exactly what he wants!

MACHIAVELL. Egmont, on the contrary, goes his way as freely as if the world were his.

MARGARET. He holds his head so high that he seems to be unaware of the majestic hand that is above him.

MACHIAVELL. The eyes of the people follow his every move, their hearts are with him.

MARGARET. He never tries to be what he is not, as if he were accountable to no one. He still calls himself Egmont, he is delighted hearing himself called Count Egmont, as if he wanted to be reminded that he has ancestors who were the lords of Gelden. Why does he not call himself Prince of Gaure as is his right? Why not? Does he intend to resurrect the dead claims of the past?

MACHIAVELL. In my opinion, he's a faithful servant of the King.

MARGARET. If he only wished, what services could he not render to the government! Instead, without advancing himself, he causes us untold annoyances. His parties, dinners and feasts have tightened the bonds between the nobles more than the most dangerous secret meetings. His toasts have made his guests permanently drunk, they will never wake from their stupor. And what a commotion he creates among the people with his jokes! How he startled the rabble with the new uniforms and silly insignia of his servants!

MACHIAVELL. I am convinced he did not mean to.

MARGARET. That's bad enough! As I said, he harms us and does no service to himself. He considers serious matters funny, while we must take jokes seriously in order not to appear lax and neglectful. Thus one thing after another; and what we try to avoid happens, it seems, with a vengeance. He is far more dangerous than the determined head of a conspiracy. I would be very much surprised, too, if all this were not carefully noted at court. I cannot deny it, more often than not he irritates me much, very much.

MACHIAVELL. It seems to me that he follows his conscience, whatever he does.

MARGARET. His conscience mirrors a pleasing image. His conduct often is insulting. He often looks like a man who is fully convinced that he is master but, being polite, does not want to let us feel it, does not exactly wish to chase us out of the country because he thinks that things will calm down anyway.

MACHIAVELL. I beg you, do not interpret his frankness, his happy nature which lets him treat important things lightly, as too dangerous a trait. That could only harm both him and yourself.

MARGARET. I do not interpret. I speak of the inevitable consequences, and I know him. Being of Dutch nobility and carrying the Golden Fleece on his breast make him more confident and more audacious. Both could serve to stave off a sudden, quick burst of the King's temper. Look closely, and you will find that he is at the root of all the misfortune that has befallen Flanders. He was the first to look the other way when the foreign teachers came; he let things slide and was perhaps secretly delighted that they gave us trouble. No, no! This is my chance to say what is bothering me. And I shall not shoot off my arrows aimlessly; I know where he is vulnerable. He, too, is vulnerable.

MACHIAVELL. Did you call the council into session? Will Orange come?

MARGARET. I sent to Antwerp for him. I will make them understand the burden of their responsibility clearly enough; they will either have to take a serious stand against the evil or declare openly that they, too, are rebels. Hurry with the letters and bring them to me for signature. Then rush the trusted Vasca to Madrid; he's tireless and loyal. He shall be the first to bring my brother the news, rumor shall not overtake him. I want to talk to him myself before he leaves.

MACHIAVELL. Your orders will be followed conscientiously and quickly.

SCENE 3. *A burgher's house. Claire, Claire's Mother, Brackenburg.*

CLAIRE. Would you like to hold the yarn for me, Brackenburg?

BRACKENBURG. Oh, please, Claire! Leave me alone!

CLAIRE. What is the matter now? Why do you refuse me this small service?

BRACKENBURG. You hold me so tight with your yarn that I cannot escape your eyes.

CLAIRE. Nonsense! Come on and hold the yarn!

MOTHER (*sits in an easy chair, knitting*). Why don't you sing a little! Brackenburg accompanies so nicely. You both used to be so gay, I always had something to laugh about.

BRACKENBURG. Used to be!

CLAIRE. Let's sing!

BRACKENBURG. Anything you like.

CLAIRE. This one is gay and lively! It's a little soldier's song, my favorite. (*She spools the yarn and sings with* BRACKENBURG.)

> Let the drums rumble,
> Let the fifes trill!
> My loved one's in armor,
> His men do his will.
> He holds his lance tight,
> Each man runs to fight.
> My heart skips a beat and
> My blood starts to boil.
> Oh, would I had doublet
> And trousers and foil!
> With bold steps I'd follow
> Him out of the gate,

All over the province,
Whatever his fate.
The foe is retreating,
We shoot at him still.
I would be a soldier
If I had my will.

(*While they were singing,* BRACKENBURG *has repeatedly glanced at* CLAIRE; *in the end, his voice fails him, tears fill his eyes, he drops the hank of yarn and steps to the window.* CLAIRE *finishes the song by herself; her mother is annoyed and gestures to her; when* CLAIRE *has finished, she gets up, takes a few steps toward* BRACKENBURG *but, undecided, turns back and sits down.*)

MOTHER. What is happening down on the street, Brackenburg? I hear sounds of marching.

BRACKENBURG. It's the Regent's Household Guard.

CLAIRE. At this hour? What does that mean? (*She gets up and joins* BRACKENBURG *at the window.*) That is not the usual guard, there are far more! Almost all her troops. Oh, Brackenburg, please run down and see what is going on! It must be something special. Go on, dear Brackenburg, do it as a favor!

BRACKENBURG. I'll go. I'll be back in a minute. (*He holds out his hand to her and she takes it; then he leaves.*)

MOTHER. Now you are sending him away again!

CLAIRE. I am curious, and also—don't be cross with me—I feel uncomfortable when he is here. I never know how to treat him. I'm doing wrong by him, and it hurts me to see how strongly he feels it. But I can't help it!

MOTHER. He's such a nice fellow.

CLAIRE. And I can't help myself, I simply have to be nice to him. Often my hand quite automatically closes on his when he touches me so gently and full of love. I blame myself for going behind his back and for letting his heart hope in vain. I'm in a bad position. God knows I haven't deceived him. I don't want him to hope, and I can't let him despair.

MOTHER. That's bad.

CLAIRE. I was fond of him and even now I wish him well with all my heart. I might have married him but I think I was never in love with him.

MOTHER. You would have been happy with him.

CLAIRE. I'd have someone to take care of me, and a quiet life.

MOTHER. You have spoiled everything now. It is your own fault.

CLAIRE. It's strange. When I think back on how it happened, I know and yet I don't. But then I only have to look at Egmont, and I understand everything so well, yes, I could understand far more! Ah, what a man he is! They adore him everywhere in the provinces, and how should I not be the happiest creature on earth when I am in his arms?

MOTHER. And what is going to happen?

CLAIRE. Oh, I only ask whether he loves me. And is there any question of that?

MOTHER. Children bring nothing but heartache. How is it going to end? Always worries and grief! It can't turn out well! You have made yourself miserable, and me, too.

CLAIRE (calmly). But in the beginning you did not object.

MOTHER. Unfortunately, I was too good to you, as I have always been.

CLAIRE. When Egmont rode by and I rushed to the window, did you scold me? Did you not look out of the window yourself? And when he looked up, smiled, nodded and saluted me, did you mind? Did you not feel honored yourself when I was so honored?

MOTHER. Now you are reproaching me!

CLAIRE (moved). Then, when he passed through our street more often and we thought he took this way because of me, did you not notice it with secret pleasure? Did you call me away when I stood behind the panes, waiting for him?

MOTHER. How could I know that it would come this far!

CLAIRE (haltingly and trying to control her tears). And when he surprised us one evening, shrouded in his cloak, as we were sitting by the lamp—who rushed to receive him while I sat gaping on my chair, as if I had been chained to it?

MOTHER. How could I know that this unhappy love would sweep my prudent little Claire so quickly off her feet? Now I must bear it if my daughter—

CLAIRE (tears welling up in her eyes). Mother! You are trying to make me cry! You seem to like frightening me.

MOTHER (weeping). And now tears! To make me even more miserable with your unhappiness! Do I not grieve enough knowing that my only daughter is depraved?

CLAIRE (gets up, coldly). Depraved! Egmont's beloved depraved? Is there a princess who does not envy this poor little Claire her place in his heart? Oh, Mother! Mother, you do not usually talk like this. Dear Mother, be good to me! The people and what they think, the neighbors and what they whisper—this room, this small house is heaven since Egmont's love has come to live here.

MOTHER. One must be fond of him, that's true. He's always kind and open-hearted.

CLAIRE. There's nothing false about him. And, you see, Mother, he is the Great Egmont, but when he comes to me, how nice, how good he is, and how much he would like to hide his position and his bravery from me! And he is always so worried about me! He's nothing but a human being, a friend—and my beloved!

MOTHER. I wonder if he's coming today?

CLAIRE. Did you not notice how often I go to the window? How I listen when there is a noise at the door? Although I know that he will not come before nightfall, I still expect him every moment, from the second I open my eyes in the morning. Oh, to be a boy! I could be with him all the time, at court and everywhere! I could carry his standard in battle!

MOTHER. You always were a tomboy; even as a small child you were now wild, now thoughtful. Are you not going to dress a little better?

CLAIRE. Perhaps, Mother. If I get bored. Just think, yesterday some of his men walked by and they sang little songs in his praise. At least his name was in the song, the rest I didn't even understand. I thought my heart would jump out of my mouth. I would have liked so much to call them back, but I didn't dare.

MOTHER. Be careful! Your recklessness will spoil everything yet. You betray your feelings in front of people, like the other day at your cousin's when you found that woodcut with the inscription and fairly screamed, "Count Egmont!" I was so embarrassed!

CLAIRE. Why should I not have shouted? It was the battle of Gravelingen, and at the top of the picture I saw the letter "C," and then I looked for "C" at the bottom, in the description, and it said: "Count Egmont as his horse is shot dead under him!" I shivered—and then, later, I had to laugh at that woodcarved Egmont who was as tall as the church tower of Gravelingen right next to him and the English ships at the side. When I think back sometimes, the way I used to imagine what a battle was like, the ideas I had about Count Egmont when I was a little girl, when they talked about him, and of all the counts and dukes—and how I now feel! (BRACKENBURG comes in.) What is happening?

BRACKENBURG. Nobody knows anything for certain. They say there have been riots again in Flanders, and that the Regent is afraid they might spread here. The castle is guarded in force, there are a lot of people near the gates, and the streets are humming with talk. I must go to my old father quickly. (*Pretends that he is leaving.*)

CLAIRE. Are we going to see you tomorrow? I must get dressed. My cousin is coming, and I look terrible. Can you help me a little, Mother? You can take this book back, but bring me another story just like it!

MOTHER. Good-bye.

BRACKENBURG (*holding out his hand*). Your hand!

CLAIRE (*holding hers back*). When you come back!

(CLAIRE *and* MOTHER *leave.*)

BRACKENBURG (*alone*). I had decided to leave, but now that she does not mind and lets me go, I become furious! Scoundrel that I am! No concern whatever about the fate of my country? About the growing unrest? Whether one of ours or a Spaniard governs, and who is right? Ha, when I was a school boy I was different! When we had to write a composition about "Brutus' Speech on Liberty, an Exercise in Oratory"—Fritz was always at the head of the class, and the teacher said if only there was a little more order in it, not everything so jumbled together. Yes, enthusiasm was boiling in me then, and it drove me on. Now, I drag myself along, my eyes on the face of this girl. I cannot tear myself away from her! She cannot love me! Oh . . . no . . . she . . . she cannot have cast me out, not quite . . . but half her love is nothing! I cannot stand it any longer! And if it's true, as a friend whispered in my ear the other day, that she opens her door to a man at night? While she is always so proper with me and sends me home before dark? No! It cannot be true! It is a lie! Claire is as innocent as I am unhappy! She spurns me, she casts my picture out of her heart, and must I continue to live like this? I cannot bear it! And now my country, in its fight against itself, is in an uproar, and it grows—and I do nothing, wither away while all around me the battles rage. When the trumpet sounds, a shot is heard, it sends a shiver down my spine, but it means nothing, the call is not for me! It does not order me to act, to help the others save what can be saved, to take my chances. Oh, it is miserable, ignominious and hateful! Much better then to end it quickly. Not long ago, I jumped into the river and sank, but then my frightened nature got the better of

me; I felt that I could swim and saved myself against my will.
—If only I could forget that there was a time when she loved
me, or so it seemed. Why did it have to take such hold of me,
that happiness? Why did my hopes consume all the pleasure of
life by showing me a Paradise far, far away? And that first
kiss! That only kiss! Here (*He puts his hand on the table.*)
we were standing, all alone. She always had been kind and
gentle to me—and now she seemed to melt—she looked at me—
the world turned somersaults around me—I felt her lips on
mine. —And—now? Die, you poor man! Why do you hesitate? (*He takes a vial from his pocket.*) Not in vain shall I
have stolen you from my brother's medicine chest, you healing
poison! You shall engulf me, dissolve my doubts, my frenzy
and my fears.

ACT II

SCENE 1. *A square in Brussels. Jetter and a Carpenter meet.*

CARPENTER. Did I not tell you? Only eight days ago I said at
the guild meeting that there would be an awful turmoil.

JETTER. Is it true that they have plundered the churches in
Flanders?

CARPENTER. They have completely ruined churches and
chapels, leaving nothing but the bare four walls. Rabble, that's
what they are! And that gives our good cause a bad name. We
should have presented our just demands to the Regent sooner,
orderly but persistently, and we should have stood our ground.
If we speak now or even meet together, they'll say that we
make common cause with rebels.

JETTER. Yes, everyone thinks first: why stick your nose out?
It's too close to the neck.

CARPENTER. I'm scared of what's going to happen once the
riffraff, the people who have nothing to lose, start setting up
a howl. They will use as a pretext the same things we plead
and tumble the whole country into misery. (SOEST *joins them.*)

SOEST. Good day, gentlemen! What's new? Is it true the
vandals are on their way here?

CARPENTER. Here they will not touch anything.

SOEST. A soldier came into my shop to buy tobacco and I

questioned him a little. He said that the Regent, such a good and prudent woman usually, is quite beside herself this time. It must really be bad if she virtually hides herself behind her guard. The castle is manned in full force. Some even say she'll flee from the city.

CARPENTER. She must not leave! As long as she is here, she will protect us, and we can offer her more protection than all her mustachioed guardians. As long as she safeguards our rights and privileges, we shall carry her above us! (*A* SOAP-MAKER *joins them.*)

SOAPMAKER. Nasty business! Bad business! It's beginning to stir and it will end badly! Just be careful, and keep quiet so they won't think you are rebels, too.

SOEST. Hear the Seven Wise Men from Greece!

SOAPMAKER. I know, there are many who secretly go along with the Calvinists, who slander the bishops and don't even have respect for the King. But a faithful subject and upright Catholic . . . (*More and more people gather around and listen.* VANSEN *enters.*)

VANSEN. God's greetings, gentlemen! What news do you have?

CARPENTER. Keep away from him! He's a bad egg.

JETTER. Is he not Doctor Wiets' secretary?

CARPENTER. He's had many masters. First he was a secretary, and when one master after the other chased him away for all the pranks and tricks he played, he quickly turned into an amateur advocate and notary. And then, he loves his liquor. (*More people gather and stand around in groups.*)

VANSEN. You, too, are congregating and sticking your noses together. That's something to talk about.

SOEST. That's what I think.

VANSEN. Now, if one or the other of you really had any courage, or the brains for it, we could easily break the Spanish chains.

SOEST. Now, mister! You mustn't talk like that! We've sworn allegiance to the King.

VANSEN. And the King to us, don't forget!

JETTER. There is a thought! Tell us what you think.

SEVERAL. Listen to him! He understands things, he knows some tricks.

VANSEN. I used to work for a man who had many parchments and letters dealing with age-old stipulations, agreements and privileges. And the rare books he had! In one of them, you could read all about our Constitution; how at first some princes governed us here in the Netherlands in accordance with our traditional rights, privileges and customs; how our ancestors showed the greatest respect for the reigning prince if he governed as he was supposed to; and how they watched when he showed signs of kicking over the traces. The states quickly went after him, for each province, no matter how small, had its states, its provincial diet.

CARPENTER. Shut up! Everybody knows that! Every decent citizen knows as much about the Constitution as he needs to know.

JETTER. Let him talk! One can always learn something new.

SOEST. He's right.

SEVERAL. Tell us more! Tell us more! One doesn't hear things like that every day of the week.

VANSEN. That's how you burghers are! You live and do not think. You follow the trade of your fathers and you let the government do with you as it likes and is able to. You don't care about tradition, history or the rights of a regent; and because you don't the Spaniards have pulled the sack down over your ears.

SOEST. Who has time to think about that? As long as one has enough to eat.

JETTER. Damn it! Why does nobody come in time to tell us these things?

VANSEN. I'm telling you now. The King of Spain, who had the good luck to get all the provinces at one stroke, still cannot govern them differently than the separate princes used to do. Do you understand?

JETTER. Explain a little more.

VANSEN. It's clear as daylight. Don't you have to be judged according to the law of your province? And why is that?

A CITIZEN. That's true!

VANSEN. Doesn't the man from Brussels have a different law than the one from Antwerp? The man from Antwerp than the man from Ghent? And why is that?

SEVERAL. By God, that's true!

VANSEN. But if you let things take their course, they'll show you a different picture. For shame! What Charles the Bold could not accomplish, nor Frederick the Warrior or Charles the Fifth, Philip can do—and all he needs is a woman!

SOEST. Yes, yes, the princes of old have tried it, too.

VANSEN. Of course! But our ancestors were wary. If they had a grudge against a master, they would catch his son and heir, perhaps, and keep him, and they would not give him back until they had obtained the greatest possible concessions. Our fathers were men! They knew where their interests lay. They knew how to seize and keep an advantage. Good men they were! And that is why our privileges are so clear and our rights assured.

SOAPMAKER. What privileges do you speak of?

MANY VOICES. Our privileges and our rights! Tell us some more about our privileges!

VANSEN. Here in Brabant we have still more than in the other provinces, although they, too, have much. I read all about them.

SOEST. Tell us about them!

JETTER. Let us hear!

A CITIZEN. Please go on!

VANSEN. To begin with, it is said: the Duke of Brabant shall be a good and faithful master.

SOEST. Good? Is that what it says?

JETTER. And faithful? Is that true?

VANSEN. Exactly as I told you. He has his duties toward us as we to him. Secondly: he shall not give evidence of force or willful acts, nor show us any signs thereof nor permit others so to act, in any manner whatsoever.

JETTER. Good! Good! Not give any evidence of force!

SOEST. Nor show us any signs thereof!

SOMEONE ELSE. That is the point. Nor permit others so to act! Not others, in any manner whatsoever.

VANSEN. Those are the express words.

JETTER. Bring us the book!

A CITIZEN. Yes, we need the book!

OTHERS. The book! The book!

SOMEONE ELSE. We must show the book to the Regent!

ANOTHER. You must speak for us, Doctor!

SOAPMAKER. Oh, what fools!

ANOTHER. Tell us some more from the book!

SOAPMAKER. I shall bash his teeth in if he says another word.

MANY VOICES. Let's see who will raise a hand against him. Tell us something about our privileges! Do we have more?

VANSEN. Quite a few, very good and useful privileges. For instance, the reigning prince shall not improve and not augment the clergy without express consent of the nobility and of the diet! Remember that! Nor shall he change the form of government.

SOEST. Is that right?

VANSEN. I shall show you the book where everything is written, back two or three hundred years.

A CITIZEN. And we accept the new bishops? The nobility must protect us, or we shall start trouble!

OTHERS. And we allow the Inquisition to intimidate us?

VANSEN. Your fault!

MANY VOICES. We still have Egmont! And we still have Orange! They will look out for us.

VANSEN. Your brothers in Flanders have started the good work.

SOAPMAKER. You dog! (*He hits him.*)

OTHERS (*restrain him and call*). Are you a Spaniard?

ANOTHER. What? Hit an honorable man?

ANOTHER. A learned man? (*They attack the* SOAPMAKER.)

CARPENTER. For Heaven's sake, peace! (*Others join in the fracas.*) Citizens, what good will that do? (*Boys whistle, throw stones and egg on their dogs; some citizens stand by and gape, more people arrive, others stroll imperturbably up and down, still others do all sorts of mischief, shouting jubilantly.*) Freedom and privileges! Privileges and freedom! (EGMONT *appears with his entourage.*)

EGMONT. Peace, people! Peace! What is the matter? Peace! Separate them!

CARPENTER. My gracious sir! You come like an angel sent from Heaven! Quiet! Don't you see? Count Egmont! Respect for Count Egmont!

EGMONT. Here too? What are you doing? Citizen against citizen! Does not even the presence of the royal Regent stop this nonsense? Go each your way, back to your work. It is a bad sign when men rest on working days. What happened? (*The turmoil gradually subsides; they all gather around* EGMONT.)

CARPENTER. They fight about their privileges.

EGMONT. In order to destroy them willfully. Who are you? You look like respectable citizens.

CARPENTER. We endeavor to be.

EGMONT. Your trade?

CARPENTER. Carpenter and master of the guild.

EGMONT. And you?

SOEST. Shopkeeper.

EGMONT. You?

JETTER. Tailor.

EGMONT. I remember you. You worked on the liveries for my men. Your name is Jetter.

JETTER. How gracious to remember, sir.

EGMONT. I do not easily forget a man I have seen and spoken with. Good people, do what befits you to preserve the peace. Your reputation is not good. Do not excite the King still more, he has the power if it comes to that. A decent citizen who honestly and diligently does his work will always have the liberty he needs.

CARPENTER. That is our trouble! It's the no-good drunkards and loafers who—begging your pardon, sir—raise a stink because they have nothing better to do and scratch for privileges because they are hungry, and tell lies to the curious and gullible for the price of a tankard of beer, and in the end will bring misery to thousands of people. That's just what they want. We keep our houses and chests too well locked to suit them, and they would like to drive us out with fire.

EGMONT. You will have all the support you need. Measures are being taken to deal energetically with this evil. Stand fast against the foreign doctrine and do not think that privileges can be safeguarded by rebellion. Stay home and do not allow them to roam the streets. Reasonable men can do much. (*Most of the people have meanwhile left.*)

CARPENTER. Our thanks to your Excellency for your good opinion! We shall do what we can. (EGMONT *leaves.*) A very gracious gentleman! A real Netherlander! Nothing Spanish about him.

JETTER. If only he were our Regent! We'd gladly follow him.

SOEST. Not likely! The King gives a position like that to his own.

JETTER. Did you notice how he was dressed? Latest fashion, Spanish cut.

CARPENTER. A handsome gentleman.

JETTER. His neck would be a Sunday dish for an executioner.

SOEST. Are you mad? What an idea!

JETTER. Of course, it's silly to think about things like that. But I can't help it. Every time I see such a beautiful long neck, I think, in spite of myself, how easily his head would come off. Those cursed executions! One never can get them out of one's head. When the boys go swimming and I see a bare back, right away I remember dozens whom I saw whipped. When I meet a nice paunch, it is as if I saw him already roasting at the stake. At night, in my dreams, every one of my limbs feels pinched. One can't enjoy a single hour's peace. I've almost forgotten what it is like to be gay and have fun. Those horrible specters are burned into my brain.

SCENE 2. *Egmont's apartment. The Secretary sits at a
table with papers; he is restless and gets up.*

SECRETARY. He is not here yet, and I've been waiting for
two hours, pen in hand, the papers before me. And just today I
wanted to leave early. I am on tenterhooks! I'm so impatient
that I can hardly get myself to stay. "Be there on time,"
was his command before he left, and now he doesn't come.
There is so much to do that I will not be able to finish before
midnight. Of course, on the other hand he is often lenient, but
I would prefer him to be strict and let a man leave at the
proper time. One could plan better that way. It is two hours
now since he left the Regent. Who knows whom he has met on
the way. (EGMONT *enters.*)

EGMONT. How do things look?

SECRETARY. I'm ready and three messengers are waiting.

EGMONT. Did I take too long to suit you? You are making a
very unhappy face.

SECRETARY. I obeyed your orders, and have been waiting for a
long time. Here are the papers!

EGMONT. Donna Elvira will be cross with me if she hears that
I'm the one who delayed you.

SECRETARY. You're joking, sir.

EGMONT. No, no! Don't be ashamed. You have good taste. She
is pretty and I don't mind at all if you have a friend in the
Castle. What are the letters about?

SECRETARY. Many things, but nothing pleasant.

EGMONT. A good thing, then, that we have our happiness at
home and need not wait for it to come from elsewhere. Was
there much mail?

SECRETARY. Enough, and three messengers are waiting.

EGMONT. Tell me what it's about, but only the most urgent
things.

SECRETARY. Everything is urgent.

EGMONT. One thing after another, then, but quickly.

SECRETARY. Captain Breda sends a report about the further
events in Ghent and its surroundings. The turmoil has subsided
for the most part.

EGMONT. But he still mentions some insubordination and fool-
hardiness, I suppose?

SECRETARY. Yes, quite a bit of that is still going on.

EGMONT. Spare me the details.

SECRETARY. They have arrested six more who toppled the

statue of Saint Mary at Verwich. He wants to know if they are to be hanged like the others.

EGMONT. I am tired of hangings. Let him give them a good flogging and send them home.

SECRETARY. There are two women among them; shall he have them flogged too?

EGMONT. Tell him to warn them and let them go.

SECRETARY. Brink, of Breda's company, wants to get married. The Captain hopes you will refuse. There are so many women around, he writes, that when they march out, the company doesn't look like soldiers on the march but like a band of gypsies.

EGMONT. For him I shall let it pass! He is a good-looking young fellow and he begged me so insistently before I left. But after this, no more! Although I'm really sorry to have to refuse their greatest pleasure to these poor devils who have enough to bear anyway.

SECRETARY. Two of your men, Seter and Hart, have played a pretty nasty trick on a girl, an innkeeper's daughter. They found her alone, and the girl could not defend herself against the two of them.

EGMONT. If it was a decent girl and they used force, he is to have them flogged three days running, and if they own anything, he is to take as much of it as is needed to buy the girl a dowry.

SECRETARY. One of the foreign teachers tried to pass secretly through Comines and was discovered. He swears that he was on his way to France. According to the orders, he is to be beheaded.

EGMONT. They are to bring him quietly to the border and warn him that he won't get off so easily a second time.

SECRETARY. There is a letter from your Collector. He writes that very little money is coming in and that he could hardly send the amount you requested within a week. Everything is in utter confusion as a result of the disturbances, he says.

EGMONT. I need the money. Let him see how he gets it.

SECRETARY. He says he will try his best and will finally have that Raymond, who has been in your debt for so long, arrested and taken to court.

EGMONT. But he has promised that he would pay.

SECRETARY. The last time he himself set a due date of fourteen days.

EGMONT. Let him have another two weeks, and after that he may proceed against him.

SECRETARY. You are right. He is well able to but does not want to pay. He will, as soon as he is sure that you mean business. The Collector also says that he plans to keep back for half a month the pensions which you have allotted to the veterans, widows and some others; meanwhile, he says, perhaps, the problem could be solved. They would have to manage.

EGMONT. What is there to manage? Those people need the money more than I. No, tell him not to do that.

SECRETARY. And where do you command him to find the money?

EGMONT. Let him worry about that. We told him already in our last letter.

SECRETARY. That is why he makes these proposals.

EGMONT. They are no good! Let him think of something else. Let him make proposals that are acceptable. But above all, let him find the money!

SECRETARY. I have put the letter from Count Oliva back here. Forgive my reminding you. The old gentleman deserves an answer more than anyone else. You planned to write him yourself. There's no doubt he loves you like a father.

EGMONT. I have no time for it. Among the many things I hate, writing letters is what I hate most. You imitate my hand so well, write him in my name. I expect Orange. I simply have no time for it, but I wish myself that he should get a reassuring answer to his letters full of anxious concern.

SECRETARY. Tell me the gist of what you wish to say. I can then draft the letter and let you see it. It will be written so that even in a court of justice it would pass as written by yourself.

EGMONT. Give me the letter! (*After glancing at it.*) That honest, good old man! I wonder if he was so prudent in his youth? Did he never scale a wall? And in a battle, did he always stay behind, as prudence certainly would counsel? Loyal and always so concerned! He wants me to live long and happily and does not realize that he is dead who only lives to be secure. Write him not to worry; tell him that I am acting as I must and shall take care that I'm not harmed; and tell him also to employ his influence at Court on my behalf, and to be certain of my gratitude.

SECRETARY. Nothing but that? Oh, he expects much more!

EGMONT. What else is there to say? Use more words if you like. It always turns around one single point: I am to live as I don't like to live. To be gay, not to take things too seriously, to live in a rush, that is what makes me happy, and I will not exchange my happiness for the safety of a tomb. Not one drop of my blood fits me for the Spanish way of life, and I do not want to suit my pace to the deliberate cadence of the Court which has become the vogue of late. I cannot live only to think of staying alive! Shall I deny myself the pleasure of this moment only to be certain that I shall live to see the next? And to consume *that* one by worrying about the one that follows?

SECRETARY. Please, sir, do not be harsh! Have patience with the good old man! You are so kind to everyone. Give me one pleasing thought that could be comfort to your noble friend. Observe how careful he is not to offend you, how gentle is his touch.

EGMONT. But he must always touch this chord! He knows, has always known, how I detest these exhortations. They irritate me and they do not help. If I walked in my sleep and had reached the dangerous edge of a roof, would it be kind to call my name, to warn, to wake and thus to kill me? Let every man choose his way and look out for his own good.

SECRETARY. It is all right for you to throw all caution to the winds, but those who know and love you . . .

EGMONT (*again reading from the letter*). He comes again with those old fairy tales, recalls again what, in an evening spent with friends in easy talk and gay with wine, we did and said, and what conclusions were drawn, cited as evidence and spread all through the realm. Very well! We did have our servants' sleeves embroidered with fool's caps and bells, and later transformed this outrageous decoration into a sheaf of arrows, an even more dangerous symbol to all those who insist on interpreting where there is nothing to interpret. In a moment of abandon we did conceive and give birth to this or that tomfoolery; we are responsible that a whole troop of nobles, beggar's pouch in hand, under false names they chose themselves, and with mock humility, reminded the King of his duty. We are guilty—of what else? Is a carnival mummery the same as high treason? Do they begrudge us the short, colored rags which we with youthful courage and inspired fantasy use to conceal the wretched nakedness of our lives? If you take life too seriously, what then remains of it? If we do not wake up with joyous expectations and there is no pleasure to look forward to in the evening, what point is there in getting dressed and taking off your clothes? Does the sun warm me today only to give me a chance to think about what happened yesterday, an opportunity to guess or to compute what cannot be foreseen, the fate tomorrow has in store for me? No, thoughts like these are not for me, let's leave them to courtiers and schoolboys! Let them think and bethink themselves, walk and creep, reach as far as they can and sneak whatever they can get. If you can use any of this, you may, but don't make a book out of your letter. The good old man takes everything much too seriously, much as a friend who has been holding your hand squeezes it one last time as he lets go of it.

SECRETARY. Pardon a mere pedestrian if he gets dizzy watching a man career past him at such rattling speed.

EGMONT. No farther, my boy, no farther! As if whipped by invisible spirits the sun horses of time bolt with fate's light carriage; we can do nothing but hold on to the reins, determined and calm, to guide the wheels now to the right, now to the left, here to avoid a rock and there a fall. Who knows where we are headed? We can barely remember whence we came.

SECRETARY. Please, sir!

EGMONT. I stand already high, but I must climb still higher. In me I feel the hope, the courage and the strength for it. The high point of my growth is not yet reached, and once arrived on top I want to stand on firmly planted feet, not fearfully. If I am meant to fall, a thunderbolt, a windstorm, even a false step may plunge me back into the depths—there I shall lie with many thousands. I never have refused to throw the dice of blood with my good comrades-in-arms for little gain, and should I be a miser when my whole life, all that I value, is at stake?

SECRETARY. Oh, sir, you do not know what words you speak! May God preserve you!

EGMONT. Take your papers now. Orange is coming. Prepare whatever is most urgent so that the messengers will be on their way before the gates are closed. The rest can wait. Leave the letter to the Count for tomorrow. Don't fail to visit your Elvira, and give her my regards. And you might listen to how the Regent feels. I understand she is not well although she tries to hide it. (*The* SECRETARY *leaves.* ORANGE *enters.*)

EGMONT. Welcome, Orange! You seem preoccupied.

ORANGE. What do you think of our conversation with the Regent?

EGMONT. I did not find her manner of receiving us extraordinary. I've seen her like that quite often. I thought she was not well.

ORANGE. Did you not notice that she was more reticent? At first she was willing to accept our conduct during the latest outbreak of riots quite calmly, even approvingly. Then she realized that this might put her in a false light and channelled the conversation into her old, well-worn discourse: that no one gives recognition to her kind and well-meaning approach, that no one gives her due credit for her friendship for us Netherlanders or that it is brushed aside, that nothing seems to turn out as it should, that she would eventually get tired and that the King would have to adopt other measures. You heard it, didn't you?

EGMONT. Not all of it. I was thinking of something else. She is a woman, my friend, and women always like to see everyone calmly bend under their gentle yoke; they wish that every Hercules shed his lion's skin and join their spinning circle, that —because they are peaceful—it were possible to settle with one kind word the ferment that grips a nation or the storm which mighty rivals arouse against each other; they would like to see the most irreconcilable elements gently lie down at their feet in perfect harmony. This is the way *she* is, and since she cannot possibly attain these goals, there is no other way for her than to become moody, to complain about ingratitude and stupidity, to point menacingly to the future where dreadful vistas open, and to threaten that she will leave.

ORANGE. Don't you think she might do it this time?

EGMONT. Never! How often have I not seen her all prepared for the journey! Where could she go? Here she is Regent, Queen. Do you think she would find it very entertaining to reel off meaningless days at her brother's court? Or to go to Italy and drag herself around in old family affairs?

ORANGE. We consider her incapable of taking that decision, because we have seen her hesitate and retreat. Yet, she is capable of doing it; new developments drive her toward the decision she has long avoided. If she went? And if the King sent someone else, what then?

EGMONT. Well, he would come and he, too, would find things to do. He would come with great projects, plans and theories, how he could bring everything into line, subject and hold together; he would be busy with trifles, this one today, another one tomorrow, and the day after he would find still more difficulties; one month he would spend planning, the next month grieving over his lack of success, and the next six would be occupied with worries about one single province. Time will pass for him, too, his head will spin, and things will go on as they did before. In the end, instead of steering a steady course across the wide oceans, he will thank God if he kept his ship away from the rocks.

ORANGE. But if someone proposed an experiment to the King?

EGMONT. Such as?

ORANGE. To see how the body would behave without a head.

EGMONT. What?

ORANGE. Egmont, for many years I have had all our affairs at heart and on my mind; I keep staring at the chessboard and refuse to consider any of the opponent's moves insignificant. And just as people who have nothing better to concern themselves studiously and conscientiously with the secrets of nature, I hold it to be the duty, yes, the true calling of a prince to know the opinions of all parties and the advice they give. I have reason to fear an explosion. The King has acted for a long time in accordance with certain principles; now he realizes that they are inadequate. What is more likely than that he will try other methods?

EGMONT. I don't believe it. When one gets old and has tried so many things, and there still is no order in the world, one should have enough of it and give up.

ORANGE. There is one thing he has not yet tried.

EGMONT. And that is?

ORANGE. To be easy on the people and to destroy the princes.

EGMONT. Oh, so many have been afraid of that for a long time! There is no danger of that.

ORANGE. Until now it was only a danger. Gradually it became a probability, and now I am certain of it.

EGMONT. But does the King have more loyal servants than ourselves?

ORANGE. We serve the King in our own way, and to each other we can admit that we know very well to weigh the King's rights against our own.

EGMONT. Who does not do that? We are his subjects and ready to serve him with everything to which he is entitled.

ORANGE. But if he felt entitled to more, and called disloyal what we call "preserving our rights"?

EGMONT. We shall be able to defend ourselves. Let him call together the Knights of the Golden Fleece, we shall submit to their justice.

ORANGE. And how would it be if the verdict preceded the investigation, the punishment the verdict?

EGMONT. That would be an injustice which Philip will never commit and a stupidity of which I believe him and his councilors incapable.

ORANGE. But suppose they are unjust and foolish?

EGMONT. No, Orange, it is simply impossible. Who would

dare to touch us? To take us prisoners would be a useless enterprise. No, they would not dare to raise the standard of tyranny
so high. The breeze which would blow such news across the
country would be enough to fan the embers into a conflagration.
And what could they do, in the end? The King alone can not
sit in judgment over us and condemn us, and would they kill
us like assassins? They cannot want to do that. In one moment
the people would form a terrible alliance. Their hate would
force the separation from Spain forever.

ORANGE. Those flames would roar above our graves, and the
blood of the enemy would flow as a vain sacrifice to our memory.
Let us think, Egmont.

EGMONT. How could they?

ORANGE. Alba is on his way.

EGMONT. I don't believe it.

ORANGE. I know it.

EGMONT. The Regent denied any knowledge of it.

ORANGE. All the more am I convinced of it. The Regent will
make room for him. I know his murderous mind, and he is
bringing an army.

EGMONT. To irritate the provinces once again? The people
will be very difficult.

ORANGE. They will seize the leaders.

EGMONT. No, no.

ORANGE. Let each of us go to his province. There let us prepare our strength. He will not use force openly.

EGMONT. Will we not have to greet him when he arrives?

ORANGE. We shall hesitate.

EGMONT. And if he demands our presence at his arrival in
the name of the King?

ORANGE. We shall find excuses.

EGMONT. And if he urges us?

ORANGE. We shall send him our apologies.

EGMONT. And if he insists?

ORANGE. Then we shall certainly not come.

EGMONT. That means a declaration of war and we would be
the rebels. Orange, don't let your cleverness lead you astray! I
know that fear will never make you retreat. Think well before
taking that step.

ORANGE. I have thought well.

EGMONT. Just think, if you were wrong, what you would have
on your conscience: the most devastating war that has ever
laid a country in ruin. Your refusal to come would be the signal
that calls the provinces to arms immediately, it would justify

all the cruelty for which Spain has always wanted a pretext. We've labored long to pacify the country, and with one wave of your hand you would throw it into the most terrible turmoil. Think of the towns, the nobility, the people! Think of the merchants, the peasants and the artisans! Think of the devastation and the murder! In a battle the soldier may see his comrade fall next to him without wincing; but when the corpses of men and children and young girls float down the rivers, you will stand transfixed by horror, not knowing whose cause you are defending, since those for whose freedom you fought will be dead. And how will you feel when you must quietly admit to yourself: I fought for my own safety.

ORANGE. We are not only individuals, Egmont. If it befits us to sacrifice ourselves for thousands of people, then it befits us also to save ourselves for thousands of people.

EGMONT. He who saves himself must be suspicious of his motives.

ORANGE. He who knows himself can safely walk either forward or backward.

EGMONT. The evil which you fear becomes a certainty by what you do.

ORANGE. It is both prudent and courageous to anticipate an inevitable evil.

EGMONT. When the risks are so great, even the smallest ray of hope is of importance.

ORANGE. We have no longer room for even a bare foothold. The abyss yawns next to us.

EGMONT. Is the King's good will so narrow a platform?

ORANGE. Not so narrow, but slippery.

EGMONT. By God, you do not do him justice! I do not like anyone thinking him unscrupulous. He is the son of Charles and is not capable of being base.

ORANGE. Kings are never base.

EGMONT. One has to know him.

ORANGE. Knowing him precisely is what makes it advisable not to take chances with a dangerous test.

EGMONT. No test is dangerous for which one has the courage.

ORANGE. You are becoming angry, Egmont.

EGMONT. I have to look at things through my own eyes.

ORANGE. Oh, how I wish that this one time you saw with mine! Because you have them open you believe that you can see. I shall leave. You wait for Alba, and may God be with you! Perhaps my refusal will be your salvation. Perhaps the dragon will disdain the meal unless it's both of us. He may delay in order to be surer of success, and meanwhile you may see the situation as it is. But when you do, be quick! Be quick! Be very quick! And save yourself! Farewell! Pay close attention, make a note of everything, how many men he brings with him, how he sets out his posts in town, what powers the Regent retains, how your friends are disposed. Send word to me—oh, Egmont!

EGMONT. What is it?

ORANGE (takes his hand). Let me persuade you! Come with me!

EGMONT. What? Tears, Orange?

ORANGE. It is not unmanly to weep for a lost friend.

EGMONT. You think that I am lost?

ORANGE. You are. Think well! You do not have much time. Farewell!   (He leaves.)

EGMONT (alone). That other people's thoughts have so much influence upon us! It never would have occurred to me, and now this man has put his apprehension into my heart. Away! This is a drop of foreign blood in my veins. Nature, eject it! And there is still a pleasant way to bathe away the furrows of anxiety and brooding from my brow.

ACT III

SCENE 1. The Regent's Palace. Margaret of Parma.

MARGARET. I should have known it, but when one lives from day to day, working and worrying, one always thinks that one is doing all that is possible, and, looking on from afar and giving his commands, the King believes that his demands are only reasonable. Oh, Kings! I never thought that it would so upset me. To rule is such a pleasure! And abdicate? I cannot understand how my father could get himself to do it. But I shall do it, too. (MACHIAVELL appears in the background.) Come in, Machiavell! I am just thinking about my brother's letter.

MACHIAVELL. Am I allowed to know what it contains?

MARGARET. As many tender attentions for me as concern for his provinces. He praises my steadfastness, diligence and loyalty in watching over his Majesty's interests in this country. He pities me because of the trouble these unmanageable people cause me. He is so convinced of the depth of my understanding and so content with my prudent conduct, that I am almost forced to say this letter is too beautiful to have been written by a king, and certainly by a brother.

MACHIAVELL. It is not the first time that he has expressed his justified satisfaction to you.

MARGARET. No, but it is the first time that it has had eloquence and form.

MACHIAVELL. I don't understand.

MARGARET. You will. After this introduction, he advances the thought that without some men, without a small army, I will always cut a pitiable figure here. We were wrong, he says, to have withdrawn our soldiers from the provinces when the population complained. An occupation force, he feels, which rides the citizens makes it impossible for them to ride too high.

MACHIAVELL. That would create quite an upheaval.

MARGARET. But the King thinks—you understand?—the King thinks that a doughty general, one who never listens to reason, would make short shrift with common people, nobles, citizens and peasants. He therefore sends, accompanied by a strong army —the Duke of Alba.

MACHIAVELL. Alba?

MARGARET. You are surprised?

MACHIAVELL. You said, "He sends." You mean, he asks you if he should, of course.

MARGARET. The King does not ask, he sends.

MACHIAVELL. So you will have an old, experienced warrior in your service.

MARGARET. In my service? Speak frankly, Machiavell.

MACHIAVELL. I did not wish to be presumptuous.

MARGARET. And I would like to pretend! It hurts, Machiavell, it hurts! I would prefer it if my brother spoke his mind instead of sending me the formal exercises of a secretary.

MACHIAVELL. Could one not make them understand?

MARGARET. I know them to the core. They like to have everything neatly swept and cleaned, and since they will not take a hand themselves they welcome anybody coming with a broom. Oh, I can see them before me, as if the King and his council were woven into this tapestry.

MACHIAVELL. So vividly?

MARGARET. Not a detail is missing. There are good men among them. The honest Roderick, experienced and moderate, who does not wish to fly too high but never stoops too low; the frank Alonzo and the diligent Freneda; the firm Las Vargas and some others who will be on their side as soon as good men gain the upper hand. But there, among them, sits the hollow-eyed Toledan with his face of iron and his deep, fiery gaze and, murmuring between his teeth, says something about women's weakness, ill-timed concessions, and the fact that women might sit well on well-trained horses but are bad riding masters and other witticisms of this kind; I had to sit and listen to the political gentlemen talking in this vein before.

MACHIAVELL. You chose a suitable palette to paint the picture.

MARGARET. You must admit, Machiavell, that among all the tints I might use none is as yellow-brown and gall-black as Alba's face and the color *he* uses for painting. Everyone is quickly classified by him as a blasphemer and offender against the Crown. For under this heading one can immediately break them on the wheel, impale them on the stake, burn, or quarter them. —The good which I have done here will look like nothing viewed from Madrid, precisely because it is good. —He clings to every malicious act that others have forgotten, keeps alive the memory of riots quelled long ago, until the King has before his eyes so many mutinies, rebellions and foolhardy attacks that he imagines people keep on eating each other alive while we have long forgotten the incident which we considered but a fleeting display of bad manners by a rough-hewn populace. So he has built up a veritable hatred against these good people; they appear to him disgusting, no better than animals and monsters. He looks to fire and sword and imagines men can thus be tamed.

MACHIAVELL. I believe you are too impetuous; you take the matter too seriously. Will you not still be Regent?

MARGARET. I know all about that. He will bring with him an instruction. I have grown up in affairs of state and know how one can push someone aside without revoking his appointment. He will have an instruction that is vague and lopsided. He will spread himself because he has the power, and if I complain he will pretend having secret instructions. If I should want to see them, he will stall. If I insist, he will show me a document which contains something quite different, and if I am not content with that, he will act as if he did not hear me. Meanwhile, he will have done what I had been afraid of and shifted far off its course what I had wished to do.

MACHIAVELL. I wish I could contradict you.

MARGARET. The people I have calmed with untold patience he will incite again by harshness and cruelty. Thus I will see my work dissolve before my eyes and even be responsible for what he does.

MACHIAVELL. Your Highness must expect it.

MARGARET. I can control myself enough to keep quiet. Let him come. I shall gracefully make room for him before he pushes me aside.

MACHIAVELL. But need you take this fatal step so quickly?

MARGARET. I find it harder than you think. Someone for whom to rule is habit, for whom it is a daily chore to weigh the fate of thousands in his hand, steps from his throne as if he climbed into his grave. But even that is better than to walk ghostlike among the living, than to attempt maintaining, with nothing but the hollow reverence which it commands, a place inherited by someone else who now possesses and enjoys it.

SCENE 2. *Claire's house. Claire and her Mother.*

MOTHER. I have never seen a love like Brackenburg's; I always thought that existed only in heroic poems.

CLAIRE (*walking up and down the room, humming a tune*).

> Happy alone
> Is the soul that loves.

MOTHER. He suspects something about your relationship with Egmont, but I think he would marry you all the same if you were only a little nice to him, if you only wanted it.

CLAIRE (*sings*).

> Joyful
> And sorrowful
> Lost in deep thought,
> Longing
> And dreading
> In lingering pain,
> Heavenly triumph
> Or death in your heart.
> Happy alone
> Is the soul that loves.

MOTHER. Oh, stop your lullaby!

CLAIRE. Don't criticize it, it is forceful song. Many a time I have sung a big child to sleep with it.

MOTHER. You really have nothing in your head but your love.

If only you didn't forget everything else over it. I tell you you should not neglect Brackenburg. He may well make you happy some day.

CLAIRE. He?

MOTHER. Yes, he! The time will come. You children never look ahead and refuse to listen to our experiences. Youth and that beautiful love, all that will come to an end, and the time comes when one thanks God to have a hole to crawl into.

CLAIRE (*shudders, remains silent for a moment and then flies up*). Mother, that time may come as death will come. To think of it now is horrible! When death comes—when we must—then —we shall conduct ourselves as best we can! Oh, Egmont, to be without you! (*With tears in her eyes.*) No, it is impossible, impossible!

(EGMONT *enters; he wears a riding cloak, his hat pushed down on his face.*)

EGMONT. Claire!

CLAIRE (*cries out and shrinks back*). Egmont! (*She rushes to him.*) Oh, you good, sweet, dear man! Did you come at last? You are here!

EGMONT. Good evening, Mother!

MOTHER. God's greetings, noble sir! My little one almost died because you are so late. She has spent the whole day again talking and singing about you.

EGMONT. Do you have some supper for me?

MOTHER. That's too much honor! If we only had something!

CLAIRE. Of course, we do. Never mind, Mother, everything is taken care of; there is something ready for him. Don't tell him, Mother!

MOTHER. It's little enough.

CLAIRE. Just wait! And then I always think: when he is with me I am not hungry at all, so he should not have such an appetite when I am with him.

EGMONT. Do you think so? (*She stamps her foot and indignantly turns away.*) What is the matter?

CLAIRE. You are so cold today! You did not even offer me a kiss. Why do you keep your arms wrapped in your cloak like a baby in swaddling clothes? That's not the thing to do for a soldier or for a lover, to keep his arms wrapped up like that.

EGMONT. Everything in due time, my darling, wait! When a soldier prepares an ambush and cunningly plans to surprise the enemy, he must control himself, take hold of his own arms and chew his plan until it's ready. And a lover . . .

MOTHER. Don't you want to sit down and make yourself comfortable? I must go to the kitchen, Claire doesn't remember a thing when you are here. You must content yourself.

EGMONT. Your good intentions are the best seasoning.

(*The* MOTHER *leaves.*)

CLAIRE. What is my love?

EGMONT. As much as you want it to be.

CLAIRE. To what would you compare it? Try, if you dare.

EGMONT. To begin with, now— (*He throws off the cloak and stands before her in resplendent dress.*)

CLAIRE. Oh, dear!

EGMONT. My arms are free now! (*He embraces her.*)

CLAIRE. No, don't! You'll spoil your clothes! (*She steps back.*) How magnificent! No, like this I can't touch you.

EGMONT. Are you content? I promised you once that I would come as a Spaniard.

CLAIRE. I've never reminded you of it; I thought you did not want to. Oh—and the Golden Fleece!

EGMONT. There it is.

CLAIRE. And the Emperor put it around your neck?

EGMONT. Yes, my darling. The chain and the insignia convey on anyone who wears them the most noble liberties. I recognize no one on earth as competent to judge my actions but the Grand Master of the Order together with the assembled Chapter of its Knights.

CLAIRE. Oh, you need not have any qualms about letting the whole world be your judge. —How beautiful this velvet is, and the gold-threaded trim, and the embroidery! One doesn't know where to begin.

EGMONT. Keep looking till you've had your fill.

CLAIRE. And the Golden Fleece! You told me the story once; you said that it's the symbol of all that is grand and precious, that one must diligently work for it and merit it. Yes, it is very precious—I could compare it to your love. I carry it on my heart the same way—but then—

EGMONT. Then what?

CLAIRE. Then again it's not comparable.

EGMONT. Why not?

CLAIRE. I did not diligently work for it, and do not merit it.

EGMONT. In love it's different. You merit it because you did not ask for it—usually only those who don't chase after it succeed in finding it.

CLAIRE. Did you draw that conclusion from your own experience? Did you make this proud observation about yourself, you whom a whole people loves?

EGMONT. If only I had done something for them! And if I only could do something for them! They love me of their own free will.

CLAIRE. Did you see the Regent today?

EGMONT. Yes, I was with her.

CLAIRE. Do you get along well with her?

EGMONT. It is like this: we are friendly and useful to each other.

CLAIRE. And in your heart?

EGMONT. I wish her well. Each has his own intentions. That does not matter. She is an excellent woman, she knows people and her eyes would penetrate quite deeply if she were not also suspicious. She has a good deal of trouble with me because she is always trying to discover secret motives for what I do— and I have none.

CLAIRE. None at all?

EGMONT. Well—some small reservations. Every wine, in time, deposits tartar in the cask. But Orange provides much better entertainment and is an ever novel problem for her. He has gained the reputation of always having secret plans, and now she always looks at his forehead to find out what he might think, and at his feet to see in which direction he will turn.

CLAIRE. Does she dissemble?

EGMONT. A regent, and you ask?

CLAIRE. Excuse me! What I meant was, is she false?

EGMONT. No more nor less than anyone who means to reach his goal.

CLAIRE. In that world I would not find my way around. But she has the mind of a man, she is a different kind of woman from us seamstresses and cooks. She is grand, courageous and determined.

EGMONT. Yes, as long as things don't go too badly. This time she is a little disconcerted after all.

CLAIRE. Why?

EGMONT. She has a little mustache on her lip, too, and suffers from occasional attacks of gout. A real Amazon!

CLAIRE. A majestic woman! I would not dare to step in front of her.

EGMONT. But you are usually not timid. And it would not be for fear, but girlish modesty. (CLAIRE *drops her eyes, takes his hand and leans against him.*)

EGMONT. My dearest girl, I understand you! Look up! (*He kisses her eyes.*)

CLAIRE. Let me be silent! Let me hold you! Let me look into your eyes and there see everything, hope, comfort, joy and sorrow. (*She embraces him and looks at him.*) Tell me something! Tell me! I don't understand. Are you Egmont? Count Egmont? The Great Egmont who is such a sensation, about whom one reads in the newspapers all the time, whom all the provinces adore?

EGMONT. No, Claire, I am not.

CLAIRE. What?

EGMONT. You see, Claire . . . let me sit down. (*He sits down, she kneels on a stool before him, puts her arms on his lap and looks at him.*) That Egmont is a gloomy, stiff, cold man who has to control himself, has to show now this and now another face, who is troubled, misunderstood and complicated when people think that he is happy and gay; who is loved by a people that doesn't know what it wants, honored and carried about by a a mob that is good for nothing; surrounded by friends whom he cannot trust, watched by people who are trying to get at him by any means they can find; who works hard and tries hard, often without purpose, usually without reward—no, let me say no more about that man, what he does and how he feels. But this Egmont, my darling, is calm, frank, happy, known and loved by the best heart in the world, a heart which he too knows intimately and which he presses to his, full of love and trust. (*He embraces her.*) This is *your* Egmont!

CLAIRE. Oh, let me die now! After this the world can offer me no greater happiness!

ACT IV

SCENE 1. *A street. Jetter, Carpenter.*

JETTER. Hey! Psht! Hey, neighbor! A word with you!

CARPENTER. Be on your way and leave me alone.

JETTER. Just one word! Any news?

CARPENTER. Nothing, except that it's forbidden again to talk.

JETTER. What?

CARPENTER. Come over here, close to the house. Be careful! The Duke of Alba had hardly arrived when he issued an order which declares that two or three people speaking to each other on the street will be considered guilty of high treason, without any further investigation.

JETTER. Oh, oh!

CARPENTER. Under threat of perpetual imprisonment it is forbidden to talk about affairs of state.

JETTER. Oh, our liberty!

CARPENTER. If anybody disapproves of measures taken by the government—the death penalty.

JETTER. Oh, our heads!

CARPENTER. And fathers, mothers, children, relatives, friends, and servants are enticed with great promises to reveal to a specially constituted court what goes on inside our houses.

JETTER. Let's go home.

CARPENTER. And those who conform are promised that they will suffer no harm, neither bodily, nor to their honor or property.

JETTER. How generous! No wonder I felt sick the minute the Duke entered the city. Since then I have felt that the sky is covered with black gossamer and reaches so far down that one has to stoop to avoid butting against it.

CARPENTER. And how do you like his soldiers? That's a different kettle of fish from what we've been used to, isn't it?

JETTER. Phew! It chokes you just to see a troop of them marching down the street ramrod-stiff, eyes straight ahead, and in step, no matter how many of them there are. And when they stand guard and you walk past one of them, it seems he wants to look right through you; and they look so tough and grouchy that you seem to see a taskmaster at every corner. I don't like them. Yes, our militia, that was a gay crowd. They carried on, standing around with legs spread apart, their hats on one ear, they lived and let live. But these fellows are like machines with a devil inside.

CARPENTER. When one of them shouts, "Halt!" and takes aim —do you think you'd stop?

JETTER. I would die on the spot.

CARPENTER. Let's go home.

JETTER. It's getting pretty bad. Adieu!

(SOEST enters.)

SOEST. Friends! Comrades!

CARPENTER. Quiet! Let's go.

SOEST. Have you heard?

JETTER. More than enough.

SOEST. The Regent has left.

JETTER. Now God have mercy on us!

CARPENTER. She stood by us, at least.

SOEST. Quietly and quickly. She could not get along with the Duke. She let the nobles know that she would come back. No one believes it.

CARPENTER. May God forgive the nobles that they let this new affliction come over us. They could have prevented it. Our privileges are gone.

JETTER. For God's sake, don't mention privileges! I sniff, and I smell executions in the morning air; the sun will not come out and the fog stinks.

SOEST. Orange has left, too.

CARPENTER. We are left all alone, then.

SOEST. Count Egmont is still here.

JETTER. Thank God! May all the saints come to his aid and let him do his best. He is the only one who can do anything.

(VANSEN enters.)

VANSEN. At last I find a few who have not crawled into their holes yet!

JETTER. Do us a favor and keep going.

VANSEN. You're not very polite.

CARPENTER. This is no time for compliments. Does your back itch again? Are you quite healed?

VANSEN. Ask a soldier questions about his wounds! If I had paid attention to thrashings, I would never have gotten very far.

JETTER. It may get more serious than that.

VANSEN. The thunderstorm that's coming up makes you feel miserably faint in all your limbs, it seems.

CARPENTER. Your limbs will twitch somewhere else pretty soon, if you don't keep quiet.

VANSEN. Poor mice who despair the minute the master of the house gets a new cat! A little differently perhaps, but we will carry on just as before, don't worry.

CARPENTER. An audacious good-for-nothing, that's what you are.

VANSEN. Cousin Numskull! Just let the Duke continue. That old tomcat looks as if he had eaten devils instead of mice and could not digest them. Just wait! He has to eat and drink and sleep like everyone else. I'm not afraid if we bide our time. In the beginning things go fast, but after a while he will find that it is much easier to live in the larder under the sides of bacon and to sleep nights than to chase mice, one at a time, in barns. Go on, I know what governors are like.

CARPENTER. What a man like that gets away with! If I had

ever spoken like that I would not have a quiet minute for the rest of my life.

VANSEN. Don't worry. You worms are not even going to tell God about it, not to speak of the Regent.

JETTER. Malicious slanderer!

VANSEN. I know some who would be better off having a tailor's heart in their bodies than their heroic courage.

CARPENTER. What does that mean?

VANSEN. Ha, I mean the Count.

JETTER. Egmont? What should he have to fear?

VANSEN. I'm a poor devil and could live a whole year on what he loses gambling in one evening. But having the use of my head for a quarter of an hour would be worth his income for a full year.

JETTER. That would mean a great deal to him, I'm sure. Egmont's hair is smarter than your brain!

VANSEN. But not finer. You talk! These great gentlemen are always the first to be deceived. He should not trust people.

JETTER. You jabber. A gentleman like Egmont!

VANSEN. Just because he doesn't have a tailor's heart.

JETTER. Watch your wicked tongue.

VANSEN. I wish he had your courage only for one hour; he would get restless soon enough, it would itch and twitch in all his limbs and drive him from the city in a hurry.

JETTER. You talk a lot of nonsense. He's as safe as a star in the sky.

VANSEN. Did you ever see a shooting star? Gone!

CARPENTER. Would you stop him? Would you start a riot if they put him in prison?

JETTER. Ah!

VANSEN. Would you risk your bones for him?

SOEST. Eh!

VANSEN (*aping them*). Ih! Oh! Uh! Go on and gape through the whole alphabet. It's true, that's it. God help him!

JETTER. Your insolence leaves me breathless. A noble, honest man like that should be in danger!

VANSEN. A knave always has the advantage. When he is the accused he makes the judge look like a fool, when he sits on the bench he takes the greatest pleasure in making the accused look like a criminal. I once had to copy a document like that, where the chief of police got high praise and a lot of money from the Court because he questioned an honest devil whom they wanted to get until he was made out a crook.

CARPENTER. Again one of your fancy lies. What can they get out of a man by questioning, if he is honest?

VANSEN. You bird-brained fool! Where you can't question anything out of a man you question it into him. Honesty makes a man careless and sometimes defiant. First, one gently asks some harmless questions, and the prisoner is proud of his innocence, as they say, and talks about everything that an intelligent man would hide. Then the questioner makes new questions out of his answers and watches for a tiny contradiction. To that he ties his rope, and if the poor devil is bewildered and admits that he said a little too much here and not quite enough there, or even for God knows what momentary whim concealed some little detail, and if perhaps he gets frightened in the end—then we are on the right track! I can assure you, the beggar women are not more careful sorting old rags out of the garbage than such a manufacturer of crooks is in concocting a straw-and-rag scarecrow from all those small, lopsided, distorted, displaced, distended, deduced, well known and denied signs and circumstances. At least he can hang the accused in effigy. And the poor devil can thank God if he gets away with the kind of hanging that he can watch.

JETTER. He surely has a well-oiled tongue.

CARPENTER. You might catch flies in that kind of a net, but wasps will laugh at it.

VANSEN. They won't laugh at the spiders. Don't you see? That tall Duke looks exactly like a spider, not one of those thick-bellied spiders, they aren't so bad, but a long-legged one with a thin body, one that doesn't get fat from eating and spins very thin threads that are all the tougher.

JETTER. Egmont is a Knight of the Golden Fleece; who can touch him? He can be judged only by his peers, only by the entire Order. Your loose tongue and bad conscience make you jabber like this.

VANSEN. I certainly don't wish him ill. I don't object to him. He is a splendid gentleman! Because of him, a few of my good friends, who elsewhere would have been strung up, got off with a good thrashing. Go home now! Go! Now I would recommend it, too. I see a patrol getting ready over there, and they don't look as if they would be our drinking companions very soon. Let's wait and quietly watch. I have a few nieces and a cousin who is a tavernkeeper; if they drink there and do not soon become domesticated, they must, indeed, be wolves with iron stomachs.

SCENE 2. *The Culenburg Palace. The apartment of the Duke of Alba. Silva and Gomez enter from different sides.*

SILVA. Did you carry out the Duke's orders?

GOMEZ. To the last detail. The regular patrols have been in-structed to arrive at the same time at their designated places; meanwhile they make their rounds as usual and maintain order in the town. None knows of the others, each believes the order applies only to his patrol; the line of posts can be drawn in at a moment's notice and all the gates to the palace will be guarded. Do you know why we have these orders?

SILVA. I am accustomed to obey unquestioningly. And whom could be easier to obey than the Duke, since the results always prove that the orders he gave were right?

GOMEZ. Very well. No wonder you are becoming as secretive and close-mouthed as he, being around him all the time. To me all this is still strange; I'm used to the less demanding service in Italy. I'm as obedient and as loyal as I ever was, but I have gotten used to chattering and arguing. None of you ever says a word, and you do not enjoy yourselves. The Duke is like an iron tower without a door; the troops that hold the tower must use wings to get in and out. The other day at the table I heard him say about some friendly person that he seemed like a dis-reputable tavern that displayed its brandy as bait for loafers, beggars, and thieves.

SILVA. But he led us here silently.

GOMEZ. Nobody can deny that. Of course, anyone who watched how cleverly he brought the army here from Italy has really seen something! How supple he was in twisting and turning between friend and foe, the French, the Royalists and the heretics, the Swiss and the Allies, always maintaining strictest discipline and completing a march that had been considered very dangerous without the least incident! That was something to watch and to learn from.

SILVA. The same way here. Everything is as quiet and peaceful as if there never had been a rebellion.

GOMEZ. Well, it was mostly quiet even when we arrived.

SILVA. But in the provinces it is much more quiet now; if any-one still moves, it's only to get away and very soon the roads will be blocked for those, too.

GOMEZ. More than ever he will be the King's favorite.

SILVA. And our greatest concern is to keep in his favor. When the King comes, there will be, I'm sure, rewards not only for the Duke but for all whom he may recommend.

Gomez. Do you think the King will come?

Silva. They are making so many preparations that it seems very likely.

Gomez. I'm not convinced.

Silva. Don't mention it anyway. For if the King does not intend to come, he surely does intend that we should think he will.

(Ferdinand *enters*.)

Ferdinand. Has my father not come out yet?

Silva. We are waiting for him.

Ferdinand. The princes should be here soon.

Gomez. Are they coming today?

Ferdinand. Orange and Egmont are expected.

Gomez (*under his breath, to* Silva). I'm beginning to understand.

Silva. Then keep it to yourself.

(*The* Duke *of* Alba *enters. As he comes forward, the others step back.*)

Alba. Gomez!

Gomez (*steps forward*). Your Grace!

Alba. Did you distribute and instruct the guards?

Gomez. Most carefully. The daily rounds—

Alba. Enough. Wait in the gallery. Silva will let you know exactly when they are to be drawn in to occupy the palace gates. You know the rest.

Gomez. I do, sir! (*He leaves.*)

Alba. Silva!

Silva. At your service, sir!

Alba. Today you have an opportunity to prove those qualities which I have always valued, your courage, your determination and your perseverance.

Silva. I am most grateful for this chance to show you that I have not changed.

Alba. As soon as they have entered, you will as quickly as you can arrest Egmont's private secretary. Have you made your arrangements to arrest the others who were designated?

Silva. You can rely on us. Their fate will overtake them, like a well-calculated eclipse of the sun, on time and terribly.

Alba. Did you have them watched carefully?

Silva. All of them, but Egmont more than any of the others. He is the only one who has not changed his habits since you have arrived in town. All day he jumps from one horse onto the next, has company, is always gay and bright at dinner, throws dice and shoots, in the evening steals to his girl. The others are quite different, they have quite noticeably paused and changed their style of life. They stay at home and their front door opens rarely, as if it bore the sign of mortal illness.

ALBA. Let us be quick then, lest against our will they once again get well.

SILVA. They will be caught. As you commanded, we eagerly heap honors on them. They shudder; they thank us timidly because they think they must, but privately they think it would be best to flee; they do not dare to act, they hesitate, cannot agree, but their esprit de corps is strong enough to stop bold action by an individual. They are so anxious to be above suspicion that they become ever more suspect. I am delighted that your entire plan already seems assured of full success.

ALBA. At best I take delight in what has happened, and even that not often; there always is enough left that we must think and worry about. Capriciously, fortune will often reward a common, odious deed and disgrace a man by letting his well-laid plans come to an ignominious end. Stay here until the princes come, then give Gomez orders to seal off the streets, while you quickly arrest Egmont's secretary and the others whose names you have been given. As soon as everything is done, return and tell my son, who then will bring the news to me while I am still in conference with them.

SILVA. Tonight I hope that I will dare to face you. (ALBA *walks toward the gallery where his son has been standing.*) I do not dare admit it even to myself, but I am doubtful. I fear that things will not turn out as he expects. I see before me spirits who, calm and thoughtful, weigh upon black scales the destinies of princes and of many thousands. Slowly the tongue wavers, back and forth; the judges ponder the issue, until at last one scale descends, the other rises, moved by capricious Fate's soft breath—and then it is decided.   (*He leaves.*)

ALBA (*coming forward with* FERDINAND). How did you find the city?

FERDINAND. All was quiet. I rode my horse, as if to while away the time, up one street, down another. The guards whom you had placed so cleverly keep fear alive so that they do not even dare to whisper. The city was like the countryside before a thunderstorm, when lightning flickers in the distance; no bird, no animal in sight that does not quickly scurry to its hole.

ALBA. Nothing else happened?

FERDINAND. Egmont rode onto the market place with some

companions, and we saluted each other. He rode a horse that he was breaking in—I had to praise it—and called out to me: "Let's hurry and break in more horses, we shall need them soon!" He said that he would see me later in the day, since he was coming to confer with you upon your invitation.

ALBA. Yes, he will see you later.

FERDINAND. He is the one among the nobles here whom I like best. I think we shall be friends.

ALBA. You are still too hasty, too careless. I always detect in you the gay abandon with which your mother threw herself unthinkingly into my arms. Appearances have tempted you into many a dangerous alliance.

FERDINAND. I try to fit myself to your desires.

ALBA. Your youth excuses your frivolous good nature and reckless gaiety, but don't forget what task I was sent here to perform, and the part I wish to assign to you.

FERDINAND. Please keep reminding me and do not hesitate to hurt if you think it is necessary.

ALBA (*after a pause*). My son!

FERDINAND. My father!

ALBA. Orange and Egmont will soon be here. It is not that I distrust you if I tell you only now what I am planning; they will come—but will not leave.

FERDINAND. What will you do?

ALBA. I have decided to arrest them. You are surprised? Hear now what you will have to do, the reasons you will know when it is done. There is no time now to explain them. You are the only one with whom I wish to talk about the most important and the secret things; a strong bond keeps us together; I love and cherish you, on you I would like to heap all that I have to give. I don't want to impress upon you only the habit of obeying; I wish to recreate in you the spirit of invention, of command and of accomplishment. I wish to leave to you a great inheritance and to the King a most valuable servant; I want to equip you with the best I have, so that you need not feel ashamed to step among your brothers.

FERDINAND. How much I owe you for this love which you give me alone, while a whole realm is trembling at the mention of your name!

ALBA. Hear then what now has to be done. As soon as the two princes have entered, all entrances to the palace will be guarded. Gomez will see to that. Silva will quickly go to arrest Egmont's secretary together with those who are the most suspect. You oversee the guard at the gates and in the courtyards. Above all, post your most reliable men in the adjoining rooms. Wait in the gallery; when Silva returns, take any sheet of paper and bring it to me as sign that he has completed his assignment. Stay in the anteroom until the Duke of Orange leaves, and follow him; I shall retain Count Egmont here as if I still had things to talk about. At the end of the gallery you ask Orange for his sword, call the guard and quickly arrest the dangerous man, while I seize Egmont here.

FERDINAND. I shall obey, my Father, for the first time with heavy heart and with uneasiness.

ALBA. I will forgive you, for it is the first great day in your experience.

(SILVA enters.)

SILVA. A messenger from Antwerp. A letter from Orange! He will not come.

ALBA. Did the messenger tell you that?

SILVA. No, my heart did.

ALBA. My evil genius speaks through your mouth. (After reading the letter, he waves both away and they retire to the gallery. ALBA remains alone in the foreground.) He will not come! He waited until the last moment to let me know. He dares not to come! So this time, against all my expectations, the clever man was clever enough not to be clever! The clock advances. A short way only for the minute hand and an important piece of work will either have been done or left undone forever; for it cannot be done at any other time nor can it be kept secret. I had weighed everything a long time ago, had also thoroughly considered this possibility, and had decided what I would do; but now that I will have to do it I cannot stop the arguments for and against from swaying back and forth anew deep in my soul. Is it advisable to seize the others if he escapes? Shall I delay and allow Egmont to get away with all his many friends who are already, and perhaps will never be again, completely in my hands? Does destiny now force my hand, too, my invincible hand? How long considered! How well prepared! How grand and beautiful a plan! How close my hopes to being realized! And now, the moment of decision comes and offers me two evils! I put my hand into the drum to draw a lot and draw a dark, uncertain future; what I hold in my hand is not unfolded yet, I do not know if it is win or lose! (He stops attentively as if he had heard something and steps to the window.) It's he! Egmont! Did your horse carry you this far and not shy at the smell of blood, not at the spirit with the glittering sword receiving you at the gate? Dismount! Now one foot in

your grave—now both! Yes, stroke him once more, pat his neck
this one last time for his brave service—I have no choice: in
such delusion Egmont will not again approach to deliver himself
into my hands! —Come here! (FERDINAND *and* SILVA *hurry in.*)
You do exactly as I ordered, I will not change my mind.
I shall retain Egmont as best I can until you bring me word that
Silva has succeeded. Stay near me, then. Fate robs you of the
honor of catching the King's most dangerous enemy with your
own hands. (*To* SILVA.) Quick now! (*To* FERDINAND.) You go to
meet him. (ALBA *remains alone for a few moments, silently
pacing up and down.* EGMONT *enters.*)

EGMONT. I come to hear the King's commands, to be ap-
prised what service we can render to demonstrate our everlasting
loyalty to him.

ALBA. He wishes above all to have your advice.

EGMONT. On what subject? Is Orange coming, too? I thought
that I would find him here.

ALBA. It grieves me that he is not with us in this most important hour. The King desires your counsel on the question
how these provinces may best be pacified. He hopes, in fact,
that you will lend your active support to calm the disturbances and to reestablish complete and durable order in the
country.

EGMONT. You are in a better position than I to know that
everything is calm, that everything was even calmer before the
arrival of another army caused fear and apprehension.

ALBA. You wish to hint, it seems, that it would have been best
if the King had not put me in the position of being able to
consult you.

EGMONT. Forgive me! Whether it was best to send the army,
or whether the force of the King's own, majestic presence might
not have been more effective, it is not up to me to judge. The
army is here, and he is not. But we would have to be ungrateful, indeed, and very forgetful if we did not remember what we
owe the Regent. We must admit that it was she who by her
clever and courageous conduct, by power and prestige, by ruse
and by persuasion, led a rebellious people back to its dutiful pur-
suits within a few months, while all the world watched in
astonishment.

ALBA. I don't deny it. The turmoil has subsided and it appears that everyone has once more been forced back behind
the boundaries of civil obedience. But cannot anyone capriciously decide to disregard these limits? Who could restrain the people from breaking out of bounds? Where is the power to control

them? Who guarantees that they will now continue to behave as loyal subjects? Their good will is the only guarantee we have.

EGMONT. But is the good will of a people not their most noble and most binding pledge? By God, when could a King feel more secure than when all stand for one, and one for all, safer from enemies within and outside his realm?

ALBA. Are we to be persuaded that this is how matters now stand here?

EGMONT. Let the King declare a general amnesty to put all doubts at rest, and it would soon become apparent that loyalty and love return in the wake of confidence.

ALBA. And everyone who outraged the King's majesty and desecrated our sacred religion would go free, would live as an example for all others that monstrous crimes will not be punished?

EGMONT. Is it not better to forgive than to pursue with cruel punishment a crime of foolishness or drunken revelry? And even more so if there is hope, nay certainty, that such evils will not recur? Have kings not thus become more secure? Were kings not praised by their contemporaries and by history for pardoning, regretting and disdaining attacks upon their dignity? Is not this why kings are compared to God, that He is far too great to be touched by every blasphemy?

ALBA. This is precisely why the King must fight to uphold the dignity of God and of religion, why we must fight to uphold respect for the King. What God does not deign to punish we must avenge and if my counsel should prevail, no one guilty of crimes shall laugh because he went unpunished.

EGMONT. Do you believe that you can reach them all? Do we not hear every day of people whom fears drive hither and thither, even out of the country? The wealthy will escape with their possessions, their children and their friends; the poor will offer their strong arms to their neighbors.

ALBA. They will, if one does not prevent them. That is why the King demands from all his princes both advice and action, from all his governors that they take matters seriously, that they not only report how things have been, and are and might be in the future if one allowed things simply to take their course. To stand by while bad things get worse, to entertain vain hopes, to hope that time will cure, perhaps once in a while to strike a blow, clown-fashion, that makes a noise but does not hurt, so that one appears to be doing something while one likes best to do nothing at all—does that not look like watching with great pleasure a rebellion which one did not incite but would like to prolong, does that not invite suspicion?

EGMONT (*on the verge of flaring up, controls himself and, after a moment's pause, speaks calmly*). Not every intention is apparent to all, and many a man's intention is to misinterpret. Thus one hears everywhere that it was not so much the King's intention to govern the provinces in accordance with uniform and clear laws, to protect the majesty of our religion and to establish general peace among the people than it is rather to bring them irrevocably and unconditionally under his yoke, to rob them of their traditional rights, to make himself the master of their properties, and to restrict the good privileges of the nobility which to preserve is the noble's only reason for consecrating himself to the King's service, body and soul. Religion, one hears it said, it only a splendid tapestry behind which dangerous schemes are all the easier hatched. The people are on their knees, praying to the sacred symbols woven into the tapestry, while the fowler sits listening behind it, ready to trap them in his nets.

ALBA. And that I must hear from you?

EGMONT. They are not my opinions! This is only what great and little men, wise men and fools, whisper and say aloud everywhere. The Netherlanders fear a double yoke, and who will warrant them their freedom?

ALBA. Their freedom? A beautiful word if it is rightly understood. What kind of freedom do they want? What do the freest call their freedom? To do right! The King will not prevent your countrymen from doing that! No, no. They do not think that they are free unless they can do harm to others and themselves. Would it not be better to abdicate than try to govern a people like that? When at the borders of the realm enemies are pressing, of whom the burgher, seeing no further than his nose, knows nothing, and the King asks for assistance, they begin to fight among themselves as if conspiring with the enemy. It is much better to restrict them like children and like children to guide them to their own advantage. Believe me, people never grow up or become less foolish; people are always childish.

EGMONT. Nor are kings too often reasonable men! Why should not, then, the many prefer to trust the many rather than a single man? And not even that one man but the few who are in his service and grow old from their master's gaze. The people have, I think, alone the right to become wise.

ALBA. Perhaps just because they are not left to themselves.

EGMONT. And because they therefore do not like to leave anyone to himself. —Do as you like, I have answered your question. I repeat: it cannot work and will not work. I know my fellow Netherlanders, they are men who are worthy of walking on God's earth, each one a man all by himself, a little king, firm, hard-working and capable, loyal and clinging to old customs. It is difficult to earn their confidence, but once earned it is easily preserved. They are rigid and solid. You can oppress, but never subjugate them. (ALBA *has glanced toward the door several times during the foregoing.*)

ALBA. Would you repeat all that in the King's presence?

EGMONT. It would be sad indeed if his presence were to deter me! Better for him and for his people if he encouraged me and gave me confidence enough to say much more than I have said.

ALBA. Whatever should be said my ears can hear as readily as his.

EGMONT. This I would tell him: the shepherd easily can drive his flock before him, the oxen pulls the plow without resisting, but if you wish to ride a noble steed, you first must learn to guess his thoughts and never give him stupid orders, or give your orders stupidly. That is why our citizens wish to preserve their old institutions and to be governed by their countrymen; they know where they are leading them and how, they know that they can count on their unselfish sympathy for them and for their fate.

ALBA. But should the Regent not have power to change these traditions? Should not just this be his most precious prerogative? If nothing in this world is permanent, why should a constitution be? In time, all relations change, and thus an overaged constitution could become the cause of a thousand evils just because it does not encompass the present condition of the people. I am afraid that these old rights are held so dear because they form hidden corners in which the clever and the mighty can conceal themselves, much to the detriment of the community.

EGMONT. But do not such arbitrary changes, such unrestricted interference by a supreme power presage intentions of letting one man's will accomplish what thousands should not be allowed to do? He wants to be the only one who is at liberty to satisfy his every desire, realize his every idea. And if we did entrust ourselves completely to a good and wise king, can he warrant us that none of his successors will reign without regard or pity for us? Who then can save us from the absolute and arbitrary power that will be wielded by his servants and his relatives whom he may send to govern us, who, knowing nothing of the country or its needs, can without opposition reign as they see fit, responsible to no one?

ALBA (*who has again glanced at the door*). Nothing more natural than that a king would govern through those, would prefer to leave the execution of his orders to those who understand his intentions best, who wish to understand them and will do as he commands, unhesitatingly and unconditionally.

EGMONT. And just as natural that citizens would rather be governed by those who were born and raised among them, who have the same conceptions of right and wrong, whom they can look upon as brothers.

ALBA. And yet the nobles did not share too equitably with their brothers.

EGMONT. That happened centuries ago and no longer rankles. But if new men appeared intending to enrich themselves at the expense of the whole nation once again, it would be looked upon as utter and audacious greed; it would call forth a ferment that could not easily be halted.

ALBA. You tell me things which are not for my ears. I am a foreigner here, too.

EGMONT. The fact that I did tell you proves that I did not have you in mind.

ALBA. I still wish that I had not heard it from your lips. The King sent me expecting that I would find support among the aristocracy. The King's will *is* his will. He saw—and he considered long and thoroughly—what he must do. Things cannot continue as they are and have been. The King intends, in their own interest, to set them limits, to force upon them what is best for them, if that is necessary; to sacrifice the harmful citizens so that the others may find peace and may enjoy a prudent government's advantages. This is the King's resolve, and to announce it to the country's nobles I am here. In his name I am asking for advice *how* to accomplish, not *what*. That has already been decided.

EGMONT. Regrettably, what you say justifies the people's fear —the general fear. He has decided then what no prince ever should decide to do. The strength of his people, their souls, the ideas which they have about themselves are to be sapped, oppressed, destroyed to make it easier to govern them. Their individuality, their inner core is to be gnawed away, no doubt to make them happier. They are to be broken so that they may grow to be something different. If the King's intentions are good, they surely are misguided. No one resists the King; but they resist a king who now has taken the first unhappy steps upon a wrong and fateful road.

ALBA. If these are your opinions, it is obvious that all attempts to find a common ground between us must be futile. You do not think much of the King and you despise his councilors if you have any doubt that all this has already been considered, thoroughly explored and weighed. I have no mandate to review once more all arguments in favor and against; what I demand now from the people is obedience; from you, the nobles of the country, I ask advice and deeds that guarantee the performance of this absolute duty.

EGMONT. Demand our heads! That would settle the matter once and for all. A noble soul does not know any difference between cowering under a yoke or bowing under the executioner's ax. All I have said was said in vain, I caused the air to vibrate, nothing else.

(FERDINAND *enters*.)

FERDINAND. Pardon me for interrupting your council. I have a letter to which the messenger demands reply immediately.

ALBA. Permit me to see what it contains. (*He steps aside*.)

FERDINAND (*to* EGMONT). The horse your people brought to take you back is beautiful.

EGMONT. It's not a bad horse. I have had it for some time and thought I might get rid of it. If you like it, perhaps we can make a bargain.

FERDINAND. Very well, let's see. (ALBA *gestures to his son who withdraws to the background*.)

EGMONT. Farewell! With your permission, I shall go, for I have nothing else to say.

ALBA. By happy chance, you have no opportunity of making further confidences. You have carelessly displayed the recesses of your heart and accused yourself far more effectively than your worst enemy spitefully could have done.

EGMONT. This accusation does not touch me. I know myself too well and know that I am serving the King far better than those who in his service only serve themselves. I do not like to leave our dispute unresolved. I only hope that we shall soon, in our master's service and for the benefit of this country, unite our forces. Perhaps, another talk, a more auspicious moment, the presence of those princes who today were missing, will accomplish what seems impossible today. In this hope, I take my leave.

ALBA (*gives his son a signal*). Halt, Egmont! Your sword!

(*The center door opens, the gallery is seen filled with soldiers of the guard who remain immobile.*)

EGMONT (*after a few moments of amazed silence*). Was this the plan? Is this why you invited me? (*Reaching for his sword as if to draw and defend himself.*) Am I then helpless?

ALBA. The King has ordered it. You are my prisoner. (*At these words, soldiers enter from both sides.*)

EGMONT (*after a moment's silence*). The King?—Oh, Orange! Orange! (*After a pause, hands over his sword.*) Take it! It has defended far more often the King's cause than protected my own breast. (*He leaves through the center door, followed by the soldiers who had entered the room and by* FERDINAND. ALBA *remains alone.*)

ACT V

SCENE 1. *A street. Dusk. Claire, Brackenburg, Citizens.*

BRACKENBURG. My dearest! For God's sake, what are you doing?

CLAIRE. Come with me, Brackenburg! You do not know the people; we surely will get him free. There is nothing like their love for him! Every one of them, I assure you, has a burning desire to save him, to avert the danger from this precious life and to restore his freedom to the freest of the free. Come! They only need to hear the voice that calls them together, for their knowledge of what they owe him is still fresh. And they know that only his mighty arm can save them from ruin. For his and for their own sake they have to risk everything. And we? What do we risk? At most our lives, which are worth nothing if he dies.

BRACKENBURG. Poor girl! You do not feel the power which has already tied us with iron bonds.

CLAIRE. That power can be overcome. But let us not waste time with useless talk. Here come some of those steadfast, honest and courageous men! Listen, my friends! Neighbors, a word with you! What is the news about Egmont?

CARPENTER. What does the child want? Tell her to be quiet!

CLAIRE. Come closer, let us talk quietly until we are agreed and therefore stronger. We must not waste one single moment! The audacious tyrant who dared to tie his hands already lifts the dagger to murder him. Oh, friends, with every step this evening takes I grow more anxious. I fear this night! Come, let us spread out and quickly run through all the quarters of the town to call the citizens! Let them take up their arms and let us meet again in the market place! Our current will sweep everyone along. The enemy will be surrounded, swamped and suffocated. How can a handful of mere mercenaries resist us? And in our midst he will return, freed by our hands, and this one time he will thank us who are so deeply in his debt. Perhaps, no certainly, his eyes will see the morning dawn upon a day of freedom.

CARPENTER. What's the matter with you, my girl?

CLAIRE. Is it possible that you don't understand? I speak of Egmont! Of Count Egmont!

JETTER. Don't mention that name! It is deadly.

CLAIRE. Not speak that name? What? The name which you had on your tongues at every opportunity? The name you read everywhere? I even saw it written in the stars, with all its letters, more than once! Not speak that name? My friends, good neighbors, are you dreaming? Come to your senses, do not look at me with those staring, frightened eyes, and shyly all around! I only speak aloud what all of you desire. Is not my voice your own heart's voice? Who would not, in this anxious night, fall on his knees before he goes to sleep and try to gain his freedom with earnest prayers? Ask each other! Ask yourselves! Who would not say, as I do: "Set Egmont free or death!"

JETTER. May the good Lord preserve us! That will end badly.

CLAIRE. Stay here! Don't slink away at the sound of his name which used to bring you running from afar! As soon as someone cried: "Count Egmont has arrived from Ghent!" who was not proud and happy to be living in a street through which he passed? No sooner did you hear his horses than you dropped your work, and from his face flashed joy and hope over the careworn and worried faces you pressed through doors and windows. You lifted up your children and you pointed to him: "Look, the tallest there is Egmont! There he is! From him you can expect the better times which your poor fathers waited for but did not live to see!" Watch out that not your children ask you later: "What happened to him? Where are those better times you promised us?" —But here we stand in idle chatter and betray him!

SOEST. You ought to be ashamed of yourself, Brackenburg! Don't let her carry on! She will cause trouble!

BRACKENBURG. My darling Claire, let us go home. What will your mother say? Perhaps . . .

CLAIRE. Perhaps what? Do you think that I'm a child, or mad? No hope you could hold out to me is good enough to chase away my awful certainty. You must listen to me and you will. I see it clearly: you are disturbed and do not recognize yourselves in your own hearts. Let just one glance at our recent past pierce through our present danger. Then turn your thoughts to all that lies ahead! Can you continue living if he dies? If he stops breathing, so will liberty! What did he mean to you? For whom did he invite this deathly peril? His wounds bled and healed only for you. The great soul, on which all of you relied, is now entombed in a prison cell and fears of vicious murder hover over him. Perhaps he thinks and sets his hopes on you, he who was accustomed only to give and to fulfill.

CARPENTER. Come, neighbor!

CLAIRE. I do not have your arms, your strength. But I have something which not one of you possesses: courage and contempt of danger. Oh, that my breath could spark you! That I could press you to my breast and warm you and inspire you! Come! I shall march with you! Defenseless as the flag leads on an army of noble warriors, my spirit will flame around your heads, my love and courage bring the wavering, scattered people together in a fear-inspiring army!

JETTER. Go, take her home. I feel sorry for her.

(*The* CITIZENS *leave.*)

BRACKENBURG. Claire! Do you know where we are?

CLAIRE. Where are we? Under the sky that seemed to arch more splendidly each time the noble man walked under it. From these windows they used to look, four and five heads, one above the other. At these doors they used to stand, scraping and nodding when he looked down at the crowd of cowards. Oh, how I loved them while they honored him! If he had been a tyrant they might well stand by and watch him fall. But him they loved! Now the hands they touched to their caps cannot hold a sword—and we, Brackenburg? Do we dare scold them? These arms that held him close to me so often, what do they do for him now? Cunning has often succeeded in this world—

You know the ins and outs, you know the castle. Nothing is quite impossible—give me a plan!

BRACKENBURG. Let us go home.

CLAIRE. Yes, let us do that.

BRACKENBURG. There, at the corner, I see Alba's guards; please, let the voice of reason penetrate to your heart. Do you think that I am a coward? Don't you believe that I would die for you? But here we are, mad both of us. Do you not see that it's impossible? You must take hold, you are beside yourself.

CLAIRE. Beside myself! Odious word! You are beside yourselves. When you gave loud approval to the hero, called him your friend, your hope and your protector, when you cheered him as he went by, I stood in my corner, barely opened the window, hid myself as I listened, but my heart beat louder than any other. And now again it beats stronger than any of yours. Now that he needs you, you hide, deny him and don't feel that you will perish if he dies.

BRACKENBURG. Come home, now.

CLAIRE. Home?

BRACKENBURG. Come to your senses! Look around! These are the streets which you would never walk except on Sundays, through which you primly went to church and where you used to vent your prudish anger on me if I dared to join you with a friendly word of greeting. Here you now stand and talk and act before the eyes of all the world. Collect yourself! What good is it?

CLAIRE. Yes, let's go home! I do remember. Come, Brackenburg, let us go home! Do you know where I am at home?

(*They leave.*)

SCENE 2. *A prison, lighted by a single lamp. A bed is in the background. Egmont alone.*

EGMONT. Old friend who never yet broke faith with me, Sleep, do you leave me now like all my other friends? How willingly you used to envelop my head when it was free! You cooled my brow like a lovely wreath of myrtle, like a wreath of love. Breathing easily like a blossoming boy I rested in your arms between my battles when I was on the crest of life's high waves. Though storms might rage through branch and leaf, though trunk and tree-top groaned under the blow, my heart's innermost core stayed calm. What is it now that shakes me?

What sets my firm and always steady mind atremble? I feel it, it's the clanging of the murderous ax that tastes my roots. Although I still stand straight, a quiver passes through me. Brute force and treachery will triumph; they sap the trunk that towers solidly, the top will crack and crash down to the ground before the bark has withered.

Why am I now—I who so often brushed the most oppressive worries off like foaming suds—why am I now unable to drive off that premonition which rises and subsides in me in a thousand different shapes? Why does Death wear this frightening grimace although I've always lived with him in all his changing forms as calmly as with all the creatures on this accustomed earth? It is not Death, the agile foe whom healthy hearts rival to meet with joy; it is the prison, antechamber of the grave from which heroes recoil as much as cowards. I used to suffer even when I sat in my soft chair, as princes, in their stately meetings, pondered in repetitive discourse what could have been resolved with ease, when the dark ceiling beams between the gloomy walls of the cavernous hall pressed down on me. Then I rushed out as soon as possible, and quickly onto my horse, my breath relieved! And out into the open air where we belong! Into the fields where Nature's coming gifts that sprout from steaming soil and all the blessings of the stars, wafting across the sky, surround us with their fragrance; where we, like earth-born giants, strengthened by our mother's touch, rise taller; where we feel one with mankind, and human appetites are strong in our veins; where the desire to push ahead, to conquer and to use our fists, to vanquish and to own burns in our youthful hunters' hearts; and where the soldier hastens his steps to claim his innate right to all the world, and, in his terrifying freedom, roams like a hailstorm through the meadows, field and woods, spreading disaster, ignoring all the boundaries which men have drawn.

I have become a distant image, a dreaming memory of happiness which I so long possessed; where has a treacherous fate now carried me? Does it deny me, does it envy me a sudden death under the open sun, which I have never feared, and offers me, instead, this hideous rottenness as foretaste of the tomb? How odious its breath that rises from these stones! Life flows no longer, my foot shies from the bed as from the grave.

Anxiety! You have begun the murder before the time has come, stand back! Am I alone, then? All alone? Doubt makes me helpless, not my fortune. The justice of the King, on which I have always relied, the Regent's friendship which was almost —I admit it—love, have they now faded like a brilliant fire in the night and left me to pursue my path into the darkness all alone? Is Orange at the head of all my friends not planning daring schemes? Will not the people gather and with surging force avenge and save their friend of old?

You walls that now confine me, you will not resist the bold push of so many well-intentioned men! The courage which once flowed from my eyes into them and gave them life, may it return from their hearts into mine! Oh yes, they are already stirring by the thousands! They're on their way, they stand by me! Devoutly they are sending urgent prayers up to Heaven, asking a miracle. But if no angel will descend to rescue me, they will take up their spears and swords. The doors will split, the gates will burst, their hands will tumble down the walls, and Egmont joyfully ascends to meet the freedom of the dawning day. How many faces of old friends will jubilantly welcome me! Oh, Claire, if you had been a man, you surely would be first to meet me, and I would thank you for what we unwillingly accept from kings—my freedom!

SCENE 3. *Claire's house. Claire comes from the bedroom, carrying a lamp and a glass of water; she puts the glass on the table and steps to the window.*

CLAIRE. Brackenburg? Is it you? What did I hear, then? Nobody yet? There's no one! I shall put the lamp in the window so that he can see that I am still awake, that I am still waiting for him. He promised to bring me news. News! Terrible certainty! Egmont condemned! What court of justice has the right to judge him? And they condemn him? Did the King condemn him? Or the Duke? And the Regent absconds! Orange hesitates and so do all his friends! Is this the world of fickleness and perfidy about which I have heard so much, but which I never felt? Is this the world? Who is so wicked as to be hostile to so good a man? Can Evil possibly be strong enough to topple one whom everyone has known and loved? Yes, it can be—it is! Oh, Egmont, I thought you as safe from God and men as if I held you in my arms! What have I been for you? You called me yours, my life was dedicated to your life. What am I now? My hand extends in vain to reach the noose which strangles you.

You are now helpless, I am free. I hold the key to my door in my hand, I am at liberty to come and go, and I do nothing for you! Oh, tie my hands to give me hope! Throw me into the deepest dungeon, and I will hit my head against the musty walls, will whine for freedom and will dream of my desire to help him if my fetters did not prevent me, of ways to help him. Yes, I am free, and in my freedom lies the fear of helplessness. I am aware of it, but I can move no limb to bring him help. Oh, it is sad that this small part of you, your Claire, is held a prisoner as much as you and, far from you, does nothing but exhaust her remaining strength in the convulsions of approaching death. Someone is coming, coughing—Brackenburg—at last he comes! You good, unhappy man, your fate's not changed; now that your sweetheart opens to you her door at night it is for such an ill-starred meeting!

(BRACKENBURG *enters.*)

CLAIRE. You look so pale, so hesitant—what is it?

BRACKENBURG. I came on a circuitous and dangerous road. The thoroughfares are occupied by soldiers, I crept to you through alleys and around the darkest corners.

CLAIRE. Tell me, what have you heard?

BRACKENBURG (*sits down*). Oh, Claire, I want to weep! I never loved him; he was rich and he enticed a poor man's only sheep to his more luscious pasture. I never cursed him; God has made me weak and faithful. My life flowed out of me in painful trickles and every day I hoped that I would die.

CLAIRE. Don't talk about that, Brackenburg! Forget yourself, speak about him! It's true? They have condemned him?

BRACKENBURG. They have, I am quite sure of it.

CLAIRE. But he is still alive?

BRACKENBURG. Yes, he is still alive.

CLAIRE. How can you be so sure? Tyranny may well murder Glory in the dark of night, his blood may flow unseen. The people in their restless sleep lie stunned and dream of rescue, dream that their helpless wish may be fulfilled, and meanwhile, vexed with us, his spirit leaves this world. Oh, he is gone! Do not deceive me and yourself!

BRACKENBURG. No, no, he is alive! The Spaniard is preparing a horrid spectacle to trample the people underfoot and with brute force to crush forever all hearts that thirst for liberty.

CLAIRE. Continue! You may calmly speak my own death sentence, too! I am approaching close and ever closer to the

Elysian fields; I can already sense the solace wafting toward me from the blessed region of eternal peace. Go on!

BRACKENBURG. The guards gave signs of it and I picked up words that people dropped here and there, that frightful preparations secretly were being made on the market place. I slunk through side streets and through passages I know until I reached my cousin's house and looked down on the market place from one of his back windows. Torches were flickering in a gigantic circle of Spanish soldiers. I strained my unaccustomed eyes, and saw a black scaffolding rising out of the night, huge, high—I shuddered at the sight. And many busily were working all around to dress whatever of the woodwork still showed white through a concealing garment of black cloth. I clearly saw how they at last covered the steps in black. It seemed that they prepared to celebrate a horrible sacrifice. High on one side they mounted a white crucifix that gleamed like silver in the night. I saw, and what I saw made the horrible certainty ever more certain. Some torches were still wavering, then slowly they receded and died out. Then, suddenly, the horrible creation of the night had once again returned into its mother's womb.

CLAIRE. Quiet now, Brackenburg, I've heard enough! Leave the last veil upon my soul. The ghosts have disappeared, and you, sweet night, lend your dark cloak to Earth; it is in ferment, it will bear no longer the abominable burden, it will split open, and the murderous scaffold will crash into the yawning, gruesome abyss. And that same God whom they profaned and made a witness to their fury will send an angel at whose sacred touch all locks and bonds will open, and who will pour a soft light round our friend. He then will lead him quietly and gently through the night to freedom. And my road, too, leads into this mysterious darkness to meet his.

BRACKENBURG (*stopping her*). Where are you going, child? What will you do?

CLAIRE. Quiet, dear man, that no one wakes, that we may not awake ourselves! Do you remember this flacon? In jest I once took it from you when you impatiently so often threatened your hasty death. And now, my friend—

BRACKENBURG. By all the saints!

CLAIRE. You cannot stop me. Death is my lot. Do not be jealous of the quick and gentle death which you yourself prepared. Give me your hand! Now as I open the dark gate through which no one returns, I wish my hand in yours could tell you how much I loved, how much I pitied you. My brother died when I was young, and I chose you to take his place. Your heart wished otherwise, it tormented both you and me, and your desire burned with ever hotter flames to own what was not meant for you. Forgive me and farewell! Let me call you Brother, a name embracing many names. Take this last, brilliant flower from me with a loyal heart as I now leave you—take this kiss. Death, Brackenburg, unites all things—and so us, too.

BRACKENBURG. Let me die with you! Share! There is enough, two lives can be snuffed out.

CLAIRE. No, you must live and you can live. Stand by my mother who without you would consume herself in poverty. Be for her what I can no longer be; live with her and together weep for me. Weep for our country and the only one who could have saved it. This generation will not rid itself of this great misery; not even furious revenge would be enough to wipe it out. You poor people, live out the time which is no time to live. Today the world stands still, stopped in its orbit, and my pulse will beat just a few minutes longer. Farewell!

BRACKENBURG. No, live with us, and we shall live for you alone! We die with you, so live and suffer! Inseparably we shall stand by you, one at each side, always watchful, and our love will offer you, embracing you with living arms, the greatest solace. Remain with us! I must not say, "Be mine!"

CLAIRE. Softly, Brackenburg! You do not know what you stir up. Where you see hope, I see despair.

BRACKENBURG. Share hope with us, the living! Stop for a moment at the abyss' rim, look down and then look back to us!

CLAIRE. I have already conquered—don't call me back to fight!

BRACKENBURG. But you are stunned, blinded by darkness you search for the depth. Not all the lights have been extinguished, and many days are still to come.

CLAIRE. Woe! Cruelly you tear the veil away that shields my eyes. Yes, yes, the day will surely dawn! Trying in vain to hide in fog, reluctantly—but it will dawn! Fearfully will the citizens look from their windows, the night will leave an ink-black spot; they look, and in the light the scaffold grows abominably. In his new torment the desecrated Christ will turn his supplicating eyes to God the Father. The sun won't dare to show its face, it will refuse to mark the hour set for his death. The clock hands go their leisurely way, one hour strikes, and then another—stop! Now is the time! The thought of dawn chases me to my grave. (*She steps to the window as if to look around and secretly drinks from the bottle.*)

BRACKENBURG. Claire! Claire!

CLAIRE (*steps to the table and drinks the water*). Here is the rest! I don't call you to follow me. Do what you think you may, farewell! Quickly and quietly put out the lamp while I lie down. Creep away carefully, close the door behind you. Softly! Do not wake up my mother! Go, save yourself! Go quickly or you may well be taken for my murderer.

(*She leaves.*)

BRACKENBURG. This last time she leaves me behind, as always. Oh, not one living soul can feel how she can tear to shreds a human heart. She leaves me to my own devices, and life and death are equally hateful to me. To die alone! You lovers, weep for me! No fate can be more cruel than is mine! She shares with me the drink of death and sends me on my way, away from her! She pulls me after her and pushes me back into life. Egmont, how glorious is your lot! She walks ahead of you; you will receive the victor's crown from her, and she will bring all heaven when she comes to meet you. And shall I follow her, standing aside again, and carrying my undying jealousy into those regions? There is no room for me on earth, and hell and heaven offer equal torment. How I would welcome feeling the fearful hand of doom!

(BRACKENBURG *leaves. For a little while, the scene remains unchanged. Music, which signifies* CLAIRE's *death, is heard. The lamp, which* BRACKENBURG *has forgotten to extinguish, flickers a few times, then goes out. The scene changes to the prison.* EGMONT *is seen sleeping on the bed. Keys rattle, and the door opens.* SERVANTS *with torches enter, followed by* FERDINAND *and* SILVA *who are accompanied by* SOLDIERS. EGMONT *starts up.*)

EGMONT. Who are you who so inconsiderately come to shake the sleep out of my eyes? What is behind your shifting, spiteful glances? Why such a terrifying parade? Have you come here to tell me, while my mind is half-asleep, a nightmare, calling it the truth?

SILVA. The Duke has sent us to announce the sentence.

EGMONT. And have you brought the executioner with you to carry it out?

SILVA. Listen and you will know what to expect!

EGMONT. The setting fits you and your wicked plans! Hatched out by night, and carried out by night. You may well wish to hide a project as audacious and unjust as yours! Boldly step forward with the sword you keep concealed beneath your cloak— here is my head, as free as any that a tyrant ever severed!

SILVA. You are mistaken. Judges who are fair do not hide their verdicts from the light of day.

EGMONT. Your insolence then is beyond imagination.

SILVA (*takes the judgment from one of the attendants, opens it and reads*). "In the name of the King and by virtue of the powers vested in me by His Majesty, to sit in judgment over all his subjects, of whatever station or rank, and not excepting the Knights of the Golden Fleece, we find . . ."

EGMONT. Can the King delegate that power?

SILVA. "We find, after painstaking, legal investigation, that you, Henry Count Egmont, Prince of Gaure, are guilty of high treason and pronounce this sentence: tomorrow at dawn, you will be led from the prison to the market place and there, in the sight of the people and as a warning to all traitors, you will be put to death by the sword. Given at Brussels, on . . ." (*He pronounces the date and year so unclearly that the audience cannot understand them.*) "Signed: Ferdinand, Duke of Alba, President of the Court of the Twelve." You've heard your fate. There is not much time for you to resign yourself, to put your house in order and to say good-bye. (SILVA *leaves with his attendants.* FERDINAND *remains with two torchbearers; the stage is in semi-darkness.* EGMONT *has been standing, without moving, deep in thought; he did not look up when* SILVA *left and now thinks himself alone. When he raises his eyes, he sees* ALBA'S *son.*)

EGMONT. You are still here? Do you intend to make my horrible surprise still greater by your presence? Do you perhaps wish to take back to your father the welcome news that you saw me in unmanly despair? Go on and tell him that his lies will not deceive me or the world! He thirsts for fame and glory, but it will be said, first in quiet whispers behind his back, then aloud and louder, in the end, once he descends from his imposing height, screamed at the top of a thousand voices, that he did not come here to further the welfare of the state, to safeguard the King's majesty, nor to establish peace in our provinces. He counseled war only for his advantage, so that a warrior might prove himself in war. He has created this immense confusion in order to be needed. I fall, a victim of mean hate and of his petty jealousy. I know it; now that I'm about to die, that I am mortally wounded, I can say it: the vainglorious man was envious of me! And he has spent much time in thinking how he could efface me.

Already when we were much younger, throwing dice, and when the heaps of gold, one after another, quickly moved from his side to mine, he wore a grim look on his face, pretended unconcern while in his soul anger consumed him, more at my luck than at his loss. I still remember his flashing eyes, his revealing pallor, when we competed in a shoot, held at a fair where thousands had gathered. He challenged me, and both the Spaniards and the Netherlanders stood and watched, made bets and hoped. I was the victor; his shot missed, mine found the mark. My men's loud shout of joy shattered the air. Now I am hit by his projectile. Tell him that I'm aware of it, that I know him and that the world despises victories which small minds surreptitiously achieve. And you! If it is possible for a son to depart from the ways of his father, learn early to blush, blush now for the one whom you wish you could honor with all your heart.

FERDINAND. I heard you out and did not interrupt you. Your accusations fall on me as blows struck with a club would hit a helmet. I feel their impact but I'm armed. You score a hit, you do not hurt me. I only feel the pain which claws my breast. To have grown up only to see this sight, to have been sent to witness such a spectacle!

EGMONT. You are complaining? What moves you, what concerns you here? Is it belated regret that you lent your hand to this despicable conspiracy? You are so young and look so happy. You were so trusting and so friendly with me. Looking at you, I could not hate your father. But as deceptive, even more than he, you tempted me into the net. You are abominable! Whoever trusts him does so at his peril. But who could think of danger in trusting you? Go! Go! Leave me alone so that I can collect myself, so that I may forget the world, above all, you!

FERDINAND. What can I tell you? I stand before you and I look at you, but I don't see you, nor do I feel myself. Shall I apologize? Shall I assure you that I only learned my father's plans at the last moment, that I was nothing but a lifeless tool through which he worked his will? What does it matter what opinion you now have of me? You are lost, and, unhappy man that I am, I can do nothing but confirm it and commiserate.

EGMONT. What strange voice, what unexpected solace do I encounter on my way to the grave? You, the son of my greatest and almost only enemy, you pity me, you are not among my murderers? Tell me, then, speak! What shall I think of you?

FERDINAND. Cruel father! By the command you gave me I recognize you. You knew my heart and my opinions which you so often vilified as my gentle mother's heritage. To make me over in your image, that is why you have sent me here to see this man at the edge of his yawning tomb, in the clutches of violent death; you want to force me to be deaf to fate and to become insensitive, whatever may become of me.

EGMONT. I am amazed! But calm yourself, talk like a man!

FERDINAND. I wish I were a woman! Then one would ask me: why are you so moved? What ails you? Name me a greater, a more monstrous evil, call me to witness a more frightful deed, and I will thank you for it; I will say that *this* meant nothing!

EGMONT. You lose yourself! Where are you?

FERDINAND. Let my passion blaze forth, let me lament without restraint! I've no desire to appear unflinching while everything within me cracks and crashes. To see you here—you—it is dreadful! You do not understand me, and how could you? Egmont! Egmont! (*He embraces him.*)

EGMONT. Explain this mystery.

FERDINAND. It is no mystery.

EGMONT. Why does the fate of a stranger stir you so deeply?

FERDINAND. No stranger. You're not a stranger to me! Ever since I was very young, your name has always stood before me shining like a heavenly star. How often I have listened for news of you, inquired after you! The child's example was the youth, the youth looked to the man. Thus you have always walked ahead of me, always ahead, and without envy I saw you before me and I followed after, on and on. At last I hoped to see you, and when I did, my heart flew toward you. Long since I had selected you, and when I saw you, I chose you again. Now I could hope to be around you, to have your company, to live your life, to understand you, to . . . All that is now cut off—and you are here!

EGMONT. If this can be a solace to you, friend, let me assure you that my heart went out to you from the first moment. Now listen to me. Let us speak calmly to each other. Tell me: is it your father's irrevocable decision to have me killed?

FERDINAND. It is.

EGMONT. The judgment, then, is not an empty phantom conjured up to frighten me, to punish me with dreadful threats, and to humiliate me only so that he can raise me up again by royal mercy?

FERDINAND. Oh no! I wish it were! At first I played myself with this elusive hope, and even then I felt terror and pain at the thought of seeing you in this condition. Where can I now find help and advice to avert the inescapable?

EGMONT. Listen to me! If your soul urges you so forcefully to rescue me, if you abhor the mighty force which fetters me, then save me! Every minute is precious. You are the son of the all-powerful and powerful yourself—let us escape! I know the way, you know the means yourself. These walls and a few miles are all that stand between me and my friends. So cut these bonds, take me to them and become one of us! The King will certainly some day be grateful to you for my rescue. Now he will be astounded, perhaps he is quite unaware of what has happened. Your father takes the risk and he compels the King to give approval to his actions, although he may be horrified. You ponder? Think of a way that leads me to my freedom! Speak, nurture the hope of a vibrating soul.

FERDINAND. No more! No more! With every word you speak you heighten my despair. There is no way here, no advice and no escape. That is what torments me, it grips and claws my breast. I was the one who drew this net around you, I know the strong tight knots that hold it. I know that all the roads that cunning and audacity might take are barred. The fetters which bind you and all the others tie me, too. Would I lament, had I not tried all possibilities? I threw myself at his feet, I talked and implored him. He sent me here so that all love of life and gaiety would be destroyed in me forever in this single moment.

EGMONT. There is no hope?

FERDINAND. None.

EGMONT (*stamps his foot*). No hope! —Sweet life, lovely and pleasant habit of living and doing, must I now leave you and leave you so calmly? Not in the turmoil of battle, amid the clanging of arms, the distracting uproar you wave a hasty good-bye; you do not leave me quickly and shorten the moment of parting. I am to take your hand, look into your eyes once more, feel more vividly than ever your beauty and worth, and then, determined, tear myself away and say, farewell!

FERDINAND. While I stand by, look on and cannot hold nor hinder you! No voice is strong enough to bewail you, no heart that would not melt its walls at such misery!

EGMONT. Compose yourself!

FERDINAND. You can compose yourself, you can renounce the world and take the grave step like a hero; necessity holds you by the hand. But what am I to do? What can I do? You conquer yourself and us, you reach the goal; I shall survive you and myself. I lost the light that shone at my table, my flag for the turmoil of battle. My future looms flat and aimless and murky.

EGMONT. My dear young friend! It's a strange fate that I should win and lose you all at once. You feel my death pains and you suffer with me; look at me now, you will not lose me. If my life was a mirror in which you liked to see your image, my death can be the same. We humans can well be together, although we are apart. One who is distant, one who is no more, can be alive for us. For you I shall continue living, I've lived enough for myself. I have enjoyed each day, each day with swift accomplishment I did my duty, as my conscience would demand. My life now ends as it might easily have ended earlier, much earlier upon the sand of Gravelingen. My life will end, but I have lived. You, too, my friend, live gladly, happily, and never be afraid of death.

FERDINAND. You could and should have saved yourself for us. You killed yourself. I listened often when wise men discussed you, well-meaning and ill-wishing men; they argued long about your worth, but in the end they all agreed, not one dared to deny, each one admitted that, indeed, you walked a perilous path. How often did I wish that I could warn you! Did you not have one single friend?

EGMONT. I have been warned.

FERDINAND. And then I read the accusations, point by point, which are contained in the indictment, and your replies! They could excuse you, to be sure, but they could not convincingly establish innocence.

EGMONT. Let's leave that now. All men believe to steer their lives, to guide themselves, yet irresistibly their destiny directs their steps. No use to think about that now! I can easily do without these thoughts; it is much harder to stop worrying about this country. But that, too, will be taken care of. If my blood flows for the many and brings my people peace, I shed it willingly. Unfortunately, it will not be thus. Yet it is hardly fitting for a man to brood when he no longer has the means to act. If you can stay or guide your father's might, then do it. But who could do that? —Farewell!

FERDINAND. I cannot go.

EGMONT. I wish to recommend my men to you. My servants are good men; do not allow them to become dispersed and miserable. What is the fate of Richard, my secretary?

FERDINAND. He went ahead of you. They found him guilty of conspiracy and treason; he was beheaded.

EGMONT. Poor soul! Just one more thing, and we shall say good-bye. I cannot stand much more. No matter how profoundly the mind is occupied, Nature demands her rights at last and will not be denied. And as a child, held in a serpent's coils, still breathes quietly in peaceful slumber, a tired man once more lies down before he passes through the gate of death and rests as if there were a long and arduous way ahead of him. Just this, then: I know a girl, and you will not despise her for the fact that she was mine. Now that I recommend her to your care, I die in peace. You are a noble man, and any woman who finds such is well protected. Is my old Adolf still alive? Was he left free?

FERDINAND. The cheerful oldster who used to ride out with you?

EGMONT. The same.

FERDINAND. He is alive and free.

EGMONT. He knows her house. Let him be your guide, and compensate him till he dies for having shown you how to reach this jewel. Farewell!

FERDINAND. I cannot go!

EGMONT (*pushes him gently toward the door*). Good-bye!

FERDINAND. Let me still stay with you!

EGMONT. No long farewell, my friend! (*He accompanies* FERDINAND *to the door, then abruptly turns away. Stunned,* FERDINAND *hurries out.*)

EGMONT (*alone*). You never planned, vindictive man, to show me kindness through your son! He has relieved me of my cares and pain, of terror and anxiety. Gently but urgently Nature now demands her final tribute. All is decided, all is past, all the uncertainties that kept me waking this last night are now unquestionable certainties that lull my senses. (*He sits down on his bed. The sound of music is heard.*) Sweet sleep! You come most willingly, like all pure happiness, when you're not asked or begged. You untie the knots of all strict reasoning, mingle all images of happiness and pain. Unhindered flows the stream of inner harmonies, and shrouded in a pleasant madness we sink down and cease to be.

(*He falls asleep. Music accompanies his slumber. Behind his*

*bed a wall seems to open and a radiant apparition becomes
visible. Liberty, clothed in heavenly garments and bathed in
bright light, is seen recumbent on a cloud. She has* CLAIRE's
*features and inclines her head toward the sleeping hero. Her
face reflects a feeling of compassion, as if she lamented him.
Soon she contains her grief and, with a gesture of encourage-
ment, shows him the sheaf of arrows, then her rod and
helmet. She exhorts him to be joyous and, hinting that his
death will mean liberty for the provinces, recognizes him as
the victor and holds out a laurel wreath. As the wreath approaches* EGMONT's *head, he makes a move like someone
stretching in his sleep and turns on his back so that he now
faces her. She holds the wreath suspended over his head.
From a great distance martial music of drums and fifes is
heard. At the first, faint sound of · his music the apparition
fades. The prison is now in the dim light of early morning.
the sound of the music becomes stronger and* EGMONT *awakes.
His first impulse is to touch his head. He arises and, his
hand still at his head, looks around.*)

The wreath is gone! Beautiful image, the morning light
has chased you away! They were united, they were one,
my heart's two sweetest friends. Freedom, the heavenly goddess, borrowed the features of my beloved; the lovely girl
was dressed in the robes of my heavenly friend. In this
somber moment they appear to me as one, more serious than
charming. With blood-stained feet she stepped before me, her
garment's flowing folds spattered with blood. That was my blood,
and the blood of many nobles. No, it will not be spilled in
vain! Pass through it, my brave people! The Goddess of Victory
leads you, and as the sea breaks through your dykes, you'll break
and tear asunder the walls of tyranny. Sweep the usurpers
drowning from the ground on which they impudently stand!
(*The sound of drums comes closer.*) Ah! How often has this
sound called me to battle and to victory! How cheerfully my
friends entered the glorious, dangerous race! Now I, too, walk
from this prison to an honorable death. I die for freedom as I
lived and fought for it; I now become its sacrificial victim.
(*Spanish soldiers with halberds form a row in the background.*)
Yes, stand together! Close your ranks! You do not frighten me.
I am accustomed to stand in front of lances and to face them.
When deadly dangers surrounded me I feel but more courageous,
I feel my life pulse doubly fast. (*Roll of drums.*) I am sur-
rounded on all sides by enemies! There are their gleaming

swords! Have courage, friends! Behind you are your parents
and your wives and children! (*He points to the guard.*) And
these are here because their master spoke an empty word, not
of their own volition! Protect your own! To save what you
love most, die gladly, as I now set you an example!

(*Roll of drums. As he walks toward the guard and the center
door, the* CURTAIN *falls. At the same time the music of a
Victory Symphony begins, which concludes the play.*)

Mary Stuart

A TRAGEDY

by
FRIEDRICH SCHILLER

❖ ❖ ❖

In June 1800, only a year after Schiller had completed the enormously taxing work on *Wallenstein*, he finished *Maria Stuart*, another grand tragedy in which he explored once again a stirring moment of history for its human motives. He examined the available sources with great care, and read extensively in English, French, and German historians; where he decided to deviate from the established evidence, he did so with a striking sense for the requirements of his dramatic design.

If Wallenstein had represented the passion of power, the pathos of Mary Stuart's end was to be the result of her pride. When the play begins, she is already condemned to die; the suspense of the subsequent action hinges on Elizabeth's approval of her execution. This dramatic tension is maintained by the subtle maneuvering among a group of exceedingly well-defined characters, each of whom produces by his calculated actions consequences which cannot be foreseen: Elizabeth is reluctant to sign the death warrant for fear of being thought cruel and of losing the respect of her court; Mary declines Mortimer's help; and Leicester's wish to please Elizabeth brings about the fateful meeting of the queens, that celebrated encounter of two radically different personalities, two temperaments, and two ambitions. What was planned as an effort to save Mary, results in her destruction: she refuses to show humility, and deeply offends the queen by her self-assurance.

This stirring scene is one of Schiller's most brilliant inventions: it is the climax of a theatrical masterpiece in which every figure, every scene, and every stage detail contributes to an overwhelming effect of dramaturgical logic. The differences in character between Elizabeth and Mary are mirrored in the four courtiers: Mortimer, the idealist who is ready to sacrifice himself—the only figure wholly invented by Schiller—and Leicester, the insecure egotist; Burleigh's cautious diplomacy has its counterpart in Shrewsbury's generous humaneness. Schiller pays here, as in all his plays, meticulous attention to the supporting figures.

Maria Stuart is not, like Schiller's next play *The Maid of*

Orleans (1801), specifically entitled a "romantic tragedy"; but its proximity to the romantic idiom is obvious. It is an account of suffering and renunciation reminiscent of the baroque drama; its religious tenor and its Catholic features—such scenes, for instance, as Mary's confession or Mortimer's account of Rome —were in keeping with German romantic sensibilities. And through the judicious use of exquisite lyrical passages and subtle rhyme schemes, Schiller manages to illuminate the historical subject matter and to transform it into what, in distinction to the "natural" form of a play such as *Egmont,* he himself called a "poetic" drama. Ideas, characters, theatrical devices, a supremely eloquent and compelling language—all these are here welded into a work whose deliberate formal intricacy corresponds to the care and insight with which a complex set of human relationships is represented.

Mary Stuart

❖

CHARACTERS

ELIZABETH, Queen of England
MARY STUART, Queen of Scotland, a prisoner in England
ROBERT DUDLEY, Earl of Leicester
TALBOT, Earl of Shrewsbury, Lord Privy Seal
LORD BURLEIGH, Lord High Treasurer
THE EARL OF KENT
SIR WILLIAM DAVISON, Secretary to Queen Elizabeth
SIR AMIAS PAULET, Mary Stuart's keeper
MORTIMER, his nephew
COUNT AUBESPINE, French Ambassador
COUNT BELLIEVRE, Extraordinary Emissary from France
O'KELLY, Mortimer's friend
SIR DRUGEON DRURY, Paulet's assistant
MELVIL, Mary's former steward
BURGOYNE, her physician
HANNAH KENNEDY, her nurse
MARGARETA CURL, her chambermaid
THE SHERIFF, English and French NOBLES, GUARDS, LACKEYS
of the Queen of England, MALE and FEMALE SERVANTS of
the Queen of Scotland.

❖

ACT I

A room in Fotheringhay Castle

SCENE 1. *Hannah Kennedy, nurse of the Queen of Scotland, in a violent quarrel with Paulet, who is about to force open a cupboard. Drugeon Drury, his assistant, is busy with a wrecking bar.*

HANNAH. What are you doing, sir? What new impertinence

Is this? Do not disturb this cabinet.

PAULET. Whence came those jewels? They were thrown
From windows on this floor to bribe our gardener!
My curse on women's tricks! Despite my vigilance
And all my searching for your valuables,
You still have hidden treasures in this room.
(*He begins to search the cupboard.*)
Where that was secreted there will be more.

HANNAH. Away! What insolence! This is the place
Where all my lady's secrets are.

PAULET. Precisely those I hope to find.
(*He pulls out some writings.*)

HANNAH. Those papers are of no importance,
They're only exercises that were written
To drive away the gloom of this sad jail.

PAULET. When wicked minds are idle—they create.

HANNAH. Those papers are in French.

PAULET. So much the worse. That is the language
Of England's enemies.

HANNAH.   They're merely drafts
For letters to the English Queen.

PAULET. I shall deliver them. But look—what's this?
(*He has touched a secret spring and now takes some jewelry
from a hidden compartment.*)
A royal diadem, encrusted richly
With precious stones, embellished with—
The lilies of the Kings of France!
(*He gives it to* DRURY.)
You keep it, Drury. Put it with the rest.   (DRURY *leaves.*)

HANNAH. Oh, shameful force which we must suffer!

PAULET. While she still has possessions she is dangerous.
In her hand everything becomes a weapon.

HANNAH. Have pity, sir! Do not deprive our lives
Of these last jewels. In her misery,
The sight of former glory brings her joy.
Now you have taken everything from her.

PAULET. It's in good hands and, in good time,
Will be restored to her.

HANNAH. Would anyone imagine that a queen
Resides within these barren walls?
No canopy above her seat! She is obliged

To put her tender foot that has been used
To gentle softness on these rough and common floors.
She finds her table set with tin, the likes of which
The meanest noblewoman would disdain.

  PAULET. That's how, at Sterlyn, she had set her husband's
    table,
While with her lover she drank wine from golden cups.

  HANNAH. She even lacks the small convenience of a mirror.

  PAULET. As long as vainly she regards her image,
She will not cease to hope and plot.

  HANNAH. She has no books to entertain her mind.

  PAULET. She has the Bible to improve her heart.

  HANNAH. They even took her lute.

  PAULET. Because she played on it lascivious melodies.

  HANNAH. What fate for her, brought up with gentleness,
A queen already in her cradle,
And at the Medici's luxurious court
Grown up amidst its lavish pleasures!
Do not begrudge her these poor baubles.
A noble heart learns, in the end, to bear
A great misfortune, but it's hard to forego
The trifles which embellish life.

  PAULET. They only make a woman vain;
She ought to contemplate and ask forgiveness.
Humiliation, want—that is the price
One has to pay for luxury and vice.

  HANNAH. If, in her tender years, she sinned,
She must make peace with God and with her heart.
No one in England can presume to be her judge.

  PAULET. She will be judged where she did wrong.

  HANNAH. Her fetters are too strong for any evil-doing.

  PAULET. And yet her fetters were not strong enough.
She reached into the world and flung the brand
Of civil war into the realm, she armed
The bands of killers whom she sent against
Our Queen, whom God may long preserve.
She was within these walls when she spurred Parry,
That evil man, and Babington
To try their cursed hands at regicide!
These iron gates were not enough to hold her back
When she snared Norfolk's noble heart!

A sacrifice to her, his head, the best
Upon this isle, fell to the executioner's ax.
And even that most pitiable sight
Did not restrain those raving maniacs
Who still compete to throw themselves
Into the abyss for her sake.
For her sake, in a never-ending stream,
Men mount the scaffold's steps to die.
And that will never end until she, too,
The real criminal, is sacrificed.
The day be cursed on which these English shores
Hospitably received this Helen.

    HANNAH. Hospitably, you say, she was received?
Poor woman! On the day she set her foot
Upon this soil, expelled, a supplicant,
And asked protection from her relatives,
She was imprisoned and she has been forced,
In bold defiance of the Law of Nations
And of her royal dignity, to mourn
The lovely years of youth in narrow prison walls.
Now she has tasted all the bitterness
That prisons hold, but that is not enough!
You drag her like a common criminal
Before the bars of justice—her, a queen—
And shamefully indict her upon pain of death.

    PAULET. She came to England as a murderess,
Chased by her people, driven from the throne
Which she had sullied by her monstrous crime.
Sworn to destroy the happiness of England,
She came with the intention of restoring
The bloody era of the Spanish Mary,
To make all England Catholic again
And to betray her to the French.
Why did she scorn to sign the treaty
Of Edinburgh? Why not renounce her claim
To England and unlock her prison doors
With one stroke of her pen? No, she prefers
Captivity, prefers ill treatment
To giving up her pompous, empty title.
And why? Because she still has faith in wily schemes,
She trusts the evil art of sly conspiracy,
She hopes, by spinning wickedness, to conquer
All of this island from a prison cell.

HANNAH. You mock her, sir. You are not only hard,
You now add bitter ridicule.
She harbor dreams like those? Immured alive,
No word of solace, not a word from friends
In her beloved country ever reaches her.
She never sees a human face, except
Her jailers' gloomy countenances.
She only recently was given yet
Another coarse-grained guard, your relative.
More bars than ever fence her in.

PAULET. No iron bars protect against her cunning.
Perhaps these bars have been filed through, these walls,
This floor, which seem so solid, hollowed out
To let a traitor enter while I sleep.
I've been assigned a cursed office,
To guard a wily woman bent on mischief.
Fear does not let me sleep in peace,
I walk by night like a tormented ghost,
I try the locks, I test the guards,
And trembling I await each morning—
My fears may have come true!
But, fortunately, there is hope that soon
All this will end. I would prefer to guard
The gates of hell, the legions of the damned,
Than guard this scheming queen.

HANNAH. Here she is now.

PAULET. The Christ she carries in her hand,
Conceit and worldly pleasure in her heart.

SCENE 2. *Hannah and Paulet; Mary enters, veiled, with a crucifix in her hand.*

HANNAH (*rushing toward* MARY).
My Queen! They put their feet upon our necks.
There is no limit to their tyranny
And to their ruthlessness. Each day they heap
New sorrows and new shame upon your head.

MARY. Now, calm yourself and tell me what has happened.

HANNAH. Look! He has forced your secretary and has seized
Your letters and the only treasure, saved
With so much difficulty, that was left,
The only piece of all the bridal jewelry

That you received from France. No regal souvenir
Remains. The robbery is now complete.

MARY. Don't worry, Hannah. Baubles do not make
A queen. If they can treat us meanly,
They cannot demean us. I've become
Accustomed to so many things in England,
That I can easily forget this, too.
You, Sir Amias, took by force
What I already had resolved
To give you voluntarily today.
Among those papers is a letter which
I have intended for the Queen, my royal sister.
Give me your word of honor that you will
Deliver it to her in person, you yourself,
And not into Lord Burleigh's faithless hands.

PAULET. I shall reflect upon what I must do.

MARY. I want you to have knowledge of its contents, sir.
I'm asking her for an important favor,
An audience with her whom I have never seen.
They've summoned me before a court of men
Whom I cannot and will not recognize
As equals, and in whom I have no confidence.
Elizabeth is of my blood, my rank,
My sex. To her, a woman and a queen,
To her, my sister, I can bare my heart.

PAULET. My Lady, you have often put
Your honor and your fate into the hands
Of men less worthy of your confidence.

MARY. I'm asking for a second favor
Which it would be inhuman to deny.
For many years now I have been
Without the consolation of my Church,
The blessing of the sacraments.
Though she has robbed me of my crown and freedom,
Although she threatens now my life, she cannot want
To bar the doors of heaven to my soul.

PAULET. Whenever you desire, the village dean—

MARY (interrupts him violently).
I do not want a dean, I want a priest
Of my own church. I furthermore demand
Some clerks and notaries to make my will.
My sorrows and the long confinement sap
My strength, I feel my days are numbered.

I am a dying woman.

PAULET. Now, these are fitting thoughts for you.

MARY. The slow effect of grief may well be hastened
By one quick blow. I can't be certain.
I therefore wish to make my testament
And to dispose of my possessions.

PAULET. That is your privilege. The Queen of England
Will not enrich herself by robbing you.

MARY. I have been separated from my faithful ladies
And from my servants. Where are they?
I can well do without their services
But I would like to be assured that they,
For being faithful, do not want or suffer.

PAULET. Your servants have been cared for.   (*He turns to go.*)

MARY. You're going, sir? You leave me once again
Without a word to soothe the torturing
Uncertainty of my alarmed and troubled heart?
Thanks to the vigilance of your informers,
I have been kept apart from all the world,
No message reaches me across these prison walls.
My fate is in the hands of enemies.
One month, painfully long, has passed
Since your forty commissioners intruded here,
Set up their court and, in unseemly haste,
Put me, quite unprepared and without aid
Of counsel, before this quite unheard-of jury;
Stunned and surprised, from memory, I was obliged
To answer grave and cleverly concocted charges.
Like ghosts they came and left again. Since then,
All have been silent, and I try in vain
To read upon your face who won, my innocence,
The fervor of my friends, or the nefarious advice
Of enemies. Now—break your silence. Let me know
What I must fear, what I may hope.

PAULET (*after a silence*). Make up your reckoning with God.

MARY. I hope for heaven's mercy—and I also hope
For justice from my judges here on earth.

PAULET. You need not doubt that justice will be done.

MARY. Has a decision been announced?

PAULET. I do not know.

MARY. Then—have I been condemned?

PAULET. My Lady, I know nothing.

MARY. In England, one is fond of acting with dispatch.
Will murderers surprise me, as the judges did?

PAULET. Assume in any case that it is so.
Thus death will find you better armed than justice did.

MARY. No, nothing would surprise me, sir.
I can imagine how a court in Westminster,
Led on by Burleigh's hate and Hutton's zeal,
Will dare to judge, for I know all too well
How England's Queen may dare to act.

PAULET. For England's rulers there is no restraint
But Parliament and their own conscience.
What justice has decreed, before the world
And fearlessly their might will execute.

SCENE 3. *The same. Mortimer, Paulet's nephew, enters and speaks to Paulet; he takes no notice of the Queen.*

MORTIMER. We have been looking for you, Uncle.
(*He leaves, again seemingly unaware of the Queen's presence. Angrily she turns to* PAULET *who is about to follow* MORTIMER.)

MARY. One more request, sir. When you wish to tell me something—
I honor your old age—from you I will accept it.
But this young man's impertinence I will not stand.
Spare me the sight of his uncouth comportment.

PAULET. I value what makes him unbearable to you.
No, he is not one of those gentle fools
Who melt when women shed deceitful tears.
He has returned from Paris and from Rheims
But has brought back his faithful English heart.
Your wiles, my Lady, will be lost on him.   (*He leaves.*)

SCENE 4. *Mary and Hannah.*

HANNAH. How does he dare, the brute, to tell you that
Right to your face! Oh, it is hard!

MARY (*musing*). In those lost days of glorious happiness
We often lent our ear too willingly
To flatterers. It's therefore just that now
We should be forced to listen to the graver sounds

Of reprimands.

HANNAH.   So humble, my dear Lady?
Why so discouraged? You have always been so gay,
And it was you who used to comfort me.
I had more cause to scold you for your giddiness
Than for despondency.

MARY.   I recognize him.
It is King Darnley's bloody shadow
That, wrathful, rises from his burial vault,
And he will never make his peace with me
Until misfortune fills my cup.

HANNAH. What thoughts—

MARY.   You, Hannah, can forget.
My memory is accurate: today
Another anniversary
Of the horrendous deed has come around,
For me a day of penitence and fasting.

HANNAH. No, you must put to rest this wretched ghost.
You have atoned for what you did with your remorse,
With all these years of agony.
The Church, which has the key to absolution,
And heaven have forgiven you.

MARY. Bleeding anew, the long forgiven guilt
Arises from its lightly covered grave.
No sacristan with tinkling bell, no priest
With host in hand, can send
My husband's vengeful ghost back to his tomb.

HANNAH. It was not you who murdered him! The others did.

MARY. I knew about it, and I let it happen,
With flattery I lured him to his death.

HANNAH. You were so young. Your tender youth
Must mitigate your guilt.

MARY.   So tender, yes—
I weighed my youth with such enormous guilt.

HANNAH. He had provoked you with his insults,
His insolence—that man whom you had raised
From his obscurity by love, as with a goddess' hand,
Whom you led through your bridal chamber to the throne,
Whom you enthralled both with your youthful bloom
And with the crown you had inherited.
Could he forget that it had been your love
And generosity which raised him to his height?

Unworthy man, he did forget!
His mean suspicion and his boorish conduct
Insulted your devoted tenderness.
Thus he became repulsive to your eyes,
The spell with which he had deceived you faded,
And you, infuriated, fled from his embrace,
Abandoning the shameless man to scorn.
And he? Instead of trying to regain
Your favor, falling at your feet
To beg forgiveness and to vow reform,
The execrable man defied you!
Your creature, he presumed to be your king!
Before your eyes he had the handsome Rizzio,
Your favorite singer, run through with a sword.
That bloody deed you bloodily avenged.

MARY. And bloody will be the revenge it wreaks on me.
Your words of solace are my condemnation.

HANNAH. When you permitted them to murder him,
You were not your own master, not yourself.
The blinding madness of a burning love
Held you enslaved to Bothwell; wretched man
And terrible seducer, he ruled you
With willful arrogance. With magic potions,
With hellish artifices he confused your mind
And fanned the flames—

MARY.   He used no artifice,
He used my weakness and his strength.

HANNAH. No, it was more! In order to succeed
In blinding all your senses with his cloak,
He had to call to aid the spirits of damnation.
The warning voices of your friends
No longer reached your ear, your eyes
No longer recognized the road of decency.
No longer were you sensitive and gentle,
Your cheeks no longer blushed with modesty.
Your face was burning with the searing flames of lust.
You threw away the veil of secrecy,
Your reticence was overcome
By Bothwell's bold display of vice, and brazenly,
For all to see, you flaunted your own shame.
You let that man, a murderer pursued
By all the people's curses, carry
The royal sword of Scotland through the streets

Of Edinburgh triumphantly ahead of you.
At last, you ringed your Parliament with arms,
And there, where Justice has her temple,
You forced the judges to take part
In an outrageous farce, to free the murderer,
Ignore his crime and to absolve him from his guilt.
You went still further—God!

MARY.   Go on!
Before God's altar I gave him my hand.

HANNAH. Enough! Let silence cover what you did.
It was revolting, horrible, the deed
Of a lost soul. But your soul is not lost,
I know you, it is I who brought you up.
Your heart is gentle, full of modesty;
Your only vice is recklessness.
There are bad spirits, I repeat, which suddenly possess
An unsuspecting heart and quickly do
Their heinous deed; then, fleeing back to hell,
They leave a horrified and sullied heart behind.
Since that first crime which blackens your whole life
You never have committed any vicious act.
I am a witness to your change of heart.
Take courage and make peace within yourself.
Whatever you may wish to see undone,
In England you are blameless. Neither Parliament,
Nor Queen Elizabeth have any right to judge you.
It's force which here oppresses you. Before
That arrogant and righteous court you may appear
With all the boldness of your innocence.

MARY. Is someone coming?
(MORTIMER *appears in the door.*)

HANNAH. It is the nephew. Leave me with him.

SCENE 5. *The same. Mortimer enters hesitantly.*

MORTIMER (*to* HANNAH). Leave us alone and guard the door.
I must talk to the Queen.

MARY (*with authority*). Hannah, you stay!

MORTIMER. You need not fear, my Lady. You will come to
know me.
(*He hands her a letter.*)

MARY (*looks at it; in consternation*). Lord! What is this?

MORTIMER (*to* HANNAH). Go, Hannah, and make sure
That we are not surprised here by my uncle.

MARY (*to* HANNAH, *who hesitates and looks questioningly
at the Queen*). Go, go, do as he says.

(HANNAH *leaves, obviously perplexed*.)

SCENE 6. *Mary and Mortimer.*

MARY. A letter from my uncle, from the Cardinal!
(*She reads.*) "Have confidence in Mortimer who brings you this.
He is your truest friend in England."
(*She looks at* MORTIMER *in great surprise.*)
It cannot be! Is this a ruse?
I find a friend close by while I believed
That I was all alone, forsaken by the world,
And this one friend—the nephew of my jailer
Upon whom I had looked as my worst enemy!

MORTIMER (*throws himself at her feet*).
Forgive me, Queen, for having worn that hateful mask
Which I despise and never used without revulsion,
But which gave me the opportunity
To come to you and offer help and rescue.

MARY. Arise, sir—please—you come upon me unawares.
It's difficult to leap from deepest misery
To hope. Please, tell me more, explain,
So I may find my fortune credible.

MORTIMER (*arises*). There's not much time. My uncle may be
here
At any moment—and with him a hateful man.
Before their frightful message takes you by surprise,
Learn how your rescue was devised in heaven.

MARY. A miracle worked by His omnipotence.

MORTIMER. Permit that first I speak about myself.

MARY. Please, speak!

MORTIMER. My lady, I was raised in strict
Obedience to my duties and was nursed
With sullen hatred for the Pope until,
When I was twenty years, an irrepressible
Desire to see the Continent drove me from home.
I left the Puritans and all their musty meeting rooms
Behind and quickly made my way through France

In ardent search of Italy—the land of promise.
It was the time then of the Church's great feast,
The roads were crowded with the host of pilgrims,
A wreath around each crucifix; it seemed
As if all mankind had begun a pilgrimage,
With heaven's kingdom as their goal.
The surging current of the faithful multitude
Soon swept me up and carried me
Into the heart of Rome. Oh, how I felt
When columns and triumphal arches
Magnificently rose before my eyes,
When suddenly the Colosseum's splendor
Held my astonished gaze, and when I sensed
The lofty spirit of creation
In the serene domain of man-made marvels!
I'd never known the power of the arts.
The church that brought me up abhors
All sensual delight, condones no image.
The disembodied word alone is held in reverence.
Ah, how I felt when I stepped into churches
Where music floated down from heaven,
Where an entire new world of images
Extravagantly gushed from walls and ceiling,
Where the Magnificent and the Supreme
Had come to life, enthralled the senses.
I saw them now, the holy figures,
The message of the angel and the birth of Christ,
Transfiguration in a glowing light,
The Holy Mother, Trinity descending.
I saw the Pope, resplendent, celebrating Mass
And blessing all the people of this earth.
Oh, what are gold and dazzling jewels
With which the kings of earth adorn themselves
Compared to him who's bathed in godliness?
His house is truly heaven's kingdom,
Because those forms are of another world.

MARY. Have pity! Stop! Don't spread the glowing carpet
Of life too temptingly before me.
I am a wretched prisoner.

MORTIMER. I, too, have been a prisoner, your Majesty.
My prison doors sprang open, and at once
My spirit soared to meet the shining day of life.
I swore undying hatred to the narrow, musty Book,

And jubilant, a wreath of flowers on my brow,
I vowed to share the company of joyous men.
My friends were many noble Scots,
The lively companies of Frenchmen.
They took me to your noble uncle,
The Cardinal of Guise. Oh, what a sure
And clear and manly man he is!
A leader born; the model of a royal priest,
A prince and churchman as I've never seen before.

MARY. You've seen him, then! You've seen his face, so dear
To me, beloved and revered by multitudes,
The man who was my guide when I was young.
Oh, tell me more about him! Does he still
Remember me? Does Fortune love him still?
Has life preserved him in his flower?
Does he still guard, a solid rock, our Church?

MORTIMER. Oh yes! He condescended to explain to me
The venerable doctrines of our faith
And he dispelled my few remaining doubts.
He showed me that man's ever-searching reason
Leads him astray and that our eyes must see
What we expect our heart to understand,
That it is necessary for the Church
To have a head that all can clearly see,
That truth presided at the councils of the fathers.
Thus soon my childish misconceptions
Evaporated in the heat of his triumphant mind
And his persuasive tongue, and I returned
Into the lap of our beloved Church.
Into his hands I disavowed my errors.

MARY. So you are one among the thousands
Whom he has led to their salvation,
Moved with his eloquence, a gift from heaven,
As once the reverend Preacher of the Mountain did.

MORTIMER. Soon afterward the duties of his office called
Him back to France, and he sent me to Rheims
Where the Society of Jesus piously
Prepares the priests for England's Church.
That noble Scotsman, Morgan, I met there
And Lessley, your devoted, scholarly
Bishop of Rosse, who spend their hapless days
Of banishment in France. I spent much time
With both these venerable men and strengthened

My new-found faith. One day, while in the bishop's study,
A strangely moving portrait of a lady caught
My eye. I stood before the picture, deeply stirred,
Unable to control my powerful emotions.
You may well stand before this picture, moved,
The bishop said to me, she's the most beautiful
Of living women, she also has the saddest fate.
She suffers for our faith, and England is
The country where she suffers.

    MARY. Not all is lost while upright men like he
Stand by me in my misery.

    MORTIMER. He told me then, so eloquently that it broke
My heart, the story of your martyrdom
And of your enemies' bloodthirsty plans.
He also told me of your family
And demonstrated your direct descent
From the exalted House of Tudor.
He thus persuaded me that you alone
Are worthy to be England's ruler—not that woman
Who masquerades as queen, who was conceived
In an adulterous bed, whom her own father, Henry,
Repudiated as a bastard daughter.
His testimony, though, was not enough.
I asked advice from legal scholars,
Consulted ancient books of heraldry,
And all who are conversant with the facts
Confirm the justice of your claim.
I am convinced now that your crime
Consists but in your just right to the throne,
That you are held, a guiltless prisoner,
In England, which is yours by right.

    MARY. That fateful, hateful right! It is
The only source of all my woes.

    MORTIMER. It was about that time when news arrived
That you had been removed from Talbot's castle
And handed over to my uncle's care.
I saw in that event the hand of God,
Miraculously pointing to your rescue.
I heard the clarion call of destiny
Which had selected me to bring you freedom.
The plans were quickly made, and I returned
To England where, as you already know,
I landed just ten days ago.

(*He pauses.*)

Then I saw you, my Queen—I saw yourself,
And not a picture. Ah, what treasure holds this castle!
This is no prison—it's a sacred hall,
More splendid than the royal court of England!
Blessed the man who is allowed to breathe
The air which you are breathing. Ah, how right
She was to bury you so deep!
For all the youth of England would rise up,
Unsheathe their swords, and with its giant head
Held high, revolt would stride across this peaceful island,
If Britons ever saw their Queen!

MARY. Luck would be hers if every Briton looked
Upon her with your eyes.

MORTIMER. They would if they, like I, saw how you suffer,
And saw the gentleness and the composure
With which you bear indignities.
From all your trials you emerge as Queen,
No prison can deprive your beauty of its sheen.
You lack the meanest ornament, yet life
And light surround you with their glow.
Each time I cross this threshold torments tear my heart,
But each time I'm enchanted by your sight.
Now, terribly, the moment of decision looms,
The danger grows with every hour, I can delay
No longer, can no longer hide the frightful news—

MARY. Has sentence been pronounced? Feel free to speak.
I'll bear it.

MORTIMER. Yes—it has. The forty-two,
Your judges, have pronounced you guilty—more,
The House of Lords, the Commons and the City
Of London are insistent that the sentence
Be swiftly carried out. The Queen alone
Still hesitates—not from a feeling, to be sure,
Of human kindness or of mercy, but waiting
Cunningly to be prevailed upon.

MARY (*calmly*). Sir Mortimer, I'm not surprised nor fright-
     ened.
I've long expected this. I know my judges.
The treatment which I have been made to suffer
Made it quite clear that they would never set me free.
I know what they intend—to keep me prisoner
In perpetuity, to bury me

Together with my vengeance and my rightful claims.

MORTIMER. No, no, your Majesty! They do not stop at that!
No tyranny can be content with leaving things
Half-done. As long as you're alive, her fears will live.
There is no dungeon deep enough to bury you.
Your death alone can guarantee her throne.

MARY. She would not dare to put the crowned head of a queen
Upon the executioner's block.

MORTIMER. She will! Don't doubt that she will dare.

MARY. She cannot wish to pull into the dust
Her majesty and that of every king.
Does she not fear the vengeance of the French?

MORTIMER. She is concluding an eternal pact with France;
She's offering the Duke of Anjou hand and throne.

MARY. The King of Spain would surely rush to arms.

MORTIMER. She does not fear a world in arms
While she's at peace at home, in England.

MARY. Would she present this spectacle to England, then?

MORTIMER. This country has in recent years seen more than one
Crowned lady leave the throne to mount the scaffold.
Her mother went that way and Catherine Howard,
A crown wore Lady Grey before she died.

MARY (*after a pause*). No, Mortimer. Your fear is blinding
      you.
It is your loyalty that makes you apprehensive
And lets you see imaginary horrors.
I do not fear the scaffold, sir.
Elizabeth has other and less noisome means
To still my claims and give her peace.
Much sooner than a hangman she could find
A murderer to do her bidding.
That is what makes me tremble, sir.
Each time I put a goblet to my lips
I shudder thinking that my royal sister
May well have filled it with her love for me.

MORTIMER. No murder, open or in secret, shall succeed.
You need not fear, all is in readiness.
Twelve noble youths, men of this country, are
In league with me; this morning they received
The sacrament and swore, by force of arms,
To aid in your abduction from this castle.
Count Aubespine, the French ambassador,

Has knowledge of our league, has offered help,
And at his palace we shall meet.

MARY. You make me tremble, sir—but not with happiness.
I feel an ill foreboding. Have you weighed well
What you are undertaking? Are you not deterred
By Babington's and Tichburn's bloody heads,
Impaled as warning upon London Bridge?
Nor by the fate of all those countless men
Who met their death in similar adventures
And made my chains still heavier?
Unfortunate, misguided man, escape!
Take flight while there's still time—unless, of course,
Lord Burleigh knows about you and has planted
A traitor in your midst. Be quick and flee the realm!
Luck does not smile on those who fight for Mary Stuart.

MORTIMER. Not Babington's and Tichburn's bloody heads,
Impaled on London Bridge as warning,
Nor the destruction of those countless men
Who lost their lives in similar adventures frighten me.
Their death brought them eternal glory.
To die for you is happiness.

MARY. It is in vain. No force, no ruse can rescue me.
The enemy is vigilant and powerful.
Not only Paulet and his throng of jailers,
All England guards my prison door.
Elizabeth alone, of her free will,
Can open it.

MORTIMER. There is no hope of that.

MARY. There is one man who might succeed.

MORTIMER. Who is?

MARY. The Earl of Leicester.

MORTIMER. Leicester? He? The man
Who raves against you more than anyone—
The favorite of Elizabeth . . . through him—

MARY. If anyone can save me it is he.
And I want you to go to him. Speak frankly.
As proof that I am sending you, bring him
This letter. It contains my portrait.

(*She draws an envelope from her bosom.* MORTIMER *steps back, hesitates to take it.*)

Accept it. I have carried it upon
My person since I wrote it long ago.

Your uncle's vigilance and strictness
Had blocked all means of reaching him. But now,
My guardian angel sent me—you.

MORTIMER. Your Majesty . . . this riddle . . . please explain.

MARY. The Earl of Leicester, I am sure, will solve it.
Trust him, he will trust you. Who's there?

HANNAH (*hurries in, busily*). Sir Paulet with some gentleman
    from court.

MORTIMER. That is Lord Burleigh. Hear him out
With equanimity. Rest calm, your Majesty.

           (*He leaves by a side door, followed by* HANNAH.)

SCENE 7. *Mary, Lord Burleigh and Paulet.*

PAULET. You asked to know your fate for certain. Now—
His Lordship brings you certainty. This is
Lord Burleigh. Hear his message humbly.

MARY. With dignity, I hope, as befits my innocence.

BURLEIGH. I come as emissary from the court.

MARY. My Lord, you eagerly accept serving the court,
Whose mind you were, now also as a mouthpiece.

PAULET. You speak as if you knew the verdict.

MARY. I know a message that Lord Burleigh brings
Before he speaks. But to the point, my Lord.

BURLEIGH. Your Majesty, you did accept
The jurisdiction of the forty-two—

MARY. Excuse me if I interrupt at once, my Lord.
Accepted jurisdiction of the forty-two?
I never did. I never could accept
Yielding so much, my rank, the dignity
Of son and people and of every king.
Does English law not give to an accused
The right of judgment by his peers?
Which of the jurors is my peer?
My peers are kings!

BURLEIGH.   You listened to the articles
Of the indictment, submitted to examination by the court—

MARY. I was misled by Hutton's cunning falsehoods.
To guard my honor, and with confidence
In the persuasive power of my arguments,

I did agree to listen to the charges
And to explain their origin—no more.
I did so also out of the esteem
In which I hold the worthy Lords as persons, not
In their capacity. That I repudiate.

BURLEIGH. Whether you recognize their jurisdiction,
Or whether you object is but an empty gesture.
It cannot influence the course of justice.
You do breathe England's air, enjoy
Her laws' protection and their benefits,
And you are therefore subject to their power.

MARY. Yes, I am breathing England's air—in prison.
Is that what you call living in your country?
Is that enjoying your laws' benefits?
I hardly know your laws. Nor did I ever swear
Obedience to them. I'm not a citizen
Of England's realm. I am a foreign queen—and free.

BURLEIGH. Do you believe that carrying a royal name
Implies the right of sowing discord
In foreign countries with impunity?
How safe would any kingdom be
If Themis' righteous sword were not so long
That it could reach a culpable, though royal guest
As easily as any beggar?

MARY. I am not trying to evade your justice.
The judges who dispense it I reject.

BURLEIGH. The judges! Why, my Lady? Why? Are they
Perhaps some nameless outcasts picked
At random from the rabble, shameless blabberers
To whom truth and justice are but goods for sale?
Or who would willingly become
The hired servants of tyrannical oppression?
Are not these judges the most noble men
In England, free enough to speak the truth,
Men who stand far above the fear of kings
And miserable bribery? These are
The very men who govern a great people
In justice and in freedom, men whose names
Alone suffice to silence any doubt
And all suspicion. At their head,
The pious shepherd, Archbishop of Canterbury,
Then come the Earl of Shrewsbury, our wise
Lord Privy Seal; the valiant Howard, the Lord Admiral—

Now, please—could England's ruler have done more
Than choose from all her kingdom the most noble men
As judges in this royal suit?
And even though among them may be some
Who could be swayed by partisan dislikes,
Could forty carefully selected men
Unite in a decision based on private passion?

    MARY (*after a silence*). I listen in amazement to your eloquence
Which always has been my misfortune.
And how can I, an unlearned woman,
Compete with such a skillful orator?
Well! —If these Lords were really
As you describe them, I could say no more;
My cause would be hopelessly lost if they condemned.
But all those names which you so highly praise,
Which are to crush me by their weight—my Lord,
I see their bearers play a different role in England's history.
I see your high nobility, your realm's
Majestic senate, flattering the whims
Of my great-uncle, Henry the Eighth,
As eunuchs fawn at the seraglio's master.
I see this noble House of Lords,
Just as subserviently as the venal Commons,
Make laws and abrogate them, close a marriage
And soon dissolve it—as their master bids;
See them brand English princesses as bastards
Or disinherit them—tomorrow crown them queens.
I see these worthy peers so true to their
Convictions that, to suit four governments,
They change their faith four times—

    BURLEIGH. You claim to be a stranger to our laws
But you're well versed in England's weaknesses.

    MARY. Those men then are my judges! You, my Lord—
I will be just in judging you, I hope
You will be just with me. I'm told
You have your Queen's, your country's interest
At heart, that you are always vigilant,
Untiring, incorruptible.
I will believe it. You do what is best
For Queen and country, do not count your own
Advantage. That is why you must be on your guard:
Do not mistake your country's interest for justice.

I do not doubt that there are other men
As honorable as yourself among my judges.
But they are Protestants, fanatic partisans
Of England's welfare who judge me—
A Papist and the Queen of Scots!
No Briton ever judged a Scotsman justly.
That is an age-old saying and is why
It has been custom since our fathers' ancient times
That Englishmen may never testify before the law
Against a Scot, nor Scots against an Englishman.
Necessity created this odd rule,
But wisdom speaks in old traditions,
And we should honor them, my Lord.
Two fiery nations Nature threw upon
This floating board, this isle, gave them unequal shares
And ordered them to fight for its possession.
The narrow river Tweed alone divides
These boisterous neighbors, and their blood
Has often mingled with its waves.
Thus, hand on hilt, they've threateningly stared
From either bank across the Tweed for a thousand years.
No enemy has ever crowded England
To whom the Scot would not extend a helping hand.
No civil war has ever burned the towns of Scotland,
For which the Briton did not carry tinder.
This hatred will not die until at last
One Parliament unites the fighting brothers,
One scepter reigns this isle.

    BURLEIGH.   And you, a Stuart, meant
To bring that happy fortune to our realm?

    MARY. Why not admit it? Yes, I nourished hopes,
I hoped to bring together these proud nations
Beneath the olive tree, both free and happy.
I never thought that I would at once become
The victim of their rivalry and hate.
I hoped to bank the fires of age-old discord,
Of their eternal jealousy,
And, as my ancestor, the Duke of Richmond, tied
Together the two Roses after bloody wars,
My hope was to unite the crowns
Of England and of Scotland in a peaceful marriage.

    BURLEIGH. You chose an evil way to reach that goal
When you inflamed the realm and sought to climb

The throne across the raging fires of civil war.

MARY. I never wanted that! Good God, whenever
Did I want that? Where is your proof?

BURLEIGH. I did not come to argue. This no longer is
A matter to be fought with words.
With forty voices against two, the jury found
That you have violated the decree
Which Parliament last year enacted,
That you are guilty under law. The act reads thus:
"If there arise disturbances within the Kingdom,
In name or fact of benefit to anyone
Pretending to the Crown, that person shall
Be prosecuted under law and punished unto death."
Now, since it's proven—

MARY.   Yes, my Lord!
No doubt, a law expressly made for me,
Conceived to ruin me, can now be used against me.
Beware, poor victim, when the mouth that gives the law
And that which passes sentence is the same.
Can you deny, my Lord, that this law aimed
At my destruction?

BURLEIGH.   It was meant to warn you.
It was you who changed it to a trap.
You saw the abyss yawning at your feet,
Were duly warned, and still plunged into it.
You were in league with Babington, that traitor,
With all his hired assassins, knew their plans,
And from your prison guided the conspiracy.

MARY. When did I do all that? Show me the documents!

BURLEIGH. You saw them recently in court.

MARY. Those copies written by I don't know whom?
Bring proof that I dictated them myself,
That I dictated them as they were read.

BURLEIGH. Sir Babington, before he died, acknowledged them
To be the documents which you had given him.

MARY. Why was I not confronted with him then
While he was still alive? Why the unseemly haste
In sending him into the other world
Before I had a chance to see him face to face?

BURLEIGH. Your clerks, too, Curl and Nau, swore that those
    letters
Were written in their hand as you dictated them.

MARY. Thus on the testimony of my servants
Am I condemned? Upon the word of men
Who could betray their Queen, betrayed their trust
The moment they agreed to testify against me?

BURLEIGH. You used to praise that Scotsman, Curl, yourself
As virtuous and most dependable.

MARY. That's how I knew him. But the character of men
Is proven only in the hour of danger.
Perhaps the torture frightened him,
And he confessed and testified to lies.
Perhaps he thought that he could save himself
By his false testimony and cause me,
His Queen, no harm.

BURLEIGH.   He swore to it on his free oath.

MARY. Not in my presence. Why, my Lord—two witnesses,
Those two, are still alive! Why may I not confront them?
Let them repeat their testimony to my face.
Do you deny a favor, no, a right to me
Which you would not refuse a murderer?
I know from Talbot, when he guarded me,
That under this, the present government
An act was passed that guarantees the right
To an accused to face the person who accuses him.
Is that not true? Am I mistaken? Paulet!
I've always looked upon you as an honorable man;
Now—prove it! Tell me, is that not the truth?
Is there not such a law in England?

PAULET. There is, my Lady. That's the law in England.
I must tell you the truth.

MARY. Well, then, my Lord! If you inflict the full severity
Of English law upon me when it harms,
Why circumvent that very law
When it may benefit me? Answer that.
Why was I not confronted, eye to eye,
With Babington, according to the law?
Why not with my domestics who are still alive?

BURLEIGH. Do not excite yourself, my Lady. Your accord
With Babington is not the only charge—

MARY. It is the only accusation which exposes me
To legal prosecution and the only one
From which I have to clear myself.
Keep to the point, my Lord! Do not evade the issue!

BURLEIGH. We also have the proof of negotiations with
His Spanish Majesty's ambassador—

MARY (*agitated*). Keep to the point, my Lord!

BURLEIGH. And that you had designs on overthrowing
The state's religion, that you schemed
To form a league of all the kings in Europe
For waging war against the Queen—

MARY. Suppose I did? I did not, but suppose I did?
I am held prisoner against the Law of Nations.
I did not come here, sword in hand; I came,
A supplicant who claimed the ancient right
Of hospitality, I came to throw myself
Into the arms of Queen Elizabeth, my relative.
But I was seized by force and chained by those
Whom I beseeched for help. My Lord,
In conscience, what do I owe England?
Do I have duties here? To search for ways
Of breaking these intolerable bonds,
To counter might with might, and to incite
And summon all the countries of the continent—
All that is nothing but my sacred right
Of self-defense. I am entitled to conduct
This war by all means that are fair and chivalrous.
My conscience and my pride will not admit
That I use foul and secret means, that I use murder.
For murder would dishonor me and soil my hands.
I say, dishonor—not subject me to your laws,
And surely not condemn me. No, what counts
Between myself and England is not right, but might.

BURLEIGH (*ominously*). Do not invoke the frightful right of
    force.
It does not favor prisoners, my Lady.

MARY. Elizabeth is powerful, and I am weak.
Well, let her use her power, let her kill me.
Let my death be the sacrifice she brings
To guarantee her safety. If she does,
She must admit she exercises force, not justice.
The sword used to remove her hated enemy
Cannot be borrowed from the law.
She cannot veil the brutish force
Of her blood-red audacity in sacred garments.
Such travesty would not deceive the world.
To murder me, she has the power—not to judge me.

Let her abandon any thought of harvesting
The fruits of crime, while she parades her virtue.
May she have courage to appear as what she is.   (*She leaves.*)

Scene 8. *Lord Burleigh and Paulet.*

BURLEIGH. Defiance! And she will keep on defying us
Up to the scaffold's steps. Unbreakable
Is her proud heart. Was she surprised
About the verdict? Did she weep?
She did not even blanch, nor ask for sympathy.
She knows too well that England's Queen
Is torn by doubts. Our fears make her courageous.

PAULET. My Lord, her vain defiance feeds, if I may say so,
On flaws which obviously mar the legal process.
Remove those flaws, and her defiance will soon vanish.
She should have been allowed to face
That Babington and Tichburn and her servants.

BURLEIGH (*quickly*). No, Sir Amias, never that! We could not
        dare.
Her power over people is too great,
So are her tears, the weapon of a woman.
If Curl, her clerk, had ever faced her to repeat
The words which spell her death, he would have turned,
Intimidated, and recanted his confession.

PAULET. But now, the enemies of England soon
Will fill the world with hateful rumors,
And the elaborate proceedings of the trial
Will seem but an audacious farce.

BURLEIGH. Precisely that is what disturbs our Queen.
Would that this mischief-maker had expired
Before she ever set her foot on English soil!

PAULET. To that I say Amen.

BURLEIGH. Or that she had succumbed to illness in her prison!

PAULET. That would have spared this country great misfortune.

BURLEIGH. But even if an accident of nature
Had put an end to her, we still would be
Her murderers.

PAULET.   Quite true. One can never
Prevent the world from thinking what it wants.

BURLEIGH. It could never be proven, and the noise
Would not be quite so shrill—

PAULET. Oh, never mind the noise. Reproaches only hurt
When they are just, not when they're loud.

BURLEIGH. Not even heaven's justice can escape
Its human censors. People always sympathize
With the unfortunate, and envy is the lot
Of the victorious. The judge's sword adorns
A man, but it is hated in a woman's hand.
The world does not believe in women's justice,
When any other woman is the victim.
It was in vain that we, as judges, followed
Our conscience. She now has the royal right
Of clemency, and she must use it.
To countenance that justice take its course
Is inconceivable.

PAULET.   And so—

BURLEIGH (*quickly interrupting him*). And so
We let her live? Oh no. She must not live.
This it is that frightens the Queen,
That is why sleep avoids her bed.
I read her inner battle in her eyes,
Her mouth would never dare to speak her wish,
But full of meaning, silently, her gaze demands:
Is there not one among my servants
Who would relieve me of this fateful choice,
To tremble on my throne in endless fear,
Or callously to let a queen, my relative,
Become a victim of the executioner's ax?

PAULET. That is the choice, and nothing can be done about it.

BURLEIGH. It could be different, the Queen must think,
If only she had more attentive servants.

PAULET. Attentive?

BURLEIGH. Yes, men who can interpret silent orders.

PAULET. Silent orders!

BURLEIGH. Men who, if given poisonous snakes to guard,
Would not protect this enemy entrusted to
Their care as thoughtfully as precious gems.

PAULET (*firmly*). The Queen's good name and blameless
    reputation
Are precious gems, indeed. One cannot be
Too careful with them, sir.

BURLEIGH. When Mary was removed from Shrewsbury's do-
    main

And Sir Amias Paulet was assigned
To guard the lady—why, one thought—

PAULET. I hope, my Lord, one thought that the most difficult
Assignment should be put into the cleanest hands.
By God, I never would have lent myself
To playing bailiff, had I not been firm
In my belief that no man but the best
In England was required for it.
Do not suggest, my Lord, that I owe my appointment
To anything other than my spotless reputation.

BURLEIGH. The rumor could be spread that she was ill,
That she was getting weaker, finally,
That she had peacefully succumbed.
She thus would fade from people's memories—
Your reputation still untarnished.

PAULET. But not my conscience!

BURLEIGH. If you don't choose to lend your hand,
You surely would not stop another man—

PAULET (interrupts him). No murderer will cross her thresh-
     old while
She is protected by my household gods.
To me her life is sacred—just as sacred as
The head of Queen Elizabeth.
You are the judges. Judge her then. Condemn her.
When it is time to have the carpenter
Come with his ax and saw to build the scaffold,
I will not bar the way to executioner or sheriff.
For now, she is entrusted to my care.
You may be sure that I will keep her safe,
So she will neither cause nor suffer harm.   (Both leave.)

ACT II

The Palace at Westminster

SCENE 1. The Earl of Kent and Sir William Davison encounter each other.

DAVISON. You here, my Lord? Is all the jousting finished,
Since you return so soon from the display?

KENT. Did you not, too, attend the tournament?

DAVISON. My office kept me here.

KENT. You missed a beautiful performance, sir.
It was most tastefully designed, and executed
With great nobility. It was a play
In which Desire attacked the citadel of Chastity
And Beauty, which the Lord Chief Justice,
The Marshal and the Lord High Steward
Defended with ten other knights.
The cavaliers from France were the attackers.
At first, a herald came who, in a madrigal,
Demanded the surrender of the fortress.
Then, from the wall, the Chancellor replied.
The turn then came for the artillery,
The dainty cannons firing flowers
And precious aromatic essences.
It was in vain! Repelled were their attacks,
Desire was forced into an ignominious retreat.

DAVISON. An inauspicious omen for the courtship of the
French.

KENT. I hardly think so. It was all in fun.
When things get serious, the fortress will,
I think, surrender in the end.

DAVISON. Do you believe so? I have given up all hope.

KENT. Why, the most complicated articles
Have been agreed, the French have given in.
Monsieur will be content to worship in his way
Behind locked doors, while publicly he will accord
Respect and give protection to the state religion.
You should have seen the jubilation of the crowds
When that news spread! For what the country feared
Was that the Queen might die without an heir
And thus surrender England once again
To Papist slavery in the event
That Mary followed her upon the throne.

DAVISON. Of that fear they can be relieved—
Into her bridal chamber steps the Queen,
While Mary Stuart mounts the scaffold's steps.

KENT. Here comes the Queen.

SCENE 2. *The same. Elizabeth enters on the arm of the Earl of Leicester. Count Aubespine, Count Bellievre, the Earl of Shrewsbury, Lord Burleigh and other French and English nobles follow them.*

ELIZABETH (*to* AUBESPINE). I do feel sorry, Count, for all
    these gentlemen
Whom their most gallant eagerness to cross
The sea brought here, and who are forced to miss
The splendor of the court of St. Germain.
I am not able to invent amusements
As elegant as those the French Queen Mother offers.
A well-behaved and happy people, apt
To crowd round my chair each time I show myself
In public—that's the only spectacle
That I can proudly show my foreign visitors.
The glitter of such noble ladies
As blossom forth in Catherine's flower garden
Would but obscure me and my dull accomplishments.

AUBESPINE. The Court of Westminster displays one lady only
To the admiring eyes of foreigners,
But in this one example they will see
Embodied all the charms of her alluring sisters.

BELLIEVRE. Your Majesty, permit us now to take our leave.
The long-awaited, happy tidings will delight
Monsieur, our royal master, whom his great
Impatience would not let remain in Paris.
He waits in Amiens, his runners spread
From there up to Calais, so that your Yes,
As quickly as your Majesty pronounces it,
May reach his ear on eagle's wings
And make him drunk with happiness.

ELIZABETH. Count Bellievre, do not press me further.
The time is not well-suited, I repeat,
To light the merry wedding torches.
The sky is black above this land,
And it behoves me more to wear deep mourning
Than sparkling bridal gowns. My heart
And my whole house are threatened by a cruel blow.

BELLIEVRE. Give us your promise, then, your Majesty,
Redeem it when the time is more propitious.

ELIZABETH. Kings are but slaves of their exalted rank.

They never may pursue the dictates of their hearts.
I've always wished to die unmarried,
I would have traded all my fame, so that
One day upon my tombstone one would read:
"Here lies the Virgin Queen." My subjects, though,
Are of a different mind; they busily
Think of the time—already now—when I am gone.
They are not satisfied to count the blessings
Which now make England such a happy place,
No, for their future, too, I am to sacrifice myself.
I am to offer up what is most dear to me,
The freedom of a virgin, to my people.
They force me to accept a master—and
Thereby give me to understand
That I am but a woman. I had thought
That I had ruled like any man and like a king.
I know full well that one does not serve God
By flouting all the rules of nature.
Praise be to them who sat upon this throne before me
For opening the monasteries and returning
To nature's duties all those thousands
Who had been victims of misguided piety.
A queen, however, does not waste her days
In idle contemplation; cheerfully
And tirelessly she performs the hardest task
Of all, and she should be exempt from nature's law
Which makes one-half of mankind servants of the other.

    AUBESPINE. Your Majesty, you've glorified upon your throne
All virtues—except one: to set all womanhood,
Whose pride you have become, in their own sphere
A proud example. It is true,
No man on earth deserves that you give up
Your freedom for his sake. But if there is
One mortal man whom birth, exalted station,
Heroic virtue and manly beauty
Make worthy of that honor, then—

    ELIZABETH. The marriage with a royal son of France
Would greatly honor me, my dear Ambassador,
There is no doubt of that, and, I admit it frankly,
If it must be, if there is nothing I can do
But yield to the insistence of my people—
And they'll be stronger, I'm afraid, than I—
I cannot think of any prince in Europe

To whom I would with less reluctance sacrifice
My greatest treasure, freedom. Now—
Let this confession be enough.

BELLIEVRE. To have this hope is priceless; still,
It's only hope. My master wished for more ...

ELIZABETH. What does he want?
(*She takes a ring from her finger and looks at it reflectively.*)
A queen is, after all, not very different
From any burgher's wife. The symbols are the same,
So are the duties and the servitude
Which they imply. A ring makes marriages,
And rings make chains. Take this, it is
A present for his Highness. It's not yet a chain,
It does not bind me yet, although in time
It may become a circlet that does bind me.

BELLIEVRE (*kneels before her to receive the ring*).
Kneeling before you, I accept
This present in his name, and in his stead
I press this kiss of homage on my monarch's hand.

ELIZABETH (*to* LEICESTER, *at whom she has gazed steadily
    during the foregoing speech*). Permit me, my Lord.
(*She takes the blue ribbon from his neck and hangs it around
    that of* BELLIEVRE.)
Pass on this decoration to his Highness,
As I now decorate you and accept you
Into the duties of my order.
Honi soit qui mal y pense!
May all suspicion fade between our nations,
And may a bond of trust henceforth unite
The crowns of England and of France.

AUBESPINE. Illustrious Queen! This is a day of joy.
May all regard it so, may there not be
A single sufferer upon this isle
Who mourns today. Oh, that a glimmer of that radiance
Which mercy's light has spread upon your features
May fall upon that most unhappy queen
Whose fate so intimately touches both our nations!

ELIZABETH. No more, Count Aubespine! Let us not mingle
Two matters which are incompatible.
If France desires our union earnestly,
She must share our concerns and not befriend our foes.

AUBESPINE. In your own eyes, she would act cowardly
If she forgot, because of our alliance,

The hapless woman, widow of her king
And sister in the faith. If nothing else,
Compassion, honor would demand—

ELIZABETH. In that sense I accept your master's intercession
And shall appraise it at its worth.
France does her duty as a friend;
With your permission, I shall act as Queen.

(*She inclines her head toward the French nobles who, with the other lords, respectfully withdraw.*)

SCENE 3. *Elizabeth, Leicester, Burleigh and Shrewsbury. The Queen sits down.*

BURLEIGH. Most glorious Majesty! Today you grant
Your people's ardent wishes. Only now
Can we enjoy the blessed days which you bestow
On us, now that we need no longer tremble
When we direct our gaze into a stormy future.
One sacrifice the people still demand from you.
Grant it, and England's welfare will forever rest
On the foundation laid today.

ELIZABETH. What do my people ask, my Lord?

BURLEIGH. They ask for Mary Stuart's head. If you
Desire to make secure the precious gift
Of freedom and the hard-won light of truth,
She must not live. The enemy must perish
Lest we always tremble for your life.
As you well know, not all your Britons think alike.
The Roman idol-worship still
Has many secret followers in England,
And all of them hatch hostile thoughts.
They have their hearts set on this Stuart,
They're allies of the brothers from Lorraine,
Whose hate for you is unremitting.
These furious partisans are sworn to fight
Their bitter war against you to the death,
A war which they pursue with hellish weapons.
They have their armory at Rheims, the Cardinal's See,
And there they fashion lightning bolts, teach regicide,
And busily dispatch to England missions
Of disciplined fanatics, well-disguised
In fanciful array. Three murderers

Already have been sent from there. That pit
Is inexhaustible and procreates
Forever secret enemies.
The Ate of this never-ending war
Sits quietly at Fotheringhay
And with the torch of love inflames the realm.
Our youths, in whom she sparks with flattery false hopes,
Risk gladly certain death for her.
Their watchword is to set her free,
Their aim to put her on your throne.
Lorraine will never recognize your sacred right,
To them you are a rank usurper of the throne,
Whom Fortune crowned. These are the men
Who viciously persuaded the deluded woman
To call herself the Queen of England!
There is no peace with her and all her tribe.
You have to strike—or else be struck.
Her life—your death; her death—your life!

ELIZABETH. My Lord, you are the advocate of gloom.
I know your zeal rests on the purest motives,
I know the wisdom of your words is unalloyed.
But wisdom which commands that blood be spilled
I hate with all my soul. Think of more lenient counsel.
My Lord of Shrewsbury, you give me your opinion.

SHREWSBURY. You gave the fervor which moves loyal Burleigh
The praise which it deserves. Though I can never speak
With equal eloquence, my heart is no less honest.
Long live my Queen, to be her people's joy
And to prolong their happy peace!
This isle has never seen more pleasant days
Since her own princes governed her.
May England never purchase happiness
With her good name. But if she does, at least,
I hope that Talbot's eyes no longer see.

ELIZABETH. May God forbid that we befoul her fame.

SHREWSBURY. Then you will think of other ways to save the
    realm.
To execute the Stuart is illegal;
You have no right to try her, for she's not your subject.

ELIZABETH. My Privy Council, then, my Parliament are wrong
And all the courts of justice are in error,
For all of them advised me that I have that right.

SHREWSBURY. Majority decisions are no proof

Of legal rights. England is not the world,
Her parliament does not include all men.
The England of today is not
The England that will be—or that once was.
Upon the waves of changeable opinion
The verdict of the court is tossed about.
Don't say that you are forced, that you obey
Necessity and the insistence of your people.
For you can prove at any moment, if you will,
That you are free to act the way you please.
Try it! Declare that you loathe bloodshed
And that you *wish* to save your sister's life.
Show openly your royal indignation
To those who want to give you other counsel—
Soon the necessity will disappear
And right will quickly change to wrong.
You must decide yourself, you cannot lean
Upon this feeble, swaying reed.
Obey your heart's advice, be merciful.
God did not put severity
Into a woman's heart. This nation's founders,
Who gave the reins of government to women, too,
Showed thereby clearly that severity
Was not to be a virtue of the English kings.

ELIZABETH. You are a most devoted advocate for her,
The enemy of England and—my own.
I do prefer a councillor
Who has my interests at heart.

SHREWSBURY. She was refused an advocate, and no one dares
To speak for her and thus incur your wrath.
Give your permission, then, to an old man,
Who, close to death, is no longer enticed
By worldly hopes, to be her advocate.
It never shall be said that in your council
The sounds of passion and of selfishness were loud,
But that compassion did not dare to speak.
All is in league against her. You yourself
Have never seen her face to face,
She strikes no chords of friendship in your heart.
I am not trying to excuse her guilt. They say
That she allowed her husband to be murdered,
And it is true she married his assassin.
That is a heinous crime. But it was done

In an unhappy, dark epoch,
Amid the pressing fears of civil war.
Then she, weak and surrounded by a host
Of importuning vassals, threw herself
Into the arms of that most powerful
And brazen man, succumbing to who knows
What wily, evil forces. Yes,
A fragile thing, indeed, is woman.

ELIZABETH. No, women are not weak. There are strong souls
Among the female sex. Do not
Speak in my presence of their weakness.

SHREWSBURY. Misfortune taught *you* many lessons,
Life had no smiles for you. You saw no throne
That beckoned in the distance—only graves
That yawned before your feet.
At Woodstock, in the Tower's gloomy night,
The gracious father of the country brought
Your duties home to you by raising you
In misery. The flatterer's seductive chatter
Was far from you, the futile noises of the world
Did not distract you. There, your mind could concentrate
And meditate upon life's genuine values.
No God saved that poor woman! At a tender age,
She was transplanted to French soil and to a court
Where nothing but frivolity and thoughtless gaiety
Surrounded her. Inebriated by unending feasts,
And blinded by the glitter of their vices,
She never heard the sober voice of truth.
The torrent of corruption carried her away.
And she was beautiful. Her bloom outshone
All other women, and that vain possession
No less than her exalted birth—

ELIZABETH. Collect yourself, Lord Shrewsbury!
Remember that we are engaged in serious council.
Her charms, indeed, must be extraordinary,
If they can fan such flames in old men's hearts!
My Lord of Leicester, you alone are silent.
Does what makes Lord Shrewsbury wag his tongue,
Tie yours?

LEICESTER. Your Majesty,
I have been silent in astonishment,
Amazed that one makes bold to fill your ear
With horror stories, fairy tales that strike

The gullible and foolish rabble on the streets
With fear. Now they are being seriously argued
In your exalted council by wise men.
I'm speechless, I admit, that Mary, Queen of Scots
Without a country, who could not maintain herself
On her own little throne, whom her own vassals mock,
An outcast, should become so dangerous to you
Now that she is in prison. What, in heaven's name,
Makes her so terrible? Her claim on England?
Is it because the House of Guise
Refuses to acknowledge you as Queen?
Can their objections weaken rights
Which you possess by birth, and which have been confirmed
By Parliament? Did Henry's testament
Not tacitly refute her claims? And will
The English, happy in their new-found light,
Now throw themselves into a Papist's arms?
Would they desert their Queen, whom they adore,
To follow Darnley's murderess?
What do these people want who so impatiently
Torment you, while you're still alive, about an heir,
Who cannot wed you soon enough because,
They say, you must save state and church?
You stand before us in the bloom of youth,
She fades, a little closer to her grave each day.
I hope, by God, that you will walk for many years
Upon her grave. There is no need for you
To push her into it.

   BURLEIGH. My Lord, that has not always been your judgment.

   LEICESTER. As member of a court of law, it's true,
I voted for her death; but I speak differently
As member of the Privy Council.
Here, law is not the issue, only interest.
Is this the time to be afraid of her,
Now that she's been abandoned by her last
Protector, France; now that you are about
To give your hand to a delighted prince;
Now that there's hope of seeing soon
A newly founded family of English kings again?
Why kill her when she is already dead?
Contempt kills most effectively. Watch out
Lest she be resurrected by compassion.
My counsel therefore is to leave the sentence,

By which she is condemned to die, in full effect,
To let her live—but live beneath
The executioner's upraised ax, and let it drop
If one man lifts his sword for her.

ELIZABETH (*rises*). I've heard your views, my Lords.
I am most grateful for your zeal.
Now, with the aid of God, who lights the way of kings,
I shall examine your opinions
And choose what I believe is best.

SCENE 4. *The same. Paulet and Mortimer enter.*

ELIZABETH. Here comes Amias Paulet. Sir Amias,
What news have you for us?

PAULET. Most gracious Majesty! My nephew,
But recently returned from far-flung travels,
Has come to kneel and pay you homage.
May he find favor in your eyes
And may the sun of your affection warm him.

MORTIMER (*kneels before the Queen*).
Long live my gracious Queen.
May happiness and glory crown her head.

ELIZABETH. Arise. I welcome you to England, sir.
Your travels, I am told, took you to France,
You were in Rheims and stayed in Rome.
Tell me what plots our enemies are hatching.

MORTIMER. May God confound them and reverse
Against the archers' breasts the arrows' flight
They aim at you, my gracious Queen.

ELIZABETH. Did you see Morgan and that spinner of intrigues,
The Archbishop of Rosse?

MORTIMER. I came to know all Scottish exiles who at Rheims
Forge their conspiracies against this isle.
I wormed my way into their confidence
In order to discover their intrigues.

PAULET. They even trusted him with secret letters,
Addressed in code to Mary, Queen of Scots,
Which loyally he handed us.

ELIZABETH. What are their latest schemes?

MORTIMER. The news that France abandons them,
Allies herself with England, hit them like a thunderbolt.

They now set all their hopes in Spain.

ELIZABETH. That is what Walsingham reports to me.

MORTIMER. The Papal Bull, which recently Pope Sixtus flung
Against you from the Vatican, arrived
As I was leaving Rheims. It will be brought
To England by the ship from France.

LEICESTER. Such weapons do not frighten England any more.

BURLEIGH. Used by fanatics, they are terrible.

ELIZABETH (*looking searchingly at* MORTIMER).
Some have accused you of attending schools
At Rheims and of abjuring your religion.

MORTIMER. I don't deny it, but it was pretense.
My eagerness to serve you went so far.

ELIZABETH (*to* PAULET, *who holds a paper out to her*).
What is that paper?

PAULET. It is a letter from the Queen of Scots.

BURLEIGH (*quickly reaching for it*). Give it to me.

PAULET (*handing it to the Queen*).
I beg your pardon, Lord High Treasurer,
She asked me to remit it to the Queen.
Although she thinks that I'm her enemy,
I only hate her vice; what I can reconcile
With my responsibilities, I'll do for her.

(*The Queen has taken the letter. While she reads it,* MOR-
TIMER *and* LEICESTER *secretly exchange a few words.*)

BURLEIGH (*to* PAULET). What can it be but meaningless
    complaints
Which we should not impose upon the Queen's kind heart.

PAULET. She did not hide from me what it contains.
She asks a favor—she desires to see the Queen.

BURLEIGH (*quickly*). Never.

SHREWSBURY. Why not? That would not be improper.

BURLEIGH. She's forfeited the right to see the Queen.
She thirsts for blood, has instigated murder!
A loyal servant of the Queen
Would never give such treacherous advice.

SHREWSBURY. But if the Queen desires to grant that favor,
Would you attempt to check that gentle impulse?

BURLEIGH. She is condemned, her head is on the block.
It is not fitting for a queen's exalted eyes

To look upon a woman doomed to die.
Once she's admitted to the presence of the Queen,
The sentence never can be carried out.
The royal presence means a royal pardon.

ELIZABETH (*has finished reading the letter and is drying her tears*).

Oh, what is Man? And what is worldly happiness?
To what point has this Queen been brought,
Who started out with such high hopes,
Whom destiny put on the oldest throne
In Christendom, who in her dreams already saw
A triple crown upon her head!
How different the language she speaks now from that
She used when she adopted England's coat of arms
And had her courtiers flatter her
As Queen of both Britannic isles!
Excuse me, gentlemen, it rends my heart,
My soul is bleeding, sadness seizes me,
As I perceive the instability
Of all that's human, and how close
The frightful fate of humans passed by me.

SHREWSBURY. God touched your heart, your Majesty.
Obey this heavenly command. Her guilt
Is terrible, but she has paid a fearful price.
The time has come to end her trials.
Descend into her dungeon's gloomy tomb,
The radiant apparition of an angel,
Reach out to lift the deeply fallen woman—

BURLEIGH. Be steadfast, Majesty. Do not let sentiment,
However praiseworthy, misguide your action.
Do not deprive yourself of your prerogative
To do what surely will be necessary.
You cannot save, you cannot pardon her.
Do not invite the odious reproach
That you, in cruel mocking triumph,
Had gloated at your victim's agony.

LEICESTER. My Lords, let us not go beyond our competence.
The Queen is wise and has no need of us
In choosing what her dignity requires of her.
A private audience in no way would affect
The course of justice. Mary was condemned
By English law, not by the Queen's decree.
It would be worthy of her noble soul

For Queen Elizabeth to heed
The dictate of her gentle heart,
If she does not obstruct the law's severity.

ELIZABETH. Leave us, my Lords. We shall find ways to do
What mercy and necessity impose on us.

(*The Lords leave. As* MORTIMER *reaches the door, the Queen
calls him back.*)

Sir Mortimer, a word with you.

SCENE 5. *Elizabeth and Mortimer.*

ELIZABETH (*after gazing at* MORTIMER *for a few moments*).
You have great courage and possess
A rare degree of self-control for one so young.
One who has mastered the demanding art
Of subterfuge so early, has reached manhood
Before his time and shortens his apprenticeship.
Your destiny calls you along the path of greatness.
It's fortunate for you that I, your oracle,
Can also make my prophecy come true.

MORTIMER. My gracious Queen, my person and abilities
Will be devoted to your service.

ELIZABETH. You've come to know the enemies of England.
You know how unrelentingly they hate her Queen,
Their inexhaustible supply of bloody schemes.
To this day, God Almighty has protected me,
But never will the crown upon my head be firm
As long as she still lives who is their hope,
And serves as pretext for their zeal.

MORTIMER. Command it, and she dies.

ELIZABETH. I thought that I had reached my goal,
But now, alas, I am no further than I was
In the beginning. Yes, I meant to leave
The matter to the law and not to soil my hands.
The law has acted now—what have I gained?
The sentence must be carried out,
And it is I who must command that it be done.
The hateful deed will come upon *my* head,
I must acknowledge it, I cannot veil it.
That is the worst.

MORTIMER.   Why be concerned about the light

In which an honest cause appears?

ELIZABETH. You do not know the world, Sir Mortimer.
What one appears to be is judged by all,
But no one judges what one is.
No one will be persuaded of my right,
And I must therefore seek to leave
The part I played in Mary's death in doubt.
When deeds have such ambiguous complexion,
Our only safeguard is obscurity.
The fateful step is that which one admits.
What one does not reveal, one has not lost.

MORTIMER. It would perhaps be best then—

ELIZABETH.   Certainly
That would be best. Oh, my good angel speaks
Through you. Continue, sir, go on,
You are a serious man, you think things through,
You're very different from your uncle—

MORTIMER (taken aback). Did you uncover your desire to him?

ELIZABETH. I did, I now regret it.

MORTIMER.   He is old.
Forgive him, for his years make him too cautious.
A daring deed needs youthful recklessness.

ELIZABETH (quickly). May I—

MORTIMER.   I lend my hand to you, but you
Must judge how you can save your reputation.

ELIZABETH. Ah, if one morning you would wake me with the
     news:
Your hated enemy, the Queen of Scots,
Expired last night!

MORTIMER. You may rely on me.

ELIZABETH. When will my head rest peacefully at night?

MORTIMER. The next new moon will end your fears.

ELIZABETH. Farewell, Sir Mortimer. Do not feel grieved
That my great gratitude will have to wear
The cloak of night—but silence is the god
Of happiness. The strongest and most tender bonds
Are tied by secrets held in common.   (She leaves.)

SCENE 6. *Mortimer alone.*

MORTIMER. Go, queen of treachery and falsehood!
As you deceive the world, so you will be deceived.
Betraying you, indeed, is right, a noble deed.
Do I look like a murderer? Did you
See in my eyes the baseness of a villain?
Yes, trust my arm—hold back your own.
Yes, show the world your pious, lying face of mercy,
While secretly you count on me to murder her.
Ah, that will give us time to rescue her.
You want to elevate me, show me in the distance,
Allusively, a far more precious prize?
Are you that prize, your favors and your love?
Poor woman, what have you to offer me?
Vainglorious fame and honors do not tempt me.
She is the only one who makes my life worth living.
The gods of grace and youthful eagerness
Perform around her their eternal dance of joy,
At her breast—heaven's happiness.
Your gifts are dead. The greatest prize,
The shining ornament of life,
A heart that gives itself in sweet forgetfulness,
Enchanted and enchanting, to a kindred heart,
That crown of womanhood you never have possessed,
No man has ever been exalted by your love—
I must wait for the Earl, give him her letter.
A hateful errand. I don't trust this courtier.
No one but I can save her. Mine shall be
The danger and the fame, and mine shall be the prize.
  (*As he turns to leave,* PAULET *enters.*)

SCENE 7. *Mortimer and Paulet.*

PAULET. What did the Queen desire of you?

MORTIMER. Oh, nothing, sir.

PAULET (*regarding him sternly*). The ground on which you
    now
Are venturing is slippery, my nephew.
The favors princes have to offer may well tempt
A youth, for youth loves honors. You, I hope,

Will not allow ambition to divert your step.

MORTIMER. You brought me here.

PAULET.   I wish that I had not.
The court is not the ground on which our family
Collected honors. Nephew, stand your ground!
Don't pay too high a price, don't go against
Your conscience.

MORTIMER.   Why? What notions!

PAULET. Mistrust her flattery, no matter what
She promises. She will not hesitate
To disavow you if you do as she commands,
And to avenge the bloody deed she hatched herself,
So that her name may not be stained.

MORTIMER. The bloody deed? What do you mean?

PAULET. No more pretense. I know exactly what the Queen
Has planned and asked of you. She hopes that you,
Young, eager and ambitious, will be more
Inclined to lend a willing ear—and hand—
Than I, an obstinate old man. Did you say yes?

MORTIMER. But Uncle!

PAULET. If you agreed, I curse and I disown you . . . I—
(LEICESTER enters.)

LEICESTER. Distinguished knight, permit me to exchange
A word with this young man. The Queen, it seems,
Has graciously received him and desires
That he from now on be entrusted with
The full responsibility of guarding Mary Stuart,
She trusts his honesty—

PAULET.   His honesty—I see.

LEICESTER. I beg your pardon?

PAULET. The Queen trusts him, I said, my Lord, and I
Rely upon myself and on my open eyes.   (He leaves.)

SCENE 8. *Leicester and Mortimer.*

LEICESTER (*perplexed*). Is something wrong with Sir Amias?

MORTIMER.   I don't know.
Perhaps this unexpected confidence . . .

LEICESTER (*giving him a searching look*).
I wonder . . . Do you merit confidence?

MORTIMER (*in the same manner*).
That very question I ask you, my Lord.

LEICESTER. You wished to speak with me in private.

MORTIMER. Give me assurance that I safely may.

LEICESTER. What proof have I that I can safely talk to you?
Don't take offense at my apparent lack
Of confidence. You show two faces here
At court. One must be false—but which?

MORTIMER. I'm in the same predicament, my Lord.

LEICESTER. Who then will be the first to drop his guard?

MORTIMER. The one who has the least to lose.

LEICESTER. Well, that is you, of course.

MORTIMER. Oh no. That's you. One word from you, my Lord,
Armed with your influence and power, easily
Could be my end. But nothing I could say
Would count against your rank and royal favor.

LEICESTER. You are mistaken. I am powerful
In every way, but in that tender point
Which I am to lay open to your view.
I'm weak, the weakest man at court.
The meanest witness could destroy me.

MORTIMER. When the all-powerful Lord Leicester stoops
To make me such a confidence, I may
Be justified in thinking higher of myself.
Then I will set a generous example.

LEICESTER. Precede me on the road of confidence,
And I shall follow.

MORTIMER (*quickly produces the letter*).
The Queen of Scotland sends you this.

LEICESTER (*terrified, quickly grabs the letter*).
Speak softly, sir. What is it? Ah, her picture!
(*He kisses it and stares at it in silent enchantment.*)

MORTIMER (*has watched him attentively while he was reading
the letter*).
My Lord, I trust you now.

LEICESTER (*has quickly run through the letter*).
Do you know what this letter is about?

MORTIMER. No, I do not.

LEICESTER.   She must have told you, surely—

MORTIMER. She told me nothing. You, she said, would clear

The mystery. To me it is a mystery how you,
The favorite of Elizabeth and Mary's enemy,
One of her judges, could yet be the man
On whom she counts to rescue her. And still,
It must be so. Your eyes betray
Too clearly what you feel for her.

LEICESTER. Before I speak, explain to me why you
Take such a fervent interest in her.
What made her put her trust in you?

MORTIMER. My Lord, that's easily explained. I changed
My faith in Rome, I'm now in league
With Cardinal de Guise, the Archbishop
Of Rheims gave me a letter to the Queen.

LEICESTER. I heard of your conversion. That awoke
My confidence in you. Give me your hand!
Forgive me for my hesitation,
But I can't be too cautious. Walsingham
And Burleigh hate me, lay in wait for me;
You might have been their creature and the bait
That was to lure me to their net.

MORTIMER. How carefully the great at court must step!
I sympathize with you, my Lord.

LEICESTER. What joy that I can now embrace a trusted friend
And throw aside the strictures which I bore so long.
You are surprised, you say, to find
My feelings toward Mary changed.
The truth is that I never hated her.
By force of circumstance alone I joined
The ranks of her oppressors. As you know,
She had been promised me before she married Darnley,
When she still stood amid the smiles of grandeur.
Unmoved, I pushed my happiness away,
But now that she's a prisoner and at the gates
Of death—I seek her out and risk my life.

MORTIMER. That's generous, indeed, my Lord.

LEICESTER. Things have a different aspect now, Sir Mortimer.
Ambition, then, made me insensitive
To youth and beauty; Mary's hand, I thought,
Was far too small a prize for me, I hoped
To win the Queen of England!

MORTIMER.   Yes, the world well knew
That she preferred you to all other men.

LEICESTER. Yes, so it seemed, but now—now that ten years
Have passed in unrelenting wooing
And hateful obligations—now my heart is overfilled.
I must give vent to my resentment, long concealed.
They call me fortunate. If they but knew
That what they envy are my chains!
For ten long, bitter years I made my sacrifices
Before the idol of her vanity,
Endured the despotism of her changing moods
With slavish meekness, a toy of her capricious whims,
One minute coddled by her tenderness,
The next repulsed by prudish pride,
Tormented equally by kindness and disdain,
Watched like a prisoner with sharp-eyed jealousy,
Called to account like any little boy
And scolded like a servant—oh, there are
No words to paint that hell!

    MORTIMER.   I pity you, my Lord.

    LEICESTER. And now, so near the goal, the prize eludes my
        grasp.
Now someone else arrives to cheat me of the fruit
Of all my pains. I lose my long-held rights
To this young man, the husband of her choice.
I am to leave the stage on which I played
So long the hero, I risk losing her,
And not alone her hand, her favor, too.
She is a woman—he a charming man.

    MORTIMER. He is the son of Catherine. There is
No better school to learn the art of flattery.

    LEICESTER. Thus all my hopes are ruined, and my eyes
Search the horizon for a plank that might
Yet save me from the shipwreck of my fortunes and—
Return to her, my first and fairest hope.
Her image stood before me suddenly,
Her radiant charm, her beauty and her youth
I saw anew—and in their proper light.
Not cold ambition but the heart compared,
And now I knew that I had lost a pearl.
With horror I perceived her plunged
Into the deepest misery—and through my fault.
My hopes aroused, I thought that there might still
Be time to rescue her, to make her yet my own.
Helped by a loyal friend I reached her ear,

Revealed my change of heart to her.
This letter which you brought from her
Gives me assurance that she pardons me,
That she will give herself to me as prize—
If I will rescue her.

MORTIMER.   But you've done nothing!
Without a word, you let them sentence her,
You even voted for her death.
It took a miracle. The light of truth
First had to fall upon her keeper's nephew,
And far away, in Rome, God's providence
Had to prepare an unexpected ally,
Before she even found her way to you.

LEICESTER. The thought of it has been a constant torment.
Just then, she was removed from Talbot's care,
Transferred to Fotheringhay, and there
Confided to your uncle's watchful guard.
All roads were blocked, and I had to continue
To play before the world the role of persecutor.
But do not think that I would let her die
A painful death. I hoped, and I still hope
To stave off that extremity, to gain
The time and find the means to rescue her.

MORTIMER. You have the means! Your noble confidence, my
          Lord,
Deserves to be returned. I want to free the Queen,
That's why I'm here. The preparations have been made.
Your powerful support assures success.

LEICESTER. What's that? You frighten me. You mean—

MORTIMER. I want to force her prison. I have friends,
All is in readiness—

LEICESTER. You have accomplices and confidants?
God help me! Don't make me a partner to your recklessness.
Do all your friends know of *my* secret, too?

MORTIMER. Don't be alarmed. Our plans were laid without
Your help, and so they would be carried out,
If she did not insist that you deliver her.

LEICESTER. Can you assure me that my name
Has not been mentioned in your league?

MORTIMER. Yes, rest assured. But why so cautious now,
My Lord, that you find help? You said you mean
To save and to possess the Queen, but now,

The moment you discover unexpected friends,
The moment that the means to do so drop
Into your lap from heaven, you appear
Embarrassed more than overjoyed.

LEICESTER. It can't be done by force. That is too risky.

MORTIMER. So is delay.

LEICESTER. I tell you, sir, it is too dangerous.

MORTIMER. For you who wish to possess the Queen!
We only want to save her—but are not so timid.

LEICESTER. You are too rash, young man, in such a dangerous
And difficult affair.

MORTIMER. You are too hesitant in matters of your honor.

LEICESTER. I see the traps which are around us on all sides.

MORTIMER. I feel the courage to demolish them.

LEICESTER. Your courage—it's audacity, it's madness.

MORTIMER. Your prudence—is that courage, sir?

LEICESTER. Are you so keen to end like Babington?

MORTIMER. You don't seem keen to rival Norfolk's generosity.

LEICESTER. Norfolk did not bring home his bride.

MORTIMER. He proved that he deserved her, though.

LEICESTER. If we should fail, we'll pull her down with us.

MORTIMER. If we are squeamish, she will not be saved.

LEICESTER. You do not think, you do not listen,
Impetuous and blind, you will destroy
What had been well along its hopeful way.

MORTIMER. Along a way which you had smoothed?
Have you done anything to rescue her?
Suppose I had been knave enough to murder her,
As I have been commanded by the Queen—
And as she even now expects of me—
Tell me, what have you done to guard her life?

LEICESTER. The Queen gave that command to you?

MORTIMER. Elizabeth misjudged me just as Mary
Misjudged the Earl of Leicester.

LEICESTER. But you agreed to carry out her order?

MORTIMER. In order to be sure she would not buy
Another pair of hands, I offered mine.

LEICESTER. Well done! That gives us elbow room. While she
Relies on you to render her this bloody service,

The sentence can't be carried out—and we gain time.

MORTIMER (*impatiently*). No, we will squander precious time.

LEICESTER. She counts on you. She therefore will not hesitate
To show the world how merciful she is.
Perhaps, with cunning, I'll persuade her
To meet her adversary face to face,
And that would tie her hands. Burleigh is right.
Once she has seen her, she can never have
The sentence carried out. Yes, I shall try with all—

MORTIMER. What good is that? When she finds out that I
Deceived her and that Mary does not die,
Is then not everything exactly as it was?
She'll never free her. Life imprisonment
Would be the mildest fate for Mary.
If thus you must act boldly in the end,
Why not begin by being bold?
You hold the power in your hands, you could
Easily raise by arming the nobility
Who live upon your property and castles!
Mary has many secret friends, yes—even now.
There are still many heroes left among
The Percys and the Howards, though the heads
Of all these noble families have tumbled.
They only wait that one of England's great
May set them an example. Yes, act openly!
Enough pretense! Guard your beloved like a knight,
Do battle, fight for her the noble fight!
You can be master of the Queen of England's person
At any time you choose. Entice her then
Where she has often followed you, to one of your castles.
Show her that you are man enough to talk
To her as master, hold her there—
Till she sets Mary free.

LEICESTER. I am aghast, you frighten me. How far
Will your insanity yet carry you?
Do you know where you are? And do you know
What things are like at court, how men
Are suffocated by this woman's regimen?
Go on, look for the heroism here,
The spirit that one used to find in England!
All is servility, and everyone
Now clings to apron strings. The springs
Of courage are unwound. Let me direct your steps.

Consider well the risks. Someone is coming! Go!

    MORTIMER. Mary still hopes. Must I return with empty sympathy?

    LEICESTER. Bring her the vows of my eternal love.

    MORTIMER. Take them yourself to her. I offered help
In saving her, not as a messenger of love.   *(He leaves.)*

SCENE 9. *Elizabeth and Leicester.*

    ELIZABETH. Who was that? Someone left, I heard you talking.

    LEICESTER *(startled, quickly turns around).*
That was Sir Mortimer.

    ELIZABETH. Is something wrong? You seem perturbed, my Lord.

    LEICESTER *(takes hold of himself).*
To see you thus before me—yes, indeed,
I never saw you looking so enchanting.
I'm blinded by your beauty. Ah, my God!

    ELIZABETH. Why do you sigh?

    LEICESTER. Do I not have sufficient reason? As my eyes
Behold your charm, the nameless pain
Of my impending loss renews itself.

    ELIZABETH. What will you lose?

    LEICESTER.   Your heart, your lovely self.
The youthful arms of your impassioned husband
Will soon bring happiness to you,
And he will own your undivided heart.
He is of royal blood, that I am not.
But no man on this earth adores you more
Than I. The Duc d'Anjou has never seen you yet,
He only loves your image and your fame—
But I love you. If you were but the poorest shepherdess
And I born to the highest throne on earth,
I would descend to where you are
And lay my crown in homage at your feet.

    ELIZABETH. Commiserate with me instead of scolding me.
I may not ask my heart. It would choose otherwise.
Oh, how I envy other women
Who are allowed to choose the man they love.
I'm not so fortunate as to have the right
To put the crown on that man's head who is

Most dear to me. The Stuart had that privilege.
She gave her hand to whom she gave her heart,
Took every liberty and drained
The well-filled cup of pleasure.

LEICESTER. She now drinks from the cup of sorrow.

ELIZABETH. For her, the world's opinion was of no account.
She chose the easy life and never bore
The yoke which I took on my shoulders.
I could have made the same demands, to taste
And to enjoy my life and earthly pleasure.
But I preferred the burden of my royal duties.
Yet she became the favorite of men,
Was courted by both young and old because—
Her one ambition was to be a woman.
Yes, such are men. Voluptuous adulterers!
In their pursuit of frivolous and passing joys,
They do not value what they should revere.
Why, did not even Talbot seem rejuvenated
When he began to talk about her charms?

LEICESTER. You must forgive him. He was once her keeper,
The wily woman caught him with her flatteries.

ELIZABETH. But is it true? Is she so beautiful?
I've had to listen to them rave about that face
So often that I'm curious how much of it is true.
Paintings can flatter and descriptions lie,
I only trust my eyes. Why do you look
At me with such a strange expression?

LEICESTER. I put you next to Mary in my thoughts.
I must confess I would enjoy, provided that
It could be done in secret, to confront
You with her. Only then would you at last
Enjoy the fullest flavor of your victory.
That shame I wish her, that with her own eyes—
And envy has sharp eyes—she could convince
Herself that you are her superior
In dignity and stature just as much
As in all other virtues of a queen.

ELIZABETH. In years she is much younger than I am.

LEICESTER. In years! To look at her, one could not tell.
Of course, she's suffered much, and that
May well have made her age before her time.
It would be still more vexing for the lady,
If she saw you as bride. Those lovely hopes

Of life to come lie far behind her now,
And she would see you walking toward happiness,
What's more, about to wed the Prince of France.
For her who always made so much and was so proud
Of her French marriage, and who even now
Insists that mighty France will rescue her,
That would indeed be bitter.

ELIZABETH (*offhand*). I'm being pressed to grant an interview.

LEICESTER. What she requests as favor, grant as punishment.
The scaffold would not pain her more
Than being overshadowed by your beauty.
That is the way to murder her, as once
She meant to murder you. For when she sees
Your beauty, guarded by your honor and enhanced
By an untarnished reputation—
Her own thrown carelessly and shamelessly away—
Exalted by the splendor of your crown,
Embellished now by tender hopes of marriage,
The hour of death has struck for her.
Yes, when I look upon you now,
You never have been better armed for victory
By beauty. When you entered here, a while ago,
I felt myself bathed in blinding rays
From an ethereal luminescence.
If you faced her this moment, as you are,
You would not live to see a finer hour.

ELIZABETH. Now? No—not now—no, Leicester—no.
I have to give it thought, and talk to Burleigh—

LEICESTER (*interrupting*). To Burleigh! He can think of
nothing but
The welfare of the country. But your womanhood
Also has rights, a subtle point
Which you have to decide and not a statesman.
Yet statecraft, too, demands that you should see her,
That by your generosity you win the public mind.
Deal later with your enemy, as you see fit.

ELIZABETH. I could not, properly and decently,
Confront a relative in want and shame.
I'm told that her surroundings are not regal.
To see her in distress, I would feel as reproach.

LEICESTER. You need not cross her threshold. Hear my counsel.
It happens that today the hunt takes place,

The way will lead past Fotheringhay, and there
She could be walking in the park,
When you, as if by chance, come by. Of course,
It must not seem deliberate, and if
You do not wish you need not even speak to her.

ELIZABETH. If this is foolishness, the foolishness
Is yours, not mine. Today I cannot look askance
At anything you might desire, Lord Leicester,
Because today I hurt you more than anyone.

(*With a tender glance at him.*)

Even if this is just a whim of yours,
Affection shows itself by being pleased
To grant a thing—yes, even though it may be wrong.

(LEICESTER *throws himself at her feet.*)

ACT III

*The Park of Fotheringhay, many trees in the foreground, a
wide view in the background.*

SCENE 1. *Mary, running, comes from behind a group of
trees. Hannah follows her slowly.*

HANNAH. You're running as if wings assisted you,
I cannot follow you so fast. Please wait.

MARY.

> Let me delight in my precious new freedom,
> Let me again be a child and rejoice
> Testing the hurrying, light-footed step
> On the green meadows' resilient carpet.
> Have I escaped the gloom of my prison?
> Am I released from my sorrowful tomb?
> Let me then drink in long, thirsty draughts
> Freedom's heady, heavenly air.

HANNAH. Oh my dear Lady, your old prison
Has only been enlarged, its walls are still

Around us, even though the trees and shrubs
May for the moment shield them from our view.

MARY. Oh, thank you, thank you, friendly trees,
Your kind green arms blot out my prison walls.
I want to dream that I am free and happy,
Why, Hannah, wake me from my sweet illusion?
I am surrounded by the vast, blue sky,
Free and unfettered my eye sweeps
Across the limitless expanse.
There where you see the clouds' grey mountains rise,
There is the boundary of my domain, my glance
Accompanies the clouds where southward lies
The goal they search beyond the ocean, France!

> Hurrying clouds, ships of the sky!
> That I could sail with you, that I could fly!
> Take my love to the land of my youth.
> I am a prisoner, I am in chains,
> You be the messengers of my pains.
> Freely you course in the infinite air,
> No one your master, no queen your despair.

HANNAH. Oh dearest Lady, you're beside yourself,
The air of freedom, missed so long, makes you extravagant.

MARY.

> There is a fisherman tying his boat!
> Frail as it is, it could be a tool,
> To take me to lands under more friendly rule.
> Scarce is the food that he catches afloat.
> I would load up his boat with the richest of treasure,
> Such fish he hauled never, try as he may,
> In his nets he would find good luck without measure,
> If his rescuing bark would take me away.

HANNAH. A forlorn hope! Do you not see the spies
Who in the distance follow us?
A dismal, cruel order chases
All sympathetic creatures from our path.

MARY. No, Hannah. No, believe me, not in vain
Have they thrown open now my prison doors.
This little favor must announce
Still greater happiness. I can't be wrong.
I see a loving hand at work,
The Earl of Leicester's mighty arm.
Yes, bit by bit they will expand the walls,
Preparing me with small for greater things

Until at last I stand before the man
Who will release me from my chains forever.

HANNAH. I see no rhyme or reason in all this:
It was but yesterday that they announced
That you must die, and now, today, this privilege.
I've also heard it said that those
May benefit from slight concessions
Whom their eternal liberty awaits.

MARY.

> Listen! The hunting horn! Did you hear
> Its mighty call across meadow and forest?
> Oh, how I wish I could mount my brave steed
> To be part of the chase!
> Again it sounds! How well I know its voice,
> Full of memories, painful and sweet!
> Often it filled my ear with delight
> On the hilly heath of the highlands,
> When the boisterous hunters approached.

SCENE 2. *Mary and Hannah. Paulet enters.*

PAULET. My Lady, have I pleased you now, at last?
Do I, for once, deserve your gratitude?

MARY. You, sir? Did you obtain this favor for me? You?

PAULET. And why not I? I gave the Queen your letter—

MARY. You did? The freedom which I now enjoy
Is the result of what I wrote the Queen?

PAULET (*significantly*). And not the only one. Prepare yourself
For even greater favors.

MARY. For greater favors, sir? What do you mean?

PAULET. You must have heard the hunting horn.

MARY (*shrinking back with a sudden suspicion*).
You frighten me.

PAULET. The Queen is hunting in this neighborhood—

MARY. The Queen—

PAULET.   —and any moment she may stand before you.

HANNAH (*hurries to MARY who, trembling, seems about to faint*).
What is it, my dear Lady? You look pale.

PAULET. Again displeased? Is this not what you asked?

The favor has been granted sooner than you thought.
You've always had a lively tongue—now use it well.
Now is the time to speak.

MARY.　　　　　Why have I not been warned?
I'm not prepared for it, I am not ready now.
What I requested as the greatest favor,
Terrifies me now—it makes me shudder.
Dear Hannah, take me to my rooms, I must
Collect myself.

PAULET.　　Stay here. This is
Where you must wait for her. I'm not surprised
That you are terrified to stand before your judge.

SCENE 3. *The same. The Earl of Shrewsbury enters.*

MARY. That's not the reason. I feel strange—
Ah, noble Shrewsbury, you come as my
Good angel, sent from heaven—no, my Lord,
I cannot see her now, I cannot bear
To see the hated woman, save me, please!

SHREWSBURY. Compose yourself. This is the fateful hour.
Now you must be courageous.

MARY.　　　　　How I've waited!
For years I have prepared myself, repeated to myself
What I would say, engraved it in my memory,
So I would surely move her. Now, at last,
The moment has arrived and now—I have forgotten.
Now I feel nothing but my burning sense
Of suffering, my heart is turned against her,
In raging hatred, all kind thoughts have fled,
Appalling shapes from hell, shaking their Gorgon's heads,
Surround me on all sides.

SHREWSBURY. Restrain your boiling blood, my Lady; conquer
The bitterness that fills your heart. No good
Can come of hatred meeting hatred in
This interview. Although you may rebel,
You must obey this moment's special law.
Humble yourself—she has the power.

MARY. To her? I can't!

SHREWSBURY.　　　You must. Speak calmly to the Queen,
Respectfully, address her generosity,

And don't stand on your rights—not now.

MARY. Ah, what I prayed for now becomes my ruin,
I'm cursed because my pleas were heard.
We should not look upon each other, never,
No good will come of it, not now—not ever.
It is more probable that fire and water
Will lovingly embrace, more likely that
The lamb will kiss the tiger—no, she's wounded me,
She has insulted me too deeply—
We never can be reconciled.

SHREWSBURY. Wait till you see her face to face.
I saw how much your letter touched her heart.
Her eyes were filled with tears, she is not heartless.
Have confidence. That's why I hurried here,
To help you calm yourself and to prepare you.

MARY (*seizes his hands*). Oh, Talbot, you have always been
my friend.
Why did they move me from your gentle prison!
Since then I've met with much adversity.

SHREWSBURY. Don't think of that. Think only that you must
Be humble when you meet the Queen.

MARY. Is Burleigh with her, my dark angel?

SHREWSBURY. No one is with her but the Earl of Leicester.

MARY. Leicester!

SHREWSBURY. You need not be afraid of him.
He's not your enemy. It is his doing
That she agreed to see you here.

MARY. I thought so!

SHREWSBURY. What did you say, my Lady?

PAULET. Here is the Queen.

ELIZABETH (*to* LEICESTER). What is the name of this estate?
(*All step aside, only* MARY *remains where she stands, leaning
on* HANNAH.)

SCENE 4. *The same. Elizabeth, Leicester and Attendants
enter.*

LEICESTER. It's Fotheringhay.

ELIZABETH (*to* SHREWSBURY). Our hunting party is to go
ahead to London.
The people push too closely on the streets.

We seek protection in this peaceful park.

(SHREWSBURY *sends the* ATTENDANTS *away.* ELIZABETH, *although now addressing* PAULET, *keeps her eyes fixed on* MARY.)

My people love me far too much, their joy
Is too extravagant, they idolize me.
That is the way to honor God, but not a mortal queen.

MARY (*has been leaning on* HANNAH *during the foregoing exchange; she was close to fainting; now she straightens up and meets* ELIZABETH's *steady gaze. Trembling she shrinks back, hiding her face at* HANNAH's *shoulder*).

Oh God! A woman with such features has no heart.

ELIZABETH. Who is the lady?
(*General silence.*)

LEICESTER. You are at Fotheringhay, your Majesty.

ELIZABETH (*pretends surprise and glowers at* LEICESTER).
Who dared to bring me here, Lord Leicester?

LEICESTER. Your Majesty, it's happened. Now that heaven
Has guided your steps here, let generosity
And pity govern you.

SHREWSBURY.   Please your Majesty
To look upon this most unfortunate of women,
Who withers at your sight.

(MARY *calms herself, takes a few steps toward* ELIZABETH *but stops again, shuddering. Her gestures express a terrible inner battle.*)

ELIZABETH. Who was it, gentlemen, who told me to expect
A woman deeply bowed? This is a woman full
Of pride, untractable for all her suffering.

MARY. So be it. I'll submit to this supreme
Indignity, I shall renounce my pride,
Forget that I'm a queen and what I suffered.
I'll throw myself upon her mercy—hers
Who pushed me into this disgrace.
(*She turns toward the Queen.*)
The heavens have decided in your favor, sister,
The victor's crown is on your happy brow.
My prayers rise to God who has exalted you.
(*She throws herself on the ground before* ELIZABETH.)
My sister, now you, too, be generous.
Don't let me lie here, shamefully,
Before you in the dust. Extend your hand

To raise me up from my abysmal fall.

ELIZABETH (*taking a step backward*).
You are where you belong, my Lady.
And I praise God and thank Him for His mercy
That He has not seen fit to let me lie
At your feet as you're lying now at mine.

MARY (*with growing passion*).
Do not forget how changeable our human fortunes are.
The gods still live who will avenge false pride.
Respect and fear those terrifying powers
Which brought me to my knees and at your feet,
Before these witnesses, honor in me yourself,
Do not disgrace and vilify the Tudor blood
Which flows in my veins as it does in yours.
Merciful God! Do not stand there before me,
As blunt and inaccessible as cliffs
Are to a drowning swimmer's vainly grasping hands.
All that is mine, my life, my fate, depend
Upon the power of my words and tears.
Relieve my heart so that I can reach yours.
When you regard me with that icy stare,
My heart contracts, my tears dry up,
Cold horror freezes on my tongue my words.

ELIZABETH (*cold and severe*). What do you wish to tell me,
    Lady Stuart?
You wished to speak with me. I will forget
That I am Queen, that you have gravely wronged me,
And I will do my duty as a sister.
I offer you the consolation of my presence.
I yield to impulse and my generosity,
Expose myself to justified reproaches
Of having stooped too low, for—you remember—
You had plans for my assassination.

MARY. How shall I start? How shall I cleverly
Compose my words so they will move but will not hurt you?
Oh God, give power to my words,
Let them be without sting to wound her.
For I cannot defend my cause without
Accusing you, and that I do not want.
You treated me unjustly. I am a queen,
Like you, but you made me your prisoner.
I came to you as supplicant, but you,
Mocking the sacred rules of hospitality

And in defiance of the Law of Nations,
Entombed me in a dungeon, tore my friends
And servants from my side, degraded me,
Exposed me to disgraceful want,
Arraigned me, finally, before an ignominious court—
No more of that! Oblivion may forever cover
The cruelties you made me suffer.
I'm willing to ascribe all that to fate.
You are not guilty, but I too am free of guilt.
An evil spirit rose from its abysmal pit
And threw the firebrand of hate into our hearts,
Divided even when we both were children.
As we grew up, so grew our hatred,
And wicked people fanned its ugly flames,
Fanatic madmen furnished swords and daggers
To arm the hands of willing interlopers—
That is the curse which fate called down on kings
That they, divided, tear the world asunder,
Set loose the storming furies of contention.
No stranger stands between us now,
    (*Confidently she steps closer to* ELIZABETH *and continues in
    endearing tones.*)
Now we stand face to face. Now, sister, speak.
Of what crime am I guilty? I shall answer you.
If you had only listened earlier
When I so urgently prayed for your presence!
It never would have come to this,
We would not have met at this dismal place
For this unfortunate and sad encounter.

   ELIZABETH. Good fortune saved me from the fate
Of nurturing a serpent at my breast.
Not destiny, your own black heart, the wild
Ambition of your family is guilty.
No enmity had been between us when your uncle,
That proud and power-hungry priest
Who reaches with his brazen hand for crowns,
Flung down the gauntlet, beguiled you to adopt
My coat of arms, to claim my royal titles,
And to engage me in a fight of life and death.
Whom did he not incite against me!
The words of priests, the arms of nations,
The dreadful weapon of religious frenzy,
And even here, in my own peaceful realm,
He fanned the flames of insurrection.

But God was on my side, the haughty priest
Did not prevail. My head was threatened—yours will fall.

MARY. My life is in God's hand. You would not dare
To stretch your power over life and death—

ELIZABETH. Who could prevent me? Why should I
Not follow the example which your uncle set?
He showed the monarchs of the world
The way to pacify one's enemies.
I'll take the night of St. Bartholomew as guide.
You speak of blood relationship,
The Law of Nations—what are they to me?
The Church cuts all the bonds of duty,
It sanctifies disloyalty and regicide.
I only do what your priests preach.
What warrant would you offer me to vouch for you,
If I were generous enough to set you free?
St. Peter's key fits any lock
That I might use to guard your loyalty.
My safety lies in force alone,
One cannot make a pact with vipers.

MARY. Oh, now your bitter, dark suspicion speaks again.
You always have considered me an enemy
And stranger. Yet, had you but named me your successor,
As was my right, my love and gratitude
Then would have made of me a loyal friend, your sister.

ELIZABETH. Abroad you have your friends, my Lady.
Your home—the Vatican; your brothers—monks.
Name you successor! You! What cunning trickery!
Let you, a sly Armida, while I'm still alive,
Seduce my people and ensnare
The noble youth of England cleverly
Into the net of your adultery,
Wait till your rising sun attracts all eyes, while I—

MARY. Ah, reign in peace! I gladly will renounce
All claims that I have ever made upon your throne.
The wings on which my spirit used to soar
Are limp now, greatness tempts no more.
You have succeeded—only Mary's shadow lives,
Her courage shattered by the endless shame of prison.
You've done your worst, you have destroyed me in my bloom.
Now, sister, make an end of it! Now say
The word which you have come to let me hear,
For I cannot believe you came to taste

Your power, cruelly to mock your victim.
Say: "Mary, you are free. I've taught you to respect
My strength, now learn that I am generous."
Say that, and gladly I'll receive
My life and freedom from your hand.
One word, and all the past will be undone.
I'm waiting—do not make me wait too long.
If you don't speak those words, then woe betide you!
Unless you part from me as a magnificent
And bounteous goddess, then—oh, sister—then
Not for the prize of this whole wealthy island,
Not for the crown of all the kingdoms of this earth,
Would I want to face you as you then would face me.

ELIZABETH. Do you admit at last that you're defeated?
Is this the end of your intrigues?
Are no more murderers abroad? Have all
Adventurers renounced their vain intent to risk
Their sorry chivalry for you?
Yes, it is finished, Lady Stuart.
No more seductions now. The world
Has other things to think about.
Not one man lusts to be the fourth,
For you're as deadly to your suitors as to husbands.

MARY (*flares up*). Sister, sister! God, grant me restraint!

ELIZABETH (*looks at her with haughty disdain*).
So these are the bewitching charms, Lord Leicester,
Which no man can behold unscathed.
This is the woman next to whom
No other woman dares to show herself.
Indeed! That fame was won at no great cost,
To be acclaimed as an uncommon beauty is not hard
If one becomes a beauty common to all men.

MARY. This is too much!

ELIZABETH (*with a derisive laugh*).
There—that is your true face; till now
You've only shown a mask.

MARY (*flushed with rage, but with dignity*).
I made mistakes, but they were human errors,
And I was young, my power tempted me.
I did not hide them, I disdained to cover them
With false appearances, I was a forthright queen.
The world has known the worst about me, and—
I think that I am better than my fame.

Beware if once the cloak of rectitude
That hides the secret of your burning appetites
Is torn away. It's not respectability
That from your mother you inherited.
We know what virtues brought Anne Boleyn to the scaffold.

SHREWSBURY (*steps between the Queens*).
Merciful God! Why did it have to come to this?
Is this your moderation, your humility?

MARY. Humility! I have submitted to as much
As anyone can bear. This is enough!
The placid lamb is dead, long-suffering patience dead!
My anger breaks its chains at last,
Emerges growling from its cave and speaks.
And you who gave the basilisk the eye that kills,
Give me a poisoned arrow that my tongue can shoot—

SHREWSBURY. She is beside herself. Forgive the raving woman.
(ELIZABETH *is speechless with rage and looks at* MARY *with a
furious expression.*)

LEICESTER (*greatly upset, tries to lead* ELIZABETH *away*).
Don't listen to her madness, come away
From this ill-favored place.

MARY. A bastard desecrates the throne of England
And dupes its noble people
With cunning trickery.
If justice reigned the world, it would be you
Who crawled before me in the dust.
For I'm your Queen.
(ELIZABETH *hurries off; her gentlemen follow her in utter
consternation.*)

SCENE 5. *Mary and Hannah.*

HANNAH. What have you done! You have infuriated her.
Now everything is lost, all hope is gone.

MARY (*still in great agitation*).
Enraged she leaves, and death is in her heart.
(*She embraces* HANNAH.)
How well I feel! At last, at last! The years
Of suffering and humiliation are avenged,
This moment of my triumph wipes them out.
The weight of mountains lifted from my heart
When deep into her breast I plunged the knife.

HANNAH. Your madness carried you away to wound

Your mortal enemy. She is the Queen,
Hers is the thunder, and you derided her
Before her lover.

MARY. I humbled her before the eyes of Leicester,
He saw it, he was witness to my victory.
As I struck out to tumble her from her pedestal,
He stood and looked, his presence gave me strength.

SCENE 6. *The same. Mortimer.*

HANNAH. Sir Mortimer, now everything—
MORTIMER.   I heard it all.
(*He signals to* HANNAH *to go back to her look-out post and
steps closer to* MARY. *His behavior and expression betray his
violent emotions.*)
You conquered her. You stamped her down into the dust.
You were the Queen, and she the criminal.
Your courage thrills me, I adore you as you stand
Before me now, a great and radiant goddess.

MARY. You talked to Leicester, handed him
My letter and my present? Tell me, please.

MORTIMER (*looking at her ardently*).
Your noble wrath was like an aureole
Around you, it transfigured you. No woman is
More beautiful than you in all the world.

MARY. Oh please, sir. I'm impatient to discover—
What did he say, what can I hope from him?

MORTIMER. Who? He? That miserable coward!
Hope nothing of him—ah, despise, forget him.

MARY. What are you saying?

MORTIMER. He save you and possess you? Let him dare!
He first would have to fight me for the privilege.

MARY. Then you did not give him my letter? Oh, I'm lost.

MORTIMER. The coward loves his life too much. A man
Who wants to save you and to call you his
Must be prepared to welcome death, too, with
A warm embrace.

MARY. He will do nothing for me?

MORTIMER.   Ah, enough of him.
What can he do? What do you want of him?
I'll rescue you myself.

MARY.   What can you do?

MORTIMER. Do not deceive yourself. Today
Is different from yesterday. Her mood
When she left you, the turn your conversation took,
Rules out a pardon. From the Queen no help will come.
Now is the time for action, boldness will
Decide, the stakes are high and high the gain.
You shall be free before the morning dawns.

MARY. What's that? Tonight? How is that possible?

MORTIMER. This is our plan. I summoned my companions
In secret to a chapel where a priest
Heard our confessions, gave us absolution
For all the sins we had committed
And in advance for trespasses to come.
We then received the sacrament, the last,
And now we're ready for our final journey.

MARY. What frightful preparations!

MORTIMER. The castle will be seized tonight. I have the keys.
We kill the guards, abduct you from your room
By force, and every living soul must die;
Not one must live who may betray the raid.

MARY. And Drury? Sir Amias? They will spill
The last drop of their blood before—

MORTIMER. They'll be the first my dagger stabs.

MARY. Your uncle who to you has been a second father?

MORTIMER. Killed by my hand, he'll fall.

MARY. Outrageous crime!

MORTIMER. All sins have been forgiven in advance.
I am prepared to do the worst—I'll do it.

MARY. How awful!

MORTIMER. And if I have to slay the Queen,
I've sworn upon the Host that I won't waver.

MARY. No, Mortimer. Before the blood begins
To run in rivers for my sake—

MORTIMER. What is my life compared to you and to my love!
Let all the bonds that hold the world together break,
Let with its rushing waves another deluge come
To swallow every living thing on earth—
I do not care. The world will see
Its day of doom approach before I shall renounce you.

MARY (steps back). My God! What language, sir—what
glances!

You frighten me.

MORTIMER (*with a strange look in his eyes and an expression of quiet madness*).
Our lives last but a moment, so does death.
Let them drag me to Tyburn and pull limb
From limb with red-hot iron tongs—
  (*With wide-open arms he takes a few quick steps toward MARY.*)
When I embrace you, my beloved—

MARY (*stepping back*). You're mad! Away from me!

MORTIMER. Ah, at this breast, from this mouth, breathing
  love—

MARY. Away, sir! Let me go!

MORTIMER. He would be mad indeed who did not hold
Good fortune in unbreakable embrace
When God presents it to his grasping hands.
You will be rescued, I shall rescue you,
No matter if it costs a thousand lives.
Yes, rescue you I will but—by the living God
I swear—I also will possess you.

MARY. Is there no God, no angel to protect me?
Terrible destiny that thrusts me cruelly
From terror on to other terrors.
Is it my fate to waken only fury?
Do hate and love conspire to frighten me?

MORTIMER. Yes, burning as their hatred is my love.
This lovely head they yearn to sever, cut
This neck, this gleaming whiteness, with an ax—
Oh, consecrate to life and happiness
What you must sacrifice to hate.
Why not bring ecstasy to your enchanted lover
With charms which are no longer yours?
This silken hair, these shining tresses,
Already forfeit to the King of Death,
Use them to bind your slave forever.

MARY. No more! If you do not respect the queen,
Hold sacred my misfortune and my suffering.

MORTIMER. The crown has tumbled from your head,
All traces of your earthly majesty are gone.
Try it, command your servants, call your friends,
And see how many rescuers will come.
Nothing is left but your celestial beauty,

Its power to enthrall and stir the heart;
It gives me strength to dare and to accomplish,
It drives me forward to the scaffold's steps.

MARY. Will no one come to save me from his fury!

MORTIMER. Audacious service merits bold rewards.
Why does a man of courage spill his blood?
To live is life's supreme reward,
And mad the man who wastes it aimlessly.
First let me rest at life's most warming hearth—
(*He embraces her passionately.*)

MARY. Must I call out for help against my rescuer?

MORTIMER. No, you are not insensitive; the world
Does not charge you with cold severity.
A lover's fervent plea can move you.
The singer Rizzio enjoyed your love,
And Bothwell was permitted to abduct you.

MARY. What impudence!

MORTIMER.   He was your tyrant;
He made you tremble—but you loved the man.
If it takes terror to seduce you, then—
By all the gods of hell—

MARY.   You are insane. Let go of me.

MORTIMER. I, too, will make you tremble.

HANNAH (*rushes in*). They're coming. They're already close.
Armed men are spreading through the park.

MORTIMER (*quickly reaching for his sword*).
I shall protect you.

MARY.   Hannah, save me from this man.
Where shall I now find refuge? To which saint
Shall I pray now? Where shall I turn?
Here it is violence, inside the house it's murder.
(*She flees toward the castle,* HANNAH *follows.*)

SCENE 7. *Mortimer; Paulet and Drury enter in great
excitement. Men of their retinue rush across the stage.*

PAULET. Lock all the gates. Draw up the bridges.

MORTIMER. What's happened, Uncle?

PAULET. Where is the murderess? Throw her
Into the deepest dungeon.

MORTIMER. What is it? What has happened?

PAULET. The Queen! What devilish audacity!
My curse on them!

MORTIMER. The Queen! Which queen?

PAULET. The Queen of England. She was killed
On her return to London.
(*He hurries toward the castle,* DRURY *follows.*)

SCENE 8. *Mortimer and, after a moment, O'Kelly.*

MORTIMER. Am I delirious? Did someone pass just now
And shout, "The Queen was killed"? No, no.
It cannot be. I must have dreamed.
A feverish illusion must present
As true and real to my mind
The horrible ideas I have nourished.
Who is it? Ah, O'Kelly—and he looks
As if the furies persecuted him.

O'KELLY (*rushes in*). Flee, Mortimer, flee. All is lost.

MORTIMER. But what is lost?

O'KELLY. Don't waste your time with questions. Flee.

MORTIMER. But what has happened?

O'KELLY. Sauvage, that madman, struck the blow.

MORTIMER. It's true then?

O'KELLY. Yes, yes, it's true. Quick, save yourself.

MORTIMER. She's dead, and Mary Queen of England.

O'KELLY. Dead? Who told you that?

MORTIMER.   You did yourself.

O'KELLY. She is alive, but you and I, we all are dead.

MORTIMER. She is alive!

O'KELLY. He missed. A mantle caught his thrust,
And Shrewsbury disarmed the murderer.

MORTIMER. She is alive!

O'KELLY. It was the Barnabite, come from Toulon.
You saw him in the chapel, sitting lost in thought,
While the Black Friar was expounding the anathema
With which the Pope has cursed the Queen.
He wanted to use any means, take any steps
To liberate the Church of God
And gain the crown of martyrdom.

Confiding only in the priest, he planned the deed,
It was accomplished on the road to London.

MORTIMER (*after a pause*). Oh, most unfortunate of women,
A grimly raging fate pursues you. Yes,
Now you must die, your downfall caused by me,
Who was to be your helping angel.

O'KELLY. Where will you flee? I shall hide out
Somewhere far in the northern forests.

MORTIMER. Flee, flee—may God direct your steps.
I stay. One more attempt to save her life;
If not, I'll die upon her coffin.

(*They leave in opposite directions.*)

ACT IV

An Antechamber

SCENE 1. *Aubespine, Leicester and Kent.*

AUBESPINE. How is her Majesty? My Lords,
I am beside myself, I'm horrified.
How did it happen? And how could it happen
In the midst of all her faithful subjects?

LEICESTER. It was not one of them who struck the blow.
A subject of your King, a Frenchman, did it.

AUBESPINE. A madman, without doubt.

KENT. A Papist certainly, Count Aubespine.

SCENE 2. *The same. Burleigh enters, in conversation with Davison.*

BURLEIGH. The orders for her execution must be drafted
Immediately and sealed. As soon as that is done,
Submit the paper to her Majesty
For signature.

DAVISON.   It will be done, my Lord.

AUBESPINE (*takes a few steps toward* BURLEIGH).
My Lord, I share this island's happiness
With all my heart. Thanked be the Lord
Who fended off the blow and saved her life.

BURLEIGH. Praise be to him who thwarted the despicable
Designs of England's enemies.

AUBESPINE. God's curse on him who dared commit
So dastardly a crime!

BURLEIGH. On him—and on the man who planned the foul
attack!

AUBESPINE (*to* KENT). My dear Earl Marshal, may it please
your Lordship
To bring me to her Majesty
So that I may duly convey to her
The greetings of my King and master.

BURLEIGH. You need not take the trouble, Count.

AUBESPINE (*very formally*). My Lord, I'm well aware of what
is fitting.

BURLEIGH. For you it will be fitting, Count,
To leave this island—now.

AUBESPINE.   What does that mean?

BURLEIGH. Today the sacred privileges still
Protect your life, not so tomorrow.

AUBESPINE. And of what crime am I accused?

BURLEIGH. Once mentioned, it becomes unpardonable.

AUBESPINE. I hope, my Lord, the right of an ambassador—

BURLEIGH. Will not protect a traitor to the realm.

LEICESTER and KENT. What's that?

AUBESPINE. My Lord, have you considered well . . .

BURLEIGH. A passport, written by your hand, was found
Upon the person of the murderer.

KENT. How is that possible?

AUBESPINE. I issue many passports and cannot divine
The private thoughts of every man.

BURLEIGH. The murderer went to confession in your house.

AUBESPINE. My house is open.

BURLEIGH.   Yes, to all our enemies.

AUBESPINE. Hold an inquiry. I demand it.

BURLEIGH. You ought to fear it, Count.

AUBESPINE. That is an insult to my sovereign.
He will tear up the treaty we have signed.

BURLEIGH. The Queen already tore it up,
England will not wed France.
My Lord of Kent, will you be good enough to escort
Count Aubespine in safety to the sea.
Enraged, the people have already stormed
His residence and found an arsenal
Of weapons. They will tear him limb from limb
If he should show himself. Conceal the Count
Until their rage subsides. You are responsible.

AUBESPINE. And I am glad to leave a country
Where pacts are toys, and where the Law of Nations
Is trampled on. My sovereign will seek
Bloody revenge.

BURLEIGH.   Let him come here and take it.

(KENT and AUBESPINE leave.)

SCENE 3. Leicester and Burleigh.

LEICESTER. So you dissolve the union now yourself
Which without warrant but with fervor you have sought.
That will not earn you England's gratitude,
My Lord, you might have saved yourself much trouble.

BURLEIGH. My purposes were honest. God decreed
That it was not to be. Happy the man
Who need not charge himself with worse offense.

LEICESTER. I see that secretive expression on your face,
The well-known sign that you hunt traitors.
This is a most propitious time for you,
My Lord. A monstrous crime has been committed
And mystery still shrouds the criminal.
A court of inquisition now will be
Installed where every word and glance are weighed
And even thoughts arraigned before the bar.
You'll be the all-important man,
An Atlas of the state upon whose shoulders
The entire weight of England rests.

BURLEIGH. My Lord, I recognize you as my master;
Your eloquence has won a victory

Such as my own has never yet achieved.

LEICESTER. What do you mean, my Lord?

BURLEIGH. Was it not you who cleverly enticed
The Queen to Fotheringhay, behind my back?

LEICESTER. Behind your back, indeed! I've never tried
To hide my actions from your scrutiny.

BURLEIGH. You lead the Queen to Fotheringhay? Oh no!
You did not lead the Queen, it was the Queen
Who graciously agreed to guide you there.

LEICESTER. What are you driving at?

BURLEIGH. That noble personage whom you let play the Queen
At Fotheringhay; and at the glorious triumph
You thoughtfully prepared for her
Who trusted you implicitly. Poor Queen!
How shamelessly you have been mocked,
How mercilessly you were sacrificed!
So that's the magnanimity, the tolerance
Which in the Council overwhelmed you suddenly.
That is why Mary Stuart was so weak
And so contemptible an enemy
That killing her would be too great an honor.
A clever plan! How finely honed! Too bad,
It was too finely honed—the point snapped off.

LEICESTER. What impudence! Come with me to the Queen
    at once,
Repeat your accusations at her throne.

BURLEIGH. I'll meet you there. Make sure, my Lord,
That you have all your eloquence at your disposal.

                                        (*He leaves.*)

SCENE 4. *Leicester alone; shortly, Mortimer.*

LEICESTER. The veil is lifted. I'm found out. How did
The spying scoundrel find my tracks?
If he has proof, I'm lost. My God,
How can I face the Queen if she discovers
That Mary and myself had understandings?
How treacherous my counsel must appear,
My urging that she go to Fotheringhay!
She must believe that I intended
The insults and the mockery, that I

Betrayed her to her hated enemy.
That she will not forget and not forgive.
Now everything must seem premeditated,
The bitter turn their conversation took,
The triumph and derisive laughter of her foe,
Even down to the murderous attempt
Upon her life, an unexpected stroke of fate,
Which now she must believe I instigated.
There is no hope, no help, no rescue.

MORTIMER (*enters in a state of great excitement and looks all around, suspiciously*).
My Lord, thank God it's you. Are we alone?

LEICESTER. Away from here, unhappy man. What brings you here?

MORTIMER. They're after us—and you. Watch out.

LEICESTER. Away from here, away.

MORTIMER. They know that there were secret meetings,
They know we were at Aubespine's—

LEICESTER. What do I care!

MORTIMER. They know that the assassin was among us—

LEICESTER. That's your concern. Do you make bold
To implicate me in your murderous schemes?
Defend your wicked enterprise yourself.

MORTIMER. But listen to me—

LEICESTER. Go to hell.
Why do you, like an evil spirit, cling to me?
Begone. I do not know your name or face.
I don't keep company with common cutthroats.

MORTIMER. I've come to warn you, listen—won't you hear?
Your dealings, too, have been betrayed—

LEICESTER. What?

MORTIMER. Lord Burleigh was in Fotheringhay
Soon after the attack. He searched the Queen's
Apartment and he found—

LEICESTER. What did he find?

MORTIMER. A letter which the Queen had just begun,
Addressed to you—

LEICESTER. Good Lord!

MORTIMER. Exhorting you
To keep your word, repeating that she promised you
Her hand and mentioning the portrait which—

LEICESTER. Hell and damnation!

MORTIMER.   And he has the letter.

LEICESTER. That seals my death.

(*In utter despair, he walks restlessly up and down while* MORTIMER *speaks the following.*)

MORTIMER. There's still a chance. Anticipate his move.
You still can save yourself and her.
Think of excuses, swear a thousand oaths,
Prevent the worst. Myself, I now can do no more.
Our league is torn assunder, my companions
Are scattered, I am on my way to Scotland. There
I hope to find new friends. It's up to you,
Now show what your prestige, what a bold front can do.

LEICESTER (*stands still, suddenly determined*).
That is what I shall do.

(*He steps to the door, opens it and calls.*)
Hey, guard!

(*To the* OFFICER *who enters with guards.*)
Arrest this traitor, guard him well.
An infamous conspiracy has been discovered.
I will inform the Queen myself.   (*He leaves.*)

MORTIMER (*at first stunned, soon recovers; with a look of utter contempt in* LEICESTER'S *direction*).
The scoundrel! I deserve it, though.
Why did I give that wretch my confidence?
He steps on me and blithely walks away,
My body is his stepping stone to safety.
Go, save yourself. My mouth is closed.
I shall not drag you with me to perdition,
Not even dying do I want your company.
The wicked only have one thing to lose, their life.

(*To the* OFFICER OF THE GUARD, *who steps forward to arrest him.*)
What do you want, you venal slave of tyranny?
I do not fear you, I am free.

(*He draws a dagger.*)

OFFICER. He's armed, quick, get his dagger.

(*The soldiers charge him, but he fends them off.*)

MORTIMER. Free in this dying moment of my life,
I finally can bare my heart and speak.
May death strike you and may damnation be your lot,

You who betrayed your God and your true Queen,
Who turned your backs on Mary, Queen of Scots
As faithlessly as on the Mary who is Queen of Heaven.
You are the servants of a bastard queen—

OFFICER. Seize the blasphemer! At him, quick!

MORTIMER. Beloved Mary, I have failed,
Your life I could not save. All I can do
Is set you an example by my death.
Saint Mary, pray for me and take me unto you,
So I may live forever in your heaven.

(*He plunges the dagger into his heart and falls into the arms of the* GUARDS.)

SCENE 5. *The Queen's chamber. Elizabeth, holding a letter in her hand, and Burleigh.*

ELIZABETH. To lure me there and have his fun with me!
In triumph to parade his Queen before his paramour!
No woman ever was so shabbily betrayed.

BURLEIGH. I cannot understand how he succeeded.
What did he do, what powers did he use,
What magic craft, to trick my prudent Queen?

ELIZABETH. I die of shame. He must have gloated at my weakness.
To humble her was my intent, instead
I was the object of her mockery.

BURLEIGH. Now you believe that I gave sound advice.

ELIZABETH. I was severely punished for not following
Your prudent counsel, but why should I not trust him?
How could I dream that he concealed a trap
Behind his oaths of loyalty and love?
Whom can I trust when he betrays me?
He whom I made the greatest of the great,
He who has always been the closest to my heart,
Whom I permitted to behave as master at my court,
To play the part of King?

BURLEIGH.   And all the time,
He was betraying you to that false Queen of Scots.

ELIZABETH. She'll die for it! Have you prepared the orders?

BURLEIGH. They're ready for your signature, your Majesty,
As you commanded.

ELIZABETH.   Yes, she will die for it.
He'll watch her die and follow her to death.
I have expelled him from my heart,
My love is gone, and hatred is my master.
High as his rise has been, as deep
And ignominious be his downfall.
He shall be a memorial to my severity,
As his aggrandizement has proved my weakness.
Let him be taken to the Tower!
I shall appoint the peers to be his judges
And let the law's full rigor deal with him.

BURLEIGH. He will attempt to speak to you
And to defend himself—

ELIZABETH.   How could he dare?
Is not the letter testimony to his guilt?
His crime is clear as day.

BURLEIGH.   But you are lenient.
Your kindness, at his sight . . . his mighty presence—

ELIZABETH. I do not wish to see him, now or ever more.
Did you convey my order to refuse
Him entry if he comes?

BURLEIGH.   I did, your Majesty.
(*A* PAGE *enters.*)

PAGE. The Earl of Leicester.

ELIZABETH. Oh, the audacity! I will not see him. Tell him that.

PAGE. I do not dare to tell that to my Lord,
And he would not believe me if I did.

ELIZABETH. So high I raised him that my servants tremble at
His sight, they fear him more than they fear me.

BURLEIGH (*to the* PAGE). The Queen forbids him to come
near.

(*Hesitantly, the* PAGE *leaves.*)

ELIZABETH (*after a pause*). And still, it may be possible—
If he were able to explain—
Could it not be a trap that Mary set
To separate me from my dearest friend?
She is a vicious viper. If—suppose
She wrote the letter only to imbed
The poison of suspicion in my heart,
To plunge the man she hates into the abyss—

BURLEIGH. Your Majesty, weigh well—

Scene 6. *The same. Leicester.*

LEICESTER (*flings the door open and enters with the bearing of a master*).
What insolence! I want to see the man
Who dares to bar this door to me.

ELIZABETH. Oh, the audacity!

LEICESTER. To turn me away! If a Lord Burleigh is allowed
To enter here, then so am I.

BURLEIGH. You're very bold, my Lord, to enter here
Without the Queen's permission.

LEICESTER. And you, my Lord, presume too much to speak.
Permission! There is no one at this court
From whom the Earl of Leicester will accept
Permission or refusal—except—
(*Humbly approaching* ELIZABETH.)
                                        —my Queen.

ELIZABETH (*without looking at him*). Out of my sight, you
    traitor!

LEICESTER. The voice is yours, my kind Elizabeth,
But yours, Lord Burleigh, are the words—
My enemy's ungracious words. I wish to speak
To my Elizabeth. You lent your ear to him,
I now demand the same.

ELIZABETH. Speak then! Deny your crime and make it worse.

LEICESTER. Let this superfluous attendant leave
Before I speak. Leave us alone, my Lord.
What I'm about to tell my Queen
Does not require a witness. Go.

ELIZABETH (*to* BURLEIGH). Stay! I command it.

LEICESTER. Why let a third one come between us two?
When I speak to my worshiped Queen,
I shall uphold the rights of my position.
They're sacred rights, and I insist that you,
Lord Burleigh, now leave us alone.

ELIZABETH. Your arrogance befits you well.

LEICESTER. It does, indeed. For I'm the happy man
On whom you graciously bestowed your favor.
That sets me above him and everyone.
Your heart raised me to this exalted rank,

And what your love gave me, that I shall guard,
That I'll defend, by God, to my last breath.
Let him be off, and it will not be long
Before we understand each other.

ELIZABETH. Vain is your hope that cunningly you will
Deceive me once again with pretty speeches.

LEICESTER. He tricked you with malicious gossip.
I want to talk straight to your heart.
What in the knowledge of your love I did,
I will defend before your heart;
I recognize no other court.

ELIZABETH. That is the court that first condemned you, brazen
man.
My Lord, show him the letter.

BURLEIGH.   Read it! Here!

LEICESTER (*quickly scans the letter, without losing his composure*).
It's Mary Stuart's writing.

ELIZABETH.   Read, and say no more.

LEICESTER (*reads the letter; calmly*).
Appearances condemn me, but I hope
That I will not be judged by specious evidence.

ELIZABETH. Can you deny your secret dealings with her,
Deny that you received her portrait or deny
That you held out the hope of liberation?

LEICESTER. If I felt any guilt, it would be easy to reject
This testimony of an enemy.
But as it is, my conscience is quite clear,
So I admit that what she writes is true.

ELIZABETH. Well then?

BURLEIGH. He stands condemned by his own words.

ELIZABETH. Out of my sight and to the Tower, traitor.

LEICESTER. That I am not. It was perhaps not right
To keep you in the dark about my plans,
But I was honest in my purpose,
To learn her schemes, the better to defeat her.

ELIZABETH. A lame excuse, my Lord.

BURLEIGH. Do you believe—

LEICESTER. I played a risky game, I know, and at this court
No one but Leicester could have dared to play it.
The world knows well enough how I hate Mary.

My rank, the confidence with which the Queen
Has honored me, will readily refute
The least suspicion of my loyalty.
The man whom your affection has distinguished more
Than any other man must have the privilege
To walk his own bold path in doing what he must.

BURLEIGH. Why, if your purpose was so pure, keep it a secret?

LEICESTER. You like to wag your tongue before you act,
my Lord.
You trumpet your accomplishments. That is
Your way. Mine is to act before I speak.

BURLEIGH. And now you speak because you must.

LEICESTER (*looking him up and down disdainfully*).
You are so proud of having saved your Queen,
You have performed a wondrously enormous feat
In sniffing out a traitor, you know everything
And nothing can escape your eagle eye.
Poor braggart! Mary Stuart would be free today,
If I had not prevented it.

BURLEIGH.   You did—

LEICESTER. Yes, I, my Lord. The Queen confided in Sir
Mortimer,
Confided him her secret hopes and went so far
As to charge him with a bloody mission against Mary
Because his uncle had refused with horror
A similar request. Is that not true?

(*The Queen and* BURLEIGH *look at each other in consternation.*)

BURLEIGH. How did you find that out?

LEICESTER. Is it not true? Well then, my Lord. Where were
Your thousand spying eyes that you did not
Become aware of Mortimer's deception?
That he, a furious Papist, was a tool
Of Cardinal de Guise, a creature of the Stuart,
A purposeful and bold fanatic who came back
To set her free and kill the Queen?

ELIZABETH. Sir Mortimer?

LEICESTER.   He was the one who carried messages
Between myself and Mary. That is how we met.
Today she was to be abducted from her prison,
As he told me himself just now.
I called the guard and, desperate

At the frustration of his plans and his
Exposure, Mortimer took his own life.

ELIZABETH. Oh, I have been imposed upon most shamelessly.

BURLEIGH. That happened now, just after I had left you?

LEICESTER. For my sake, I regret exceedingly
That he so ended, for his testimony,
If he were still alive, would totally
Absolve me, clear me of the last suspicion.
That's why I wished to see him in the hands
Of Justice. I was sure that I could prove
Before a court of law, before the world
That I am innocent.

BURLEIGH.   You said he killed himself.
You're sure he did? It was not you who killed him?

LEICESTER. What reprehensible suspicion!
The officer to whom I handed him may speak.
    (*He opens the door and calls the* OFFICER OF THE GUARD,
    who enters promptly.)
Make your report, so that her Majesty
May know the details of Sir Mortimer's demise.

OFFICER. I guarded with my men the antechamber,
When suddenly the door flew open and my Lord
Gave me the order to arrest the knight
As traitor to the Crown. He flew into a rage,
Drew out his dagger, screaming calumnies
Against the Queen, and plunged it deep into his breast.
Before we could prevent it, he fell dead—

LEICESTER. The Queen has heard enough, sir; you may go.
    (*The* OFFICER *leaves.*)

ELIZABETH. What an abyss of abominations!

LEICESTER. Who was it then that saved you? Burleigh?
Did Burleigh know what dangers threatened you?
Did he avert them? Your good angel was—
The Earl of Leicester.

BURLEIGH. This Mortimer died most conveniently, my Lord.

ELIZABETH. I don't know what to say. I do believe you and—
I don't. I think that you are guilty and—
That you are not. That cursed woman is
The cause of all my sorrow.

LEICESTER.   Now she has to die.
Now I, too, vote in favor of her death.

I counseled you to leave the sentence in suspense
Until someone would lift his arm for her.
That's happened now, and I insist
On carrying the sentence out at once.

BURLEIGH. That's your advice?

LEICESTER. I am appalled by extreme measures,
But I am now convinced the welfare of the Queen
Requires this sacrifice. I therefore ask
That orders for her execution
Be instantly prepared.

BURLEIGH (*to the Queen*). My Lord seems so sincere and
    serious,
That I propose he be appointed
To have the sentence carried out.

LEICESTER. I!

BURLEIGH.   You. There is no better way to lay at rest
All lingering suspicion than that you,
Who's been accused of having loved her,
Be named to supervise her execution.

ELIZABETH (*fixing her gaze on* LEICESTER).
My Lord's advice is good. So be it.

LEICESTER. My rank should properly excuse me
From missions of so sad a nature,
Which are in every way more suitable
For a Lord Burleigh. Someone who's as close
To his beloved Queen as I should not
Take part in such unhappy tasks.
However, I shall prove my eagerness
And do all that my Queen may ask of me.
I waive the privileges of my rank,
I'll undertake this hateful duty.

ELIZABETH. You'll share your task with my Lord Burleigh.
    (*To* BURLEIGH.)
See that the orders are prepared at once.

(BURLEIGH *leaves. Tumultuous voices are heard outside.*)

SCENE 7. *The same. The Earl of Kent enters.*

ELIZABETH. What is this uproar in the streets, my Lord?

KENT. Your Majesty, the people are beleaguering
Your palace, clamoring to see their Queen.

ELIZABETH. What do my people want?

KENT. They're terrified by rumors spreading through
The streets of London that your life is threatened,
That murderers are still abroad sent by the Pope,
That there's a vast conspiracy of Catholics
To force the Stuart's prison, free her and—
Proclaim her Queen. The mob believes these tales
And is enraged. Nothing will pacify
Their fury but the Stuart's head—today.

ELIZABETH. Am I to be compelled to act?

KENT. They are determined to maintain their siege
Until the sentence is confirmed and signed.

SCENE 8. *The same. Burleigh and Davison enter with a document.*

ELIZABETH. What do you bring me, Davison?

DAVISON (*solemnly approaches the Queen*). Your Majesty
   commanded—

ELIZABETH. What is it?
(*As she moves to take the document, she recoils with a shudder.*)
                    Oh, my God!

BURLEIGH. Obey the people's voice, it is the voice of God.

ELIZABETH (*struggling with her emotions, undecided*).
My Lords, how can I know that this is really
The voice of all my people and of all the world,
That a different voice will not rise tomorrow
If I obey what is the people's wish today?
Precisely those who urge me now to act
May well severely blame me when the deed is done.

SCENE 9. *The same. Shrewsbury enters.*

SHREWSBURY (*enters in great agitation*).
They want to hurry you, your Majesty,
Stand fast.
(*He notices the document in* DAVISON's *hand.*)
            Am I too late? Has it been done?
That is a fateful paper. It must not be put

Before her Majesty just now—not now.

ELIZABETH. Lord Shrewsbury, they would compel me—

SHREWSBURY. Who could compel you? You are Queen.
Now is the time to show them your authority.
Command those vulgar voices to be silent
That insolently try to force your hand
And to be masters of your will.
Blind fear and wild emotions rule the crowd,
You are upset yourself, grievously hurt,
And you are human. Now you cannot justly judge.

BURLEIGH. She has been judged. The judgment that has been
Pronounced needs only to be executed.

KENT (*who had left at* SHREWSBURY's *entrance, returns*).
The crowd is growing. It's impossible
To hold the mob in check.

ELIZABETH (*to* SHREWSBURY).

You see, I am compelled.

SHREWSBURY. I only plead postponement. Your life,
Your happiness and peace, will be decided
By this one stroke your pen will make.
For years you have been weighing what to do,
Let not one stormy moment now decide
On your behalf. A short postponement only,
Collect yourself, await a calmer hour.

BURLEIGH. Wait, hesitate, delay until at last
The realm will be ablaze, until she finally
Succeeds with her foul plans of murder.
God has averted an assassin's blow three times,
Today it almost found its mark. To hope
For one more miracle would be to tempt your fate.

SHREWSBURY. That God who held His saving hand
Above your head four times, who gave today
An old man's trembling hand the force to overcome
A madman, that God does deserve your trust.
I will not raise the voice of justice now,
There will be time for that. But think of this:
You tremble now before the living Mary.
You need not fear her while she lives,
Mary beheaded, Mary dead—that is the danger.
Arising from her grave, she will, a goddess of dissension,
Sow discord in your people's hearts,
A Spirit of Revenge, she'll stalk your realm

Until your people turn away from you.
Because they fear her now, they hate her,
When she is dead, they will avenge her.
They will no longer look
Upon her as an enemy of their religion,
But mourn her as the daughter of their kings,
A victim of your hate and jealousy.
You'll quickly note the change. Walk through the streets
Of London, once her blood is spilled,
And show yourself among your people
Who used to crowd around you, cheering you;
You'll see another England and another people.
No longer will the aureole of justice,
Which conquered every heart, adorn you. Fear,
That dreadful mate of tyranny, will roam the streets,
Precede you on your path, and where you go
Deserted streets will lie before your eyes.
If her head falls, the worst will have been done,
For if a queen's life is not sacred,
Whose life then is secure?

    ELIZABETH. Oh, Shrewsbury, you saved my life today,
You fended off the murder sword,
Why did you not allow the blow to fall?
It would have ended all my battles.
Relieved of all my doubts, unsoiled by guilt
And peaceful, I would lie in my still grave.
I'm tired of life, I'm tired of ruling lives.
If one of us, the rival queens, must die
So that the other one may live—
And I do recognize that this is so—
Why cannot I give way? My people may decide,
I give them back their sovereignty.
God is my witness that I lived my life
Not for myself, but for my people's welfare.
If they expect that fawning Mary,
The younger queen, to bring them greater happiness,
I'll gladly leave my throne to her, return
To Woodstock and its quiet solitude.
That is where unpretentiously I spent my youth
And where I found, far from the vain ambitions of the world,
Nobility within myself.
I am not made to rule. A ruler must be capable
Of being hard; my heart is soft.
For many years I've ruled this island happily

Because I needed only give it happiness.
But now the harsher side of royal office faces me,
And now I feel my weakness.

    BURLEIGH. When I must hear my Queen speak such unqueenly
        words,
I would betray my duty and the realm
Were I to listen and be silent.
You say you love your people most,
More than yourself. Now is the time to prove it.
You cannot choose to be at peace yourself
And let the country flounder on the stormy waves.
Think of the Church! Are all the old,
Discarded superstitions to return
With Mary Stuart? Are the monks to rule again?
Are Roman emissaries to be given franchise
To come and lock our churches, to dethrone our kings?
From you I now demand the souls of all your subjects.
As you act now, they will be lost or saved.
This is no time for softness and compassion,
Your supreme duty is the country's weal.
Your life was saved by Shrewsbury today,
I want to save the life of England. That is more.

    ELIZABETH. I wish to be alone, my Lords. No man
Can offer comfort or advice in such
An important matter. I'll consult a higher judge.
As He instructs me, I shall act. For now,
Leave me alone, my Lords.

    (*To* DAVISON.)

                    You, sir, please stay nearby.

SCENE 10. *Elizabeth alone.*

    ELIZABETH. It's slavery to serve the people, shameful servitude.
I'm tired of flattering this idol
Which, deep within myself, I do despise.
Will ever I be free upon my throne?
Public opinion must be pleased, I must
Debase myself to win the rabble's praise,
Do what the mob that only loves a fool
May think is right. He is not truly king
Who has to please the world. He only is
Who need ask no man's approbation when he acts.

I've hated arbitrary power all my life,
I have been just, and thus I've tied my hands
For this inevitable act of violence.
The standard which I set myself condemns me now.
But had I been a tyrant like the Spanish Mary,
My predecessor on the throne, I now
Could shed the blood of kings without reproach.
Was it by my own choice that I was just?
All-powerful necessity, which bends
The will of kings as it controls all men,
Decreed that justice be my foremost virtue.
Surrounded on all sides by enemies,
The people's will alone has kept me on the throne.
All powers of the Continent seek to destroy me;
Implacable, the Pope hurls his anathema
Against me; France betrays me with a Judas kiss,
The Spaniards arm for furious warfare on the seas.
Thus I must fight against a world, alone,
An unarmed woman. I've been forced to use
Imposing virtue to conceal my threadbare rights,
The stain upon my royal birth
With which I was disgraced by my own father.
In vain I've tried to cover it.
The furious hatred of my enemies
Exposed it to the world and pitted Mary,
A frightening and unrelenting specter,
Against me. No, this fear must end.
Her head must fall. At last, I want my peace.
She is the Fury of my life, a vengeful sprite
Which fate glued to my heels to torture me.
Wherever I plant hope or happiness,
This hellish serpent coils before me in the grass.
She tears my lover from my arms, she steals
My bridegroom. Mary Stuart—that's the name
By which I call all my misfortune.
Once she is extirpated, I am free as mountain air.
    (*After a silence.*)
With what contempt she looked upon me,
As if to grind me with her eyes into the dust!
But you are powerless, I have the better weapons.
Their blow is mortal—and you are no more.
    (*She steps quickly to the table and takes the pen.*)
You call me bastard? Fool! I am
A bastard only while you breathe, all doubts

About my royal birth will be erased
As soon as I have crushed you.
When Britons have no other choice but me,
I'll be at once a child of holy wedlock.

(*She signs the document with quick, firm strokes; then, with
an expression of terror, she drops the pen and steps back.
After a while, she rings the bell.*)

SCENE 11. *Elizabeth and Davison.*

ELIZABETH. Where are the other lords?

DAVISON. They went outside
To calm the raging crowd. The uproar died,
Indeed, at once when they saw Shrewsbury.
"That's he! It's he," a hundred voices roared,
"He is the one who saved the Queen. He is
The bravest man in England. Hear his words."
He spoke to them and in his gentle, forceful manner
Rebuked them for their violence and soon
Persuaded them. Calm was restored, and quietly
They slunk away.

ELIZABETH. The vacillating crowd
That changes with the wind. Beware the man
Who leans upon this slender reed.
Thank you, you may withdraw.

(*As he turns to leave.*)
Oh yes, this sheet.
I give it back to you, it's in your trust.

DAVISON (*glances at the document, shrinks back*).
Your Majesty, your name—have you decided then?

ELIZABETH. I was to sign—I did. A piece of paper
Does not decide. It bears my name, but names don't kill.

DAVISON. Your name, your Majesty, upon this document
Decides and kills. It's like a bolt of lightning
That strikes and kills in a single flash.
This paper orders both commissioners
And sheriff to proceed at once to Fotheringhay,
There to announce her death to Mary Stuart,
And with the rising light of morn to have
The sentence executed. There is no doubt,
There will be no delay. The Queen of Scotland
Will be dead as I pass on this document.

ELIZABETH. Quite true, sir. God has put, you see,
Into your feeble hands a matter fraught with destiny.
Implore Him to enlighten you with wisdom.
I leave you to your duties. I must go.

(*She turns to go.*)

DAVISON (*steps quickly in front of her*).
No, no, your Majesty, you cannot leave
Without informing me of your desire.
Can there be any other wisdom here
Than to obey your orders to the letter?
You put this sheet into my hands, I presume,
So that I may pass it on at once for action?

ELIZABETH. If, in your wisdom, you—

DAVISON (*interrupts her, terrified*).
Not in my wisdom! God forbid! Obeying you
Is all my wisdom. Nothing must be left
For me, your servant, to decide.
A small mistake might lead to regicide,
To unforeseeable disaster.
Let me remain your willing tool, without a will.
Put your intentions into crystal words—
What shall I do with this death warrant?

ELIZABETH. That is precisely what it is.

DAVISON. That means—you wish it carried out at once?

ELIZABETH (*hesitatingly*). I didn't say that, and I shudder at
    the thought.

DAVISON. You wish me to withhold it, then?

ELIZABETH (*quickly*).
At your own risk. You'll be responsible for the results.

DAVISON. At my risk? God! Please it your Majesty
To tell me—what do you desire?

ELIZABETH (*impatiently*). It's my desire that this unfortunate
    affair
Be now forgotten, that I finally
Be rid of it—for good, that I have peace.

DAVISON. One word is all I ask. Please say it!
Command what's to become of this.

ELIZABETH. I told you. Don't torment me further.

DAVISON. You told me? But you told me nothing. Please,
Your Majesty, remember!

ELIZABETH (*stamps her foot*).

This is intolerable.

DAVISON. Have patience with me, please! I've come
Into this office only recently.
I don't yet understand the words of kings.
I have grown up in simple customs. Please,
Be patient with your servant, don't begrudge
Me the one word that makes my duty clear.

(*He approaches her in an attitude of supplication; she turns
her back. He stands in silent despair, then says with great determination:*)

Take back this document. Please, take it back.
It turns to fire, it burns my hands.
Do not choose me to serve you in this fearful task.

ELIZABETH. Discharge the duties of your office.

(*She leaves.*)

SCENE 12. *Davison; shortly, Burleigh.*

DAVISON. She goes. And I stand here, perplexed and full of
doubts,
This frightful paper in my hand.
What am I now to do? Withhold it? Pass it on?

(*To* BURLEIGH, *who enters.*)

Good, good that you have come, my Lord!
You introduced me to my office, now
Relieve me of my duties. I was unaware
Of the responsibilities I would assume.
Let me return to the obscurity
From which I came. The court is not for me.

BURLEIGH. What happened to you, sir? Compose yourself.
The Queen called you. Where is the warrant?

DAVISON. She left me, in a rage. Advise me, help me, please!
Release me from this hell of doubt and fear.
Here is the sentence, it is signed.

BURLEIGH (*quickly*). She signed? Give it to me!

DAVISON.   I cannot do that.

BURLEIGH.

                                                        What?

DAVISON. She has not told me clearly what she wants.

BURLEIGH. Not clearly! She has signed it. Let me have the
sheet!

DAVISON. I am to have it carried out—and I am not—

Oh God, who knows what I must do!

    BURLEIGH (*increasingly insistent*).
At once, this instant you're to have it executed.
Give it to me, you're lost if you delay.

    DAVISON. I'm lost if I'm too hasty.

    BURLEIGH.   You're a fool.
You must be mad. Give me the document!

    (*He snatches the paper from* DAVISON's *hands and hurries out.*)

    DAVISON (*follows him quickly*).
What are you doing? Stay! You'll ruin me!

ACT V

The scene is the same as in Act I.

SCENE 1. *Hannah Kennedy, in deep mourning, is seen sealing packages and letters. Her eyes are tear-swollen, her face expresses deep but quiet grief. Overcome, she frequently interrupts her task to immerse herself in silent prayer.*
Paulet and Drury enter, also dressed in black. They are followed by a great number of servants who carry in silver vessels, mirrors, paintings and other precious objects which they deposit in the background, almost filling that part of the room. Paulet hands Hannah a small jewel box and a paper, indicating to her by gestures that it constitutes an inventory of the objects brought into the room. At the sight of the treasures, Hannah is again overcome by grief. She sinks into deep mourning, as the others leave the room. Melvil enters.

    HANNAH (*calls out as she notices* MELVIL).
You, Melvil! It is you! Oh, to see you again!

    MELVIL. Yes, loyal Hannah, here we meet again.

    HANNAH. It's been so long, a long and painful separation.

    MELVIL. And now it is a cruel, sad reunion.

    HANNAH. Oh God, you've come—

    MELVIL.   To bid my Queen a last farewell.

    HANNAH. Now finally, the morning of her death,

She is allowed to have her long-missed friends
Around her. I won't ask how you, good sir,
Have fared, nor tell you how the Queen has suffered
Since you were taken from our side. Some day,
Alas, there may be time for that. Oh, Melvil,
Why did we have to live so long
That we must see the dawn of such a day!

    MELVIL. Let us not weaken one another. I shall weep
As long as there is life in me. My face
Shall never brighten with a smile again,
And I shall never shed these gloomy garments.
I'll mourn forever, but today
I will be resolute. You too must promise me
That you will check your tears although the others
May yield to their inconsolable grief.
Let us be her example, nobly poised,
So she may lean upon us as she walks to death.

    HANNAH. You are mistaken, Melvil, if you think
The Queen needs our support to help her face
Her fate unflinchingly. She is the one
Who sets us an example with her noble poise.
No, have no fear! The Queen will die a queen.

    MELVIL. Did she take calmly the announcement of her death?
I heard she was quite unprepared.

    HANNAH. She was, but other horrors frightened her.
Not death, her liberator made her tremble.
She had been promised freedom. Mortimer
Had vowed that he would take us this last night
Away from here, and torn between her fears and hope,
Not sure if she could really entrust
Her honor and her person to the bold young man,
She waited for the day to break.
Then a great uproar burst upon the castle,
Our ears were frightened by the noise of pounding,
The sound of many hammers, and we thought
We heard our rescuers. Hope beckoned sweetly,
Irresistibly the will to live
Once more awoke in her. Then suddenly,
The door is opened, Sir Amias comes
To tell us that, below, the carpenters—
Have started to erect—the scaffold.

    (*Overcome by grief, she averts her face.*)

    MELVIL. Merciful God! How did she take that terrifying news?

HANNAH (*after a pause, during which she has calmed herself*).
One does not shed one's life in little pieces.
In one swift movement the transition
From life on earth to life eternal must be made.
God granted her, in that decisive moment,
The strength to thrust all earthly hope aside
And resolutely to embrace eternity.
No sign of fear, no blanching, no complaint
Dishonored her. Not till she heard the news
Of Leicester's shameful treason, of the sacrifice
The noble youth had brought her by his death,
Not till she saw his uncle's tragic grief,
Whose last hope now had died because of her,
Then only flowed her tears. Not her fate, no,
The grief of others made her weep.

MELVIL. Where is she now? Can you conduct me to her?

HANNAH. She spent the time that still remained before the
    dawn
Awake, she prayed, wrote letters to her friends
And signed her testament. Now she is resting.
May her last sleep on earth refresh my Lady.

MELVIL. Is anybody with her now?

HANNAH. Burgoyne, her personal physician, and her women.

SCENE 2. *The same. Margareta Curl enters.*

HANNAH. What news? Is she awake?

MARGARETA (*drying her tears*).   She is already dressed.
She wants you.

HANNAH.   I shall go at once.
(*To* MELVIL, *who is about to follow her.*)
Not yet. First let me warn her of your coming.
(*She goes into the next room.*)

MARGARETA. Oh, Melvil! Our old steward!

MELVIL.   Yes, I'm he.

MARGARETA. This house no longer needs a steward.
You come from London, Melvil; have you news
For me about my husband?

MELVIL. He will be freed, I hear, as soon—

MARGARETA. As soon as our beloved Queen is dead!
The coward, the abominable traitor!

He is the murderer of our dear Lady,
His testimony, I am told, condemned her.

MELVIL. That's so.

MARGARETA. His soul be damned to hell. He lied!

MELVIL. Now, Margareta, watch what you are saying!

MARGARETA. I'll swear to it before the bars of justice,
I will repeat it to his face, I'll fill
The world with it: he lied, and she is innocent!

MELVIL. So help us God.

SCENE 3. *The same. Burgoyne enters; shortly, Hannah.*

BURGOYNE (*discovering* MELVIL). Melvil!

MELVIL.   Burgoyne!

BURGOYNE (*to* MARGARETA).   Quick, get a cup of wine.

MELVIL. Why? Is the Queen not well?

BURGOYNE.   Oh, she feels strong.
Her courage gives her a deceptive strength,
And thus she does not feel the need to eat,
But she still has a cruel test before her.
Her enemies shall have no cause to boast
That she was pale from fear of death,
When only nature's weakness blanched her cheeks.

MELVIL (*to* HANNAH, *who enters*).
She will come presently herself.
You seem to look around, surprised; your eyes
Demand: why all this splendor in a room
Where death has come to dwell? Oh, Melvil,
We suffered want while there was life and hope,
Abundance has returned to us with death.

SCENE 4. *The same. Two of Mary's chambermaids enter,
also in mourning. At the sight of Melvil, they break out in
tears and lamentations.*

MELVIL. Oh, that I must see you again—like this!
Gertrude and Rosamund!

SECOND CHAMBERMAID. She sent us out.
She wants to be alone to talk to God.

(*Two more servants enter, in mourning like the others, and
express their grief by silent gestures.*)

SCENE 5. *The same. Margareta comes back carrying a golden cup filled with wine. She puts it on a table and, pale and trembling, holds on to a chair.*

MELVIL. What is it? What has frightened you?

MARGARETA.   Oh God!

MELVIL. What is the matter?

MARGARETA.   Oh, I saw—

MELVIL. Please, calm yourself and tell us what it is.

MARGARETA. As I came up the stairs to bring this cup
I passed the lower hall, the door was open,
I looked in—and saw—oh God!

MELVIL. What did you see? Compose yourself.

MARGARETA. The walls were draped in black, a giant scaffold,
All covered with black cloth, rose from the floor
And on its top, right in the middle, a dark block,
A pillow and beside it gleamed a well-honed ax.
The hall was filled with people crowding round
The scaffold, in their eyes hot lust of blood.

CHAMBERMAIDS.   May God have mercy on our Queen!

MELVIL. Be calm now! Here she comes.

SCENE 6. *The same. Mary enters, dressed in a white, festive gown; a chain made of small beads, from which an Agnus Dei is suspended, hangs around her neck; a rosary is fastened to her belt; she carries a crucifix. Her head is adorned with a tiara, her long, black veil is thrown back. As she enters, all step aside with expressions of their grief. In an instinctive gesture, Melvil drops to his knees.*

MARY (*looking all around with calm dignity*).
Why do you grieve? Why do you weep? You should
Rejoice with me that I am near the end
Of all my trials, that my chains will drop,
My prison open and my joyous soul
Will float on angels' wings to its eternal freedom.
While I was in the power of my haughty foe
And suffered such indignities
As no queen should be made to suffer,

Then was the time to weep for me.
Soothing and healing, death comes closer now,
My solemn friend. His great, black wings will cloak
My shame. When man has seen the bottom of the pit,
He finds a new nobility in this encounter.
I feel the crown upon my head again,
And in my soul the proud serenity I used to know.
(*She advances a few steps.*)
You here, Sir Melvil? Not like this, dear sir.
Arise! You have not come to see the death,
You're here to see the triumph of your Queen.
It is an unexpected happiness for me
That you, a friend who shares my faith,
Will be a witness when I die, for how I die
Will thus be known not only to my enemies.
Tell me, Sir Melvil, how have you been treated
In this barbarian, hostile land since I lost sight
Of you? Your fate has often troubled me.

MELVIL. What weighed upon me was not want, it was
My grief for you, the knowledge of my helplessness.

MARY. What has become of Didier, my chamberlain?
The loyal man has probably been in his grave
For many years now; he was very old.

MELVIL. That mercy God did not bestow on him.
He is alive and now must bury his young Queen.

MARY. How I have wished that I, before my death,
Could once more have embraced my dearest relatives.
But I must be content to die among
You, friendly strangers, and to see you weep for me.
To you, my loyal Melvil, I entrust
My last farewell to all my family.
I bless my husband's brother, the most Christian King
Of France and all the royal family.
I bless the Cardinal, my uncle, and Henri de Guise,
My cousin. I also bless the Pope,
The Holy Vicar of Christ, who blesses me, I know,
And give my blessing to that Catholic King
Who nobly offered rescue and revenge.
My testament lists all their names,
And they will not, I hope, despise the gifts
I leave them, poor as they may be.
(*She turns to her servants.*)
The King of France, my royal brother,

To whom I've recommended all of you,
Will care for you and give you once again a home.
Accept this last request of mine:
Do not remain in England, do not let
The overbearing Britons gloat at your misfortune,
Do not allow them to humiliate
A single one because he served me faithfully.
Give me your promise on this crucifix
That you will leave this wretched land when I am gone.

    MELVIL (*his hand on the crucifix*). I swear for all of us.

    MARY. What I, poor woman who was robbed so viciously,
Possess and can dispose of at my will,
I have distributed for you to share.
I hope my testament will be respected.
This, too, all that I wear upon my walk to death,
Is yours. Do not begrudge me this last use
Of worldly splendor on my way to heaven.

    (*To her* CHAMBERMAIDS.)

To you, dear Alix, Gertrude, Rosamond,
I give my pearls and garments. You are still so young,
You will enjoy this finery.
You, Margareta, are the next who has a claim
Upon my generosity, for you will be
The most unhappy one of all I leave behind.
My will shows that I don't take my revenge
On you for what your husband did.
You, faithful Hannah, are not tempted
By gleaming gold and sparkling stones, the memories
You have of me will be your greatest treasure. Still,
This shawl is yours; I have embroidered it
For you myself, and all the tears I've wept
Are part of its design. Use it to blindfold me—
When that time comes. That service is the last
That I shall ask of you, dear Hannah.

    HANNAH. I cannot bear it, Melvil!

    MARY.   Come now,
Come, all of you, and let me say good-bye.
    (*She holds out her hands, and one after the other kneels before her and, weeping, kisses her hand.*)
Farewell, my Margareta—farewell, Alix—
Thank you for all you did for me, Burgoyne—
Your mouth is hot, Gertrude. I have been hated much,
But many, too, have loved me. May a noble man

Make you, my Gertrude, happy, for your burning heart
Needs love— You, Bertha, chose the better part,
You want to be the virgin bride of heaven.
Do hurry to complete your vows!
All worldly goods are so deceptive,
That lesson you may learn from me. Enough!
Farewell! Good-bye! Farewell forever!

(*She quickly turns away; all her attendants, except* MELVIL, *leave.*)

SCENE 7. *Mary and Melvil.*

MARY. All the affairs of this world I have ordered,
I hope that I depart this life
A debtor to no living soul.
But one thing, Melvil, still prevents my troubled soul
From soaring, free and joyous, heavenward.

MELVIL. I am your old and trusted friend. To me
Reveal your troubles; ease your burden.

MARY. I stand upon the threshold of eternity
And soon must step before my Supreme Judge,
But I am not yet reconciled with God.
I am denied a priest, the presence of my Church,
And I refuse the Holy Sacrament
Presented to me by their own, false priests.
I wish to die without surrendering my faith,
For it alone can bring salvation.

MELVIL. Rest calm, for God accepts a fervent, pious wish
In place of actions. Tyranny can only tie
Your hands, your heart's devotion reaches God.
The word is dead, the faith gives life.

MARY. No, Melvil, that is not enough. Faith does not need
Itself alone, it needs a token to assure
Possession of the supreme grace.
That is why God became a man, that is why He
Mysteriously enshrined the gifts of heaven,
Not visible to us, in His substantial body.
It is the Church, our Holy Church, that builds
For us a ladder to eternity.
We call our Church the Catholic, the all-embracing Church,
Because the faith of the community
Strengthens the faith in each of us.

When thousands worship, thousands pray together,
The embers of our faith flare up in searing flames,
Bewinged, our spirit soars to heaven.
Oh, happy those who joyously assemble
For common prayer in a house of God!
The altar splendidly bedecked, the candles glow,
The fragrance of the incense—then the bell,
The bishop in his shining vestments
Holds up the chalice, blesses it, announces
The miracle of the transfiguration,
And in the presence of their living God,
The faithful fall upon their knees—
Oh, I alone am barred, the benediction
Does not reach me forsaken in my prison cell.

    MELVIL. It reaches you! It is close by. Have faith
In omnipotent God. The driest branch
May yet sprout leaves if only we have faith.
The One who could release a spring from solid rock
Can also build an altar in your prison,
Transform this cup, the worldly food that it contains,
Into a sacred vessel and eternal nurture.
    (*He takes the cup from the table and holds it up.*)

    MARY. Oh, Melvil—it is hard to comprehend—
But yes—I understand! There is no priest, no church,
No Host, but our Redeemer said: "Where there are two
Who come together in my name,
There I am present in their midst."
What is the consecration of a priest?
What gives him power to proclaim the Word?
His blameless heart, his spotless life.
Thus you can be, for me, a priest,
Albeit unconsecrated, and a messenger
Of God to bring me peace. To you, then, I shall make
My last confession and from you
I will receive my absolution.

    MELVIL. Since faith drives you so powerfully, learn
That God has worked a miracle to comfort you.
You say there is no priest here and no Host,
No church? You are mistaken! Here's the priest,
And he has brought the body of our Lord.
    (*With these words, he uncovers his head and shows her the Host in a golden bowl.*)
I am the priest. So that I might receive

Your last confession and bring peace to you
As you walk to your death, I have received
The seven consecrations, and I bring
This Host to you, sent by the Holy Father;
It has been consecrated by His Holiness.

MARY. Heavenly joy that comes to me,
Now even at the gates of death!
As an immortal God descends to earth
On golden clouds, as once the angel broke
The prison chains that fettered the apostle—
Not sentries' swords nor iron bars can hinder him
As he strides mightily through walls and doors—
A messenger from heaven now surprises me,
I stand in awe before his glory,
Now that all human rescuers have failed.
And you who once served me are now God's servant,
His holy words come to me through your mouth.
As you once bent your knee before your Queen,
Thus I now lie before you in the dust.

(*She falls on her knees.*)

MELVIL (*makes the sign of the cross over her head*).
In the name of God the Father, God the Son
And of the Holy Ghost! Queen Mary, did you search
Your heart, and do you vow and swear that you will speak
The truth before the God who is the Truth?

MARY. My heart lies open before Him and you.

MELVIL. Of what sins does your conscience blame you, sins
Committed since you last propitiated God?

MARY. My heart was filled with jealousy and hate,
The thought of vengeance raged within my mind.
I who had sinned and prayed forgiveness
Did not have strength enough to pardon her
Who was my enemy.

MELVIL.   Do you repent,
And is it now your firm resolve
To pass from life, at peace with her?

MARY. As truly as I hope for God's forgiveness.

MELVIL. And of what other sins do you accuse yourself?

MARY. Oh, even more than by my hate I have affronted God
By sinful love. My heart was vain,
It was attracted by the man
Who faithlessly deserted me.

MELVIL. Do you regret your failing? Has your heart
Returned to God from the false idols it adored?

MARY. It was the hardest fight I had to win,
The last of all my earthly bonds is torn.

MELVIL. Is there another sin with which your conscience
    charges you?

MARY. A deed of blood, committed long ago
And long ago confessed, returns to me
With doubled terror in this hour of final reckoning,
And black it looms between me and the gate of heaven.
I had the King, my husband, murdered,
I gave my heart and hand to the seducer.
I did atone for it with all the penalties
The Church imposed, but in my soul
The viper lives and will not let me sleep.

MELVIL. Are there no other sins, not yet confessed
And not yet expiated, which oppress your heart?

MARY. I've told you all that weighed upon my heart.

MELVIL. Remember the proximity of the Omniscient,
Think of the penalties the Church decrees
For incomplete confession! That sin means
Eternal death, it outrages the Holy Ghost.

MARY. May heaven's everlasting mercy grant me victory
In my last struggle, I hide nothing knowingly.

MELVIL. What? Do you hide from God the crime
Of which the world accuses you?
You tell me nothing of your share in Babington's
And Perry's treacherous offense?
For that crime you will lose your life on earth,
Do you intend to forfeit life eternal, too?

MARY. I'm now prepared to face my Supreme Judge.
It will be only minutes till I stand
Before His throne, and I repeat,
I've made complete confession.

MELVIL.   Weigh your words!
The mind deceives. Perhaps you did avoid,
With cunning ambiguity, the word
That would condemn, but shared the crime by willing it.
But juggler's tricks will not deceive
The flaming eye that looks into your heart.

MARY. I summoned all the princes of the Continent
To free me from demeaning bonds,

But never did I touch, in thought or deed,
The life of my opponent.

MELVIL. The testimony of your clerks then was a lie?

MARY. It is as I have said. God be the judge
Of what they testified.

MELVIL. Convinced, then, of your innocence you mount the
scaffold?

MARY. God has seen fit to let me expiate
My early crime by dying innocently.

MELVIL (*makes the sign of the cross over her*).
Go then, and by your death atone for it,
Put down your life as sacrifice before the altar.
Blood can redeem a deed of blood.
Your crime was but a woman's frailty,
And mortal weakness stays behind
When our transfigured souls ascend to heaven.
By virtue of the power to unite
And to dissolve, which has been given me,
I now absolve you from all sin.
As you believed, thus be done unto you.
(*He gives her the Host.*)
This is the body that was sacrificed for you.
(*He takes the cup from the table, consecrates the wine with a
silent prayer, then offers it to her. She hesitates and refuses
the cup with a gesture of her hand.*)
Accept the blood which Jesus shed for you.
Accept it, for the Pope grants you this favor.
The noblest right of kings, the sacerdotal right,
It shall be yours unto your death.
(*She accepts the cup.*)
And as your God is now mysteriously joined
With you in this, your earthly shell,
Thus you shall be united with your God
In all eternity, to live,
A blessed angel, in His joyous realm
Where neither guilt nor tears exist.
(*He puts down the cup. Hearing a noise, he covers his head
and steps to the door. MARY remains on her knees, in silent
prayer.*)

MELVIL (*returning from the door*).
One painful struggle still remains for you.
Do you feel strong enough to vanquish
All bitterness or hate that you may feel?

MARY. I'm not afraid of their return. I've sacrificed
My hate and all my love to God.

MELVIL. Prepare yourself, then, to receive
The Earl of Leicester and Lord Burleigh. They are here.

SCENE 8. *The same. Burleigh, Leicester, and Paulet enter.
Leicester stands far back and does not raise his eyes.
Burleigh, noticing his behavior, steps between him and
Mary.*

BURLEIGH. I come, my Lady, to receive your last commands.

MARY. Thank you, my Lord.

BURLEIGH.   My Queen desires
That any fair request be granted you.

MARY. My testament contains my final wishes.
I've given it to Sir Amias, and I hope
That it be executed faithfully.

BURLEIGH. You may rely on that.

MARY. I also ask that you allow my servants
To leave for France or Scotland without hindrance,
Wherever they themselves may wish to go.

BURLEIGH. It will be done as you desire.

MARY. And since my body may not rest in consecrated ground,
I ask that you permit this loyal servant
To take my heart to France. There it has always been.

BURLEIGH. So be it. Is there any other wish—

MARY. Take to the Queen of England my sincere
And sisterly regard. Tell her
That in my hour of death I pardon her
With all my heart, and that I ask of her
Forgiveness for my violence of yesterday.
May God preserve her and grant her a happy reign.

BURLEIGH. Have you not reconsidered? Do you still refuse
The consolations of the dean?

MARY. I've made my peace with God. Oh, Sir Amias,
I've caused you, much against my wish, great pain.
I've robbed you of the comfort and support
Of your old age. Please, let me hope
That you won't hate my memory.

PAULET (*takes her hand*). Go peacefully, and God be with
    you!

SCENE 9. *Hannah and the other women of Mary's retinue return, visibly terrified; they are followed by the Sheriff who carries a white staff. Behind him, armed men are seen through the open door.*

MARY. What is it, Hannah? Yes, the time has come.
Here is the sheriff who will lead us to our death.
Now we must part. Farewell! Farewell!
    (*Her women cling to her; to* MELVIL.)
You, sir, and Hannah shall accompany
My last steps in this world. Lord Burleigh,
You will not deny me this last favor.

BURLEIGH. I've no authority to grant it.

MARY. You would refuse me this one small request?
Do you have no respect for women?
Who, then, shall render me the final service?
It cannot be my sister's wish
That you insult, in me, all womanhood,
That men shall touch me with their uncouth hands!

BURLEIGH. No woman is allowed to mount the scaffold's steps
With you. Her screams and lamentations would—

MARY. Hannah will not lament. She will be calm
And strong, I warrant you. Be kind, my Lord!
Don't separate me from my faithful nurse
In this last hour. On her arms I was carried
Into life, let her guide me to death
With gentle hands.

PAULET (*to* BURLEIGH). Grant her request.

BURLEIGH.   So be it, then.

MARY. Now I have finished with this world.
    (*She kisses the crucifix.*)
My Savior and Redeemer, as your arms
Were stretched upon the cross, now spread them wide
To welcome me!
    (*As she turns to go, her eyes fall upon* LEICESTER *who had, startled by her departure, roused himself and looked at her. At his sight,* MARY *begins to tremble, falters and is about to fall;* LEICESTER *catches her in his arms. For a moment, she gazes at him, silently and solemnly; he averts his eyes. Finally, she speaks.*)
        You keep your promise, Leicester.

You vowed to lead me from my prison on your arm,
And now you do.
(*He stands in silence, crushed by her words. She continues
in a soft voice.*)
           Yes, Leicester, I expected
Not only freedom from your hands,
You were to make my freedom dear to me.
I hoped that on your arm, rejoicing in your love,
I would begin a new, delicious life.
Now that I am about to leave this world
And to become a blessed spirit
Whom worldly love no longer tempts,
Now I admit that weakness without blushing.
Farewell and, if you can, live happily!
You had the privilege to woo two queens;
You scorned the tender, loving heart of one,
To win the proud heart of the other.
Kneel, then, before Elizabeth!
I hope your prize will not become your punishment.
Farewell! Now I have finished with this earth.
(*She leaves, preceded by the* SHERIFF, *at her side* MELVIL
and HANNAH. BURLEIGH *and* PAULET *follow, while the others
stare after her in silent grief until she is out of sight. Then
they leave by the other two doors.*)

SCENE 10. *Leicester alone.*

LEICESTER. I'm still alive? How can I bear to live?
Why does this roof not fall and crush me with its weight?
Why does no abyss open up to swallow me?
What have I lost! What jewel have I thrown away!
The bliss of heaven I have squandered.
She goes, already a transfigured spirit,
And I remain to suffer the despair of hell.
What happened to my firm resolve to choke
My senses and to suffocate my heart,
Unfeelingly to watch her die?
Is it the sight of her that reawakened
My shame which I had killed? Does she,
Even in death, ensnare me with the bonds of love?
I am abominable and I have no right
To melt in womanly commiseration.
The happiness of love does not lie on my path,

I must protect my breast with iron armor, be a rock.
Proceed! I must complete the infamy that I began
Lest I be cheated of its fair reward.
Compassion—die! Eyes—turn to stone!
I shall be witness, I shall see her die.

(*He takes a few determined steps toward the door through
which* MARY *left the room; before reaching it, he stops.*)

In vain! In vain! Hell's horror grips my soul
I cannot face the terrifying sight,
I cannot see her die. Ah! What was that?
They are already in the hall,
The ghastly work proceeds below my feet.
Now I hear voices—no! Away! Away
From this abode of death and horror!

(*He tries to escape through another door but finds it locked.
He recoils in terror.*)

What? Does a vengeful God encage me here?
Am I compelled to hear what I don't dare to see?
The deacon's voice—he cautions her—
She interrupts—there—now she prays aloud—
Her voice is firm—now she is quiet—all is still—
So still—there is no sound but that
Of weeping women and of sobs—
Now they undress her—there—they move the stool—
She kneels upon the pillow—now she puts her head—

(*He has spoken the last lines with steadily mounting terror;
then, suddenly his body twitches and he falls to the floor, unconscious. At the same moment, the dull roar of many voices
is heard from below and continues for some time.*)

SCENE 11. *The Queen's chamber. This is the same room as
in the second part of Act IV. Elizabeth enters through a
side door; her movements indicate her extreme agitation.*

ELIZABETH. No one here yet—no messenger! Will night not fall
Today? The sun stands still in its celestial course.
How long am I to suffer torture waiting for
The long-awaited news? Has it been done
Or has it not? I shudder at the thought of both.
I dare not ask. No sign of Leicester or of Burleigh,
Whom I have named to carry out the sentence.
If they left London, it has happened.
The arrow has been shot, it flies, it finds its mark.
Not for my kingdom could I stop it now. Who's there?

SCENE 12. *Elizabeth and a Page.*

ELIZABETH. You come alone? Where are the lords?

PAGE. The Earl of Leicester and Lord Burleigh—

ELIZABETH (*with bated breath*). Where are they?

PAGE. They're not in London.

ELIZABETH. They're not? Where are they, then?

PAGE. No one could tell me, but it seems they left
The city before dawn in haste and secrecy.

ELIZABETH (*bursts out*). Then—I am Queen of England!
(*She paces up and down in great agitation.*)
Go—call—no, stay! She's dead! She's dead.
At last there is room enough for me on earth.
Why do I tremble? Why am I afraid?
My fear lies in her grave, and who can say
I did it? I shall not lack tears to mourn her death.
(*To the* PAGE.)
Are you still here? I want my secretary,
Davison, to come at once. Send for
The Earl of Shrewsbury. Ah, here he is.

(*The* PAGE *leaves.*)

SCENE 13. *Elizabeth and Shrewsbury.*

ELIZABETH. Welcome, my Lord. What news have you?
It must be an important matter that directs
Your steps to me so late at night.

SHREWSBURY. Your Majesty, today my troubled heart
And fear for your good name impelled me to the Tower,
Once more to test the truthfulness of Curl and Nau,
The Stuart's clerks, who are imprisoned there.
Embarrassed, the Lieutenant of the Tower
At first refused to let me see the prisoners.
My threats, at last, gained me admittance.
God, what a sight my eyes beheld!
Unkempt, a wild look in his eye, the Scotsman, Curl,
Lay on his bed as if pursued by Furies;
No sooner did he recognize my face,
The wretch fell on his knees before me, clutched

My legs and, twisting like a worm and screaming,
Implored and begged of me to tell him Mary's fate.
A rumor, so it seems, that she had been condemned
To death had penetrated to the Tower's depth.
When I confirmed that this was true and said
Moreover that his testimony was
The reason of her death, the man sprang to his feet
And in a rage attacked his fellow prisoner;
He pushed him down, and with a madman's strength
He tried to strangle him. We barely managed
To tear the man from his infuriated grip.
But now he turned his rage against himself
Clawed at his breast with his fierce hands and cursed
Himself and his companion to eternal hell.
His testimony had been false, he cried,
The letters to Sir Babington which he had sworn
Were true had been a forgery, the words
Which he had written were not those
That Mary had dictated. Nau
Had talked him into this treachery.
With that, he ran and tore the window open
And screamed into the street, where people quickly gathered,
That he was Mary Stuart's clerk, the fiend
Who had accused her falsely and that now,
As a false witness, he was damned.

ELIZABETH. You said yourself that he was mad.
The words that madmen speak prove nothing.

SHREWSBURY. His madness, by itself, proves all the more.
Your Majesty, I do implore you not to act
Too hastily. Command a new inquiry.

ELIZABETH. That I shall do—because you ask, my Lord,
And not because I can believe my peers
Have judged the matter hastily.
Yes, to appease your conscience I command
That the investigation be renewed.
Good that there is still time. There shall not be
The faintest doubt to cast a shadow on our royal honor.

SCENE 14. *The same. Davison enters.*

ELIZABETH. Where is the sentence, sir, which I put in your
hands?

Where is it?

DAVISON (*perplexed*). What? The sentence?

ELIZABETH.   Yes, the document
I gave you yesterday to keep—

DAVISON.   To keep!

ELIZABETH. The crowd insisted that I sign, I had
To grant their wish, and so I did.
I was compelled to sign, and to gain time,
I put the document into your hands,
And you remember what I told you. Well?
I want it back.

SHREWSBURY. Please, sir, return it. Things
Are different now. A new inquiry will be made.

ELIZABETH. Do not waste time. Where is the paper?

DAVISON. Oh, I am lost! This is my death!

ELIZABETH (*quickly*). I hope you did not—

DAVISON. I do not have it any more—I'm ruined!

ELIZABETH. What did you say?

SHREWSBURY.   Merciful God!

DAVISON. Lord Burleigh has the document—since yesterday.

ELIZABETH. You wretch! Is that how you obey my orders!
It was my strict command that you retain it.

DAVISON. No, that, your Majesty, was not your order.

ELIZABETH. Do you propose to make a liar of me, scoundrel?
When did I say to give the sheet to Burleigh?

DAVISON. Not in so many words—not clearly—but—

ELIZABETH. Do you, then, dare interpret my commands
And give them the unholy meaning you pretend
To see in them? If a misfortune should result
From what you did on your, and only your,
Authority, you'll pay for it. I'll have your life!
Oh, Shrewsbury, you see how they misuse my name!

SHREWSBURY. I see it clearly. Oh, my God!

ELIZABETH.   What did you say?

SHREWSBURY. If this man did presume to act
At his own risk and without your approval,
He must be tried before his peers for having made
Your name repulsive for all time.

SCENE 15. *The same. Burleigh; at the end, Kent.*

BURLEIGH (*enters and kneels before the Queen*).
Long live my Queen! May all the enemies
Of England end as Mary Stuart ended!
(SHREWSBURY *covers his face;* DAVISON *wrings his hands in despair.*)

ELIZABETH. Tell me, my Lord, did you receive from me
The order for her death?

BURLEIGH. No, I did not, your Majesty.
I had it from this gentleman.

ELIZABETH. Did Davison give you the order in my name?

BURLEIGH. No, not exactly—

ELIZABETH. But you were quick to execute it without first
Confirming my desire? Just was the sentence,
The world cannot find fault with us.
But to forestall my clemency you had no right.
Therefore you're banished from my presence.
(*To* DAVISON.)
You may expect a stricter judgment,
For you have overstepped your competence
And with impertinence abused a sacred trust.
Conduct him to the Tower! It is my desire
That he be tried on pain of death.
You, Noble Talbot, I have found to be
The only one among my councillors
Who has been just. You be my friend and counsel.

SHREWSBURY. Don't banish your most faithful friends,
Do not imprison those who acted in your stead
And now are silent for your sake.
I, gracious Majesty, ask your permission
To put again into your hands the seal
With which for twelve years you have trusted me.

ELIZABETH (*taken aback*). No, Shrewsbury, you cannot leave
me now—

SHREWSBURY. Forgive me, I'm too old and this straight hand
Too stiff to seal your novel actions.

ELIZABETH. The man who saved my life would now abandon
me?

SHREWSBURY. What I did was not much. The nobler part of
you

I could not save. Live long, reign happily!
Your enemy is dead. You now need have
No fear and no respect for anything.   *(He leaves.)*

   ELIZABETH *(to* KENT *who enters).*
I wish to see the Earl of Leicester.

   KENT. The Earl of Leicester asks to be excused.
He has embarked for France.

   *(*ELIZABETH *controls herself and remains calm and composed.)*

CURTAIN

The Prince of Homburg

A PLAY IN FIVE ACTS

by
HEINRICH VON KLEIST

❖ ❖ ❖

The genius and power of no other play in the canon of German drama has been more slowly discovered and admired than that of Heinrich von Kleist's *Prinz Friedrich von Homburg*. Written in 1809–10 at a time when Kleist's anti-Napoleon convictions made the patriotic subject matter especially appealing to him, and published in 1821, ten years after his suicide, it was for long regarded as merely a romantic spectacle with a specifically Brandenburg setting and a plot motivated by a curiously ambiguous moral argument. The story of the prince's defiance of orders during the Battle of Fehrbellin (1675), his decisive contribution to victory, and his surprising court-martial was an incident familiar enough to students of Prussian history. Kleist modifies it in some respects but retains the central episode: the middle-aged prince is in Kleist's play a youthful enthusiast, equally preoccupied with love and a desire for fame. He disobeys the order of the day, is condemned to death for insubordination, comes to accept the justice of the verdict, is pardoned, and eventually celebrated as a hero.

This simple and austere anecdote becomes in Kleist's terse and exceedingly concentrated plot an impressive vehicle for an intellectual and moral issue characteristic of the German classicist drama. The prince, an impulsive and noble but somewhat naïve human being, is confronted by a system of law and order which he "naturally" finds irksome, absurd, and inhuman. He is brought, through a series of incidents which Kleist motivates with great skill, first to submit to the judgment of the Elector and eventually to understand his motives. His understanding is mirrored in the attitude of the Elector who is himself tested and examined: what seems in him at first a rigid and purely formal Prussian sense of duty is shown to be dedication to a code of values, and an intelligent identification with them, which must be—for Kleist—the prerequisite of any social order.

The sympathies of the audience and indeed of all the figures in the play itself, lie altogether with the prince: his offense seems trivial, it can easily be excused and argued away. The Elector himself is deeply attached to the prince; but he is resolved to bring him to the point where he must himself judge whether or not he should be pardoned. In the famous scene where the prince, at first terrified but gradually composed and resolute, faces the prospect of his death, Kleist portrays an existential crisis which leads beyond animal despair to comprehension and responsibility. The prince must learn to accept life in the full knowledge of its ultimate dependence upon death: "There is nothing more sublime in life," Kleist wrote on another occasion, "than that you can sublimely throw it away."

The Prince of Homburg is thus a parable of the paradoxical relationship between freedom and order, and of the threat to the balance between the two by the extremes of irresponsibility and inhumanity. The harmony which is precariously achieved in the final scene of the play—a brilliant piece of romantic theatre—has as much to do with grace and forgiveness as with the prince's eventual acceptance of his own share in the efficacy of the law.

The recent success of Kleist's drama in France and Germany is undoubtedly due to the relevance of Kleist's argument for a generation that has itself experienced the contradictory claims of freedom and obedience, of allegiance and of skepticism toward the law. But beyond the fascination which the intellectual issue of the play may exercise, it is the superb craftsmanship, the economy and discipline of the dramatic construction, and the breathless consistency with which the dialectical movement of the central idea is developed that is now so profoundly admired.

The Prince of Homburg

✤

CHARACTERS

Friedrich Wilhelm, Elector of Brandenburg
The Electress
Princess Natalie of Orange, the Elector's niece and chief
    of a regiment of dragoons
Field Marshal Dörfling
Prince Friedrich Arthur of Homburg, General of Cavalry
Colonel Kottwitz, of the Regiment of the Princess of Orange
Hennings
Count Truchss } Infantry Colonels
Count Hohenzollern, of the Elector's suite
Captain von der Golz
Count George von Sparren
Stranz } Cavalry Captains
Siegfried von Mörner
Count Reuss
A Sergeant
Officers, Corporals and Cavalrymen, Courtiers, Ladies-
    in-Waiting, Pages, Haiduks, Servants and People of both
    sexes and all ages.

The year is 1675.

✤

ACT I

Scene 1. *Fehrbellin. A garden in the traditional French
style. In the background is a palace, from which a ramp
leads down into the garden. It is night. The Prince of Homburg sits on a bench under an oak tree, his head bare and
his shirt open at the neck, half-awake; he is making a
wreath. The Elector, the Electress, Count Hohenzollern,
Captain Golz, Princess Natalie, and others come furtively*

out of the palace and look at the Prince from the top of the
ramp. Pages hold torches that light up the scene.

HOHENZOLLERN. The Prince of Homburg, our intrepid
    cousin,
For the last three days has been in brisk pursuit
Of the escaping Swedes with all his cavalry
And did not reach our quarters here in Fehrbellin
Until today, ending the breathless chase.
You ordered him to stay just the three hours
He needs to feed his horses, then again
To hurry off in search of Wrangel,
Who wants to dig his forces in along the Rhyn,
And to push forward to the Hackel Hills.
Is that correct?
    ELECTOR.   That's so.
    HOHENZOLLERN.   Well then,
He did instruct the chiefs of all his squadrons
To leave the town at ten o'clock tonight
According to your plan; but he, exhausted
And panting like a bird dog, threw himself
Upon the straw to rest his weary limbs awhile
Before the battle that will start at dawn.

    ELECTOR. I heard about that. Well?

    HOHENZOLLERN.   The hour arrives,
The entire cavalry is mounted,
The horses paw the field before the gate,
But who is missing? Yes, their general,
The Prince of Homburg! So they look for him
With lanterns and with torches and, at last,
They find him—where?
    (*He takes a torch from one of the pages.*)
             You see? Upon that bench.
You never would believe that he walks in his sleep,
But there, lured by the moonlight, he now sits,
Asleep and dreaming, busily engaged
In winding for himself a wreath of glory,
As if he were his own posterity.

    ELECTOR. Impossible!

    HOHENZOLLERN.   And yet it's true. See for yourself!
(*He lets the light from his torch fall on the* PRINCE.)
    ELECTOR. Asleep? I can't believe it.

HOHENZOLLERN.   Fast asleep.
Call out his name, and he'll collapse.
  (*A pause.*)

ELECTRESS. The young man is not well.

NATALIE.   He needs a doctor.

ELECTRESS. We ought to help him, not waste time with mocking him.

HOHENZOLLERN (*handing the torch back to the* PAGE).
You ladies are compassionate and kind,
But he's as well as I am. That the Swedes
Will soon find out when they meet up with him
Tomorrow on the battlefield.
It's nothing, you may rest assured,
But a peculiar habit of his mind.

  ELECTOR. I always thought it was a fairy tale.
Come, friends, let's take a closer look at him.
  (*They descend the ramp.*)

A COURTIER (*to the* PAGES).
Stay back! No torches!

  HOHENZOLLERN.   Let them shed their light.
The village could go up in flames,
And he would be no more aware of it
Than would the diamond he wears.
  (*They stand around the* PRINCE; *the* PAGES *light up the
  scene.*)

ELECTOR (*bending over the* PRINCE).
What are those leaves he uses for his wreath?
Not willow leaves?

  HOHENZOLLERN. What? Willow leaves? Oh, no!
He uses laurel leaves, as he has seen
On heroes' portraits in the armory.

  ELECTOR. But how did he find laurels in our sand?

  HOHENZOLLERN. That only God can tell.

THE COURTIER.   The gardener
Grows many foreign plants back in the garden.
That's where he found the leaves perhaps.

  ELECTOR. It's very strange. I wonder what may drive
The mind of this young fool to such behavior.

  HOHENZOLLERN. Oh, that! It is tomorrow's battle, sir.
He sees star-gazers fashion him
A victor's crown from suns.

(*The* PRINCE *inspects the wreath.*)

THE COURTIER.   Now he has finished, sir.

HOHENZOLLERN. It is a shame that there's no mirror here.
He would step up like a coquettish girl,
Put on the wreath, now this way and now that,
As if it were a bonnet made from gossamer.

ELECTOR. By God, I want to see how far he'll go.
(*He takes the wreath from the* PRINCE. *The* PRINCE *blushes
and looks at him. The* ELECTOR *then takes his chain off and
wraps it around the wreath, giving both to* NATALIE. *The*
PRINCE *quickly gets to his feet, while the* ELECTOR *and the*
PRINCESS, *who is holding the wreath up above her head,
step back. The* PRINCE *follows her with outstretched arms.*)

PRINCE (*whispers*). Oh, Natalie . . . my dearest girl . . . my
     bride!

ELECTOR. Let's leave now, quickly!

HOHENZOLLERN.   What did he whisper?

THE COURTIER.   What was that?
(*The entire party goes back up the ramp.*)

PRINCE. My father . . . Frederic . . . my sovereign!

HOHENZOLLERN. Hell and damnation!

ELECTOR (*stepping backward*). Quick now, open up the doors.

PRINCE. My mother!

HOHENZOLLERN.   He's mad, he is . . .

ELECTRESS.   Whom does he call?

PRINCE (*reaching for the wreath*).
Beloved, why do you escape? O Natalie!
(*He snatches a glove from* NATALIE's *hand.*)

HOHENZOLLERN. The devil, what was that he took?

THE COURTIER.   The wreath?

NATALIE. No, no.

HOHENZOLLERN (*throws open the portal*).
                  In here, your Highness, quickly let
The vision fade from view again.

ELECTOR. Back to the void, my Prince of Homburg! Back
Into the void! We'll see each other, if you please,
Tomorrow on the battlefield.
So great a prize is never won in dreams.
(*They all enter into the palace. The door is shut behind them,
slamming noisily in the* PRINCE'S *face.*)

SCENE 2. *A pause. Puzzled, the Prince stands for a moment in front of the door, then, musing and pressing the hand in which he holds the glove to his forehead, he descends the ramp. When he arrives at the bottom, he turns and looks once more at the closed door.*

SCENE 3. *The Prince. Hohenzollern enters through a garden gate below, followed by a Page.*

PAGE (*softly*). Please listen to me, gracious sir!

HOHENZOLLERN (*irritated*).
Stop chirping! Well, what do you want?

PAGE. I've come to tell you, sir—

HOHENZOLLERN.   Don't wake him up!
Well now, you've come to tell me what?

PAGE. His Highness, the Elector, sends me and he asks
That nothing should be mentioned to the Prince,
When he awakes, about the jest
His Highness has allowed himself to play just now.

HOHENZOLLERN (*under his breath*).
I knew that anyhow. Go back to sleep!

(*The PAGE leaves.*)

SCENE 4. *The Prince and Hohenzollern.*

HOHENZOLLERN (*standing several paces behind the PRINCE, who is still staring up at the ramp*).
Oh, Arthur!
    (*The PRINCE falls to the ground.*)
                There he lies. A bullet
Could not have brought him down more quickly.
    (*He steps closer.*)
I'm curious what fantastic fairy tales
He'll tell me to explain why he selected
This garden bench to serve him as a bed.
    (*He bends over him.*)
Hey, Arthur! Are you mad? What are you doing here?
Is this a place to spend the night?

PRINCE. Why . . . good old friend . . .

HOHENZOLLERN. I really must say! The cavalry

That you command has left an hour ago,
And you lie here and sleep!

    PRINCE.   What cavalry?

    HOHENZOLLERN. The Mamelukes! By God, he does not even
        know
That he commands the cavalry of Brandenburg!

    PRINCE (*rising*). Quick now, my helmet—my cuirass!

    HOHENZOLLERN. Hm, hm—but where are they?

    PRINCE.   Oh, Heinrich, over there,
Right on that stool.

    HOHENZOLLERN.   What stool? And over where?

    PRINCE. I put them over there, it seems to me ...

    HOHENZOLLERN (*looking at him*).
Well then, just take them from the stool yourself.

    PRINCE. What's this? A glove?
    (*He looks at the glove which he is still clasping.*)

    HOHENZOLLERN.   How would I know?
(*Aside.*) Confound it! That is what he snatched
Unnoticed from the Princess' arm up there.
(*Sharply.*) Be quick now, don't waste time.

    PRINCE (*throws the glove away*).   I'm coming. Franz!
Where is the scoundrel? He was told to wake me up.

    HOHENZOLLERN (*looking at the* PRINCE, *aside*).
He's raving mad.

    PRINCE.   I swear, my friend,
I don't know where I am.

    HOHENZOLLERN.   In Fehrbellin,
You crazy dreamer, on a garden path
Behind the palace.

    PRINCE (*aside*). That the night would swallow me!
I have been walking in my sleep again.
    (*Getting control of himself.*)
Forgive me, now I know. It was so hot
Last night, I simply could not stay in bed.
Exhausted thus, I stole into this garden,
And since the night embraced me so delightfully,
Its hair caressing me, so full of fragrance,
I laid my head into her lap,
A bridegroom lovingly received by his dark bride.
What is the time?

HOHENZOLLERN. Half past eleven.

PRINCE. The squadrons have already left, you say?

HOHENZOLLERN. Of course! At ten o'clock, as they were ordered.
The Princess of Orange's regiment has undoubtedly
Already reached the heights near Hackelwitz,
Where it will cover, as the vanguard,
The army's noiseless march tomorrow morning.

PRINCE. All right. Old Kottwitz leads them, and he knows
Exactly what he is to do. What's more,
I would have had to come back here in any case,
At two o'clock, when we are to receive
The orders of the day. It's just as well
I stayed behind. Come on, let's go.
Does the Elector know about this?

HOHENZOLLERN. How could he? He has been asleep for hours.
(*As they start to go, the* PRINCE *suddenly stops, turns back
and picks up the glove.*)

PRINCE. I had the strangest dream. It seemed to me
That from a royal palace, glittering
With gold and silver, suddenly emerged
A whole procession of the people I love most,
Descending down a marble staircase toward me;
Among them the Elector and his spouse,
And then a third one—what's her name again?

HOHENZOLLERN. Whose name?

PRINCE (*trying to remember*). The one—I mean. Why, anyone,
Though deaf and dumb, would know her name!

HOHENZOLLERN. The Countess Platen?

PRINCE.   No, of course not, Heinrich.

HOHENZOLLERN. Ramin?

PRINCE.   No, no.

HOHENZOLLERN.   The Winterfeld? Or Bork?

PRINCE. No, really! You do not see the pearl
For all the splendor of its setting.

HOHENZOLLERN. You name her, then. How can I guess her face?
Which lady was it?

PRINCE.   Never mind. Now that I am awake,
I can't recall. It does not matter anyhow.

HOHENZOLLERN. All right, then. Go ahead.

PRINCE.   Don't interrupt.
He—the Elector—with the head of Zeus,
Held in his hand a laurel wreath; he stepped
In front of me and wrapped his chain of gold
Around the wreath, then gave both wreath and chain,
To crown my head with them, to . . .

HOHENZOLLERN.   Whom?

PRINCE.   Oh, friend!

HOHENZOLLERN. Who was it?

PRINCE.   Well, it must have been the Platen.

HOHENZOLLERN. The Countess Platen? But she is in Prussia now.

PRINCE. I'm sure—I think. Or else, the Countess von Ramin.

HOHENZOLLERN. Ramin? Aha, the redhead! Yes, I know,
You like her violet, coquettish eyes.

PRINCE. I like her, yes.

HOHENZOLLERN.   Well then? She gave the wreath to you?

PRINCE. High in her hand, a deity of glory,
She held the wreath, the chain attached to it,
As if she were about to crown a hero.
Moved in a way I've never felt before,
I stretch my hands to take it, ready
To throw myself upon the ground before her feet,
But as the mist that wafts across a valley
Will disappear before the lightest breath of air,
The group recedes, retreating up the ramp.
Beneath my steps the ramp extends
Unendingly to heaven's gate.
I reach for someone, something, right and left,
In terror try to grasp a human hand—
In vain. The palace doors burst open suddenly,
A flash of lightning swallows all of them,
The portal clatters shut, alone outside,
I'm left with nothing but a glove,
Snatched from the lovely apparition's arm
In my pursuit. A glove, almighty gods,
I still hold in my hand as I awake!

HOHENZOLLERN. Amazing! And you think the glove is hers?

PRINCE. Whose?

HOHENZOLLERN. Why, the Countess Platen's.

PRINCE.   Yes, the Platen's.
Or else the Countess von Ramin's.

HOHENZOLLERN (*laughing*).
You rogue! With all your dreams and apparitions,
Who knows what tender tryst with flesh and blood
You kept here, wide awake, from which this glove
Remains a sweet memento in your hand.

PRINCE. What? I? As surely as—

HOHENZOLLERN.   All right, all right.
It's no concern of mine. For all I care,
The glove belongs to Countess Platen or Ramin.
The stagecoach leaves for Prussia early Sunday,
And that would be the fastest way to ascertain
If your beloved has mislaid a glove.
Let's go. It's twelve o'clock, and here we stand and chatter.

PRINCE (*musing*). You're right. Let's go to bed. There's something, though,
I meant to ask you—yes, are the Electress and her niece,
The lovely Princess Natalie, who recently
Arrived in Fehrbellin, still here?

HOHENZOLLERN. Why do you ask? (*Aside.*) I think, the fool . . .

PRINCE. I'll tell you why. I was to furnish her
A guard of thirty men to take them back.
I gave the order to Ramin.

HOHENZOLLERN. Ah, nonsense. They have left long since, or else
They're ready now. Ramin was waiting at the gate
For them all night. Let's go. It's twelve o'clock.
I want to rest awhile before the battle starts.

(*Both leave.*)

SCENE 5. *A hall in the palace of Fehrbellin. Shooting is heard in the distance. The Electress and Natalie enter, followed by their ladies. Dressed for traveling, they are escorted into the hall by a Courtier and sit down at one side. A moment later, the Elector enters with Field Marshal Dörfling, the Prince of Homburg, who has pushed the glove into his doublet, the Count of Hohenzollern, Count Truchss, Colonel Hennings, Captain von der Golz and several other generals, colonels and officers of lower rank.*

ELECTOR. Where does the shooting come from? Is that Götz?

FIELD MARSHAL. Yes, that is Colonel Götz, your Highness,
Who left here with the vanguard yesterday.
He sent an officer to bring us warning,

So that you should not be alarmed by it.
A Swedish force, a thousand strong, has pushed ahead
Up to the Hackel Hills, but Götz has guaranteed
That he will take the heights and asks you to proceed
As if they were already in his hands.

ELECTOR. The Marshal has the battle plan.
Please write it down, as he explains it.

(*The officers gather around the* MARSHAL *and bring out their pads.*)

ELECTOR (*to the* COURTIER).
Has Count Ramin brought up the carriage yet?

THE COURTIER. He will be here at once, your Highness.
They're hitching up the horses now.

ELECTOR (*sitting down behind the* ELECTRESS *and* NATALIE.)
Ramin will drive you, dear, and thirty cuirassiers
Will be your guard. You'll go to Kalkhuhn's castle,
Near Havelberg, beyond the Havel River,
Where Swedes no longer dare to show themselves.

ELECTRESS. Have they repaired the ferry boat?

ELECTOR. At Havelberg? They're working at it; more,
It will be daylight long before you reach the spot.

(*A pause.*)
Why is my darling Natalie so still?
Is something wrong?

NATALIE.　　　　　I am afraid, dear uncle.

ELECTOR. And yet you never have been more secure,
Not even in your mother's lap.

(*A pause.*)

ELECTRESS. When do you think that we shall meet again?

ELECTOR. As soon as God grants me the victory
I hope to win, perhaps within these next few days.

(PAGES *come with breakfast for the ladies. Meanwhile the* FIELD MARSHAL *begins to dictate his orders. The* PRINCE, *pad and pencil in hand, stares at the ladies.*)

FIELD MARSHAL. The battle plan his Highness has drawn up
Aims, gentlemen, at cutting off
The entire army of the Swedes, in flight
Already, from the bridgehead which they hold
As cover for their rear along the Rhyn,
And to destroy it. Colonel Hennings—

HENNINGS.　　　　　　　　　Here!

(He begins to take notes.)

FIELD MARSHAL. Who will, according to his Highness' wish,
Command our right today, will quietly
Advance through the depression of the Hackel Hills
And thus attempt to flank the foe's left wing.
He'll throw his troops between the enemy
And the three bridges in their rear, and then,
Together with Count Truchss—Count Truchss!

TRUCHSS. Here! *(He begins to write.)*

FIELD MARSHAL. Then, with Count Truchss . . . *(He pauses.)*
                        Who meanwhile has set up
His cannon on the heights and faces Wrangel . . .

TRUCHSS *(writing)*. His cannon on the heights and faces
Wrangel . . .

FIELD MARSHAL. You have that written down? Will seek to
drive
The Swedes into the swamps behind their right.

(A HAIDUK enters.)

THE HAIDUK. The carriage, gracious Lady, has pulled up.

(The ladies rise.)

FIELD MARSHAL. The Prince of Homburg . . .

ELECTOR *(also rising)*.   And Ramin is ready?

THE HAIDUK. He's mounted and awaits her Highness at the
gate.

                  (The ladies take their leave from the ELECTOR.)

TRUCHSS *(writing)*. The Swedes into the swamps behind
their right.

FIELD MARSHAL. The Prince of Homburg . . . Is the Prince of
Homburg here?

HOHENZOLLERN *(under his breath)*.
Hey, Arthur!

PRINCE *(starts)*.
          Here!

HOHENZOLLERN. Have you gone mad?

PRINCE. What are your orders, sir?
(Blushing, he gets his pencil and pad ready.)

FIELD MARSHAL.   To whom his Highness
Again entrusts, as previously at Rathenow,
Command of all his mounted troops . . . *(He pauses.)*
Though without disrespect for Colonel Kottwitz,
Who'll let him benefit from his advice . . .

(*In a low voice to* CAPTAIN GOLZ.)
Is Kottwitz here?

GOLZ.   No, sir. I have been delegated
To take your orders in his stead.

(*The* PRINCE *again stares fixedly at the ladies.*)

FIELD MARSHAL (*continuing*).
Will take position on the plain,
Close to the village, Hackelwitz,
And opposite the enemy's right wing,
But well beyond his cannon's range.

GOLZ (*writing*). But well beyond his cannon's range.

(*The* ELECTRESS *ties a scarf around* NATALIE'S *throat.*
NATALIE, *about to put on her gloves, looks around as if she
were looking for something.*)

ELECTOR (*stepping up to her*).
Something amiss, my girl?

ELECTRESS.   Is something lost?

NATALIE. I wonder, aunt . . . one of my gloves . . . I had . . .
(*Everyone starts looking for it.*)

ELECTOR (*to the* LADIES-IN-WAITING).
Would you be good enough to help, fair ladies?

ELECTRESS (*to* NATALIE).
It's in your hand, dear child.

NATALIE.   The right one is;
What could have happened to the left one, though?

ELECTOR. Perhaps you left it in the bedroom?

NATALIE.   Please,
Dear Bork, would you . . . ?

ELECTOR (*to that lady*).   But please, be quick.

NATALIE. Look on the mantelpiece.

                        (*The* LADY-IN-WAITING *leaves.*)

PRINCE (*aside*). Good God, did I hear right?
(*He takes the glove from his doublet.*)

FIELD MARSHAL (*looking at the paper in his hand*).
And well beyond his cannons' range. (*He continues.*)
The Prince will not . . .

PRINCE.   She's looking for her glove!
(*He looks repeatedly from* NATALIE *to the glove and back
again.*)

FIELD MARSHAL. According to our Chief's express command . . .

GOLZ (*writing*). According to our Chief's express command . . .

FIELD MARSHAL. No matter how the battle may develop,
Move from the point to which he is assigned . . .

PRINCE. I must find out if this is really the one.
(*He drops the glove together with his handkerchief, then
picks the handkerchief up, leaving the glove on the floor
for all to see.*)

FIELD MARSHAL (*dismayed*). What is your Highness doing?

HOHENZOLLERN (*under his breath*). Arthur!

PRINCE. Here!

HOHENZOLLERN. You have gone mad.

PRINCE. What are your orders, sir?
(*He gets ready to write. The MARSHAL looks at him dubiously. A pause.*)

GOLZ (*having written down the words*).
Move from the point to which he is assigned.

FIELD MARSHAL (*continues*).
Until, pressed by the Colonels Truchss and Hennings . . .

PRINCE (*in a low voice to GOLZ, looking at his pad*).
Who, my dear Golz? Is that for me?

GOLZ. Yes, you; who else?

PRINCE. I'm not to move?

GOLZ. That's right.

FIELD MARSHAL. Well? Did you put that down?

PRINCE (*aloud*). I'm not to move from where I've been assigned . . . (*He writes.*)

FIELD MARSHAL. Until, pressed by the Colonels Truchss and
Hennings . . . (*He pauses.*)
The left wing of the enemy, dispersed,
Is pushed upon his right and all his regiments
Are faltering and seek to gain the open field,
Upon whose marshy ground, crisscrossed by ditches,
It is our plan to finish their destruction.

ELECTOR. Here, pages, light! Your arms, dear ladies.
(*He starts for the door, the ELECTRESS and NATALIE taking his
arms.*)

FIELD MARSHAL. Then he will let the bugles sound the signal.

ELECTRESS (*acknowledging the bows of several officers*).
Don't let us interrupt you, gentlemen. Good-bye!
(*The FIELD MARSHAL also bows to her.*)

ELECTOR (*stops suddenly*).
There is the glove! Look, over there!

A COURTIER. But where, your Highness?

ELECTOR.   There, right at our cousin's feet.

PRINCE (*chivalrously*). At my feet? Oh, is that your glove?
(*He picks it up and takes it to* NATALIE.)

NATALIE. I thank you, Prince.

PRINCE.   Is that your glove?

NATALIE. Yes, that's the glove I have been looking for.
(*She takes it and puts it on.*)

ELECTRESS (*on her way out, to the* PRINCE).
Farewell, good luck, make sure that soon
We'll meet again as happily as ever.
(*The* ELECTOR *leaves with the ladies, followed by the* COUR-
TIERS, LADIES-IN-WAITING *and* PAGES.)

PRINCE (*stands motionless for a moment, as if struck by
lightning, then, triumphantly, he returns to the circle of officers*).
Then he will let the bugles sound the signal.
(*He pretends to write.*)

FIELD MARSHAL (*glances at the paper in his hand*).
Then he will let the bugles sound the signal.
However to make sure that he will not
Erroneously attack too early, the Elector . . .

GOLZ (*writing*). Erroneously attack too early, the Elector . . .

PRINCE (*softly, to* HOHENZOLLERN, *in great excitement*).
Oh, Heinrich!

HOHENZOLLERN (*irritated*). What? What is it now?

PRINCE. Did you not notice?

HOHENZOLLERN.   No! For God's sake, quiet now.

FIELD MARSHAL. Will send an officer of his own suite,
Who will, note well, transmit the order to attack.
The bugles will not sound till then.
(*Daydreaming, the* PRINCE *stares at his feet.*)
Did you make note of that?

GOLZ (*writing*). The bugles will not sound till then.

FIELD MARSHAL (*louder than before*).
Your Highness, do you have that?

PRINCE.   Sir?

FIELD MARSHAL. I asked if you made note of that.

PRINCE. About the bugles, sir?

HOHENZOLLERN (*under his breath, irritated and emphatically*).
The devil with the bugles! Not till then . . .

GOLZ (*in the same manner*).
Not till he has received . . .

PRINCE (*interrupting them*). Oh yes, of course.
Not till . . . But then he will let sound the signal.
(*He writes. A pause.*)

FIELD MARSHAL. I wish to speak to Colonel Kottwitz, Baron
    Golz,
Before the battle starts, if possible.
Please make a note of that.

GOLZ (*significantly*).   I certainly will tell him, sir.
You may rely on it.
(*A pause.*)

ELECTOR (*returning*). Well, gentlemen,
The dawn is graying. Have you finished?

FIELD MARSHAL. Your Highness, we are done. Your battle
    plan
Has been passed on to your commanders carefully.

ELECTOR (*taking his hat and gloves*).
To you, my Prince, I recommend the greatest calm.
Along the Rhyn, you recently cost me
Two victories, as you well know. Control yourself.
Don't let me miss another one today,
Which means as much to me as throne and country.
(*To the* OFFICERS.)
Come with me, gentlemen. Hey, Franz!

A GROOM (*enters*). Yes, sir!

ELECTOR.   Quick, bring me my white charger.
I wish to reach the battlefield before the sun is up.
(*He leaves, followed by the officers. The* PRINCE *remains
alone.*)

SCENE 6. *The Prince of Homburg alone; he steps forward.*

PRINCE. Roll closer on your sphere, enormous Fate!
Today the breeze that fills the sail of ships
Will lift your veil, Fortuna. Roll to me!
You have already touched my head, and thrown
A token from your horn of plenty down to me

As you were passing me on floating clouds.
Today, fleet child of gods, I will pursue
And seize you on the battlefield,
And empty all your blessed treasures at my feet,
Though you be tied with seven iron chains
To Swedish chariots of victory.   (*He leaves.*)

ACT II

SCENE 1. *Battlefield near Fehrbellin. Kottwitz, Hohenzollern, Golz and other officers enter at the head of a column of cavalry.*

KOTTWITZ (*offstage*). Halt, cavalry! Dismount!

HOHENZOLLERN and GOLZ (*entering*).   Halt! Halt!

KOTTWITZ (*offstage*). Who'll help me off my horse, good friends?

HOHENZOLLERN and GOLZ. I'll help, old man; I'm coming.
                                        (*They leave again.*)

KOTTWITZ (*still offstage*).
Ouff . . . Thank you, friends. The devil take . . .
For helping me, may God give sons
To both of you, who will someday, when you begin
To fall apart, be just as kind to you.
     (*He enters, followed by* HOHENZOLLERN, GOLZ *and other officers.*)
Yes, when I'm on my horse I'm youth itself,
But I'm no sooner off then there's a battle on,
As if my soul and body tried to pull asunder.
     (*He looks around.*)
Where is the Prince?

HOHENZOLLERN.   He will be here at once.

KOTTWITZ. Where did he go?

HOHENZOLLERN.   He took a side road through the trees
That hide the village which you passed alongside.
He will be back in just a moment.

An Officer. I hear he had a nasty fall last night.

Hohenzollern. Yes, I believe so.

Kottwitz.   What? A fall?

Hohenzollern (*turning away*).
Nothing important. Over by the mill,
His horse shied, but he did not hurt himself,
Just slid off sideways gently to the ground.
It isn't worth a moment's worry, sir.

Kottwitz (*climbs a hillock*).
This is a lovely day, by God, a day
Which He made certainly for sweeter things than war.
The sun sends rosy smiles through clouds,
Our hearts soar jubilantly with the larks
Toward the cheerful fragrance of the sky.

Golz. Did you find Marshal Dörfling, sir?

Kottwitz (*coming forward*).   Damnation, no!
What does his Excellency think?
Am I a bird, a thought, a flying arrow,
That I could chase him all across the battlefield?
I galloped to the vanguard on the heights
And to the rearguard in the Hackel Valley,
But who's invisible? The Marshal. So,
I went where I belong, here with my cavalry.

Golz. I'm sure he will regret that you have missed him, sir.
It seems that he had something of importance
That he wished to confide to you.

An Officer.   Here comes the Prince!

Scene 2. *The same. The Prince of Homburg enters, a black
bandage on his left hand.*

Kottwitz. Welcome, your Highness! Look how I've deployed
The cavalry down on the valley road
While you were in the village. I hope
You will approve what I have done.

Prince. Good morning, Kottwitz, and good morning, friends!
You know that I have never yet found fault with you.

Hohenzollern. What did you do back in the village, Arthur?
You look so solemn.

Prince.   I . . . I visited
The chapel that gleamed white and quietly

Among the trees. As we passed by, the bells
Announced the service, and I felt compelled
To enter and to pray before the altar.

KOTTWITZ. A pious gentleman, indeed.
What you begin with prayer, that, my friends,
Will certainly be crowned with fame and victory.

PRINCE. I meant to ask you something, Heinrich . . .
(*He leads* COUNT HOHENZOLLERN *forward.*)
What did the Marshal bring up yesterday
With reference to me, when he read out
The orders of the day?

HOHENZOLLERN.   You were distracted, to be sure.

PRINCE. Distracted, absent-minded . . . that is true.
I don't know what was wrong with me.
Dictation always irritates me terribly.

HOHENZOLLERN. It's fortunate that there was really
Not much for you this time. Hennings and Truchss
Will lead the infantry into the first attack;
Your mission is to hold the cavalry
Here in the valley and to be prepared
To join the battle when you get the orders.

PRINCE (*stares dreamily into space; after a pause*).
A strange event.

HOHENZOLLERN. What's that, my friend?
(*He looks at him. A cannon shot is heard.*)

KOTTWITZ. Hello, my friends! Hey, gentlemen, let's mount!
That's Hennings. Now the battle starts.
(*They all climb the hillock.*)

PRINCE. What's that? Who is that shooting?

HOHENZOLLERN.   Hennings, friend,
Who quietly has crept around the Swedish lines.
Come up; from here you have a splendid view.

GOLZ (*on the hillock*). Look how he now deploys along the
Rhyn.

PRINCE (*shielding his eyes with his hand*).
Is that Hennings over there, on our right?

AN OFFICER. That's right, your Highness.

PRINCE.   But—what's going on?
He had the left wing yesterday.
(*Cannon fire in the distance.*)

Kottwitz. The devil! Look, now Wrangel opens up
With twelve volcanoes spitting fire against his men.

First Officer. Those Swedish gun emplacements are not bad.

Second Officer. By God, the steeple of the village church
Behind them is no taller than those walls.

(*Shooting close by.*)

Golz. That's Truchss.

Prince.   What? Truchss?

Kottwitz.   That's Truchss who now arrives
In Hennings' aid, attacking frontally.

Prince. How is it that Count Truchss today commands the
    center?

(*Violent cannon fire.*)

Golz. Good heavens! Look, I think the village is on fire.

Third Officer. That's right, it's burning like a torch.

First Officer.   And how!
It seems the fire already climbs the steeple.

Golz. Look how the Swedish messengers dart left and right.

Second Officer. They're falling back!

Kottwitz.   Who? Where?

First Officer.   Their right is giving way.

Third Officer. That's right .... in columns ... three whole
    regiments.
It seems they want to reinforce their left.

Second Officer. And so they are. There comes their cavalry,
Advancing to protect them on their march.

Hohenzollern (*laughing*). Eh, they will quickly leave again,
Once they find out that we are hidden here.

(*Musket fire.*)

Kottwitz. Look, friends, look over there!

Second Officer.   Hey, listen!

First Officer.   Musket fire.

Third Officer. Now they are fighting hand to hand at the
    emplacements.

Golz. So help me God, I've never heard the likes
Of such a cannonade in all my life.

Hohenzollern. Keep shooting! Shoot! Shoot till the earth
    cleaves open.
The cleft shall be your grave and your memorial.

(*A pause. Shouts of "Hurrah" in the distance.*)

FIRST OFFICER. O Lord in heaven who gives victory . . .
The Swedes are turning heel!

HOHENZOLLERN.   Impossible.

GOLZ. As sure as I am standing here . . . look on the left!
They're pulling back their cannon from the field emplacements.

ALL. The battle's over, victory is ours!

PRINCE (*stepping down from the hillock*).
Come, Kottwitz, follow me.

KOTTWITZ. Now, children, let's keep calm and cool.

PRINCE. It's time to let the bugles sound attack.

KOTTWITZ. Keep calm, I say.

PRINCE (*wildly*).   Hell and damnation!

KOTTWITZ. His Highness was explicit yesterday:
We are to wait until we get an order.
Golz, read the Prince the orders of the day.

PRINCE. Await an order? Kottwitz, is that how you ride?
Did you not get an order from your heart?

KOTTWITZ. An order?

HOHENZOLLERN.   Please!

KOTTWITZ.   An order from my heart?

HOHENZOLLERN. Please, Arthur, understand.

GOLZ.   Please listen, sir.

KOTTWITZ (*offended*). O ho, young Prince, is that the way you
    feel?
I'm not too old yet, I can still drag you
And your old mare along, tied to my horse's tail!
Into the battle! Forward march, my friends!
Let then the bugles signal the attack.
Old Kottwitz is not one to stay behind.

GOLZ (*to* KOTTWITZ). Don't do it, Colonel, don't! You cannot
    do it.

SECOND OFFICER. Hennings has not yet reached the Rhyn.

FIRST OFFICER. Relieve him of his sword.

PRINCE.   What? Me? My sword?
    (*He pushes him back.*)
Why, you presumptuous puppy, have you not yet learned
The ten commandments we obey in Brandenburg?
    (*He tears off* OFFICER'S *belt with its scabbard and sword.*)
Here is your sword, together with its sheath!

FIRST OFFICER (*staggering*).

By God, your Highness, that . . .

PRINCE (*advancing on him*).   Do you still speak?

HOHENZOLLERN (*to the* OFFICER).
Be quiet! Are you mad?

PRINCE (*passing on the sword*). Guards! Take this man
To headquarters as prisoner.
 (*To* KOTTWITZ *and the other officers.*)
And now the watchword is: a scoundrel he
Who does not follow his commander into battle!
Does anyone prefer to stay behind?

KOTTWITZ. You've heard what I have said. Why all the noise?

HOHENZOLLERN (*soothingly to the* PRINCE).
We thought we ought to give you our advice.

KOTTWITZ. You take the blame for it. I follow you.

PRINCE (*assuaged*). I'll take the blame. Now, brothers, fol-
    low me!

(*All leave.*)

SCENE 3. *A cottage in the village. A peasant and his wife
sit at the table, working. A Courtier in riding boots enters.*

COURTIER. Good morning, my good people. Have you room
To take in company?

PEASANT.   Of course, we gladly will.

WOMAN. May I ask whom?

COURTIER.   You may. None less
Than the most gracious Mother of our Country.
The axle of her carriage broke
Precisely as we came into the village.
Now, since we've heard that victory is won,
There is no need for her to travel further.

PEASANT and WIFE (*rising quickly*).
The battle's over? God be thanked!

COURTIER. You hadn't heard? The Swedish army is defeated,
If not forever, certainly until next year.
The country will be safe from fire and sword.
Here she is now, the Princess of the land.

SCENE 4. *The same. The Electress, pale and worried,
enters with Natalie and several Ladies-in-Waiting.*

ELECTRESS (*in the doorway*).

Bork! Winterfeld! Please come, give me your arms.

NATALIE (*hurrying to help her*).
Oh, Mother!

THE LADIES. God! She blanches, she will fall!
(*They support her.*)

ELECTRESS. Let me sit down. Bring me a chair. He's dead?
Did he say, dead?

NATALIE.   My dearest mother!

ELECTRESS. I want to hear the messenger of gloom myself.

SCENE 5. *The same. Captain von Mörner enters; he is
wounded and is being assisted by two cavalrymen.*

ELECTRESS. What news, herald of terror, do you bring?

MÖRNER. Unfortunately, what I've seen, your Highness,
To my eternal grief with my own eyes.

ELECTRESS. Tell me your story.

MÖRNER.   The Elector is no more.

NATALIE. Merciful God! That is a frightful blow.
(*She covers her face.*)

ELECTRESS. Tell me, then, how he died. Illumine the last mo-
    ment.
As with the traveler, hit by a bolt of lightning,
The world for one quick moment flashes up
In a display of glorious color one last time,
Your words will paint for me a final vision;
When you have finished, I shall drown in waves of night.

MÖRNER (*supported by the two soldiers, steps in front of her*).
The Prince of Homburg had moved down into the plain
Against the Swedes, when after Truchss' attack
The enemy began to waver.
He had already broken through two lines
When he came up against a strong point
And met a rain of lead so murderous
That it laid low his men as reapers mow the wheat.
He had to halt, and between hills and trees
He gathered up the remnants of his scattered corps.

NATALIE (*to the ELECTRESS*).
Oh dearest Mother, please be calm.

ELECTRESS.   I will, my dear.

MÖRNER. That was the moment when we saw

That the Elector, far from the swirling dust,
Was riding with the Corps von Truchss against the foe.
He was a splendid sight on his white horse,
As in the glaring sunlight he rode on,
A beacon on the road to victory.
Concerned to see him in the midst of heavy fire,
We gathered on a hill to get a better view.
Then suddenly, before our eyes, they fell,
The rider and his horse, into the dust.
Two standard bearers fell on top of him
And hid his body with their flags.

NATALIE. Oh, Mother—no!

FIRST LADY-IN-WAITING. Oh God!

ELECTRESS. Continue, sir.

MÖRNER. Beholding that calamity, the Prince,
Whose heart was gripped by nameless grief,
Sprang up and, like a bear spurred on
By furious hate and thirst of vengeance, charged
The fort with us. In one attack we overran
The trenches and broke through the earthwall guarding it.
We overwhelmed and scattered and wiped out the garrison,
And took their cannon, flags and drums and standards,
The entire Swedish baggage train, as booty.
Had not their bridgehead at the Rhyn at last
Brought to a halt our furious assault,
We would have slain each one of them;
None would have reached his father's hearth to say:
I was at Fehrbellin and saw the hero fall.

ELECTRESS. That was a costly victory.
I do not want it. Give me back the price
We had to pay for it!
(*She faints.*)

FIRST LADY-IN-WAITING. She is unconscious! Help!
(NATALIE *breaks down in tears.*)

SCENE 6. *The same. The Prince of Homburg enters.*

PRINCE. My dearest Natalie!
(*Greatly moved at the sight of her, he puts her hand on his heart.*)

NATALIE. So it is true?

PRINCE. I wish I could say No! I wish that I could drain

My heart and with its blood bring his heart back to life.

NATALIE (*drying her tears*).
Have they brought back his body from the field?

PRINCE. Until this moment I have had no thought
But Wrangel. I have had no time for other cares.
But I've sent out a troop to search for him,
No doubt, before the night descends
Upon the field of death they'll bring him back.

NATALIE. Who now will keep the Swedes in check
And carry on this gruesome fight?
Who will protect us from that world of enemies,
Which his great fame and fortune have created?

PRINCE (*taking her hand*).
I'll make your cause my own, my dearest girl.
An angel with a flaming sword, I'll guard
The orphaned throne of Brandenburg.
Before this year has run its course,
He meant to see this country free, and I shall be
The executor of his will and testament.

NATALIE. My dearest cousin!
(*She withdraws her hand.*)

PRINCE.   Natalie!
(*He pauses for a moment.*)
How do you look upon your future now?

NATALIE. What can I do, now that the ground
Beneath my feet is rent by sudden lightning?
My parents have been in their grave in Amsterdam
For many years, and Dortrecht, my ancestral home,
Lies ruined and in ashes. That's my heritage!
My cousin, Maurice, sorely pressed by Spain's
Armed tyranny, can hardly find a way
To rescue his own children. Now my last support,
The staff that held my fortune's slender vine,
Is gone. A second time I have been orphaned.

PRINCE (*putting his arm around her*).
My dearest Natalie, if this hour
Were not consecrated to our sorrow, I would say:
Let then your branches twine around my breast
That in its solitary bloom has craved
For years the lovely fragrance of your blossoms.

NATALIE. My dear, good cousin!

PRINCE.   Will you, Natalie?

NATALIE. May I grow into it, into its inmost core?
(*She puts her head on his chest.*)

PRINCE. What did you say?

NATALIE.   Away!

PRINCE (*holding her*).   Into its core!
Oh, Natalie, into its heart and core!
(*He kisses her; she tears herself away.*)
If only he for whom we weep could be here now,
To look upon our union! We could say
To him: give us your blessing, Father.
(*He covers his face with hands.* NATALIE *turns to the* ELEC-
TRESS.)

SCENE 7. *The same. A Sergeant rushes in.*

SERGEANT (*to the* PRINCE).
Your Highness, there's a rumor . . . I don't dare
To tell you . . . the Elector is alive!

PRINCE. Alive?

SERGEANT.   Count Sparren came and brought the news.

NATALIE. Good God in heaven, Mother, did you hear?
(*She sinks down at the* ELECTRESS' *feet and puts her arms
around her.*)

PRINCE. Who did you say reported that?

SERGEANT.   Count Sparren.
He saw him safe and sound at Hackelwitz,
Where he was visiting the Corps von Truchss.

PRINCE. Quick, Sergeant, bring him here.

                                    (SERGEANT *leaves.*)

SCENE 8. *The same. Count Sparren and the Sergeant enter.*

ELECTRESS. I hope I won't be plunged again into an abyss.

NATALIE. But Mother, he has seen—

ELECTRESS.   He saw him—alive?

NATALIE (*supports her with both hands*).
Life's summit welcomes you once more.

SERGEANT (*enters*). Here is Count Sparren now, your Highness.

PRINCE. I'm told that you have seen our illustrious master

Alive and well at Hackelwitz with Truchss?

SPARREN. I saw him in the courtyard of the parsonage,
Surrounded by his staff, where he gave orders
To give the dead of both the armies decent burial.

THE LADIES-IN-WAITING.
What news from heaven . . .
(*They embrace each other.*)

ELECTRESS.   Oh, my daughter . . .

NATALIE. This happiness is more than I can stand.
(*She puts her head into the* ELECTRESS' *lap.*)

PRINCE. But, watching from afar, I was convinced
I saw him sink into the dust amid a hail of bullets.

SPARREN. It's true, his horse went down; so did the man
Who rode the horse, but that, my Lord, was not,
As you surmised, his Highness the Elector.

PRINCE. Not the Elector?

NATALIE.   I could shout with joy!
(*She rises and stands next to the* ELECTRESS.)

PRINCE. Speak, tell us how that happened, Count. Your words
Fall heavily, like gold, into my heart.

SPARREN. It's the most moving story you have ever heard.
As always, the Elector rode, against
All warning and advice, that stallion, glaring white,
That Froben recently bought him in England,
And as always happens, so again
He was the foremost target of the enemy.
Within a circle of a hundred paces,
It was well nigh impossible approaching him,
For the grenades, the bullets and the shots
Roared like a torrent of destruction toward him,
And every living soul retreated to its banks.
A dauntless swimmer, he alone persisted,
And, waving to his friends, swam bravely on
To reach the still unconquered heights, the torrent's source.

PRINCE. That was, indeed, a fearful sight.

SPARREN. Then Froben, who as equerry was nearest him,
Called out: "That stallion's glaring white be damned!
I bought that horse in London for a mint of gold,
But now I would pay fifty ducats to the man
Who painted him the color of a mouse."
With that, he galloped off, and getting close

To the Elector, called, full of concern:
"My Lord, the battle noise still makes your stallion shy;
Allow me, please, to put him once more through his paces."
Thus speaking he gets off his chestnut, grasps
The Master's stallion by his bridle,
His Highness, too, dismounts and smiles.
"The art that you would like to teach him, Froben,
He'll never learn while daylight shines.
Take him behind those hills, so that his fault
Will not be so apparent to the enemy."
With that he mounts the chestnut Froben rode
And gallops off to where his duty calls.
But Froben, barely mounted, falls,
Both man and horse hit by the deadly fire
The Swedish field redoubt spewed forth.
He died a victim of his loyalty,
And no one heard him speak another word.

(*A short pause.*)

PRINCE. He's paid the price, and if I had ten lives
I could not put them to a better use.

NATALIE. Good, faithful Froben!

ELECTRESS. What an exemplary man!

NATALIE. A lesser man would merit that we weep for him.
(*They weep.*)

PRINCE. Enough. Now to the point. Where is his Highness
now?
Did he set up his headquarters at Hackelwitz?

SPARREN. No, sir. He started back immediately
And asked his generals to join him in Berlin.

PRINCE. What? In Berlin? Is this the end of the campaign?

SPARREN. I am surprised that you've not heard the news.
Count Horn, the Swedish general, arrived in camp,
And shortly afterward a truce was signed.
The Marshal says, if I have understood him right,
That negotiations have commenced, and peace
Quite possibly will follow soon.

ELECTRESS. How splendidly the night makes way for day!
(*She rises.*)

PRINCE. We must set out at once to follow him.
Would you, dear aunt, to speed my journey, be so kind
As to concede a carriage seat to me?
Before we go, I'll quickly write a line

To Kottwitz. I shall join you instantly.

ELECTRESS. I'll be delighted to have you along.

PRINCE (*finishing the letter, folds it and gives it to the*
SERGEANT. *Turning back to the* ELECTRESS, *he gently puts
his arm around* NATALIE).

There is one favor which I still must ask of you.
I shall confide it to you when we're on our way.

NATALIE (*freeing herself from the* PRINCE).

Please, Bork, my scarf!

ELECTRESS.   Ask me a favor?

FIRST LADY-IN-WAITING.

It is around your neck, your Highness.

PRINCE (*to the* ELECTRESS).   Can't you guess?

ELECTRESS. I've no idea.

PRINCE.   None at all?

ELECTRESS. No matter. On a day like this,
I could not answer No to anyone
Who asked me for—whatever it may be,
And least of all, in all the world, to you,
The victor on the battlefield. Enough!

PRINCE. May I interpret what you said
In any way I please?

ELECTRESS.   Enough, I said.
We'll talk about it in the carriage. Please,
Give me your arm.

PRINCE.   O Caesar Divus,
The ladder which I now ascend will reach your star!

(*He leaves, with the* ELECTRESS *and* NATALIE *taking his
arms. The others follow.*)

SCENE 9. *Berlin. The garden in front of the Old Castle. In
the background is the chapel, with steps leading up to its
entrance. The chapel is brightly illuminated and the bells
are ringing. Froben's body is carried past and placed on
a magnificent catafalque. The Elector, Field Marshal Dörfling, Colonel Hennings, Count Truchss and several other
officers enter from the opposite side; other officers appear
with dispatches for the Elector. A throng of people of both
sexes and all ages crowds the chapel and the open square
in front of it.*

ELECTOR. Whoever led our cavalry the day of Fehrbellin
And ordered, on his own authority,
The charge that forced the enemy to flee
Before the troops of Colonel Hennings could destroy
The bridges and before I had myself
Commanded the attack, that man deserves,
I solemnly declare, the penalty of death.
Forthwith, I order him to be court-martialed.
The Prince of Homburg was not their commander?

TRUCHSS. No, he was not, my Lord.

ELECTOR.   How do you know?

TRUCHSS. Before the battle had begun, I was assured
By several men that they had seen him in a church,
Severely wounded in the head and thighs,
And he was being bandaged by a surgeon.
He'd fallen off his horse, they said.

ELECTOR. I see. It was a splendid victory,
However, and I will thank God for it
In church tomorrow. But had it been ten times greater,
That would be no excuse for the commander
Who won it for me by mere accident.
There will be other battles to be fought,
And I demand obedience to the law.
Whoever, I repeat, led that attack
Has forfeited his head, and I command
That he be judged by military law.
But now, my friends, please follow me into the church.

SCENE 10. *The same. The Prince of Homburg enters carrying three Swedish flags, followed by Colonel Kottwitz
carrying two and by Count Hohenzollern, Captain Golz, and
Count Reuss, each carrying one flag. Several other officers,
corporals, and cavalrymen carry flags, drums, and battle
standards.*

FIELD MARSHAL (*at the sight of the* PRINCE).
The Prince of Homburg? Truchss, what did you say?

ELECTOR (*startled*).
From where do you come, Prince?

PRINCE (*advancing a few steps*).
                              From Fehrbellin,
To bring these trophies of our victory to you.

(*He lays the flags at his feet; the others do likewise.*)

ELECTOR. I heard you were severely wounded. Truchss!

PRINCE (*gaily*). Please pardon me—

TRUCHSS.   I don't know what—

PRINCE. My chestnut fell before the battle started.
This hand here, bandaged by an army surgeon,
Does hardly merit to be called a wound.

ELECTOR. Then it was you who led the cavalry?

PRINCE (*looks at him*).
Of course! Am I the first to tell you that?
I've put the evidence before your feet.

ELECTOR. His sword! He is a prisoner.

FIELD MARSHAL (*taken aback*).   Whose sword?

ELECTOR (*stepping between the flags*).
Be welcome, Kottwitz!

TRUCHSS (*aside*).   Hell!

KOTTWITZ.   I am extremely—

ELECTOR (*with a glance at* KOTTWITZ).
What's that you said? Look at this harvest, reaped
To add more lustre to our fame. I think
This is the standard of the Swedish Guards.
    (*He takes one of the flags, unfurls it and looks at it.*)

KOTTWITZ. My Lord?

FIELD MARSHAL.   Your Highness?

ELECTOR.   So it is, indeed.
It dates from King Gustavus Adolf's time.
What is inscribed on it?

KOTTWITZ.   I think—

FIELD MARSHAL. *Per aspera ad astra*, sir.

ELECTOR.   That promise
It did not keep at Fehrbellin.
    (*A pause.*)

KOTTWITZ (*hesitantly*).
Your Highness, may I . . . just a word—

ELECTOR.   What do you want?
Take all the drums and flags, all of the trophies,
And hang them on the pillars in the church.
I'll use them when we celebrate our victory.
    (*He turns to the couriers, takes their dispatches, opens them
    and reads.*)

KOTTWITZ (*aside*). By God, that is too much!
(*After hesitating for a moment, he takes his two flags; the others do likewise. At last, when only three flags are left, he takes those, too, and now holds five of them.*)

AN OFFICER (*stepping in front of the* PRINCE).
Your Highness, please, your sword.

HOHENZOLLERN (*holding his flag, steps beside him*).
Keep calm, my friend.

PRINCE.   Is this a dream?
Am I awake? Am I alive? Or am I mad?

GOLZ. Your Highness, please, hand him your sword
Without a single word, I would advise.

PRINCE. I am a prisoner?

HOHENZOLLERN.   You are.

GOLZ.   You heard his words.

PRINCE. Am I allowed to ask a question? Why?

HOHENZOLLERN. No, don't ask now. You charged too soon,
Just as we told you then. Your orders were
To wait until he sent the order.

PRINCE. Help, friends! I'm going mad!

GOLZ (*interrupting him*).   Keep quiet now.

PRINCE. Then—did we lose the battle?

HOHENZOLLERN (*stamps his foot*).   That's irrelevant.
The law must be obeyed.

PRINCE (*bitterly*).   I see. I see.

HOHENZOLLERN (*moving away*).
It won't cost you your head.

GOLZ (*following* HOHENZOLLERN).
                    Tomorrow you'll be free.
(*The* ELECTOR *folds the letters and rejoins the group of officers.*)

PRINCE (*unbuckling his sword*).
My cousin Frederic has serious thoughts
Of playing Brutus, and he sees himself
Already painted, sitting on the curule chair,
The Swedish flags arrayed before his feet,
The articles of war upon the table.
By God, I'm not a son who will admire
His greatness, while the executioner
Holds high his axe above my head.
My heart is still old-fashioned German

And used to generosity and kindness.
When he adopts the ancients' rigid stance,
I cannot help but pity him.

> (*He gives his sword to the waiting officer and leaves.*)

ELECTOR. Take him to Fehrbellin, to our headquarters,
And summon the court-martial that will judge him.

> (*He goes into the church. The flags are carried in after him and are hung up on the pillars while he and his entourage kneel down at* FROBEN's *coffin and pray. Funeral music.*)

ACT III

SCENE 1. *A prison in Fehrbellin. The Prince of Homburg. In the background two soldiers who guard him. Hohenzollern enters.*

PRINCE. Hello, my friend! Be welcome to my cell!
Am I released?

HOHENZOLLERN (*surprised*). Are you? Praise be to God!

PRINCE. What did you say?

HOHENZOLLERN.   Are you released?
Did he return your sword?

PRINCE. To me? Not yet.

HOHENZOLLERN.   He didn't?

PRINCE.   No, I said.

HOHENZOLLERN. Then—what is that you said about release?

PRINCE (*after a pause*).
I thought you brought it with you. Never mind.

HOHENZOLLERN. I don't know anything about it.

PRINCE. I told you, never mind. So he'll send someone else
To bring the welcome news to me. Sit down.
Has the Elector left Berlin? Has he returned?

HOHENZOLLERN (*distracted*).
Yes, he came back last night.

PRINCE.   And did he celebrate
The victory in church as he had planned?

I know he must have. Was he in the chapel?

HOHENZOLLERN. Yes, he attended, the Electress, too,
And Princess Natalie of Orange.
The church was beautifully lit.
The batteries, drawn up before the castle,
Added their solemn roar to the *Te Deum*.
The Swedish flags and banners waved
Like trophies from the pillars, and,
Upon express command of the Elector,
Your name was mentioned from the pulpit as the victor.

PRINCE. I heard about that. Well, what else has happened?
You don't look very gay, my friend.

HOHENZOLLERN. Has anyone been here to talk to you?

PRINCE. I talked to Golz not long ago,
When I was in the palace for the hearing.

(A pause.)

HOHENZOLLERN *(looks at him dubiously)*.
What do you think about your situation,
Since it has changed so strangely, Arthur?

PRINCE. The same that you and Golz, and the judges, too,
Are thinking: the Elector did no more, no less
Than what he had to do, but that he now
Will certainly obey his heart's command.
"You have done wrong," he'll tell me solemnly,
"But I will give you back your liberty."
As token of his favor he may even wind
Some decoration round the sword that won him victory.
But if not that, it does not matter.
For that, I know, I don't deserve.

HOHENZOLLERN. Oh, Arthur— *(He breaks off.)*

PRINCE.   Well? What is it?

HOHENZOLLERN.   Are you sure?

PRINCE. Yes, I imagine so. He values me,
That much I know, and loves me like a son.
He's proven that a thousand times from childhood on.
What doubts are there to worry you?
He seemed delighted, even more than I,
To see my fame grow bright, and everything I am,
I am because of him. Why should he now
Step jealously upon the plant he raised himself
And hate it just because it blossomed
Too soon and too luxuriantly? No,

Not his worst enemy would see him in such light,
Much less a man like you, who knows him well
And loves him dearly.

HOHENZOLLERN.   Arthur, you were tried
By a court-martial. Do you still believe all that?

PRINCE. Because I have been tried, I do. By God,
He would not go so far unless he planned
To use his right of pardon in the end.
Before the bar of justice I restored my faith.
For was it really a crime so great
That only death is proper punishment,
To stamp the Swedish might into the dust
Two seconds earlier than my instructions had foreseen?
What other crime did I commit?
How could he ask me to appear
Before those heartless judges who like owls
Recite their litany of death to me,
Unless he meant to step amongst them like a god,
Dispassionately to pronounce the final word?
No, no, my friend, he draws this night of clouds
Around my head, because he wants to rise
Before me like the sun that breaks their foggy veil.
That pleasure I do not begrudge him, friend.

HOHENZOLLERN. But they have reached a verdict, I have heard.

PRINCE. Yes, so I understand. They've sentenced me to death.

HOHENZOLLERN (*surprised*).
You know that?

PRINCE.   Golz was present at the sentencing,
And he has told me what the judgment was.

HOHENZOLLERN. And that—that fact means nothing to you,
    Arthur?

PRINCE. To me? Nothing at all.

HOHENZOLLERN.   You must be mad!
What gives you that assurance?

PRINCE.   Intuition.
I think I know how he will act.
    (*He gets up.*)
                    Now please,
If you don't mind, let's change the subject. Why
In all the world should I let useless doubts
Torment me? No court-martial could do otherwise
Than sentence me to death. That is the law.

But he will never have the sentence carried out,
Expose this heart that loves him loyally
To bullets fired upon a signal with a cloth.
He would much rather stab himself
And let his blood drip, drop by drop, into the dust.

HOHENZOLLERN. But, Arthur, I assure you—

PRINCE (*annoyed*). Please!

HOHENZOLLERN. The Marshal—

PRINCE (*irritated*). My friend, I said before, let's change the subject.

HOHENZOLLERN. Two words I want to tell you, then;
If they mean nothing to you, I'll be silent.

PRINCE (*turning toward him again*).
You see, I know what has been happening. Well?

HOHENZOLLERN. The Marshal went himself—and that is strange—
To take the verdict to the palace,
And the Elector asked to have it brought to him
For signature, instead of exercising
At once the right of pardon which it gives to him.

PRINCE. No matter. I have told you more than once—

HOHENZOLLERN. No matter?

PRINCE. The Elector . . . for signature?

HOHENZOLLERN. That's what I said, and that is certain.

PRINCE. The sentence? No! The document itself?

HOHENZOLLERN. The death sentence.

PRINCE. Who told you that?

HOHENZOLLERN. The Marshal.

PRINCE. When was that?

HOHENZOLLERN. Just now.

PRINCE. When he returned from the Elector?

HOHENZOLLERN. As he came down the steps, just after seeing him.
When he became aware of my alarm,
He added that, as yet, nothing was lost;
Tomorrow was another day, he said,
And just as suitable for clemency.
But his expression did not match his words;
His eyes said, "I'm afraid it is not so."

PRINCE (*rising*). Do you believe that he is capable . . . ?

He cannot be! He could not possibly
Turn over in his mind such monstrous thoughts;
He cannot plan to trample into dust
Someone who just gave him a diamond,
Merely because he found a flaw in it
That even with a glass is hardly visible.
No, such a deed would make the Dey of Algiers look
As white as snow, would let King Ashurbanipal
Appear to us as angel, silver-winged,
And make the entire dynasty
Of ancient Roman tyrants seem like babes
Who die, as innocent as they were born,
Peacefully in their mothers' arms
And sit at God's right hand for all eternity.

HOHENZOLLERN (*also rising*).
And yet you must convince yourself of that.

PRINCE. The Field Marshal had nothing else to say?

HOHENZOLLERN. What could he say?

PRINCE.　　　　　　　　O God, my hopes are shattered!

HOHENZOLLERN. Did you perhaps, at any time,
Do something, inadvertently or by design,
That might have been offensive to his pride?

PRINCE. No, never.

HOHENZOLLERN. Please, remember carefully.

PRINCE. I never did, so help me God! To me,
Even his shadow has always been sacred.

HOHENZOLLERN. Don't be offended, Arthur, if I have my
doubts.
Count Horn, the Swedish emissary, has arrived,
And I have been assured his mission here
Concerns the Princess Natalie.
In that connection, something that your aunt
Has said to the Elector has, it seems
Upset and wounded him; it would appear
That the young lady has already chosen.
Are you in any way involved in that?

PRINCE. My God, is that it?

HOHENZOLLERN.　　　　　Then it's true?

PRINCE. Yes, it is I. Now everything is clear.
Count Horn's proposal is my downfall. Yes,
I am the cause of her refusal—we're engaged.

HOHENZOLLERN. Dim-witted, careless fool, what have you
    done?
How often have I warned you to watch out!

PRINCE. Give me your helping hand, or I am lost.

HOHENZOLLERN. But where is there a way from this predica-
    ment?
Perhaps you ought to speak about it to your aunt.

PRINCE (*turning around*). Hey, Guard!

SOLDIER (*in the background*).   Your Highness!

PRINCE.   Call your officer.
(*He snatches a coat from the wall and puts on his plumed
hat, which has been lying on the table.*)

HOHENZOLLERN (*helping him to get ready*).
That step, well-executed, might be your salvation.
For if, in fact, the price which Charles demands
From the Elector for a treaty is
What we believe it is, you'll see,
He'll make his peace with you at once,
And within hours you will be free.

SCENE 2. *The same. An Officer enters.*

PRINCE (*to the* OFFICER).
Stranz, I'm committed to your custody;
May I have your permission to absent myself
On urgent business from this prison for an hour?

OFFICER. Your Highness, I have no authority
To keep you, for my orders are
To let you go wherever you may wish.

PRINCE. That's odd. I thought I was a prisoner?

OFFICER. I beg your pardon, sir, you are quite right.
Your word of honor is a bond.

PRINCE (*leaving*). All right. That suits me well enough.

HOHENZOLLERN. Your shackles follow you like faithful dogs.

PRINCE. I'm going to the palace, to my aunt,
And shall be back immediately.

                                       (*All leave.*)

SCENE 3. *The apartment of the Electress. The Electress and Natalie enter.*

ELECTRESS. My daughter, come, the hour has struck;
Count Horn, the Swedish emissary,
Has left the palace. All the guests are gone,
But in your uncle's study—look—the light still burns.
Quick, take your wrap and steal into his room.
Perhaps there is still time to save his life.

(*They are about to leave.*)

SCENE 4. *The same. A Lady-in-Waiting enters.*

LADY-IN-WAITING. The Prince of Homburg, gracious Lady
waits outside.
I don't believe my eyes to see him here.

ELECTRESS (*startled*). My God!

NATALIE.   He's here?

ELECTRESS.   I thought he was a prisoner.

LADY-IN-WAITING. He is outside this door, in coat and hat,
And urgently requests an audience.
He seems distressed and greatly agitated.

ELECTRESS (*irritated*). The stupid man! To break his word!

NATALIE.   Who knows
What's weighing on his mind!

ELECTRESS (*after a moment's hesitation*). Go, show him in.
(*The* LADY-IN-WAITING *leaves. The* ELECTRESS *sits down.*)

SCENE 5. *The same. The Prince of Homburg enters.*

PRINCE. Oh, Mother!
(*He falls on his knees before the* ELECTRESS.)

ELECTRESS.   Prince, what are you doing here?

PRINCE. Please, let me kneel before you, Mother!

ELECTRESS (*controlling her emotion*).
You are a prisoner, and yet you come?
Why add this new offense to your guilt?

PRINCE (*urgently*). Have you not heard what happened?

ELECTRESS.   I have heard.
What can a helpless woman do for you?

PRINCE. Oh, Mother, you would not speak so complacently
If you were terrified by death, as I am now.
You seem endowed with heaven's powers to bring help,
Yourself, the Princess and your ladies—all of you.
I could embrace the meanest stable boy
Who feeds your horses, and implore him: help!
I am alone in all this world,
Abandoned, helpless, powerless.

ELECTRESS. You are beside yourself. What happened?

PRINCE. Ah, on my way to you, I saw the grave
That, by the light of torches, men were digging,
That is tomorrow to receive my bones.
Look at my eyes which now meet yours—
They will be shaded by eternal night;
This breast is to be riddled with their bullets.
They have already rented all the windows
That give upon the market place, to watch
The better the abominable spectacle.
Today I stand upon the summit of my life,
Scanning my future that lies like a fairyland
Before my eyes, tomorrow I shall molder
Between the four confining boards, a stone
That says, "He was," all that is left of me.

(NATALIE, *who has been standing in the background, leaning on the shoulder of a* LADY-IN-WAITING, *now sits down
at a table and, overcome by grief, breaks out in tears.*)

ELECTRESS. My son, if Heaven wills it so, you'll meet
What comes with courage and composure.

PRINCE. I love this world that God has made so beautiful.
Don't let them chase me to the realm of shades
Before my time has come. If I've done wrong,
He can find other punishment for me—
Why does it have to be the bullet?
Let him dismiss me from the offices I hold,
Let him discharge me without honor from the army,
If that is what the law demands. Oh God!
Since I have seen my grave I have but one desire:
To live! No longer do I care if life is honorable.

ELECTRESS. Get up, my son. What kind of talk is that?
You are upset. Compose yourself.

PRINCE. Not till you swear that you will go to him

And, on your knees, beg for my life. Before she died,
My mother gave me in your care, your childhood friend,
And said: "You be his mother when I am no more,"
While you kneeled at her bedside, deeply moved,
Bent over her and promised solemnly,
"He will be like my son, and I his mother."
I now remind you of those words.
Go, plead with him as if your own son's life
Hung in the balance, beg for mercy, beg, I say,
And then come back to tell me: "You are free."

ELECTRESS (*in tears*). My dearest son, that I have done a
    ready,
But all my imprecations were in vain.

PRINCE. I have renounced all claims to happiness,
I've given up all thought of Natalie—
And don't forget to tell him that!
All tender feelings for her are extinguished,
She is as free as deer upon the heath
And she may give her heart and word to anyone,
As if I were a dream she had, no more.
If she accepts the Swedish King, I'll praise her choice.
Myself, I'll go and live on my estates
Along the Rhine; there I will build and tear apart
Until the sweat stands on my brow,
There I will sow and harvest as I would
For wife and children—but I'll live alone.
And when the harvest's in, I'll sow again,
I'll chase my life in never-ending circles,
Until, at last, the evening comes and I shall die.

ELECTRESS. For now, return to prison, whence you came.
That is the precondition of my favor.

PRINCE (*rises and turns to* NATALIE).
You weep, poor girl. Today, the sun has been
The light by which you buried all your hopes.
I was the first for whom your heart decided,
And on your face I read that, true as gold,
You never will devote your life to any other man.
What can I say, as I am now, to comfort you?
Go to your cousin, that is my advice,
Live in the convent by the Main with her,
Look in the mountains for a boy, blond-haired as I,
Buy him with gold and press him to your breast,
Teach him to call you Mother, bring him up,

And when he's grown, instruct him how to close
The eyes of those who are about die.
That's all the happiness you can expect.

NATALIE (*arises and puts her hand in his; with courage and determination*).
Go back, young hero, to your prison now,
And on your way look calmly once again
Into the grave that has been opened to receive you.
It is no darker and no deeper than all those
You've seen a thousand times upon the battlefield.
I shall be faithful to you unto death.
I'll dare to speak the words that may bring rescue;
Perhaps I shall succeed in moving my uncle's heart,
And free you from your heavy load of sorrows.
    (*A pause.*)

PRINCE (*fixedly gazing on* NATALIE, *folds his hands*).
If I saw wings grow on your shoulders, Natalie,
I would be sure I looked upon an angel.
Did I hear right? You want to speak for me?
Where did you hide the quiver of your words,
That you would dare approach the sovereign in my cause?
A light of hope shines brightly through the night!

NATALIE. The Lord will give me arrows that will reach the
    mark.
But if my uncle cannot change the verdict,
Then you, brave man, will know how to submit
Courageously to the inevitable.
The man who won a thousand victories
In life, will win one more in death.

ELECTRESS. Let's hurry! The propitious moment passes.

PRINCE. May all the saints be with you and protect you!
Farewell! Whatever you achieve,
Give me a sign of your success.

    (*All leave.*)

ACT IV

SCENE 1. *The Elector's study. The Elector stands at a table set with candles; he is studying papers. Natalie enters through the center door and immediately drops to her knees.*

NATALIE (*kneeling*). My noble uncle, Frederic of Brandenburg!
ELECTOR (*puts down the papers*).
Why, Natalie!
(*He makes a gesture of lifting her up.*)
NATALIE. No, leave me on my knees.
ELECTOR. What do you wish, my dear?
NATALIE. I want to beg you, on my knees as it befits
A supplicant, for mercy for my cousin Homburg.
It's not for my sake that I ask for clemency,
Although my heart desires him, I admit.
Still, not for my sake have I come to plead his cause.
Let him be married to whomever he may choose,
I only want, dear uncle, that he be alive,
That for his own sake he be left to grow,
Free, self-sufficient like a flower that delights
My eye. That is, my friend and sovereign, all I ask.
I know that you will heed my plea.
ELECTOR (*lifts her up*). My daughter, do you know what you
        demand?
You know what grave offense your cousin has committed.
NATALIE. Oh, dearest uncle!
ELECTOR.   Well? Do you think he is blameless?
NATALIE. Oh, that mistake which he in blue-eyed innocence
Committed and for which you should have pardoned him
Before he even had the time to ask!
You cannot kick him brutally away for that.
If for no other reason, for his mother's sake,
You'll press him to your breast and say: "Don't weep,
You are as dear to me as loyalty itself!"
Was it not eagerness to serve your fame
That in the heat of battle tempted him
To break the rules which law provides?

And once he crossed the boundaries of law
In youthful fervor, did he not put manfully
His foot upon the dragon's head?
To crown him victor first, then kill him—no!
Posterity does not demand such sacrifice.
That would be so majestic it would be inhuman,
And God did not create a kinder man than you.

ELECTOR. My dearest child, were I a tyrant, yes,
Your words would melt my iron heart, I know.
But let me ask you, do I have the right
To disregard the verdict of the court?
What, if I did, would be the consequences?

NATALIE. For whom? For you?

ELECTOR.   No, not for me.
Do you not recognize a higher principle than me,
My person and my crown? Have you not heard
The sacred word which in our camps resounds—
The Fatherland?

NATALIE.   Is that what you're concerned about?
Our country will not shatter into a thousand pieces
And perish, if you heed your heart's advice.
Quite the contrary: what you,
Who have been raised a soldier, call disorder,
That is in this case, arbitrarily
To tear the sentence which the court has passed
To shreds, that, in my eyes, is the most precious order.
I know, the articles of war must govern,
But kindly sentiments must have their place.
The country which you founded for us is secure,
A mighty fortress that will yet withstand
Far greater storms than this too early victory;
It will keep growing splendidly until,
When it is governed by your children's children,
Embellished and enlarged, its towers glittering
Luxuriantly like a fairy castle's,
Its strength will be impregnable,
The friend's delight, the terror of the enemy.
It does not need the blood of your best friend,
That cold and sterile mortar, to endure
Beyond the peaceful, glorious autumn of your life.

ELECTOR. Is that what cousin Homburg thinks?

NATALIE.   Why, I—

ELECTOR. Does he believe it does not matter
If order reigns or arbitrary rule?

NATALIE. Oh, he . . . he is so young!

ELECTOR.   Well? Does he?

NATALIE. Oh, Uncle, I have no replies but tears to that.

ELECTOR (*startled*). But why, my little daughter? What has
  happened?

NATALIE (*hesitantly*). He thinks of nothing but his rescue
  now.
The rifles, rigid at the marksmen's shoulders,
Their muzzles staring at him horribly,
Appal and stagger him. The wish to live
Is all he feels and thinks and cares about.
The country could be split by lightning
Or plunge into an abyss—he would never ask
A single question. You have broken his heroic heart.
  (*She averts her face and weeps.*)

ELECTOR (*stunned*). I can't believe it, dearest Natalie!
He begs for mercy? No, that is impossible.

NATALIE. Oh, that you never had condemned him!

ELECTOR. He begs for mercy? God in heaven, what has hap-
  pened?
Why do you weep? Now tell me what you know.
You talked to him?

NATALIE (*leaning her head against his chest*).
                          Just now, in the apartments of my aunt,
Where he had crept, protected by the feeble light of dusk,
Bewildered, frightened, ignominious,
A woeful, a repulsive sight to see.
I never thought a man whom history
Acclaims as hero could descend into such misery.
I am a woman, and I shrink
From contact with a worm that slithers near my feet,
But if I should encounter Death,
And though he took a frightful lion's shape,
He would not find me so entirely crushed,
So utterly devoid of courage.
Oh, what is human greatness, human fame!

ELECTOR (*confused*). If that is so, my child, take heart.
If that is so, by God, he will be free.

NATALIE. What did you say?

ELECTOR.   I'll pardon him. I shall at once

Prepare the necessary orders.

NATALIE. Oh, dearest Uncle, is that true?

ELECTOR.   You heard my words.

NATALIE. You'll pardon him? He will not die?

ELECTOR.   I swear.
How could I set my own opinion up
Against the judgment of that mighty warrior?
You know that I have great esteem for him;
If he believes the sentence is unjust,
Then I shall abrogate it—he is free.
    (*He brings her a chair.*)
Please, Natalie, sit down for just a moment.
    (*He sits down at the table and writes. A pause.*)

NATALIE (*aside*). Why do you beat so violently, heart?

ELECTOR. The Prince is still within the palace?

NATALIE. He has returned and now is back in prison.

ELECTOR (*finishes and seals the letter, then gives it to Natalie*).
My little niece was crying! There! And I,
To whom her happiness has been entrusted,
Have been the one who caused those clouds
To shroud her eyes' enchanting sky.
    (*He puts his arm around her.*)
How would you like to take this letter to the Prince yourself?

NATALIE. Go to his prison?

ELECTOR (*giving her the letter*). Yes. Why not? Hey, guards!
    (GUARDS *enter.*)
Bring up a carriage for the Princess.
She has some urgent business with the Prince of Homburg.
                                   (GUARDS *leave.*)
Thus he can thank you for his life in person.
    (*He embraces her.*)
My dearest child, have you forgiven me?

NATALIE (*after a pause*).
I do not know and do not question why
Your kindness was so quickly roused.
But this I feel deep within my heart: I know
That you would never mock me callously.
No matter what this letter's message is,
I feel that it will mean his liberty.
For that I thank you, Uncle.
    (*She kisses his hand.*)

ELECTOR. Of course, it does, my daughter, certainly.

As surely as he really desires it.

(*They leave.*)

SCENE 2. *Natalie's room. Natalie enters, followed by two Ladies-in-Waiting and Count Reuss.*

NATALIE (*hurriedly*). What news have you, Count Reuss? Is it important?
Something about my regiment?
Can we postpone it to the morning?

REUSS (*hands her a letter*). This is from Colonel Kottwitz, gracious Lady.

NATALIE. Well, quickly then. What does it say?
(*She opens the letter.*)

REUSS. It's a petition to his Highness, as you see,
Composed with frankness but with due respect,
In favor of our general, the Prince.

NATALIE (*reads*). "Petition most respectfully submitted
To the Elector by the Regiment Princess of Orange."
(*A pause.*)
Who drafted the petition, Count?

REUSS. As you will probably have guessed, considering
The shaky writing, Colonel Kottwitz did.
Besides, he heads the list of signatures.

NATALIE. The thirty signatures that follow are . . . ?

REUSS. The names of all the officers, in order of their rank.

NATALIE. And why is this petition brought to me?

REUSS. To ask you most respectfully, your Highness,
If you, as Chief, would fill the place
Which at the top is open for your signature.
(*A pause.*)

NATALIE. The Prince, I hear, is to be pardoned by his Highness
Upon his own decision, and this step
Therefore will not be necessary.

REUSS.   Is that true?

NATALIE. But be that as it may, I won't refuse
To sign a letter which, if wisely used,
Might tip the scales, and the Elector
May even welcome it as added argument.
I therefore will, as you request, put down my name
To head the list of signatures.

(She steps to a table, ready to sign.)

REUSS. We would, indeed, be most obliged to you.

NATALIE *(turning to* REUSS *again).*
I only see my regiment, Count Reuss.
Why are there not the names of Bomsdorf's cuirassiers
And those of the dragoons of Götz and Anhalt-Pless?

REUSS. Not, as you may suspect, because their hearts
Don't beat as strongly for the Prince as ours.
It is unfortunate for this petition
That Kottwitz has been stationed at some distance,
In Arnstein, while the other regiments
Are in encampments close to Fehrbellin.
We lacked the freedom thus to have this sheet
Gain strength by circulating it more widely.

NATALIE. Still, is this paper not a little light?
Are you quite certain, Count, that, if you stayed
And talked to all the other officers
Who come together here, they would approve
Of this petition?

REUSS.   Here in town, your Highness?
The entire cavalry would sign their names.
Yes, more than that, I'm sure we could successfully
Have the petition circulated
In Brandenburg's entire armed might.

NATALIE *(after a pause).* Why did you not send officers
To gather signatures here in the camps?

REUSS. I beg your pardon, Princess, that's one step
That Colonel Kottwitz would not take.
He did not wish to do a single thing
Which might give our démarche an evil name.

NATALIE. A curious old codger, Colonel Kottwitz.
Now bold, now timid. Well, it's fortunate
That the Elector, pressed by other business,
Has asked me to instruct my regiment—
Kottwitz declares that he lacks stable space—
To move to Fehrbellin forthwith.
I'll write the orders out at once.

(She sits down and starts writing.)

REUSS. That's excellent, your Highness! I can't think
Of anything more fortunate for our petition.

NATALIE *(still writing).*
Make use of this, Count Reuss, as best you can.

(*She finishes the letter, seals it and gets up.*)
But for the moment, keep it in your pocket.
Don't leave for Arnstein and remit the order
To Colonel Kottwitz yet. I'll tell you when to leave.
    (*She gives him the letter.*)

A HAIDUK (*entering*). The carriage which his Highness
    ordered, Princess,
Is ready in the yard, awaiting your command.

NATALIE. Let it pull up. I'm coming down at once.
    (*A pause. Lost in thought,* NATALIE *steps to the table and
    puts on her gloves.*)
Would you accompany me, Count?
I'm on my way to see the Prince. There is a seat
At your disposal in my carriage.

REUSS. I'm greatly honored by your offer, Highness.
    (*He offers her his arm.*)

NATALIE (*to the* LADIES-IN-WAITING).
Please follow me, my friends.
    (*To* REUSS.)   It may well be
That I'll decide about the letter while I'm there.

                                        (*All leave.*)

SCENE 3. *The prison. The Prince hangs up his hat, then
nonchalantly sits down on a cushion on the floor.*

PRINCE. Life is a journey and, at that—the Dervish claims—
A short one. So it is. It takes the traveler
From five or six feet this side of the ground
To five or six below. I shall sit down
And rest awhile midway between the two.
Today a man may proudly wear his head held high,
Tomorrow it may droop, though still in place,
But the day after he may find it near his heels.
It may be true, as many people say,
That in the land beyond another sun
Shines over fields more gaily colored than on earth.
I will believe it, but it's sad to think
That our dead eyes will never see that splendor.

SCENE 4. *The Prince. Natalie enters, escorted by Count
Reuss, and followed by her ladies. A runner with a torch
leads the way.*

RUNNER. Her Highness, Natalie, Princess of Orange!

PRINCE (*rises*). Natalie!

RUNNER. Here comes her Ladyship.

NATALIE (*inclining her head toward* REUSS). Leave us alone
For a few minutes, Count.

(REUSS *and the* RUNNER *leave.*)

PRINCE. My dearest lady!

NATALIE. My dear, good cousin!

PRINCE (*leading her forward*). Tell me, please—
What news have you about my fate?

NATALIE. Good news.
You will be pardoned, just as I foresaw.
You're free! And here is proof of it, a letter
Which the Elector wrote himself.

PRINCE. It can't be true, I must be dreaming.

NATALIE. Read!
Read what he writes and you will see yourself.

PRINCE (*reads*). "My dearest Prince, when I commanded your
    imprisonment
Because of your unauthorized attack,
I had no other thought than doing what I must.
I counted on your full agreement;
But if you feel that an injustice has been done,
Please tell me so in a few words,
And I'll return your sword immediately."

(NATALIE *turns pale. A pause. The* PRINCE *looks at her
    questioningly.*)

NATALIE (*apparently overjoyed, bursts out*).
What did I tell you? Now you see yourself.
A few words are all that's needed, my sweet friend!
(*She presses his hand.*)

PRINCE. Oh, my beloved Natalie!

NATALIE. What a happy hour now dawns! Here—take the pen.

PRINCE. Is this his signature?

NATALIE. That is the "F"
He uses as his sign. Oh, Bork, rejoice with me.
His kindness, like the sea, is limitless.
Quick, bring a chair, so he can write at once.

PRINCE. He says, if I believe—

NATALIE (*interrupting*). Of course. Sit down
And quickly write a line. Shall I dictate?
(*She puts a chair next to him.*)

PRINCE. I want to read the letter once more. Please—

NATALIE (*pulls the letter from his hand*).
But why? Did you not see the tomb extending you
With open jaws its grisly welcome?
Don't hesitate, sit down and write.

PRINCE (*smiling*). You sound as if the tomb might, like a
    panther,
Come leaping at my throat.
    (*He sits down and takes the pen.*)

NATALIE (*averting her face and in tears*).
                    Don't make me angry. Write!
(*The PRINCE rings for a SERVANT, who enters promptly.*)

PRINCE. Bring paper, wax, and seal.
(*After gathering together the writing utensils and putting
them before the PRINCE, the SERVANT leaves. The PRINCE
begins his letter. After writing a few words, he tears the letter
up and throws the pieces under the table.*)
                    A stupid opening.
(*He takes another sheet of paper.*)

NATALIE (*picks up the pieces of the first letter and reads*).
What did you say? That's fine, that's excellent.

PRINCE (*aside*). Bah, that's how scoundrels write, but not a
    Prince.
I'll think of something else.
(*A pause. He tries to pull the ELECTOR's letter out of
NATALIE's hand.*)
                    What did he say again?

NATALIE. You know it very well. There's nothing else.

PRINCE. Give me the letter.

NATALIE.   You have read it twice.

PRINCE. And yet I want to read it once again,
To know how I should formulate my own.
(*He gets hold of the letter, unfolds it and reads.*)

NATALIE (*aside*). Oh God, this is the end. Now he is lost.

PRINCE (*startled*). Look, this is strange. I'm sure you did not
    see
This passage here before.

NATALIE.   No. Which?

PRINCE. He asks me—me!—to be the judge myself.

NATALIE. And so?

PRINCE.   He is so frank and dignified;

That is exactly how a man of stature
Would put the matter.

NATALIE.   I agree,
His generosity is boundless. Now—
You do your part and write what he demands.
You can see readily that this is nothing
But a formality, a pretext that he needs.
As soon as your few words are in his hands,
He will forget this silly quarrel.

PRINCE (*putting the letter aside*).
No, no. I'll think about it till tomorrow.

NATALIE. Mysterious man, what is the matter now?
Why won't you write the letter and be done with it?

PRINCE (*gets up, passionately*).
Don't ask me, please. Apparently
You don't quite understand just what he says.
I cannot write him that he was unjust,
Which he makes the condition of his pardon.
If you insist that I give my reply
This minute, in my present mood I'd write:
You acted justly.
   (*He sits down again and, folding his arms on the table, looks
   at the letter.*)

NATALIE (*pale*). What is this? You are insane!
(*Deeply moved, she bends over him.*)

PRINCE (*presses her hand*).
Wait just a minute; I believe . . . (*He ponders.*)

NATALIE.   Yes? What?

PRINCE. I'll know what I must write him presently.

NATALIE (*pained*). Oh, Arthur!

PRINCE (*taking the pen*). Yes? I'm listening.

NATALIE. My dearest friend, I praise the sentiment
That moves you now, but I assure you,
The orders have been issued to the regiment
That has been picked to celebrate with carbines
The reconciling obsequies above your grave.
If, noble as you are, you won't contest the verdict,
If you refuses to do what must be done,
According to his terms, to have it voided,
Then, I assure you, he will just as nobly take
The matter as it is and, though regretfully,
Command the sentence to be carried out tomorrow.

PRINCE (*writing*). That doesn't matter.

NATALIE. What? It doesn't matter?

PRINCE. Let him act as he may, and I'll act as I must.

NATALIE (*steps closer to the table, apprehensively*).
Have you already finished, monstrous man?

PRINCE (*reading the final words as he writes them*).
"Homburg. Given at Fehrbellin, this twelfth day . . ."
It's done! Franz!
(*He puts the letter into the envelope and seals it.*)

NATALIE. God have mercy!

PRINCE (*gets up*). Quick, this letter
Must be in the Elector's hands at once.
(*The* SERVANT *leaves.*)
I do not wish to stand as worthless knave
Before a man who has such dignity.
I recognize too well that I am guilty.
If he cannot forgive that grave offense
Unless I argue with him, I will have
No part of clemency.

NATALIE (*kisses him*). This kiss
Will tell you that, although twelve bullets riddled you,
I could not help myself, I would rejoice
And weep and say: I love you very much.
Meanwhile, if you do as your heart dictates,
I shall feel free to follow the advice
Which my heart gives to me. Count Reuss!
(*The* RUNNER *opens the door through which* COUNT REUSS *enters.*)

REUSS. Your Highness, I am at your service.

NATALIE. The time has come for you to ride to Arnstein
And to deliver what I've given you to Kottwitz.
Our sovereign orders that the regiment break camp,
And I'll expect the Colonel here by midnight.
(*All leave.*)

ACT V

SCENE 1. *A large room in the palace at Fehrbellin. The Elector, half-dressed, comes from the adjoining room, followed by Count Truchss, Count Hohenzollern, and Captain von der Golz. Pages enter with candles.*

ELECTOR. Kottwitz? With the Dragoons of the Princess of
  Orange?
He's here in town?

TRUCHSS (*opening a window*).
He is, your Highness.
He has drawn up his regiment before the palace.

ELECTOR. Well, gentlemen? Would one of you perhaps
Supply me with the answer to this riddle?
Who ordered him to Fehrbellin?

HOHENZOLLERN.   That I don't know,
Your Highness.

ELECTOR.   My instructions were to stay
In Arnstein where I ordered him.
Quick, one of you go out and bring him here.

GOLZ. He will appear before you presently, your Highness.

ELECTOR. Where is he now?

GOLZ.   I've heard that he is in the Town Hall,
Where all your generals have gathered.

ELECTOR. Why that? What do they plan?

HOHENZOLLERN.   I do not know.

TRUCHSS. May we have your permission, sir, to join them
  there?
We won't be long.

ELECTOR.   Where? At the Town Hall?

HOHENZOLLERN. Yes, in their meeting, sir. We promised we
  would come.

ELECTOR (*after a short pause*).
You are dismissed.

GOLZ.   Come with me, gentlemen.
                          (*The* OFFICERS *leave.*)

SCENE 2. *The Elector alone. Later, two servants.*

ELECTOR. That's strange! If I were Dey of Tunis,
I certainly would sound alarm at once
At such ambiguous proceedings. I would put
A silken cord upon my desk,
Would barricade the gates and draw up cannon
And howitzers before the palace walls.
But since it is Hans Kottwitz from the Priegnitz
Who has arrived without authority
And of his own accord, I shall conduct myself
As it is custom here in Brandenburg.
I'll seize him by one of his silvery locks
And lead him with his squadrons quietly
To Arnstein where he ought to be right now.
So—why arouse the town from peaceful slumber?
   (*He steps to the window and, after a moment, back to the
   table. He rings the bell. Two* SERVANTS *enter.*)
Go down and ask, as if from idle curiosity,
What happens in the Town Hall at this moment.
   FIRST SERVANT. At once, your Highness.

                                             (*He leaves.*)

   ELECTOR (*to the other* SERVANT).
                                You, get me my clothes.
   (*The* SERVANT *goes and comes back with the clothes. The*
   ELECTOR *dresses and puts on his insignia.*)

SCENE 3. *The same. Field Marshal Dörfling enters.*

FIELD MARSHAL. Rebellion, sir!
   ELECTOR (*still occupied with his clothes*).
Please, Marshal, keep your head!
You know that I detest being disturbed
By anyone without announcement. Well?
   FIELD MARSHAL. Please pardon me, your Highness; an event
Of very special import brings me here.
Colonel von Kottwitz has arrived in town;
He had no orders; and almost a hundred officers
Are gathered in the Town Hall at this moment;
They circulate a document

Intended to infringe upon your rights.

ELECTOR. I know. What can it be but a petition,
A move to save the Prince, who is condemned
By law to die?

FIELD MARSHAL. Exactly, sir. By God,
That is precisely what they want, your Highness.

ELECTOR. In that case—very well, I share their feelings.

FIELD MARSHAL. They are insane! They're planning to present
The document to you before the morning dawns,
And, should your anger be implacable,
Should you insist on standing by the verdict—
I hardly dare to say it—they intend
To liberate the Prince by force!

ELECTOR (*grimly*). Who told you that?

FIELD MARSHAL. Who told me? Lady Retzow,
Whom you can trust. She is a cousin of my wife's.
This evening she was at her uncle's,
The Count von Retzow's house, where officers
Who came from the encampments spoke about
Their bold designs quite openly.

ELECTOR. That I shall not believe before a man
Confirms it. I shall mount the guard myself
Before his house to save the Prince from these young hotheads.

FIELD MARSHAL. If you have any thought at all, your Highness,
Of pardoning the Prince, please do it now,
Before irreparable harm is done.
You know all armies love their heroes.
Do not allow this dimly glowing spark
That animates them now to grow into devouring flames.
Kottwitz and his companions have no knowledge yet
Of my forewarning you, as loyalty demands.
Send back the Prince's sword before they come,
As, after all, is only equitable.
Thus one more noble deed, one misdeed less,
Will be recorded in your history.

ELECTOR. I first would have to ask agreement from the Prince,
Who, as you know, was not imprisoned arbitrarily
And cannot arbitrarily be freed.
I want to see the gentlemen when they arrive.

FIELD MARSHAL (*aside*). None of my arrows penetrates his
armor.

SCENE 4. *The same. Two Haiduks enter, one of them carrying a letter.*

FIRST HAIDUK. The Colonels Kottwitz, Hennings, Truchss and
   others
Respectfully request an audience.

ELECTOR (*to the other* HAIDUK, *who hands him the letter*).
That's from the Prince of Homburg?

SECOND HAIDUK.   Yes, your Highness.

ELECTOR. Who gave it to you?

SECOND HAIDUK.   The sentry at the gate,
Who had received it from his Highness' orderly.

ELECTOR (*steps to the table and reads the letter, then turns
   and calls a* PAGE).
Prittwitz! Bring me the death sentence. I also want
The passport for Count Horn, the Swedish emissary.
   (*The* PAGE *leaves. He turns to the* FIRST HAIDUK.)
Ask Kottwitz and his followers to enter.

SCENE 5. *The same. Colonel Kottwitz enters with Colonel
Hennings, Count Truchss, Count Hohenzollern, Sparren,
Count Reuss, Captain von der Golz, Stranz, and other officers.*

KOTTWITZ (*holding the petition*).
Allow me to present to you, your Highness,
In all humility and in the name of all your troops,
This document.

ELECTOR.   Before I take it, Kottwitz,
Would you mind telling me who ordered you
To Fehrbellin?

KOTTWITZ (*looking at him*). You mean my regiment?

ELECTOR. Yes, your dragoons. It seems to me,
I had assigned you Arnstein as your garrison.

KOTTWITZ. You did, but then you ordered me to move.

ELECTOR. I did? Show me the orders.

KOTTWITZ.   Here they are.

ELECTOR (*reads*). "Signed, Natalie, at Fehrbellin,
On the instructions of my august uncle, Frederic."

KOTTWITZ. I surely hope, your Highness, that these orders

Do not come as a surprise to you.

ELECTOR.   Oh no!
Please understand . . . Who brought these orders, Kottwitz?

KOTTWITZ. Count Reuss.

ELECTOR (*after a moment's hesitation*). I see. That's right. I
  welcome you.
You and your squadrons have been picked
To render final honors to the Prince tomorrow,
Whom, as you know, the law has judged.

KOTTWITZ (*startled*). What's that, my Lord?

ELECTOR (*returning the orders to* KOTTWITZ). Your regiment
  is still drawn up
In night and fog, before the palace gates?

KOTTWITZ. In night and fog . . . I beg your pardon, sir . . . ?

ELECTOR. Why don't you billet them?

KOTTWITZ.   They have been billeted.
As you commanded, they are quartered here in town.

ELECTOR (*with a quick movement toward the window*).
Why . . . just a little while ago . . . God knows,
You've found them stables quickly, then.
Well, all the better. Once again, be welcome here.
Now to your business. What has brought you here?

KOTTWITZ. Sir, this petition from your loyal army.

ELECTOR. Well, let me see it.

KOTTWITZ.   Here, your Highness, but the words
You spoke just now have drowned all hope.

ELECTOR. Then, what I yet may say, will possibly revive them.
  (*He reads.*)
"Petition, pleading clemency for our beloved leader,
Accused on pain of death, our general,
Prince Friedrich Hessen-Homburg." Yes, indeed,
  (*To the* OFFICERS.)
A noble name, and worthy of the efforts
Which you expend on his behalf
In such great numbers, gentlemen.
  (*Looking again at the petition.*)
And who composed this document?

KOTTWITZ.   I did, my Lord.

ELECTOR. The Prince, of course, has been informed of this?

KOTTWITZ. No, in no manner whatsoever, sir.
It was conceived and executed in our midst.

ELECTOR. Allow me to take a moment, gentlemen.

(*He steps to the table and reads through the petition. A long pause.*)

That's very strange. You, Kottwitz, an old warrior,
Defend the action of the Prince? You find
Excuses for the premature attack
He made against my orders?

KOTTWITZ.   Yes, your Highness,
That is what Kottwitz does.

ELECTOR.   But at the time,
You had a different opinion.

KOTTWITZ. That, sir, was ill considered, poorly judged.
I should have quietly accepted what the Prince,
Who knows his strategy, was setting out to do.
The left wing of the Swedes was giving way,
They were about to reinforce their right.
Had he held back until your order came,
They would have taken hold in the ravines,
And you would not have won your victory.

ELECTOR. Hm, that's how you prefer to see things now.
You know that I had ordered Colonel Hennings
To seize the bridgehead that protected Wrangel's rear.
He would have carried off that stroke,
If you had followed orders, and within two hours
He would have burned the bridges, taken up
Positions on the river bank, and Wrangel's army
Would then have perished in the swamps and ditches,
Destroyed, exterminated, root and branch.

KOTTWITZ. Leave it to smaller men than you to reach
For fate's supreme rewards in every case.
Until today, you've always taken what it offered you.
The dragon that laid waste your provinces
With impudence was chased away with bleeding fangs.
What more could you accomplish in one day?
Why worry if he lies exhausted in the sand,
To lick his wounds, another week or two?
We've learned the art of beating him by now
And have a mind to practice that art.
Let us meet Wrangel face to face again,
And we'll complete what we auspiciously began;
We'll chase him to the Baltic Sea and drown him there.
Rome was not built, your Highness, in one day.

ELECTOR. What right have you, old fool, to hope for victory,

If anyone is free to seize the reins?
Do you think fortune will reward forever
All disobedience with the crown of victory,
As it did this time? I don't want those victories
That only lucky circumstance makes possible.
I will uphold the reign of law, the mother of my crown,
Who bore an entire family of victories for me.

    KOTTWITZ. The supreme law that governs your commanders'
      hearts
Should never be the letter of your will;
That law should be the country's welfare and the crown,
And he who wears that crown—yourself.
Why be so much concerned about the rules
By which the enemy is fought, if in the end
You see him prostrate at your feet, with all his flags?
The rule by which the enemy is beaten
Should always be the rule that we obey.
Do you desire to make your army,
That is so fervently attached to you,
Into a lifeless tool that, like a sword,
Hangs from your golden sash, but cannot act alone?
It was a sorry mind that thought of such a doctrine.
Ill-starred, short-sighted is the art of government
Which would forget, because it failed one time,
That intuition in ten other cases
Was indispensable to victory.
Am I prepared to shed my blood for wages,
For gold and honors, when the cannons roar?
My blood, your Highness, is too good for that!
I find my satisfaction and my joy
In contemplating quietly, all by myself,
Without constraint, your excellence and glory,
The growth and lustre of your fame.
Those are the wages which I will accept.
Suppose that I, while roaming through the woods
And fields with my twelve squadrons, like a shepherd,
By chance caught sight of victory, unbidden as the Prince,
Would I not be a scoundrel if I failed
To follow gaily in the Prince's footsteps,
And did so even though you just had doomed the Prince
For winning such a victory without your orders?
Then, if you said, your book of rules in hand,
"That foolishness will cost your head," I would reply,
"I knew that. Take it, sir, my head is yours."

The oath that ties me, soul and body, to your crown
Includes my head. You're only taking what belongs to you.

ELECTOR. With you, peculiar old gentleman,
I find it difficult to tilt.
Your wily eloquence may easily seduce
A man like me, who as you know quite well,
Has always been your friend. I have to call
Upon an advocate to plead my case
And put an end to our dispute.
(*He rings the bell, a* SERVANT *enters.*)
See that the Prince of Homburg is brought here at once.
(*The* SERVANT *leaves.*)
He will instruct you, I assure you, Kottwitz,
In matters of obedience and discipline.
At least, he wrote a letter to me which sounds different
From the sophistic theories of freedom
You have expounded here in schoolboy fashion.
(*He steps again to the table and reads.*)

KOTTWITZ (*surprised.*)
Have whom brought here?

HENNINGS.   The Prince?

TRUCHSS.   Impossible!
(*Uneasily, the* OFFICERS *huddle together and talk among themselves.*)

ELECTOR. Who wrote this second letter?

HOHENZOLLERN.   I, your Highness.

ELECTOR (*reads*). "Proof that the Prince of Homburg's action
Was caused by what Elector Frederic himself . . ."
By God, that I call brash!
You lay at my feet all responsibility
For his deliberate and willful crime?

HOHENZOLLERN. I do, your Highness, I, Count Hohenzollern.

ELECTOR. Well! That is more fantastic than a fairy tale.
The one claims that the Prince is innocent,
The other even that it's I who is to blame.
How will you prove that allegation, sir?

HOHENZOLLERN. Your Highness will remember that one night
We found the Prince asleep upon a bench,
Beneath the oak tree in the palace garden.
He had a wreath of laurels in his hand
And dreamed, we surmised, of the next day's victory.
You took—maybe to probe his inmost nature—

The wreath away from him and smiling wound the chain
You wore around it; then you handed both of them,
Thus intertwined, to Princess Natalie.
At this remarkable, enchanting sight,
Blushing, the Prince arose and tried to snatch
The lovely treasure from the gracious hands
That offered it to him. But you withdrew,
Together with the Princess, and in haste escaped.
The open palace door received
The lady with the wreath and chain, yourself
And all your retinue—then clattered shut.
The Prince stayed back, alone again,
Imbedded in the midnight's lap—
But in his hand remained a glove which he had seized
From someone—whom, he did not know himself.

ELECTOR. What glove?

HOHENZOLLERN.   Allow me to complete my story.
The thing had been a farce, of course,
But, as I soon discovered, for the Prince,
Of great significance. For when I presently
Stole back to him through the small garden gate,
As if by accident, and roused him from his sleep,
He still remembered the event and glowed
With happiness as he recalled its image.
Most touchingly he told me all that happened,
Down to the most minute detail, and added
That he had never yet dreamed quite so vividly.
He soon was thoroughly convinced the dream
Had been a sign from heaven to announce
That God would grant him all that he had seen—
The wreath, its decoration and the girl—
The day of the impending battle.

ELECTOR. Hm, that is strange. But what about the glove?

HOHENZOLLERN. The glove, transubstantiation of his dream,
Destroyed the dream as dream, but strengthened his belief
In the significance of the event.
Wide-eyed he stared at it—the glove was white
And, judging by its cut and trim, a lady's glove—
But since he had not spoken to a lady all that night
To whom it might belong, and since I presently
Cut short his musing, taking him along
With me to get our orders at the palace,
He soon forgot what he could in no way understand,

And simply slipped the glove into his doublet.

ELECTOR. And then?

HOHENZOLLERN. He dutifully came along, armed with his pad
    and pencil,
To give the Marshal his complete attention.
But the Electress and the Princess were by chance
Dressed for their journey, present in the hall.
Imagine his surprise, when suddenly
The Princess started looking for her glove,
The very one that he had put into his doublet.
The Marshal called on several occasions,
"The Prince of Homburg—is he here?" And he,
"What are my Marshal's orders?" trying to collect his wits.
Thus in the midst of all these strange events
The trumpets of the Day of Judgment might have sounded—

    (*He stops.*)

ELECTOR. Was it the Princess' glove?

HOHENZOLLERN.   Indeed, it was.

    (*The* ELECTOR *stands lost in thought.*)

He stood transfixed; although he seemed alive,
Still with his pad and pencil in his hands,
All thought and all emotion had deserted him,
As if he had been touched by a magician's wand.
And not until the morning when the cannons roared
Did he return to life. Then suddenly he asked,
"What did the Marshal say last night, my friend,
Concerning me, when he announced the battle orders?"

FIELD MARSHAL. That part I can confirm, your Highness. I recall
That he did not perceive one word of all I said.
I've often seen the Prince distracted,
But never yet as absent-minded as that night.

ELECTOR. Now, if I understand you right, your reasoning
Leads to this conclusion: had I not in jest—
Perhaps, it's true, ambiguously—played
Upon the dreamer's curious state of mind,
He would not have committed an offense,
Would not have been distracted at the conference,
And not have been so obstinate in battle.
That's what you think, am I not right?

HOHENZOLLERN. It's up to you, my Lord, to draw conclusions.

ELECTOR. You harebrained fool! If you had not aroused

My curiosity and called me down
Into the garden, I would not have had
My harmless fun with him, our sleeping beauty.
I therefore claim with equal logic
That you're the veritable cause of his offense.
The Delphic wisdom of my officers!

HOHENZOLLERN. Sir, let this be enough. I'm certain
That you will give my words their proper weight.

SCENE 6. *The same. An Officer enters.*

OFFICER. The Prince will be here presently, your Highness.
ELECTOR. Good, let him enter.
OFFICER.   He will be here at once.
When passing by the graveyard on his way,
He asked the keeper to admit him for a moment.
ELECTOR. The graveyard?
OFFICER.   Yes, my Lord.
ELECTOR.   Why that?
OFFICER. To tell the truth, I'm not quite sure. It seemed
That he desired to see the tomb
Which you have ordered opened for his bones.
(*The* OFFICERS *stand together in a group and talk among
themselves.*)
ELECTOR. I see. As soon as he arrives, please show him in.
(*He steps to the table again and studies the papers.*)
TRUCHSS. Here come the guards who bring the Prince.

SCENE 7. *The same. The Prince enters, followed by the Officer and Soldiers of the guard.*

ELECTOR. I've called you here because I need your help.
Von Kottwitz has submitted a petition
In your behalf—here, take a look at it—
Which has been signed by a hundred noblemen.
The army, it declares, demands that you be freed
Because they disapprove of the court-martial's verdict.
Read it yourself, so you may be informed.
(*He gives the petition to the* PRINCE.)

PRINCE (*glances at the petition, then turns and looks around among the* OFFICERS).
Kottwitz, give me your hand, old friend;
You're doing me a greater honor
Than I deserved of you the day of Fehrbellin.
But still, go back to Arnstein whence you came
And do not stir from there. I've reconsidered
And have decided to accept
The sentence of the court as just.
(*He hands him the petition.*)

KOTTWITZ (*stunned*). Oh no, your Highness, you can't mean
what you are saying!

HOHENZOLLERN. He wants to die?

TRUCHSS.   He must not and he shall not die.

SEVERAL OFFICERS (*pushing closer to the* ELECTOR).
Your Highness, listen to us, please!

PRINCE. Please, quiet! I've made up my mind,
And my decision is unalterable.
I want to glorify the sacred law of war
By dying of my own free will.
How little value has another paltry victory,
That I might wrest from Wrangel yet, for you, my brothers,
Measured against the glorious triumph
That I can win tomorrow over arrogance
And blind defiance, our most deadly foes!
Let all who wish to subjugate us perish
And let the men of Brandenburg walk freely
Upon the soil they have inherited,
For it is theirs; for them alone
The splendor of its fields and forests was created.

KOTTWITZ (*deeply moved*). My son, my friend—what shall I
call you?

TRUCHSS. God!

KOTTWITZ. I want to kiss your hand.
(*They press close to the* PRINCE.)

PRINCE (*turning to the* ELECTOR). My Lord and Master—
I used to have the privilege, now forfeit,
To call you by a gentler name—
I kneel before you with an overflowing heart.
Excuse my fault if I was overzealous
In serving you on that decisive day.
My death will wash away my guilt.

Console my heart, that without rancor, smilingly,
Accepts your judgment, by assuring me
That you, too, have renounced all enmity,
And in this hour of parting graciously
Betoken it by granting me a last request.

ELECTOR. What is your wish, young hero? Speak.
Upon my word and on my princely honor,
Whatever it may be, it will be done.

PRINCE. My Lord, do not buy peace from Charles Gustavus,
With Natalie as purchase price.
Expel the emissary who made bold
To offer such dishonorable terms,
And write your answer with a volley.

ELECTOR (*kissing his forehead*).
So be it! With this kiss, my son,
I grant your last request. What need is there
For such a sacrifice, which could be forced
Upon me only by the war's misfortunes?
From every word you speak blooms forth a victory
That grinds my enemies to dust.
I'll write him that she is the Prince of Homburg's bride,
The man who for his victory at Fehrbellin
Became a victim of our laws,
And that to gain her he will have to fight
The Prince's spirit on the battlefield,
Where he will bear our flags to victory.

(*He kisses him again and raises him up.*)

PRINCE. Now you have given me another life to live.
I pray that all the blessings which the seraphim
Pour jubilantly down from heaven's throne
Upon the heads of heroes will be yours.
Go forth and fight and vanquish all the world
That dares defy you! You deserve the prize.

ELECTOR. Guards! Take the Prince back to his prison.

SCENE 8. *The same. Natalie and the Electress appear in the doorway, followed by their Ladies-in-Waiting.*

NATALIE. Oh, Mother, please! Why talk about propriety?
The only proper thing in such a moment is
To love. My most unfortunate, my dearest friend!

PRINCE (*starting to go*). Now let me go!

TRUCHSS (*holding him back*).   No, that must never be!
(*Several* OFFICERS *bar his way.*)

PRINCE. Take me away!

HOHENZOLLERN.   Your Highness, can your heart—

PRINCE (*tearing himself away*).

Don't try to drag me to my death with chains!

Make way! I've finished my accounting with the world.

                              (*He leaves with the* GUARDS.)

NATALIE (*leaning her head against her aunt's bosom*).

O Earth! Let me return into your womb!

Why look upon the sun, now that its light is gone?

SCENE 9. *The same, without the Prince.*

FIELD MARSHAL. Dear God, why did it have to come to this?
(*The* ELECTOR *speaks softly but urgently to an* OFFICER.)

KOTTWITZ (*coldly*). Your Highness, after what has happened,
May I assume that we're excused?

ELECTOR. Not yet. I'll tell you when it's time to go.
(*He gazes at* KOTTWITZ *for a moment, then takes the papers,
which a* PAGE *has brought, from the table and turns to the*
FIELD MARSHAL.)

This is the passport for Count Horn. Give it to him.

Tell him the Prince of Homburg has requested,

And I feel duty-bound to grant his wish,

That in three days the war will be resumed.

(*A pause. He glances at the death sentence.*)

Well, gentlemen, now I ask you to be the judges.

By his defiance and by carelessness,

The Prince has cost me two important victories

This year and put a third in serious jeopardy.

Now that he has gone through the school

Of these last days' events, are you prepared

To take another chance with him?

KOTTWITZ and TRUCHSS (*simultaneously*).

You mean . . . My gracious sovereign . . . Is it true—

ELECTOR. Are you prepared to do that? Are you really?

KOTTWITZ. You might be standing at the brink of utter ruin,

I swear that he would not unsheath his sword

To save you if you do not order him to act.

ELECTOR (*tears the death sentence to shreds*).

Come to the garden with me then.

(All leave.)

SCENE 10. *The palace with the ramp, as in Act I. Again it is night. Stranz leads the Prince, who is blindfolded, into the garden through the gate below. Officers and Guards. In the distance, the drumbeat of a funeral march is heard.*

PRINCE. Now, Immortality, you are entirely mine.
Your light streams through my blindfold, and I see
The dazzling splendor of a thousand suns.
Wings grow upon my shoulders, and my soul
Floats upward through the quiet ether.
And as the bustling harbor fades from view
When lively breezes carry off the ship,
All life begins to dim before my eyes.
Now I can still distinguish forms and colors,
And now the mist shrouds everything below.
  (He sits down on the bench under the oak tree in the center.
  STRANZ *quietly steps aside and looks up the ramp.)*
How lovely is the perfume of the violet!
Do you not sense their fragrance, Stranz?

  STRANZ *(coming closer again).*
They're gillyflowers and carnations, sir.

  PRINCE. Carnations? How did they get here?

  STRANZ. I am not sure. Perhaps a girl has planted them,
But . . . would you like to have one?

  PRINCE. That's very kind. I'll put it in a vase at home.

SCENE 11. *On the ramp appear the Elector, holding the laurel wreath around which a gold chain is wound, the Electress, Natalie, the Field Marshal, Colonel Kottwitz, Hohenzollern, Golz, and other Officers, Ladies-in-Waiting and Pages with torches. Hohenzollern steps to the balustrade and signals to Stranz with a white handkerchief. Stranz leaves the Prince and talks to the guards in the background.*

  PRINCE. There seems to be a brilliant light. What is that, Stranz?

  STRANZ *(coming back).*
Your Highness, will you kindly rise?

  PRINCE. What is it?

STRANZ. Nothing that will frighten you.
I only want to take your blindfold off.

PRINCE. Has my last hour of suffering arrived?

STRANZ. It has. God bless you, sir. You merit it.
(*The* ELECTOR *gives wreath and chain to* NATALIE *and leads her down the ramp. The* LADIES *and* GENTLEMEN *follow them. Surrounded by torches,* NATALIE *steps in front of the* PRINCE, *who rises in utter consternation, and puts the wreath on his head, the chain around his neck and presses his hand to her heart. The* PRINCE *faints.*)

NATALIE. Oh, heaven help us! The joy is killing him!

HOHENZOLLERN (*helping the* PRINCE *to his feet*).
Come quickly, friends, and help me wake him up.

ELECTOR. No, let the roar of cannon wake him up.
(*Cannon shots. A march. The palace is brilliantly illuminated.*)

KOTTWITZ. Hail to the Prince of Homburg, hail!

THE OFFICERS. Hurrah!

ALL. Long live the victor of the day at Fehrbellin!
(*Momentary silence.*)

PRINCE. No. . . . No. . . . Is this a dream?

KOTTWITZ. Of course, a dream!

SEVERAL OFFICERS. To war! To war!

TRUCHSS. Forward into the battle!

FIELD MARSHAL. Into the battle! On to victory!

ALL. Into the dust with all the enemies of Brandenburg!

CURTAIN

Danton's Death

by
GEORG BÜCHNER

❧ ❧ ❧

Of Georg Büchner's three dramatic works, *Dantons Tod* (1835) is the most impressive: he wrote it in five weeks at the age of twenty-two, almost surreptitiously "on the dissecting table" during his preparations for a university medical school examination, and as he was sought by the police for his participation in political disturbances against the reactionary government in Hessen. A year later he fled to Switzerland, became a lecturer at the University of Zurich, and died in 1837. Büchner's vigorous involvement in revolutionary activities seems curiously in conflict with the profoundly fatalistic sentiments expressed in his letters and represented so radically in *Dantons Tod*.

In the play, the French Revolution has reached a critical phase; Danton, earlier one of its most ardent defenders, has withdrawn and is now engaged only in a weary epicureanism and in skeptical reflections on life and death. He is indifferent to Robespierre's devious moralizing and to his advocacy of terror in the service of utopian ideals. He refuses to counteract the intrigues against him, even when he learns of his own imminent arrest. His grand and stirring oration is too late to save him; he and his friends are condemned to die—among them Desmoulins, from whom he parts in a moving farewell scene. His own wife and Desmoulins's voluntarily join them in death.

It is, once again, the topic of history as the ineluctable condition of human life that Büchner represents in this powerful drama. But he is not, like Schiller or Kleist, concerned with the opportunities of freedom and heroic defiance that the course of history may offer to the resolute character. Büchner's philosophy of history, very different from that of the idealistic tradition, is altogether negative and deterministic; it is founded on the scientific materialism which is later expounded in his brother Ludwig's influential book, *Kraft und Stoff* (*Energy and Matter*) (1855). What he wished in part to provide in *Dantons Tod* was a detached yet stirring account of the inexorable law by which men will use the language of idealism to destroy one another. At the same time, his interest in the single figure of Danton overrides his fascination with the intellectual impulses of revolution. Danton is to be destroyed; yet, he dies not so much in consequence of his defeat in the maneuvering for power as because he is himself drained of life and without the energies either of religious certainty, of intellectual conviction, or of romantic passion. He becomes increasingly isolated, lonely, and weary; he wants above all to be left alone. "We are mere puppets led by unknown powers." Peace for him is to be found only in non-being, and toward this absolute state of mind he moves with a full awareness of his tragic nihilism.

Büchner's aim as a dramatist was "not merely to give descriptions but characters," and few other German plays are so crowded with such superb figures as move here in the quick and brilliant succession of thirty-two scenes. Danton's oration and the encounters in prison are the dramatic and lyrical high points of an action that moves with extraordinary speed and force. Whether Büchner used passages from the actual speeches made during the Revolution or whether he invented minor figures, he managed to combine a technique of realistic reporting with elements (for instance in the love scenes between Desmoulins and Lucile) of tender and romantic lyricism.

Later in the century, Büchner's essentially passive hero became the prototype of the naturalistic character drama; the sharp social criticism of the play struck Gerhart Hauptmann and Frank Wedekind as eminently congenial; and when the play was first performed in 1910, its language and its sparse structure were at once felt to have many of the features of the new expressionist style and sensibility.

Danton's Death

❧

CHARACTERS

GEORGES DANTON
LEGENDRE
CAMILLE DESMOULINS
HÉRAULT-SÉCHELLES
LACROIX } deputies
PHILIPPEAU
FABRE D'EGLANTINE
MERCIER
THOMAS PAYNE

ROBESPIERRE
SAINT-JUST
BARÈRE } members of the Committee
COLLOT D'HERBOIS of Public Safety
BILLAUD-VARENNES

CHAUMETTE, Attorney for the City of Paris
DILLON, a general
FOUQUIER-TINVILLE, Public Prosecutor
AMAR } members of the Committee
VOULAND of Security
HERMAN } presidents of the
DUMAS Revolutionary Tribunal
PARIS, a friend of Danton's
SIMON, a prompter
LAFLOTTE
JULIE, Danton's wife
LUCILE, Camille Desmoulins's wife
ROSALIE
ADELAIDE } grisettes
MARION

MEN and WOMEN of the people, GRISETTES, DEPUTIES, EXECUTIONERS, etc.

❧

405

ACT I

SCENE 1. *Hérault-Séchelles and several Ladies seated at a card table. Danton and Julie sit apart, Danton on a footstool at Julie's feet.*

DANTON. Look how nicely that pretty lady deals the cards! She really has a knack for it. They say that she always deals a heart to her husband and diamonds to everyone else. You women could make a man fall in love with a lie!

JULIE. Do you believe in me?

DANTON. Who knows! We know so little about each other. We are thick-skinned. We reach out for each other, but it is no good; we only manage to rub against each other and to irritate the coarse leather. We are very lonely.

JULIE. You know me, Danton.

DANTON. Yes, what we call knowing! You have dark eyes, curly hair and a delicate complexion, and you always say "dear Georges" to me! But (*Pointing to her eyes and her forehead.*) there . . . there . . . what is behind that? Look, our senses are not very refined. To know each other, we would have to crack open each other's skulls and pull the thoughts out of the fibres of our brains.

A LADY (*to* HÉRAULT). What are you doing with your fingers?

HÉRAULT. Nothing.

THE LADY. Don't tuck your thumb in like that! It looks terrible!

HÉRAULT. Oh, but you see, that has a special meaning.

DANTON. Julie, I love you like the grave.

JULIE (*turning her head away*). Oh!

DANTON. No, don't turn away! Listen to me! They say that there is peace in the grave, that being buried is the same as resting. If that is true, I'm buried when I lie in your lap. Sweet grave, your lips are funeral bells, your voice my deathknell, your breast the mound above my grave and your heart my coffin.

THE LADY. You have lost!

HÉRAULT. It was a romantic adventure that cost money, as they always do.

THE LADY. You must have declared your love with your fingers, like a deaf mute.

HÉRAULT. And why not? Some people even insist that deaf mutes are easier to understand than anyone else. I was arranging a love affair with a card queen. My fingers were bewitched princes in the shape of spiders, and you, Madame, were the Good Fairy. But it didn't work out; the queen was constantly pregnant and gave birth to one knave after the other. I wouldn't allow my daughter to play games like this, with gentlemen and ladies most indecently tumbling over each other, and little knaves turning up shortly after.

(CAMILLE DESMOULINS and PHILIPPEAU *enter*.)

HÉRAULT. Philippeau, how sad your eyes are! Did you tear a hole in your red cap? Did Saint Jacob give you a stern look? Or was it raining during the guillotine performance? Or did you have a bad seat and couldn't see anything?

CAMILLE. You are parodying Socrates. Do you know what the Divine One asked Alcibiades one day when he saw him downcast and brooding? "Have you lost your shield on the field of battle? Did someone beat you in a race or in a fight? Did someone else sing better or play the zither better than you?" Oh, what classical minds we Republicans have! Compare it with the romanticism of our guillotine!

PHILIPPEAU. Twenty more victims died today. We were wrong; they sent the Hébertists to the scaffold only because they were not systematic enough; perhaps also because the Decemvirs thought themselves lost if there were men who even for one single week had been feared more than they.

HÉRAULT. They would like to make us into antediluvians. Saint-Just would not mind at all if we walked again on all fours; then the attorney from Arras could start all over inventing hats, school benches, and a God for us, in accordance with the system of mechanics established by the watchmaker from Ghent.

PHILIPPEAU. If that would do it, they would be quite willing to add some zeros to the record Marat set. How long are we supposed to remain dirty and bloody like new-born babes, have coffins for cradles and play with heads? We must go forward! The Clemency Committee must become reality and the expelled deputies must be readmitted!

HÉRAULT. The Revolution has reached the period of consolidation.—The Revolution must end, the Republic must begin.—

In the fundamental principles of the state, right must take the place of duty, contentment the place of virtue, and defense the place of punishment. Everyone must count, and must be allowed to follow his natural inclination. Whether he is reasonable or unreasonable, educated or uneducated, good or evil—that is not the government's concern. All of us are fools and no one has the right to force his particular brand of foolishness on anyone else. Everyone should be allowed to enjoy himself according to his taste, as long as it is not at the expense of others, nor by interfering with their preferred form of enjoyment.

CAMILLE. The form of government must be a transparent gown which closely hugs the body of the People. The pulsing of the veins, the flexing of the muscles, each twitching of the sinews must show through it. The body may be beautiful or ugly, it has the right to be as it happens to be. We have no right to tailor it a little dress to suit our fancy. We shall slap the hands of those people who would like to drape a nun's veil over the naked shoulders of that most enticing of sinners, France. We want nude gods, we want Bacchantes, Olympic games, and love, sung by melodious lips, that makes our limbs unbend—oh, wicked love! We shall not stop the Romans from sitting in a corner and cooking turnips, but let them not insist on treating us to gladiatorial games! Let the divine Epicurus and Venus with the glorious behind stand guard at the doors of the Republic instead of St. Marat and St. Chalier. Danton, you are the one to mount the attack in the Convention!

DANTON. I am, you are, he is. If I am still alive, said the old woman. After one hour, sixty minutes have passed, is that not true, my boy?

CAMILLE. What does that mean? It is self-evident!

DANTON. Oh, everything is self-evident. And who, if I may ask, is to get all these beautiful things started?

PHILIPPEAU. We—and all honest men.

DANTON. That "and" is a very long word! It keeps us rather far apart! The way is long, and Honesty may lose its breath before we get together! However . . . one can lend money to honest men, one can become godfather to their children and give them one's daughters in marriage—but that is all!

CAMILLE. If that is your opinion why did you start the fight?

DANTON. I detest those people. I have never been able to look at such blown-up paragons of virtue without giving them a kick. That is the way I am. (*He rises.*)

JULIE. You are going?

DANTON (*to* JULIE). I must go. Their talk of politics rubs me the wrong way. (*As he leaves.*) Standing between pillar and post, I shall make you a prophecy: the statue of liberty has not yet been poured, but the furnace is glowing and we all have a chance to burn our fingers. (*He leaves.*)

CAMILLE. Let him go! Do you think he will be able to keep out of it once we start to act?

HÉRAULT. That's true, but he will do it only as a pastime, like playing chess.

SCENE 2. *A street. Simon and his Wife.*

SIMON (*beating his wife*). You procurer! You shriveled quicksilver pill! You worm-eaten apple of sin!

WIFE. Help! Help!

PEOPLE (*running in*). Get them apart! Pull them apart!

SIMON. No! Leave me alone, Romans! I want to break your bones, you vestal virgin!

WIFE. I—a vestal virgin? That I would like to see!

SIMON. From your putrid shoulders I tear your robe, and naked in the sun your corpse shall lie. You whore! Every wrinkle of your body is a seat of lechery! (*The* CITIZENS *separate them.*)

FIRST CITIZEN. What's wrong?

SIMON. Where is the virgin? Tell me! No, I can't call her that! The girl! No, not that, either! The woman, the wife! No, no, not even that! There is only one word! Oh, it strangles me! I don't have enough breath to speak it.

SECOND CITIZEN. A good thing that, too; it would reek of brandy.

SIMON. Old Virginius! Veil your bald head! The Raven of Shame is sitting on it, trying to peck at your eyes. Hand me a knife, Romans! (*He collapses.*)

WIFE. Oh, he's really not a bad man, only he can't hold his drink. The brandy quickly trips him up by giving him another leg.

SECOND CITIZEN. He walks on three legs, then.

WIFE. No, he falls, on his face.

SECOND CITIZEN. That's right. First he walks on all three legs, then he shifts his weight onto the third until that falls too.

SIMON. You are the vampire's tongue that licks the warm blood of my heart.

WIFE. Just leave him alone. This is the moment where he always gets sentimental. He'll get over it.

FIRST CITIZEN. What is the matter?

WIFE. You see, I was sitting on a stone in the sun, warming myself, you see—because we don't have any firewood, you see—

SECOND CITIZEN. Why don't you use your husband's nose?

WIFE. —and my daughter had gone down, just around the corner—she is a good girl and takes care of her parents.

SIMON. Ha, she confesses!

WIFE. Judas! Would you have a single pair of pants to put on if the young gentlemen didn't take off theirs when they're with her? You brandy barrel, wouldn't you die of thirst if the fountain stopped flowing, eh? We work with all our limbs, why not with that one? Her mother worked with it when she brought her into the world, and it hurt. So why shouldn't she work with it for her mother? And does it hurt? You blockhead!

SIMON. Ha, Lucretia! A knife, give me a knife, Romans! Ha, Appius Claudius!

FIRST CITIZEN. A knife—yes. But not to use on that poor whore. What has she done? Nothing! It's her hunger that whores and goes begging. A knife—yes, but to use on those who buy the flesh of our wives and daughters! Your stomach rumbles and theirs is stuffed. Your jackets are torn, but they have warm coats. Your hands are callused, theirs are soft as velvet. Which means you work and they do not; which means that you have earned what you possess and they have stolen it; which means that you must beg and prostitute yourselves if you want to regain a few pennies of the property that they have stolen from you; which means that they are scoundrels and that we must kill them!

THIRD CITIZEN. There is no blood in their veins but the blood they have sucked from ours. They told us, "Kill the Aristocrats, they are wolves!" And we strung them up on the lanterns. They told us, "The Veto is eating your bread," and we killed the Veto. They told us, "The Girondists are starving you," and we guillotined the Girondists! But they stole the clothes from the dead and we are still running around on naked feet and freezing. We shall peel the skin off their legs and make pants from it! We shall melt their fat and put it into our soup! Go to it! Kill everyone who does not have a hole in his coat!

FIRST CITIZEN. Kill everyone who knows how to read and write!

SECOND CITIZEN. Kill everyone who walks with his toes turned out!

ALL (*shouting*). Kill them! Kill them!

(A YOUNG MAN *is dragged in by several people.*)

SEVERAL VOICES. He has a handkerchief! He is an Aristocrat! On the lantern with him! On the lantern!

SECOND CITIZEN. What? He doesn't blow his nose with his fingers? String him up! (*A lantern is being let down.*)

YOUNG MAN. Oh, but gentlemen!

SECOND CITIZEN. There are no gentlemen here! Up with him!

SOME VOICES (*sing*).
> If you're buried in the ground
> Worms will eat you without sound.
> Hanging in the air is better
> Than to rot beneath a mound.

YOUNG MAN. Mercy!

THIRD CITIZEN. It's just a little game with a piece of hemp around your neck! It only lasts a moment. We are much more charitable than you people. Our whole life, we are murdered by work, we hang on the rope for sixty years and kick our legs, but we'll cut ourselves loose! On the lantern with him!

YOUNG MAN. Go ahead then! It won't make the light any brighter for you.

PEOPLE AROUND HIM. Bravo! Bravo!

SOME VOICES. Let him go! (*He escapes.* ROBESPIERRE *appears with a retinue of women and* SANS-CULOTTES.)

ROBESPIERRE. What is going on, Citizens?

THIRD CITIZEN. What do you think? Those few drops of blood that dripped in August and September weren't enough to give the people red cheeks. The guillotine works too slowly. We need a downpour!

FIRST CITIZEN. Our women and children are crying for bread and we are going to feed them Aristocrats' meat. Let's go! Kill everyone who doesn't have a hole in his coat!

ALL. Kill them! Kill them!

ROBESPIERRE. In the name of the law!

FIRST CITIZEN. What is the law?

ROBESPIERRE. The will of the people.

FIRST CITIZEN. We are the people! And our will is not to have any law. Which means that in the name of the law there is no law, which means, kill them!

SEVERAL VOICES. Listen to Aristides! Listen to the Incorruptible!

A WOMAN. Listen to the Messiah who was sent to choose and

to judge! He will kill those who are evil with his sharp sword. His eyes are the eyes of selection, his hands the hands of justice!

ROBESPIERRE. Poor, virtuous People! You are doing your duty, you sacrifice your enemies. You great People! You manifest yourself with thunder and lightning. But your blows, People, must not wound your own body, or else you will murder yourself in your wrath. Your enemies know that you can be vanquished only by your own strength. Your legislators are on guard and will guide your hands. Their eyes are unerring, your hands are inescapable. Follow me to the Jacobins! Your brothers will open their arms to receive you and we shall sit in bloody judgment over our enemies.

MANY VOICES. To the Jacobins! Long live Robespierre! (*All leave except* SIMON *and his* WIFE.)

SIMON. Woe! All alone! (*He attempts to get up.*)

WIFE. There! (*She helps him.*)

SIMON. Oh, mine own Baucis! You are gathering fiery coals on my head!

WIFE. There! Stand on your feet now!

SIMON. You are turning from me? Can you forgive me, Portia? Did I beat you? It was not my hand, not my arm that beat you—it was madness!

Then Hamlet did it not, Hamlet denies it.
His madness is poor Hamlet's enemy.
Where is our daughter? Where is my little Sanna?

WIFE. There, around the corner.

SIMON. To her! Come with me, virtuous spouse!

(*Both leave.*)

SCENE 3. *The Jacobin Club.*

A MAN FROM LYON. Our brothers in Lyon have sent us to pour into your breasts their bitter discontent. We are not sure if the tumbril on which Ronsin rode to the guillotine was the hearse of Liberty; but we are certain that since that day the feet of Chalier's murderers are once again firmly planted on the ground as if there was no grave big enough to hold them. Have you forgotten that Lyon is a blemish upon the ground of France that must be covered with the bones of traitors? Have you forgotten that this whore of kings can wash away her scabs only in the water of the Rhone? Have you forgotten that Pitt's navy will have to run aground on the corpses of aristocrats carried to the Mediterranean by this revolutionary river? Your clemency is murdering the revolution. The breath inhaled by an aristocrat is the death rattle of Liberty! Only cowards die for the Republic; a Jacobin will kill for her! Remember this: if we do not find in you the energy possessed by the men of the tenth of August, of September and of the thirty-first of May, only one choice will be left us, the same that was left to that great patriot Gaillard—the dagger of Cato! (*Applause and tumultuous shouts.*)

A JACOBIN. We shall empty the cup of Socrates with you!

LEGENDRE (*jumping upon the platform*). There is no need for us to turn our eyes to Lyon. People who wear garments of silk, ride in carriages, occupy the boxes in the theatre, and talk like the dictionary of the Academy seem to have carried their heads firmly anchored to their shoulders for some time now. They are even witty and say that Marat and Chalier should be given the benefit of a double martyrdom by guillotining them in effigy. (*Strong movement among the crowd.*)

SEVERAL VOICES. Those people are already dead—their tongues have guillotined them.

LEGENDRE. The blood of these saints may come upon them! I ask the members of the Committee of Public Safety who are present here, since when are your ears so deaf . . .

COLLOT D'HERBOIS (*interrupts him*). And I ask you, Legendre, whose voice is it that gives expression to such thoughts, so that they come to life and dare to speak? The time has come to pull off the masks! The cause accuses its effect, the shout its echo, the premise its conclusion. The Committee of Public Safety is better versed in logic, Legendre! Rest assured that the busts of the saints will not be touched; like the head of Medusa they will turn the traitors into stone.

ROBESPIERRE. I demand the floor!

THE JACOBINS. Listen to him! Listen to the Incorruptible!

ROBESPIERRE. We only waited, before speaking, to hear the cry of discontent which now sounds from all sides. Our eyes were open. We saw the enemy arming, making ready to rise up, but we did not sound the alarm. We let the people guard itself, and it was not asleep, it clanged its arms! We let the enemy come out of hiding and approach; now he stands in the open, without cover in the bright light of day, and every blow we strike will find its mark. He will be dead the moment you lay eyes on him. I have told you before that the internal enemies of the Republic are divided into two groups, like two armies. Under flags of different colors, on different roads, they march toward the same goal. One of these factions no longer exists. In their con-

ceit and madness they attempted to push the tried and tested
patriots aside as worn-out weaklings, and thus to rob the Republic of her strongest arms. They declared war on God and
on Property, as a diversion in favor of the kings. They parodied
the sublime drama of the Revolution in order to confute it by
their studied excesses. If Hébert had triumphed, the Republic
would have disintegrated into chaos, and despotism would have
reigned supreme. The sword of the law descended upon the
traitor. But what do the foreigners care, as long as they have
other criminals at their disposal ready to help them reach the
selfsame end? We have accomplished nothing if we do not ex-
terminate that other faction, too.

That faction is the other's opposite. These men exhort us to
be weak. Their war cry is, "Have mercy!" They want to tear the
weapons from the people's hands and sap the strength with which
they handle them, in order to deliver them naked and unnerved
to the kings. Republic's weapon is the Terror, its strength is
Virtue. Virtue, because without it Terror is corrupt; Terror, because without it Virtue is powerless. Terror flows from Virtue,
for it is nothing but swift, stern, and inflexible justice. They
say that the Terror is the weapon of a despotic government, that
our government, therefore, is despotism. Indeed! But only if
the sword a fighter wields for freedom is like the sabre that a
satellite swings fighting for the tyrant whom he serves. If a
despot governs his animal-like subjects through terror, he exercises only the right of a despot. If you shatter the enemies of
freedom through terror, you are no less right, you, the founders
of the Republic. The revolutionary government is the dictatorship of freedom against tyranny. From certain quarters, we hear
the shout, "Have pity on the Royalists!" Have pity on scoundrels? No! We reserve our pity for the innocent, for the
weak and the unfortunate, we pity mankind! Only the peaceful
citizen has a right to protection by society. In a republic, only
republicans are citizens; royalists and foreigners are enemies. It
is merciful to punish the oppressors of mankind; to forgive
them would be barbaric. All these signs of a false sensitivity
seem very much like sighs heaved toward Austria or England.
But they are not content with wresting the arms from the hands
of the People; they want to poison the most sacred sources of its
power by Vice. This is the most subtle, the most dangerous, and
most despicable attack on liberty. Vice is the mark of Cain
borne by the aristocracy. In a republic, vice is not only a moral
but a political offense. The depraved are freedom's political
enemies, and they are all the more dangerous, the greater the

services they seem to have rendered it. The most dangerous citizen is the one who uses up a dozen red caps before doing one single good deed.

You will understand what I mean when you think of the people who used to live in garrets and who are now riding in carriages, wenching with former marquises and baronesses. We may well ask: have not the people been robbed, do we not shake the gold-plated hands of the kings when we, the legislators of the People, parade the vices and the luxuries of erstwhile courtiers before the People, when we see these counts and barons of the Revolution marry rich women, give sumptuous banquets, gamble, surround themselves with servants, and wear luxurious clothes? We may well prick up our ears when we hear their new ideas, their precious discourse, and their pretty speeches. Not long ago, someone impertinently parodied Tacitus; I could reply with quotations from Sallust and with a travesty on Catiline, but I believe there is no need to add more details to the picture—the portraits are complete. Let us not make peace nor even make a truce with those who have thoughts only for robbing the people, with those who hope to get away with robbery, with those for whom the Republic is a game of fortune and the Revolution nothing but a trade. Terrified by the examples they have seen passing before their eyes in a roaring cataract, they are now carefully trying to cool the fires of justice. It almost seems as if they said to themselves: "We are not virtuous enough to be terrible. Have pity on our weakness, philosophic legislators! I do not dare admit to you that I'm depraved; I rather say: do not be cruel!"

Be confident, virtuous People! Have faith, Patriots! Tell your brothers in Lyon that the sword of Justice will not rust in the hands of those to whom you have confided it! We shall set the Republic a great example! (*General applause.*)

MANY VOICES. Long live the Republic! Long live Robespierre!

PRESIDENT. The meeting is adjourned.

SCENE 4. *A street. Lacroix. Legendre.*

LACROIX. What have you done, Legendre! Do you have any idea at whose head you are aiming with your busts?

LEGENDRE. The heads of a few fops and elegant women. That's all.

LACROIX. You are committing suicide! You are a shadow that murders its original and thus itself.

LEGENDRE. I don't understand.

LACROIX. I thought Collot had made himself quite plain.

LEGENDRE. What of it? He was drunk again.

LACROIX. Fools, children and—well?—drunks speak the truth. Whom do you think Robespierre meant when he mentioned Catiline?

LEGENDRE. Well?

LACROIX. It's so simple. They sent the atheists and ultra-revolutionaries to the scaffold. But that didn't help the people, they are still walking the streets barefoot, bent on making shoes from aristocrats' hides. So the temperature of the guillotine must not be allowed to drop; let the thermometer show only a few degrees less and the Committee of Public Safety will find that their beds have been moved to the Place de la Révolution.

LEGENDRE. What do my busts have to do with all that?

LACROIX. Don't you understand yet? You have given official recognition to the counterrevolution; you have forced the Decemvirs to show some energy, you have guided their hands. The people are like the Minotaur; they must have their corpses every week, or they will eat the Committee itself.

LEGENDRE. Where is Danton?

LACROIX. Who knows? He is trying to find the Venus of Medici piecemeal in all the grisettes of the Palais-Royal. He is putting a mosaic together, as he calls it. God only knows with which part of the body he is busy right now. What a shame that Nature has dismembered beauty, like Medea her brother, and deposited the fragments in different bodies. Let's go to the Palais-Royal.   (*Both leave.*)

SCENE 5. *A room. Danton, Marion.*

MARION. No, let me sit like this—at your feet. I want to tell you a story.

DANTON. I could think of a better use for your lips.

MARION. No, let me sit like this—just this once!—My mother was a wise woman. She used to tell me that chastity was a great virtue. When people came to the house and started to talk about all sorts of things, she always sent me out of the room. When I asked her later what the people had wanted, she used to reply that I ought to be ashamed of myself. When she gave me a book to read, I always had to skip some pages. But she let me read the Bible as much as I wanted; there everything was sacred.

Still, there were some things in it that I did not understand, but I didn't like to ask anybody about it; I just brooded about it. Then spring came, and things were going on all around me in which I had no part. I became enveloped in a peculiar atmosphere, and it almost suffocated me. I looked at my limbs and sometimes I seemed to be two, and then again I melted into one. At that time, a young man used to come to the house. He was handsome and often said crazy things. I didn't quite know what he wanted, but he made me laugh. My mother asked him to come more often, and that suited both of us. Finally, we didn't see why we couldn't just as well lie next to each other between two bed sheets as sit next to each other on two chairs. I liked that better than his conversation and couldn't understand why I should be deprived of the greater and be allowed only the smaller pleasure. We did it secretly. And thus it went. But I became like the sea, devouring everything, and churning deeper and deeper. Only one difference existed for me—all men blended into one body. That's how I was, and who can jump out of his skin? He finally noticed it. One morning he came and kissed me as if he wanted to choke me. His arms knotted around my neck and I was terribly afraid. Then he let go of me, laughed and said he had almost done something foolish; I should keep my dress and wear it; it would wear out eventually anyway and he didn't want to spoil my fun too soon; after all, he said, it was the only thing I had. Then he left. Again I didn't know what he meant. That evening I sat by the window. I am very sensitive; I am connected with the world around me only by my senses; I drowned in the waves of the sunset. Then a crowd came down the street, the children were running ahead, and women looked out of the windows. I looked down; they were carrying him past in a basket, the moon fell on his pale forehead and his hair was damp. He had drowned himself. And I started to cry. That was the only break in my life. Other people have Sundays and weekdays, they work for six days and pray on the seventh, they become emotional once a year on their birthday and think a little once a year on New Year's Day. I don't understand any of this; there are no intermissions or changes in my life. My life is only one thing: an uninterrupted yearning and holding, a furnace, a river. My mother died of a broken heart. People point their fingers at me. That's stupid. It's all the same, whether one enjoys bodies, pictures of Christ, flowers, or children's toys. It's all the same feeling. The one who enjoys most, prays the most.

DANTON. Why can't I absorb your beauty completely, wh
can I not encircle all of it?

MARION. Danton, your lips have eyes.

DANTON. I wish I were a part of the ether, so that I coul
bathe you, so that I could break myself on every wave of you:
beautiful body. (LACROIX, ADELAIDE *and* ROSALIE *enter.*)

LACROIX (*remains standing in the doorway*). This really make:
me laugh! It is too funny!

DANTON (*cross*). Well?

LACROIX. I was just thinking of the street.

DANTON. So?

LACROIX. There were two dogs on the street, a great Dane anc
a tiny, long-haired lap dog. They had a hard time.

DANTON. What about it?

LACROIX. The thought just occurred to me and I had to laugh.
It really was an edifying sight! The girls were watching from
the windows. One shouldn't even let them sit in the sunshine:
the mosquitoes might carry on right on their hands, and tha•
makes them think. Legendre and myself have been chasing
through almost all of the cells, and the little nuns of the
Revelation through the Flesh were hanging on to our coattails
they wanted us to bless them. Legendre is helping one of them
do penance, but he will have to fast a month for it. Here are
two of the Priestesses of the Body.

MARION. Good day, Demoiselle Adelaide! Good day, Demoiselle Rosalie!

ROSALIE. We haven't had the pleasure for a long time.

MARION. I have missed you.

ADELAIDE. My God, we are so busy day and night.

DANTON (*to* ROSALIE). Eh, little girl, your hips have really
become supple!

ROSALIE. Oh yes, I'm improving every day.

LACROIX. What is the difference between an Adonis of antiquity
and one of our time?

DANTON. And Adelaide has become interestingly modest. What
a stimulating change! Her face looks like a fig leaf that she is
holding in front of her whole body. A fig tree like this, standing
on such a busy thoroughfare, offers the most delightful shade.

ADELAIDE. I would be a cow path if Monsieur—

DANTON. I understand. Don't be angry, Mademoiselle!

LACROIX. Now listen to me! A modern Adonis is not torn apart
by a wild boar but by sows. He is wounded, not in the thigh,
but in his groin. And not roses grow from his blood, but
blossoms of quicksilver.

DANTON. Mademoiselle Rosalie is a restored torso: only the hips and feet date back to antiquity. She is a magnetic needle: what the pole "head" repels, the pole "foot" attracts. In the middle is the equator, and everyone who passes the line is baptized with quicksilver sublimate.

LACROIX. They are two Sisters of Charity. They serve in a hospital, that is, each in her own body.

ROSALIE. You ought to be ashamed to make us blush!

ADELAIDE. You really ought to have better manners!

(ADELAIDE *and* ROSALIE *leave.*)

DANTON. Good night, my pretty children!

LACROIX. Good night, you quicksilver mines!

DANTON. I feel sorry for them. They have been cheated out of their dinner.

LACROIX. Listen, Danton. I'm coming from the Jacobins.

DANTON. Is that all?

LACROIX. The people from Lyon read a proclamation. They felt all that was left for them to do was to wrap themselves in the toga. They all made faces as if each was about to say to his neighbor: Paetus, it does not hurt! Legendre shouted that there were men about who were prepared to smash the busts of Chalier and Marat. I believe he is trying to paint his face red again. He has completely lost touch with the Terror; even the children pull his coattails on the street.

DANTON. And Robespierre?

LACROIX. He shook his finger from the rostrum and said that Virtue has to rule through Terror. That phrase gave me a pain in the neck.

DANTON. It planes planks for the guillotine.

LACROIX. And Collot shouted like mad, he said the masks should be torn off.

DANTON. The faces would come off, too, if they were.

(PARIS *enters.*)

LACROIX. What's new, Fabricius?

PARIS. I went from the Jacobins to Robespierre and demanded an explanation. He tried to make a face like Brutus sacrificing his sons. He talked about duty in general and said that he would do anything for the defense of liberty, that he would be willing to sacrifice everything, himself, his brother, his friends.

DANTON. That was plain, I would say. One only has to reverse the order and he stands at the bottom, holding the ladder for his friends. We have to be grateful to Legendre; he has made them talk.

LACROIX. The Hébertists are not yet dead and, physically,

the people still suffer. That is a terrible lever. The scale with blood must not be allowed to rise or it will become the lantern on which the Committee of Public Safety will hang. He needs ballast on the other side of the scales, he needs a heavy head.

DANTON. I know, I know very well—the Revolution is like Saturn; she devours her own children. (*After some reflection.*) Yet, they will not dare.

LACROIX. You are a dead saint, Danton. But the Revolution has no use for relics; the bones of the kings were thrown out on the street and the statues out of the churches. Do you think for a moment that they will let you stand as a monument?

DANTON. But my name! The People!

LACROIX. Your name! You are a moderate, like myself, like Camille, Philippeau and Hérault. The mob knows no difference between weakness and moderation; they kill the stragglers. The tailors in the division of the Red Caps will feel the entire history of Rome in the point of their needles, if the Man of September should look like a moderate compared with them.

DANTON. That's very true. Besides, the masses are like children. They have to break everything to see what's inside.

LACROIX. What's more, Danton, we are wicked men, as Robespierre calls us. That is, we are able to enjoy ourselves. The masses are virtuous, which is to say that they enjoy nothing because work has dulled their organs of enjoyment; neither do they drink—because they have no money. Nor do they go to a brothel—because they reek of cheese and herring, and the girls find that disgusting.

DANTON. He hates anyone who enjoys life as a eunuch hates men.

LACROIX. They call us scoundrels, and (*Bending down until his mouth almost touches* DANTON's *ears.*)—between ourselves—there is a kernel of truth in that. Robespierre and the masses will remain virtuous, Saint-Just will write a novel and Barère will tailor a Carmagnole and drape the robe of blood around the shoulders of the Convention and—I can see it all!

DANTON. You are dreaming. They never had courage without me and they will not have any against me. The Revolution is not yet finished and they may need me again. They are likely to keep me in storage in their arsenal.

LACROIX. We must act.

DANTON. We shall see.

LACROIX. We shall see—when we are lost.

MARION (*to* DANTON). Your lips have grown cold. Your words have smothered your kisses.

DANTON (*to* MARION). To waste all this time! It was not worth it! (*To* LACROIX.) I'll go to Robespierre tomorrow. I shall make him so angry that he won't be able to keep silent. So —tomorrow! Good night, my friends, good night! I thank you!

LACROIX. Off with you, my good friends, off with you! Good night, Danton! The thighs of Mademoiselle will be your guillotine, her Mound of Venus your Tarpeian Rock!

(*He and* PARIS *leave.*)

Scene 6. *A room. Robespierre, Paris, and Danton.*

ROBESPIERRE. I tell you, anyone who tries to stop me when I draw my sword is my enemy—no matter what his intentions. Anyone who prevents me from defending myself kills me as much as if he had attacked me.

DANTON. Where self-defense ends, murder begins. I see no reason that forces us to continue killing.

ROBESPIERRE. The social revolution has not been completed. Leaving a revolution half-finished means digging your own grave. The aristocracy is not yet dead, the healthy forces of the people must take the place of this class that is decadent in every way. Vice must be punished, Virtue must rule by Terror.

DANTON. I don't quite understand this word, "punishment." You and your virtue, Robespierre! You have never taken money, you don't have any debts, you never sleep with a woman, you always wear a decent suit of clothes and you never get drunk. Robespierre, you are outrageously righteous! I would be ashamed of myself for chasing around between heaven and earth for thirty years with the same moral expression on my face just for the miserable pleasure of being able to look down on everybody else. Is there really nothing in you that tells you sometimes, very quietly and secretively: you are a liar, you are a liar!

ROBESPIERRE. I have a clear conscience.

DANTON. Conscience is a mirror, and only monkeys torment themselves in front of it. Everyone decks himself out as well as he can and tries to have his fun on his own way. It's hardly worthwhile to get into each other's hair about that! Let everyone defend himself if somebody else spoils his pleasure. Do you have any right to make the guillotine into a washtub for other people's dirty linen, and their heads into a ball of soap to wash their dirty clothes, merely because your coat is always immaculately clean? Yes, you have a right to defend yourself if they spit on your coat or tear holes in it. But if they leave you alone, what do you care? If they don't mind walking around the way they are, what right have you to lock them into their graves? Are you heaven's policeman? If you can't bear to look at it as easily as your Good Lord, why—hold a handkerchief before your eyes!

ROBESPIERRE. Are you denying Virtue?

DANTON. Virtue and Vice. All men love pleasure, some are crude and some refined; Jesus was the most refined of all. That is the only difference between men I have been able to discover. Everyone acts according to his nature, that is, he does what does him good. It is cruel, Incorruptible, is it not, to make you walk without your shoes like this?

ROBESPIERRE. Danton, at times Vice is high treason.

DANTON. You must not banish Vice, for heaven's sake, do not do that! It would be most ungrateful; you owe Vice too much —by contrast, that is. But even if one thinks the way you do, our blows must be of benefit to the Republic. We must not punish the innocent along with the guilty.

ROBESPIERRE. And who says that one man was punished who was innocent?

DANTON. Did you hear that, Fabricius? Not one man has died innocent! (*He turns to leave; while he is walking to the door, to* PARIS.) We must not waste one single moment. We must show ourselves.   (*Both leave.*)

ROBESPIERRE (*alone*). Go! Go! He wants to halt the steeds of the Revolution in front of a brothel like a coachman his well-trained horses. They will be strong enough to drag him to the scaffold. Make me walk without shoes! If one thinks the way I do!—But wait! Stop! Is that perhaps it?—They will say that his towering stature had cast too long a shadow on me, and that I therefore had made him step aside. And if they're right? Is it really necessary? Yes, it is! For the sake of the Republic! He must go. It's ridiculous how my thoughts keep an eye on each other.—He must go. If a man who is part of moving masses stops, he resists as much as if he tried to halt their march. He'll perish under their feet.

We will not allow the ship of the Revolution to run aground on the mud banks of these people's shallow calculations. We must chop off the hand which dares to stop it—even if he tries to hold on with his teeth!

Let us wipe out this crowd that has stolen the clothes of dead aristocrats and has inherited their leprosy! No virtue!

Virtue one of my shoes! If one thinks the way you do!—How that keeps coming back to me. Why can I not forget it? His bleeding finger keeps pointing there, at that one spot! No matter how many bandages I wrap around it, the blood still oozes out. (*After a pause.*) I don't know which part of myself is lying to the other. (*He steps to the window.*)

The night snores across the face of the earth and tosses in a wild dream. Thoughts and desires, barely suggested, confused and shapeless, which timidly hid from the light of day, now take on form, dress up and creep into the quiet house of dreams. They open doors, look out of windows and almost become flesh. The sleeping limbs stretch in their sleep and lips begin to murmur words.—And is not waking just a clearer dream? Are we not sleepwalkers? Do we not act awake just as we do in dreams, if more distinctly, more decisively and more effectively? Who can blame us? The mind performs more acts of thought in sixty minutes than our bodies' leaden organism is able to enact in years. The sin is in our thoughts. Whether the thought becomes an act, whether the body imitates the mind—is merely accident.

(SAINT-JUST *enters.*)

ROBESPIERRE. Heh, who is that in the dark? Light, bring light!

SAINT-JUST. Do you know my voice?

ROBESPIERRE. Oh, it is you, Saint-Just! (A MAID SERVANT *brings a candle.*)

SAINT-JUST. Were you alone?

ROBESPIERRE. Danton just left.

SAINT-JUST. I met him on the way, in the Palais-Royal. He had put on his revolutionary face and talked in epigrams. He called the Sans-Culottes by their first names and the grisettes ran after him looking at his calves. People stopped and whispered to each other what he had said. We are going to lose the advantage of the attack. Do you still hesitate? In that case, we shall act without you. We are determined.

ROBESPIERRE. What do you propose to do?

SAINT-JUST. We are going to call the Legislative Committee and the Committees of Security and Public Safety into solemn session.

ROBESPIERRE. Very ceremonious.

SAINT-JUST. We must bury such an important corpse with all the decencies, like priests and not like murderers. It must not be mutilated—all its limbs must go into the grave together.

ROBESPIERRE. Be a little more explicit!

SAINT-JUST. We must bury him in all his armor and kill his horses and his slaves above his grave. Lacroix—

ROBESPIERRE. An unmitigated scoundrel, former law clerk, now Lieutenant General of France. Go on!

SAINT-JUST. Hérault-Séchelles.

ROBESPIERRE. A handsome face.

SAINT-JUST. He was the illuminated letter at the head of the Constitution. Since we no longer have any need for decorations of this kind, he will be erased.—Philippeau. Camille.

ROBESPIERRE. He, too?

SAINT-JUST (*handing him a paper*). I thought so. Read this!

ROBESPIERRE. Aha! "Le Vieux Cordelier"! Is that all? He is a child. He laughs at you.

SAINT-JUST. Read this—here! (*He points to a passage in the paper.*)

ROBESPIERRE (*reads*). "Robespierre, the Bloody Messiah, on his Calvary between the two thieves, Couthon and Collot, on which he sacrifices rather than is sacrificed. Below him stand the Saintly Sisters of the Guillotine like Mary and Magdalen. Saint-Just, embracing him like John, announces the Master's apocalyptic revelations to the Convention. He carries his head like a monstrance."

SAINT-JUST. I'll make him carry his like St. Denis.

ROBESPIERRE (*continues reading*). "Is it possible that the clean frockcoat of the Messiah is France's shroud and that his thin fingers, twitching all over the rostrum, are the knives of the guillotine? And you, Barère, who said that money could be coined on the Place de la Révolution! But—I do not want to rummage in that old bag. He is like a widow who has had half a dozen husbands and has buried them all. Who can help that sort of thing? He simply has that special, hippocratic gift to see death in the face of people six months before they die. Who wants to sit with corpses and smell the stink?"—So you, too, Camille? Away with them! And quickly! Only the dead don't return. Is the indictment ready?

SAINT-JUST. It was easy. You gave enough hints at the Jacobins.

ROBESPIERRE. I wanted to frighten them.

SAINT-JUST. I only had to follow through. The forgers will supply the egg, the foreigners the apple. I give you my word, the meal will be deadly for them.

ROBESPIERRE. Quick then, tomorrow! No long drawn-out

death struggle! I have become sensitive these last few days. Make it quick!

(SAINT-JUST *leaves*.)

ROBESPIERRE (*alone*). Yes, a Bloody Messiah who sacrifices and is not sacrificed. He redeemed them with His blood, I save them with theirs. He made them sin, I take the sin upon myself. He had the voluptuous pleasure of pain—I suffer the torments of the hangman. Whose abnegation was greater, His or mine? And still, this thought contains some kind of foolishness. Why do we always look at Him? Truly, in each of us the Son of Man is crucified and each of us sweats blood struggling in his own Garden of Gethsemane, but none of us saves any other with his wounds. My dear Camille! They leave me, all of them—all is an empty desert—I am alone.

ACT II

SCENE 1. *A room. Danton, Lacroix, Philippeau, Paris, Camille Desmoulins.*

CAMILLE. Quick, Danton, we have no time to lose!

DANTON (*getting dressed*). But time loses us. How boring always to put on first the shirt and then on top of it the trousers, to creep to bed at night and out of it again next morning, and always to put one foot in front of the other. And there's no prospect that these things will ever change. How sad to think that millions before us did it just like we, that millions coming after us will keep on doing it, and that, to top it all, we consist of two parts doing both the same, so that all that is done is duplicated—how sad to contemplate all this.

CAMILLE. You talk like a child.

DANTON. The dying often become childish.

LACROIX. Your hesitations are your ruin, and you pull all your friends with you into the abyss. Give notice to the cowards that the time has come to rally round you; call those who sit on the Mountain and the others below! Denounce the tyranny of the Decemvirs, speak of daggers, refer to Brutus—and you will frighten the galleries and bring to your side even those who are threatened as associates of Hébert! Give your wrath free rein! At least don't let us die disarmed and humiliated like that miserable Hébert!

DANTON. You called me a "dead saint," remember? There was more truth in that than you suspected. I have been talking to all the Sections; they showed respect, but looked like undertakers. I am a relic, and one throws relics into garbage cans; you were quite right.

LACROIX. Why did you let it come to this?

DANTON. To this? Yes, I believe I was bored in the end. To wear the same coat and the same expression all the time! Pitiful! To be such a poor instrument that one string can only produce one sound—it is unbearable! I wanted to have an easy life, and I succeeded; the Revolution lets me rest, although a little differently than I thought. Besides, on whom can we rely? True, our whores would be a match for the Pious Sisters of the Guillotine; but that is all! You can figure it out on your fingers: the Jacobins have declared that Virtue is the order of the day, the Cordeliers call me Hébert's hangman, the City Council is doing penance and the Convention—now there might be the answer! But it would take another thirty-first of May, they would not willingly give in. Robespierre is the dogma of the Revolution, and you do not erase a dogma. Nor would it work. We did not make the Revolution, the Revolution made us! But even if it worked—I'd rather be guillotined than order others to the guillotine. I am fed up with it. Why should men fight each other? We should sit down side by side and have some peace. When we were created, someone made a mistake; there is something missing in us—I don't have a name for it, but we are not going to dig it out of each other's entrails. So why cut open our bellies? Go on—we're miserable alchemists!

CAMILLE. Put a little more solemnly, you might say: How long will humanity continue gulping its own limbs to satisfy its endless hunger? Or: Shall we shipwrecks continue forever sucking the blood out of each other's veins to still our unquenchable thirst? Or: how long shall we who do our algebra with flesh, continue writing our accounts with lacerated limbs while we search for the unknown X that is eternally refused us?

DANTON. You are a powerful echo.

CAMILLE. A pistol shot makes as much noise as a clap of thunder. So much the better for you; you should always have me around!

PHILIPPEAU. And we leave France to her hangmen?

DANTON. What of it? It does not seem to bother anyone. They are unfortunate. What more could they ask, if they want to feel sentimental, noble, virtuous or witty, and above all for constant entertainment? What does it matter whether they die under the guillotine or of a fever or old age? All things considered, it is preferable that they should take their bow and leave the stage while they are in good health; as they withdraw, they still can make some pretty gestures and even hear the audience applaud. That is quite gracious and very suitable for us. We always have been on the stage, although at last we're stabbed in earnest.

It is a good thing that our life-span is reduced a little. Our coats are much too big for us, we do not fill them. Life becomes an epigram and that will do. For who has enough breath and wit to write an epos of fifty or sixty cantos? It's time that we stopped drinking the tiny bit of elixir allowed us from washtubs, and that we started using liqueur glasses instead. At least we'll get a mouthful that way while we could hardly make a few drops roll together in the clumsy vessel.

And finally, I would have to shout; that is far too much trouble. Life is not worth the effort we make to preserve it.

PARIS. Flee then, Danton!

DANTON. Can you take your country with you on the soles of your shoes? Finally—and that is the most important thing: they will not dare. (*To* CAMILLE.) Come, my friend; I tell you, they won't dare. Adieu, adieu!   (DANTON *and* CAMILLE *leave*.)

PHILIPPEAU. There he goes.

LACROIX. And does not believe one word of all he said. Nothing but laziness! He'd rather put his head under the guillotine than make a speech.

PARIS. What can we do?

LACROIX. Go home and study how to make a decent exit, like Lucretia.

SCENE 2. *A promenade. People strolling.*

A CITIZEN. My good Jacqueline—I meant to say Corn . . . I mean Cor . . .

SIMON. Cornelia, Citizen, Cornelia.

CITIZEN. My good Cornelia has presented me with a little boy.

SIMON. Borne the Republic a son!

CITIZEN. The Republic—that sounds a bit too general; you might say . . .

SIMON. That's just it! The individual and the general must . . .

CITIZEN. Ah yes, that's what my wife says, too.

STREET-SINGER (*sings*).

          What is this, what is this
          That a man would hate to miss?

CITIZEN. Only, about the names—I just can't make up my mind.

SIMON. Call him Pike Marat!

STREET-SINGER (*continues to sing*).
      To grief and sorrow we are born,
      We must toil from early morn
      Till the sun goes down.

CITIZEN. I would like to give him three names; there is something about the number three; and also names that would be useful and proper. Now I have it: Plow, Robespierre. But what about the third one?

SIMON. Pike.

CITIZEN. Many thanks, neighbor. Pike—Plow—Robespierre— they are nice names, they have a pretty sound.

SIMON. I can tell you, your Cornelia's breast will swell like the udder of the Roman she-wolf—no, that won't do at all. Romulus was a tyrant, that won't do. (*They pass.*)

A BEGGAR (*sings*). "A handful of earth and a little moss . . ." Dear Gentlemen, beautiful Ladies!

FIRST GENTLEMEN. Scoundrel! Go and work! You don't look exactly starved!

SECOND GENTLEMAN. There! (*He gives him some money.*) His hands are like velvet! What impudence!

BEGGAR. Sir, where did you get your coat?

SECOND GENTLEMAN. I work! Work, that's what paid for it! You could have one just like it. I'll give you work. Come around and see me. I live—

BEGGAR. Sir, why did you work?

SECOND GENTLEMAN. So I could buy this coat, you fool!

BEGGAR. So you have slaved in order to have some pleasure. For to have a coat like that gives you pleasure. Rags would do the same thing.

SECOND GENTLEMAN. Of course, there's no other way.

BEGGAR. I'd have to be a fool! The one offsets the other. The sun is warm at the corner and that makes it easy. (*Sings.*)
      "A handful of earth and a little moss . . ."

ROSALIE (*to* ADELAIDE). Hurry up, there are soldiers coming! We haven't had anything warm in our stomachs since yesterday.

BEGGAR. ". . . as last greeting on my grave they toss." Gentlemen, kind ladies!

SOLDIER. Halt! Where are you going, girls? (*To* ROSALIE.) How old are you?

ROSALIE. As old as my little finger.

SOLDIER. You're pretty sharp.

ROSALIE. And you're very dull.

SOLDIER. Then you be my whetstone! (*Sings.*)

> My dear Christine, Christine, my dear,
> The damage hurts you much, I fear.
> Much I fear, much I fear.

ROSALIE (*sings in reply*).

> Oh no, dear soldier, that's not true.
> I'd like some more, some more like you,
> More like you, more like you.

(DANTON *and* CAMILLE *enter*).

DANTON. Isn't this merry? I smell something in the air—it feels as if the sun was breeding obscenities. Don't you feel like jumping right into the middle, pulling down your trousers and copulating from behind like dogs in the street? (*They pass.*)

YOUNG GENTLEMAN. Ah, Madame, the sound of bells, the evening sun seen through the trees, the distant glimmer of a star . . .

MADAME. The perfume of flowers! Yes, these natural, pleasures, the pure enjoyment of nature! (*To her daughter.*) You see, Eugenie, only virtue has eyes for this.

EUGENIE (*kisses her mother's hand*). Oh, Mamma, I can see only you!

MADAME. You are a good child!

YOUNG GENTLEMAN (*whispers into* EUGENIE'S *ear*). Do you see the pretty young lady with the old gentleman over there?

EUGENIE. I know her.

YOUNG GENTLEMAN. I'm told her hairdresser set her hair—à l'enfant.

EUGENIE (*laughing*). Wicked tongues!

YOUNG GENTLEMAN. The old gentleman walks next to her; he sees the little bud swell, takes it for a walk in the sunshine, and thinks that he was the thundershower that started it.

EUGENIE. Oh, how naughty! I feel like blushing!

YOUNG GENTLEMAN. That would make me blanch.

(*They leave.*)

DANTON (*to* CAMILLE). Don't ask me to be serious! I simply cannot understand why people don't stop in the street and laugh in each other's faces. It seems to me they ought to be laughing from the windows and even from their graves, and the sky ought to split and the earth roll with laughter. (*They leave.*)

FIRST GENTLEMAN. I assure you, it is an extraordinary discovery! It puts all technical knowledge into a completely different light. Mankind is rushing toward its supreme destiny with giant strides.

SECOND GENTLEMAN. Did you see the new play? A Tower of Babylon! A maze of vaults, little stairs, corridors, and everything so airy and bold as if thrown high into the air. One gets dizzy with every step. A bizarre face. (*He stops, embarrassed.*)

FIRST GENTLEMAN. What's the trouble?

SECOND GENTLEMAN. Oh nothing! Please, give me your hand, sir! This puddle—there. Thank you so much. I almost didn't make it. That might have become dangerous!

FIRST GENTLEMAN. You weren't afraid, were you?

SECOND GENTLEMAN. Well, the earth has such a thin crust. I'm always afraid I might drop right through when there are holes like that. One has to step carefully—it's easy to break through! But you must go to the theatre, I really recommend it.

SCENE 3. *A room. Danton, Camille, Lucile.*

CAMILLE. I tell you, if you don't serve it to them in wooden copies spread all over the theatres, concert halls, and art exhibitions, they have neither eyes nor ears for it. If someone carves a marionette that shows the thread by which it is made to move, and that creaks in the joints at every step in five-footed iambics —oh, what character, how impressive! When somebody takes a trite little emotion, an aphorism or some idea, dresses it up in coat and pants, makes hands and feet for it, paints its face and lets it squirm its way through three whole acts, until finally it either gets married or shoots itself—that is perfection! When someone fiddles an opera that reflects the floating and sinking of the human soul as accurately as a water-filled clay pipe the song of the nightingale—ah, what art!

Take the people out of the theatre and into the street—that is miserable reality. They cannot see their creator for all his pitiful imitators. They see nothing and hear nothing of the creation which glows and roars and shines around and within them and is born anew every moment. They go to the theatre, read poetry and novels, grimace like the caricatures about which they read—and to God's creatures they say: how common! The Greeks knew whereof they spoke when they told the story about Pygmalion's statue which came to life but did not procreate.

DANTON. And all the artists have the same attitude toward Nature as David when he cold-bloodedly drew pictures of the September victims just as their bodies were being thrown from the prison into the street; he said: I am catching the last spasm of life in these scoundrels!

(DANTON *is called out of the room.*)

CAMILLE. What do you say, Lucile?

LUCILE. Nothing. I like to see you talk.

CAMILLE. Do you hear me, too?

LUCILE. Why, of course!

CAMILLE. Am I right? Do you know what I said?

LUCILE. No, I really don't.

(DANTON *comes back.*)

CAMILLE. What is the matter?

DANTON. The Committee of Public Safety has decided on my arrest. I have been warned and have been offered a hide-out. They want my head—so be it. I'm tired of all the trouble. Let them take it! What does it matter? I'll know how to die courageously. It's easier than living.

CAMILLE. Danton, there is still time!

DANTON. Impossible. But I didn't think . . .

CAMILLE. You are so lazy!

DANTON. I'm not lazy, I'm tired. The soles of my feet are burning.

CAMILLE. Where are you going?

DANTON. Oh, if I knew that!

CAMILLE. Seriously, where to?

DANTON. For a walk, my boy, for a walk.   (*He leaves.*)

LUCILE. Oh, Camille!

CAMILLE. Be calm, dear child!

LUCILE. When I think that this head . . . Oh, Camille! It isn't true, is it? Am I mad?

CAMILLE. Be calm! Danton and I are not one.

LUCILE. The world is huge, there are so many things in it. Why do they want just this one thing? Why do they want to take it from me? That would be terrible. What do they want to do with it?

CAMILLE. I repeat what I told you, don't worry! I talked to Robespierre only yesterday, and he was friendly. It's true, there is some tension between us, there are differences of opinion, but that is all.

LUCILE. You must go and talk to him!

CAMILLE. We sat on the same bench in school. He was always gloomy, always alone. I was the only one who sought him out and sometimes made him laugh. He has always been loyal to me. I'll go and talk to him.

LUCILE. So soon, my friend? Yes, go! Come, just this! (*She kisses him.*) And this! And now go quickly! (CAMILLE *leaves.*)

These are hard times. That is the way it goes. Who can resist it? We must bear it. (*She sings.*)

> Oh, parting, oh parting, oh parting!
> Who ever has thought of it first?

How did this song get into my head just now? It is not good that it should find its way all by itself like that—when we left, I felt as if he would never be able to turn back and would leave me farther and farther behind, farther and farther. How empty this room is! The windows are open as if a body had been lying here. I can't stand it any longer inside.   (*She leaves.*)

SCENE 4. *An open field. Danton.*

DANTON. I don't want to walk any farther. I don't want to break this silence with the chitchat of my marching feet, the gasping of my lungs. (*He sits down. After a pause.*) I have been told of an illness which robs you of your memory. Death is supposed to be somewhat like that. But sometimes I have hopes that death is still more powerful, that it takes everything. If this were true! Then, like a Christian, I would run to save an enemy—my memory. That place may well be safe, yes, for my memory; but not for me. For me, the grave is safer; at least it lets me forget, it kills my memory. But there, my memory would stay alive and kill me! My memory or I? The answer is so simple! (*He gets up and turns back.*) I flirt with Death. It is quite pleasant to ogle Death like this, through my lorgnette and from a comfortable distance. But when I think about it, this whole business makes me laugh. I have a feeling of stability that tells me tomorrow will be like today, and so the day after tomorrow, and thus always as it is now. It is a false alarm; they want to frighten me. But they won't dare! (*He leaves.*)

SCENE 5. *A room. It is night. Danton.*

DANTON (*at a window*). Will it never stop? Will the light never fade, the sound never rot? Will there never be darkness and peace, so that we need no longer see and hear each other's beastly sins? September!

JULIE (*calls from the next room*). Danton! Danton!

DANTON. What?

JULIE (*enters*). What were you shouting?

DANTON. Did I shout?

JULIE. You talked of beastly sins, and then you groaned, "September!"

DANTON. Did I? No, no, I did not talk. I barely thought these things; they were but very quiet, secret thoughts.

JULIE. You are trembling, Danton!

DANTON. Isn't it enough to make you tremble when the walls start to speak? When my body is so shattered that my thoughts flicker and roam and talk with the lips of the stones? That's strange.

JULIE. Georges, dearest Georges!

DANTON. It's very strange, Julie. I'd rather not think at all any more if my thoughts immediately turn into words. For some thoughts, Julie, there should be no ears. They should not cry like babes as soon as they are born. It is not fitting.

JULIE. May God preserve your reason, Georges! Georges, do you recognize me?

DANTON. Why not? Of course I do! You are a human being, you're a woman and, finally, you are my wife, and then there are five continents, Europe, Asia, Africa, America, and Australia, and two times two is four. You see, I am in full possession of my senses. Didn't something shout, "September"? Didn't you say something like that?

JULIE. Yes, Danton. I could hear it through all the rooms of the house.

DANTON. When I stepped to the window . . . (*He looks out.*) The city is quiet, all the lights are out . . .

JULIE. A child is crying not far away.

DANTON. When I stepped to the window . . . it shouted and it screamed through all the streets, "September!"

JULIE. You had a dream, Danton. Now calm yourself!

DANTON. A dream? Yes, I was dreaming. But it was something different, I'll tell you all about it in a minute . . . oh, my poor head . . . it is so weak . . . in just a minute. There—now I remember: the earth groaned under me with its mighty thrust and I gripped it like a wild steed, burying enormous hands in its mane and pressing gigantic feet into its ribs, my head turned to one side, my hair flying above the abyss. Thus I was dragged along. In my fright I cried out—and awoke. Then I stepped to the window—and there I heard the shout, Julie.

Why just this word? Why this and not another? What does it matter to me? Why does it reach for me with its blood-stained hands? I did not strike it. Julie, help me, my senses are dull! Wasn't it in September, Julie?

JULIE. The kings were within forty hours of Paris . . .

DANTON. The fortifications had been taken, the aristocrats were in the city . . .

JULIE. The Republic was lost.

DANTON. Yes, it was lost. We would have been fools to leave the enemy at large at our rear. Two enemies together on one plank, we or they—the stronger of the two pushed off the weaker one. Was that not fair?

JULIE. Of course.

DANTON. We beat them and that was not murder, it was civil war.

JULIE. You saved the country.

DANTON. Yes, I did. It was self-defense, we had no choice. The Man on the Cross took the easy way out; trouble is bound to come but woe betide the man who causes it! We must. This was a "must." Who can condemn the hand on which the curse of "must" has fallen? Who spoke the "must"? Who was it? Was it that part of ourselves which lies, whores, steals, and murders?

We're puppets, and unknown powers manipulate our wires. Ourselves we're nothing, nothing! We are the swords wielded by ghosts who fight each other, their hands remain unseen as in a fairy tale. Now I am calm.

JULIE. Quite calm, my dearest?

DANTON. Yes, Julie; come to bed.

SCENE 6. *Street before Danton's house. Simon. Citizen Soldiers.*

SIMON. How far is the night?

FIRST CITIZEN. What about the night?

SIMON. How far is the night?

FIRST CITIZEN. As far as from sundown to sunup.

SIMON. Scoundrel, what time is it?

FIRST CITIZEN. Look at your dial. It's the hour when the pendulum swings under the bed covers.

SIMON. We must go up! Forward, Citizens! We answer for it with our heads. Dead or alive? He has powerful limbs. I'll go ahead, Citizens. A path for liberty! Take care of my wife! I'll leave her a cluster of oak leaves.

FIRST CITIZEN. With acorns on them? It seems enough acorns fall into her lap every day as it is!

SIMON. Forward, Citizens! You'll deserve well of the country!

SECOND CITIZEN. I wish the country deserved well of us. For all the holes we rip into other peoples' bodies not one in our pants has yet been mended.

FIRST CITIZEN. Do you want the fly of your pants sewn up? Ha, ha, ha!

THE OTHERS. Ha, ha, ha!

SIMON. Forward, forward! (*They push into* DANTON's *house*.)

SCENE 7. *The National Convention. A group of Deputies.*

LEGENDRE. Will the butchering of deputies never end? Who is safe if Danton falls?

A DEPUTY. What can we do?

ANOTHER DEPUTY. He must get a chance to appear before the Convention. The result is certain. What could they do against his voice?

ANOTHER. Impossible. There is a decree which prevents it.

LEGENDRE. It must be repealed or an exception must be granted. I shall move that this be done, and I count on your support.

THE PRESIDENT. The meeting will come to order.

LEGENDRE (*mounts the rostrum*). Four members of the National Convention were arrested last night. Danton is one of them, this much I know. I don't know who the others are. Whoever they may be, I demand that they be heard before these bars. Citizens, I assure you that Danton is, in my opinion, as untainted as I am myself, and I do not believe that anyone can bring an accusation against me. I do not wish to attack any members of the Committees of Public Safety and Security, but there are sound reasons for my concern that private hatred, private passions may in the end rob Liberty of defenders who in the past have rendered her the greatest services. The man whose energy saved France in 1792 deserves to be heard. He must have a chance to defend himself if he is accused of high treason. (*Violent commotion.*)

SOME VOICES. We second Legendre's motion.

A DEPUTY. We sit here in the name of the people. We cannot be pushed off our seats without the consent of our constituents.

ANOTHER. Your words smell of cadavers. You must have taken them out of the mouths of the Girondists. Are you asking for privileges? The sword of Justice is suspended over the heads of all of us.

ANOTHER. We cannot permit our Committees to push legislators from the sanctuary of the law to the guillotine.

ANOTHER. Crime has no sanctuary, only crowned criminals find sanctuaries—on their thrones.

ANOTHER. Only scoundrels claim the right of sanctuary.

ANOTHER. Only murderers do not recognize it.

ROBESPIERRE. We have not seen this assembly in such confusion for some time. That it exists proves that most important matters are before us now. We shall decide today whether a few men shall be allowed to defeat the nation. How could you go so far in denying your own principles that you would grant some individuals today what yesterday you refused Chabot, Delaunay, and Fabre? Why such a distinction in favor of some few? The speeches which men make to praise themselves and all their friends mean nothing to me. We have had adequate experience to know what they are worth. We do not ask whether a man has one or another patriotic achievement to his credit; we look at his entire political career. Legendre does not seem to know the names of the arrested men. The whole Convention knows them. His friend Lacroix is one of them. Why does Legendre pretend not to know that? Because it would take audacity to come to Lacroix's defense. He named no one but Danton because he thinks that privileges attach to his name. But no, we want no privileges, we want no idols! (*Applause.*) In what respect is Danton superior to Lafayette, to Dumouriez, to Brissot, Fabre, Chabot, or Hébert? What could be said of them that would not be true of him? And did you spare them for all that? Why does he deserve to be treated with greater respect than his fellow citizens? Perhaps because some dupes, and also some who were not duped, gathered around him because they hoped that in his retinue they were bound to find fortune and power? The more he deceived the real patriots who put their trust in him, the more he now must feel the wrath of all the friends of liberty.

They are trying to make you wince at the misuse of a power which you have exercised yourselves. They shout about the despotism which the Committees exercise, as though the confidence which the people placed in you and which you transferred to the Committees, were not an ample guaranty of their patriotism. They will have you believe that everyone is trembling with fear. But I tell you that anyone who trembles now is guilty. For innocence has never trembled at the sight of public vigilance. (*General applause.*)

They have tried to frighten me, too. They gave me to understand that the fate now closing in on Danton might engulf me, too. They wrote me, Danton's friends besieged me, all in the hope that the memory of a long association and blind faith in fake virtues would be able to temper my zeal and my passion for freedom. But I tell you that nothing will stop me, not even the thought that Danton's present peril might become my own. All of us need a little courage and some measure of greatness. Only criminals and small minds fear the prospect of seeing men of their own kind fall at their side, because when they can no longer hide behind a crowd of accomplices they are exposed to the glaring light of truth. But if there are some souls like these in this assembly, there are heroic men here, too. The number of scoundrels is not great. We need to strike only at a few heads, and the nation will be saved. (*Applause.*) I demand that Legendre's motion be rejected. (*The* DEPUTIES *rise to signify general approval.*)

SAINT-JUST. There are, it seems, some sensitive ears in this assembly which cannot stand the sound of the word "blood." A few general observations will perhaps convince them that we are not any more cruel than Nature and Time. Nature follows her laws calmly and irresistibly. Man is destroyed if he comes into conflict with them. A slight change in the composition of the air, a sudden flaring-up of the tellurian fires, a change of equilibrium in masses of water, an epidemic, the eruption of a volcano or a flood may be the death of thousands. What is the result? An infinitesimal, hardly noticeable change of physical nature which would have passed with hardly a trace, if we did not see the corpses in its path. I therefore ask: should spiritual Nature be more considerate in accomplishing its revolutions than physical Nature? Should an idea not be permitted to destroy what obstructs it as much as a physical law? Should an event which changes the entire structure of morality, that is the structure of humanity, not be allowed to find its way through blood? The Spirit of the Universe makes use of our arms in the realm of the mind just as it uses floods and volcanoes in the physical sphere. What difference whether men perish in epidemics or in revolutions?

Mankind progresses slowly; its paces can be measured only in centuries, and behind each of these century-long paces rise the funeral mounds of generations. To make the simplest inventions and to establish the most modest principles has cost the lives of millions who fell by the wayside. Is it not then a simple truth that when history quickens the pace more people are likely to lose their breath? We are quickly led to the simple conclusion that, since all men were created under the same circumstances, all men are equal, excepting only those differences which Nature itself has made between them. Therefore, while anyone may have superior traits, none may have privileges, either as individuals or in a smaller or a larger group.

Each part of this proposition has demanded its victims when translated into reality. The fourteenth of July, the tenth of August, the thirty-first of May are punctuation marks. It took four years to bring it to success, to give it life while under normal circumstances a century would have been necessary, and generations would have been the punctuation marks. Is it then so remarkable that the great river of the Revolution leaves corpses at every cliff and at every bend?

There still are some conclusions we must add to our proposition. Should a few hundred corpses really prevent us from drawing them? Moses led his people through the Red Sea and into the desert until the old, corrupted generation had perished, and only then he founded his new state. Legislators! We have neither a Red Sea nor a desert, but we have war and the guillotine. The Revolution is like the daughters of Pelias: she tears mankind to pieces to make it young again. Mankind will emerge from the cauldron of blood as the earth emerged from the waves of the Flood, with strong and healthy limbs as they were at the time of Creation. (*Sustained applause. In their enthusiasm, some* DEPUTIES *rise from their seats.*) We call upon all secret enemies of tyranny, who here in Europe and all over the globe carry the dagger of Brutus hidden under their cloaks, to share with us this sacred moment. (*The* DEPUTIES *and the public intone the "Marseillaise."*)

ACT III

SCENE 1. *A large room in the Palais Luxembourg. Chaumette, Payne, Hérault-Séchelles and other prisoners.*

CHAUMETTE (*pulling* PAYNE'S *sleeve*). Listen, Payne, it may well be, after all. It passed through my mind a little while ago . . . I have a headache today. You might help me a little with your logic . . . I feel very strange.

PAYNE. Come then, Anaxagoras, you philosopher, I shall catechize you! *There is no God,* for either God created the world or He did not. If He did not create it, the world carries its cause of its creation within itself; in that case, there is no God, for God becomes God only by virtue of His being the source of all existence. Now, God cannot have created the world, for either creation is perpetual like God or it has had a beginning. In the latter case, God must have created the world at a definite point in time, which means that God, after having rested for an eternity, must suddenly have become active, and thus must have experienced a change within Himself, which would make it possible to apply to Him the notion of *Time.* Both of these assumptions contradict the essence of God. Therefore, God cannot have created the world. Since we know, on the other hand, that the world, or at least that our ego exists, and since our existence, according to our previous conclusions, must carry its origin within itself or in something that is not God, therefore then, there can be no God. *Quod erat demonstrandum.*

CHAUMETTE. Indeed, I can see light again! Thank you! Thank you very much!

MERCIER. Just a minute, Payne! What if creation is, in fact, perpetual?

PAYNE. In that case it is no longer creation, for it would be one with God, or an attribute of God, as Spinoza said. In that event, God would be in everything, in you, my good friend, in our philosopher Anaxagoras and in me. That wouldn't be bad at all, but you must admit that there wouldn't be much to the heavenly majesty if the dear Lord can, in each of us, get a toothache or the clap, be buried alive, or at least have the very unpleasant premonitions of it.

MERCIER. But there must be some first cause.

PAYNE. Who denies that? But who can affirm that this cause is what we think of as God, that is as perfection? Do you consider the world perfect?

MERCIER. No.

PAYNE. So how do you want to deduce from an imperfect effect a perfect cause? Voltaire didn't dare to get himself into trouble with God any more than with kings; that's why he came to that conclusion. Somebody who has nothing but a reasoning mind and does not even have the ability or courage to use it consistently is only a dilettante.

MERCIER. I on the other hand ask: can a perfect cause have a perfect effect, that is, can something perfect create something perfect? Is that not impossible because something that was created can never have its cause within itself—which, as you said, is part of being perfect?

CHAUMETTE. Be quiet! Stop it!

PAYNE. Calm yourself, philosopher! You are right. If God really has to create, but can create only something imperfect, He'd do better to leave it alone. Isn't it very human to be unable to think of God otherwise than as a creator? Just because we have to keep being active and always on the move, to tell ourselves over and over again: we exist! But do we have to ascribe this sorry urge to God as well? Must we, the moment our mind tries to immerse itself into the essence of an eternal being, harmonious and at rest within itself, must we, I say, immediately assume that it cannot do otherwise than reach across the table for the bread and knead little figures because of a prodigious need to love, as we discreetly whisper into each other's ears? Must we really do all that just so that we can call ourselves sons of God? I'll be content with a less imposing father. At least I won't have to complain behind his back that he brought me up beneath his station, in a pig sty or as a galley slave.

Do away with imperfection, for only then can you demonstrate God; Spinoza tried it. You can deny evil but you can't deny pain. Only reason can prove the existence of God, the emotions revolt against it. Remember this, Anaxagoras: why do I suffer? This is the bedrock on which atheism stands. The faintest twitch of pain, be it but in one single atom, fissures creation from one end to the other.

MERCIER. And morality?

PAYNE. First you deduce God from morality and then morality from God! What about your morality? I don't know if there is any absolute good or evil but that is no reason for me to change my conduct. I act according to my nature. What agrees with it is good for me, and I do it; what is against my nature is bad for me, and I don't do it, I fight against it if it gets in my way. One can very well be, as they call it, "virtuous" and fight against so-called vice, without despising one's opponents, which is a very sad feeling.

CHAUMETTE. Very true.

HÉRAULT. Yes, Anaxagoras, you philosopher, but one could also say that God, in order to be everything, must also be His own opposite, which means that He must be both perfect and imperfect, both good and evil, blessed and suffering. Of course, the result would be zero, one would counterbalance the other and we would arrive at Nothingness. Be happy, for you are gaining your ends. You may keep right on worshipping Madame Momoro as Nature's masterpiece. At least she's left the rosaries you need for your devotions in your groin.

CHAUMETTE. My most sincere thanks to you, gentlemen!
(*He leaves.*)

PAYNE. He is still unconvinced. In the end, he'll accept extreme unction, will point his feet toward Mecca and have himself circumcised, to make sure that no possible route will be barred.

(DANTON, LACROIX, CAMILLE, *and* PHILIPPEAU *are led in.*)

HÉRAULT (*quickly walks to* DANTON *and embraces him*). Good morning! Good night, I should say! I can't ask you, how did you sleep? The question is rather, how *will* you sleep?

DANTON. Well, one had better go to bed laughing.

MERCIER (*to* PAYNE). This bulldog with the wings of a dove! He is the evil genius of the revolution. He even defied his mother, but she was stronger than he.

PAYNE. His life and his death are equally great misfortunes.

LACROIX (*to* DANTON). I did not expect them to get you so soon.

DANTON. I knew about it. I had been warned.

LACROIX. And you said nothing?

DANTON. Why should I? A stroke is the best death. Would you like to be ill first? And—I did not think that they would dare. (*To* HÉRAULT.) It is better to lie in the earth than to get corns treading it. I'd rather have it as a pillow than as a footstool.

HÉRAULT. At least we won't have calluses on our hands when we pat the cheeks of that beautiful lady, Decay.

CAMILLE (*to* DANTON). Don't try so hard! You can stick your tongue out as far as it will go, it won't be long enough to lick the death sweat off your forehead. Oh, Lucile! This is too pitiful!

(*The prisoners crowd around the new arrivals.*)

DANTON (*to* PAYNE). What you did for the good of your country I have been trying to do for mine. I have been less fortunate; they now send me to the scaffold. All right, I shall not stumble.

MERCIER (*to* DANTON). You are drowning in the blood of the Twenty-two.

A PRISONER (*to* HÉRAULT). The power of the people and the power of reason are the same thing.

ANOTHER (*to* CAMILLE). Well, Attorney General of the Lanterns, the improvements you made in lighting the streets did not make France any brighter.

ANOTHER. Leave him alone! These are the lips which formed

the word "mercy." (*He embraces* CAMILLE; *several other prisoners follow his example.*)

PHILIPPEAU. We are priests who have prayed with the dying. Now we have caught the disease ourselves, we will die of the same epidemic.

SEVERAL VOICES. The blow that falls on you kills all of us.

CAMILLE. Gentlemen, I regret exceedingly that our labors were to no avail. I mount the scaffold because I shed tears over the fate of some unfortunates.

SCENE 2. *A room. Fouquier-Tinville and Herman.*

FOUQUIER. Is everything ready?

HERMAN. It will be very difficult; if Danton were not one of them, it would be easier.

FOUQUIER. He has to lead the dance.

HERMAN. He will scare the jury. He is the scarecrow of the Revolution.

FOUQUIER. The jury will have to be determined.

HERMAN. I have thought of a way, but it would be against the rules of legal procedure.

FOUQUIER. Go ahead!

HERMAN. We won't choose them by lot but pick the most robust.

FOUQUIER. That should be possible. It will be a nice bonfire. There are nineteen of them, and they are a very cleverly mixed company. Four counterfeiters, a few bankers and foreigners— that is a very tempting dish. That's what the people need. Yes, reliable men! Who, for example?

HERMAN. Leroi. He's deaf and won't hear a thing of what the accused will say. Danton can shout until he's hoarse for all he cares.

FOUQUIER. Excellent! Go on!

HERMAN. Vilatte and Lumière. The one sits in the tavern all day, the other one is always asleep. Both will open their mouths only to pronounce the word "guilty." Then there's Girard, who acts according to the principle that no one must escape who has been put before the bars of the Tribunal. Renaudin . . .

FOUQUIER. He, too? He assisted some clerics once.

HERMAN. Never mind! A few days ago he came to see me and demanded that all the condemned men be bled before the execution to weaken them a little. He found their usually defiant attitude most vexing.

FOUQUIER. Ah, excellent! I shall rely on you, then.

HERMAN. Leave it to me!

SCENE 3. *A hallway in the Palais Luxembourg. Lacroix, Danton, Mercier and other prisoners are walking back and forth.*

LACROIX (*to a prisoner*). What? So many unfortunates in such miserable condition?

THE PRISONER. Didn't the tumbrils ever tell you that Paris is a slaughterhouse?

MERCIER. Lacroix, it's true, is it not, that Equality swings its scythe above the heads of all of us, the lava of the Revolution flows, the guillotine makes Republicans! This kind of talk brings applause from the galleries and the Romans rub their hands in delight. But they do not hear that every one of these words is a victim's death rattle. Follow your phrases just for once to the point where they become reality. Take a look around! All you see you have said! This is a pantomimic translation of your words. These miserable beings, their hangmen and the guillotine are your speeches come to life. You constructed your systems, like Bajazet his pyramids, from human heads.

DANTON. You are right. These days, all our work is done in human flesh. That is the curse of our time. My body, too, will now be used. It's just a year ago that I created the Revolutionary Tribunal. I apologize to God and humanity for doing it; I meant to forestall another September massacre and hoped to save innocent lives. But this slow formal murder is more horrible and just as inescapable. I had hoped, gentlemen, that what I did would serve to let all of you leave this place.

MERCIER. Oh, we shall leave it all right!

DANTON. Now I am one of you. Heaven knows how it will end.

SCENE 4. *The Revolutionary Tribunal.*

HERMAN (*to* DANTON). Your name, Citizen!

DANTON. The Revolution calls my name. Soon I shall live in the Void and my name in the Pantheon of History.

HERMAN. Danton, the Convention accuses you of having conspired with Mirabeau and Dumouriez, with Orléans, with the Girondists and with foreigners, and with the faction of Louis XVII.

DANTON. My voice, which has so often sounded to defend

the cause of the people, will easily refute this calumny. Let those miserable creatures who accuse me appear here, confront me—and I shall cover them with shame. Let the Committees come before this court, I shall reply only in their presence. I shall need them as accusers and as witnesses. Let them show themselves!

Besides, what do I care about you and your verdict? I have already told you that I shall soon find sanctuary in the Void. Life is a burden to me; tear it from me! I yearn to shake it off!

HERMAN. Danton, audacity is the earmark of the criminal; the innocent are calm.

DANTON. No doubt, personal audacity is reprehensible. But that national audacity which I have often demonstrated, with which I so often fought for freedom, that audacity is the greatest of virtues. That is my kind of audacity and I use it now for the benefit of the Republic and against my miserable accusers. How can I be calm when I must stand here and listen to these despicable slanders? Do not expect a cold, detached defense from a revolutionary like me! Men of my cast are invaluable in revolutions, for the genius of liberty hovers over their heads. (*Signs of applause among the public.*)

I am accused of having conspired with Mirabeau, with Dumouriez and with Orléans, of having scraped at the feet of contemptible despots. I am asked to answer these charges before the bars of inescapable and inflexible justice. Wretched Saint-Just, you will be responsible to posterity for this calumny!

HERMAN. I demand that you give your replies calmly. Think of Marat; he stood before his judges with respect.

DANTON. They lay hands upon my whole life. My whole life, therefore, stands up and faces them. I shall bury them under the weight of each one of my actions. I am not proud of them. Fate guides our arms, but only powerful natures become its instruments. I declared war on the monarchy on the Field of Mars; I defeated the monarchy on the tenth of August and I killed it on the twenty-first of January. I flung all other kings a royal head as gauntlet. (*Repeated signs of applause.* DANTON *takes the Bill of Particulars.*) Just glancing at this slanderous document makes me tremble to the core of my being. Who are those who had to appeal to Danton that he show himself on that memorable day, that tenth of August? Who are those privileged men from whom he borrowed his energy? Let my accusers appear! I demand it in full possession of my mental powers. I shall unmask those shallow scoundrels and fling them back into the Nothingness from which they never should have crawled.

HERMAN (*ringing the bell*). Don't you hear the bell?

DANTON. The voice of a man who defends his honor and his whole life must be stronger than the sound of your bell. In September, I nourished the young cubs of the Revolution with the torn bodies of aristocrats. It was my voice which forged arms for the people from the gold of aristocrats and of the rich. My voice was the gale which buried the satellites of the despots under waves of bayonets. (*Loud applause.*)

HERMAN. Your voice is getting hoarse, Danton. You are too excited. You may complete your defense at the next session. You do need rest. The court is adjourned.

DANTON. Now you know Danton. Only a few more hours and he will fall asleep in the arms of glory.

SCENE 5. *A prison cell in the Palais Luxembourg. Dillon, Laflotte and a Jailer.*

DILLON. Brute! Don't stick your nose right in my face! It won't make me see any better. Ha, ha, ha.

LAFLOTTE. Keep your mouth shut! Your half-moon has a halo. Ha, ha, ha.

JAILER. Ha, ha, ha! Do you think, sir, that you can read by its light? (*He points to a piece of paper he holds in his hand.*)

DILLON. Give me that!

JAILER. Sir, my half-moon is at low tide.

LAFLOTTE. Your trousers look as if the tide was high.

JAILER. No, no, the moon is in the clouds. (*To DILLON.*) It is hiding before your sun, sir. You'll have to give me something to make it come out again if you want to have enough light to read by.

DILLON. There, you scoundrel! Off with you! (*He gives him some money. The JAILER leaves. DILLON reads.*) Danton has frightened the Tribunal. The jury vacillates and the public grumbles. The crowd around the Palace of Justice reached all the way to the bridges. A handful of money, an arm—hm, hm! (*He walks up and down, filling his glass from a bottle now and then.*) If I only had my feet on the street! I am not going to let them kill me just like that. Yes, if I were only on the street!

LAFLOTTE. And on the tumbril, that's the same.

DILLON. Do you think so? There are a few steps in between, a distance long enough to measure with the bodies of Decemvirs. The time has come for honest people to raise their heads.

LAFLOTTE (*aside*). All the better. They are easier to hit that way. Go on, old man. A few more glasses, and I shall be afloat.

DILLON. Scoundrels! Idiots! In the end they'll guillotine themselves! (*He paces rapidly up and down.*)

LAFLOTTE (*aside*). One could begin once more really to love life, like one's own child, if one has brought it forth oneself. That doesn't happen so often, to have a chance of committing incest with fate and to become one's own father. Father and child in one! A cozy Oedipus!

DILLON. One cannot feed people with corpses. Let Danton's and Camille's women throw assignats among the people! That would be better than heads!

LAFLOTTE (*aside*). I wouldn't tear my eyes out afterward. I might need them to cry for this good general.

DILLON. To lay hands on Danton! Who is still safe? Fear will unite them.

LAFLOTTE (*aside*). He's lost anyhow. What of it then, if I step on his corpse to climb out of my grave?

DILLON. Only to be on the streets! I would find enough people, old soldiers, Girondists, and former noblemen. We would break open the jails, we must come to an understanding with the prisoners.

LAFLOTTE (*aside*). Of course, it does smell a little of perfidy. What does it matter? I would like to try that. I have been in a rut. My conscience would bother me, and that would be a change. After all, it isn't too bad to smell one's own stink. I'm bored with the prospect of the guillotine, after waiting so long. I've tried it out in my mind at least twenty times and there is no spice left; it has become most ordinary.

DILLON. We'll have to send a letter to Danton's wife.

LAFLOTTE (*aside*). And then—I'm not afraid of death, I am afraid of pain. It might hurt; who can guarantee that it won't? They say it's just a moment, but pain measures time on a subtler scale, it counts in minute fractions of seconds. No! Pain is the one and only sin, and suffering the only vice. I shall stay virtuous!

DILLON. Listen, Laflotte, what happened to that rascal? I have money, and it must work. We'll have to forge the iron now, my plan is made.

LAFLOTTE. Immediately! I know the jailer, I shall talk to him. You can count on me, General, we shall get out of this hole— (*Aside, while he walks to the door.*)—and enter another one: I, the biggest hole there is, the wide world, and you the smallest one, the grave.

SCENE 6. *The Committee of Public Safety. Saint-Just, Barère, Collot d'Herbois, Billaud-Varennes.*

BARÈRE. What does Fouquier write?

SAINT-JUST. They have finished the second session. The prisoners demand that several members of the Convention and of the Committee of Public Safety appear before the court. They appeal to the people against the refusal to hear their witnesses. The excitement seems to be indescribable. Danton parodied Jupiter and shook his mane.

COLLOT. It will be that much easier for Samson to grab it.

BARÈRE. We must not show ourselves. The fishwives and ragpickers may not find us very imposing.

BILLAUD. The people have an instinct for being kicked, even though it be with mere glances. They love insolent faces like his, although their expressions are worse than a nobleman's coat-of-arms; for they reflect the subtle aristocracy of those who are contemptuous of all humanity. Everyone who dislikes being looked down upon should help bash in these faces.

BARÈRE. His skin is as horny as Siegfried's. The blood he shed in September has made him invulnerable. What does Robespierre say?

SAINT-JUST. He pretends having something to say. The jury will have to declare themselves adequately informed and close the debate.

BARÈRE. Impossible! We cannot do that.

SAINT-JUST. We have to get rid of them, at any price, and if we have to throttle them with our own hands. Be bold! Danton taught us the word, his lesson shall not have been in vain. The Revolution will not stumble over their corpses; but if Danton stays alive, he will tug at her dress, and there is something about him that makes you think he could rape Liberty.

(SAINT-JUST *is called out. A* JAILER *enters.*)

JAILER. There are prisoners dying at St. Pelagie. They want a doctor.

BILLAUD. That's quite unnecessary. That much less trouble for the executioner.

JAILER. There are pregnant women among them.

BILLAUD. So much the better. We won't need coffins for the babies then.

BARÈRE. Every time an aristocrat comes down with consumption we save the Tribunal a session. Medicine would be downright counterrevolutionary.

COLLOT (*takes a piece of paper and reads*). A petition! And signed by a woman!

BARÈRE. Probably one of those who would like to be forced to choose between a crouch under the guillotine and the couch of a Jacobin. Like Lucretia, they die after they have lost their honor, only they wait a little longer than the Roman lady; they die in child-birth, or of cancer or old age. It may not even be unpleasant to chase a Tarquin out of a virgin's virtuous republic!

COLLOT. This one is too old. Madame demands death, and she knows how to express herself quite well: prison, she says, weighs upon her like the lid of a coffin. And she's been in prison only four weeks! The answer is very simple. (*He reads the words as he writes them down.*) "Citizeness, it has not yet been long enough that you have longed for death."

(*The* JAILER *leaves.*)

BARÈRE. Well said. But I don't like to see the guillotine starting to laugh, Collot. People won't be afraid of it any more. One should not become so familiar!

(SAINT-JUST *comes back.*)

SAINT-JUST. I have just received word from an informer. There is a conspiracy in the prisons, and a young fellow called Laflotte has discovered it all. He shared a room with Dillon, and Dillon got drunk and babbled.

BARÈRE. He will cut his throat with the bottle. That has happened before.

SAINT-JUST. According to Laflotte, Danton's and Camille's women are to throw money among the people, Dillon is to break out, the prisoners are to be liberated and the Convention is to be blown up.

BARÈRE. That sounds like fairy tales.

SAINT-JUST. But we will sing them to sleep with these fairy tales! I have the information in my hands, and if you add to that the impudence of the accused, the grumbling of the people and the consternation of the jury—I shall make a report.

BARÈRE. Go ahead, Saint-Just, and spin your periods so that each comma is a blow struck with a sword, each period a severed head!

SAINT-JUST. The Convention must decree that the Tribunal

is to bring the trial to conclusion without delay, and that it is empowered to exclude from the debate any one of the accused who does not conduct himself with due respect to the court or who causes scenes which disrupt the proceedings.

BARÈRE. You have the instincts of a revolutionary! This sounds very moderate and yet it will do the trick. They can't remain silent; Danton, for one, must shout.

SAINT-JUST. I count on your support. There are some people in the Convention who are as sick as Danton and afraid of the same medicine. They have become bold again and will scream about irregular procedure . . .

BARÈRE (interrupting him). I shall tell them that the Roman consul who uncovered Catiline's conspiracy and sentenced the criminals to death on the spot was also accused of having violated the rules of procedure. And who were his accusers?

COLLOT (with great fervor). Go, Saint-Just! The lava of the Revolution flows. Liberty will suffocate in her embrace those weaklings who make bold to impregnate her mighty womb! As Jupiter appeared to Semele, the people, in their majesty, will appear to them with thunder and lightning and turn them into ashes. Go, Saint-Just! We shall assist you in hurling the thunderbolt upon the heads of the cowards!

(SAINT-JUST leaves.)

BARÈRE. Did you hear him say "medicine"? They will finish by making a specific against venereal disease out of the guillotine. They do not fight the Moderates, they battle against Vice.

BILLAUD. Our road has been the same so far.

BARÈRE. Robespierre would like to transform the Revolution into an auditorium for lectures on Morals, and to use the guillotine as his lectern.

BILLAUD. Or as his prayer stool.

COLLOT. On which he should, however, lie—not kneel.

BARÈRE. That will be easy. The world would have to be upside down if so-called scoundrels were to be hanged by so-called righteous people.

COLLOT (to BARÈRE). When will you come to Clichy again?

BARÈRE. When the doctor stops coming to see me.

COLLOT. It's true, isn't it, that above that place hangs a comet whose burning rays are shriveling your marrow?

BILLAUD. It won't be long until the charming Demaly will use her adorable hands to pull it out of its casing and make him wear it down his back like a pigtail.

BARÈRE. Psh! The Virtuous One must never know a thing about this.

BILLAUD. He is an impotent free-mason.

(BILLAUD *and* COLLOT *leave*.)

BARÈRE (*alone*). The monsters! "It has not yet been long enough that you have longed for death." Those words should have withered the tongue that formed them.

And I? When the Septembrists pushed into the prisons, one of the prisoners took his knife and, mingling with the murderers, plunged it into the breast of a priest. He was saved! Who can argue against it? Whether I join assassins or sit as a member of the Committee of Public Safety, whether I take the blade of a penknife or the blade of the guillotine—it is the same; the circumstances are a little more involved, but fundamentally the situation is the same. Now, if it was permissible to kill one man, was he allowed to kill two—three—or still more? Where does it end? And here we arrive at the famous question of the grains of barley: do two grains make a pile? Or three, or four, or how many? Come, conscience, come little chicken, cluck, cluck, cluck, here is some food for you! But—was I like that prisoner? I was suspect, and that amounts to the same thing. My death was certain.   (*He leaves*.)

SCENE 7. *The Conciergerie. Lacroix, Danton, Philippeau, Camille.*

LACROIX. Well shouted, Danton! If you had tried as hard to save your life a little earlier, things would be different now. When death so impudently snuggles up to you, so that you can smell his foul breath, and becomes more and more insistent— you see now, don't you?

CAMILLE. If at least death came like a man and raped you and wrestled his prize from your hot limbs in a hard-fought struggle! But like this, with all the formalities, like a wedding with an old woman where the contract is signed, the witnesses called, the Amen spoken, and then the bed covers lifted and it crawls in with its cold limbs . . .

DANTON. If only it were a battle where arms and teeth become enmeshed! I feel as if I had fallen into the gears of a mill, as if my limbs were being systematically wrenched off by cold, brute force. To be killed so mechanically!

CAMILLE. And then to lie there, all alone, cold and stiff, in the dank fumes of decay . . . perhaps death tortures life slowly out of your fibres . . . to be conscious, perhaps, that you're rotting away!

PHILIPPEAU. Be calm, my friends! We are like autumn flowers whose seed ripens only after the winter has passed. We differ from flowers that are transplanted only in that we start stinking a little in the attempt. Is that so bad?

DANTON. An edifying prospect! From one dung heap to another! That is the theory of the divine school classes again, is it not? From first grade into second, from second to third and so on? I am tired of school benches—like an ape I have calluses on my rear end from sitting on them.

PHILIPPEAU. Then what do you want?

DANTON. Rest.

PHILIPPEAU. You'll find it in God.

DANTON. I'll find it in Nothingness. Can you immerse yourself into anything more restful than Nothingness? So if God is supreme peace, is not Nothingness God? But I'm an atheist. And there is this damned maxim that something cannot become nothing! I am something, that is the trouble! Creation has spread itself so widely that there is not an empty spot. It's teeming everywhere. Nothingness has committed suicide, Creation is its wound, we are drops of its blood and the world is the grave in which it rots. This sounds crazy, and yet there is much truth in it.

CAMILLE. The world is like the Wandering Jew, Nothingness is like death—but death is impossible. Oh, not to be able to die, not to be able to die, as the song goes!

DANTON. All of us have been buried alive, put to rest in triple and quadruple coffins like kings, under the sky, in our homes, in our coats and shirts. For fifty years we claw at the coffin lid. Yes, if one could only believe in complete destruction, that would be a help! There is no hope in death. Death is only a more simple life, a more complicated and higher organized form of decay. That's the whole difference. But I happen to be used to this particular sort of decay and the devil knows how I'll adjust to another.

Oh, Julie! If I had to go by myself! If she left me alone! Even if I disintegrated utterly, if I dissolved entirely, I would be a handful of tormented dust and every atom of me could find rest only with her. I cannot die. No, I cannot die! We must scream! And they will have to press each drop of life out of my limbs.

LACROIX. We must stand by our demands. Our accusers and the Committee must appear before the Tribunal.

SCENE 8. *A room. Fouquier, Amar, Vouland.*

FOUQUIER. I don't know any more what to tell them. They now demand a commission.

AMAR. We have caught them, the scoundrels. This is what you want. (*He hands* FOUQUIER *a piece of paper.*)

VOULAND. That will satisfy them.

FOUQUIER. Yes, indeed, we needed this.

AMAR. Now hurry up, so both we and they get this business off our necks!

SCENE 9. *The Revolutionary Tribunal.*

DANTON. The Republic is in danger—and he has no instructions! We appeal to the people. My voice is still strong enough to speak the funeral oration for the Decemvirs. I repeat, we demand a commission; we shall make important revelations. I shall retreat into the citadel of reason, bring into play the guns of truth and squash my enemies. (*Signs of applause.* FOUQUIER, AMAR, *and* VOULAND *enter.*)

FOUQUIER. In the name of the Republic, silence! Respect for the law! The Convention has passed the following resolution: "Whereas there have been discovered signs of insurrection in the prisons, and whereas Danton's and Camille's women are throwing money among the people; and whereas further General Dillon is to escape from prison and to put himself at the head of the rebels with the aim to liberate the accused, and whereas, finally, the accused themselves have attempted to create disorders and to insult the Tribunal, be it resolved that the Tribunal is empowered to continue the inquiry without interruption and to exclude from participation in the proceedings any of the accused who shall fail to accord due respect to the law."

DANTON. I ask those present here, did we mock this Tribunal, the people or the National Convention?

MANY VOICES. No, no!

CAMILLE. The wretches! They want to kill my Lucile!

DANTON. Some day the truth will be known. I foresee a great misfortune for France. That is a dictatorship! It has already torn away the veils; it carries its head high, and it advances over our bodies. (*Pointing to* AMAR *and* VOULAND.)

Look at the cowardly murderers! There they are, the vultures of the Committee of Public Safety! I accuse Robespierre, Saint-Just and their hangmen of high treason. They want to drown the Republic in blood. The ruts made by their tumbrils are the high-roads on which the foreigners are to push straight into the heart of the fatherland.

How much longer are graves to be the footprints of liberty? You ask for bread, and they throw you heads. You are thirsty, and they make you lick the blood off the steps that lead to the guillotine. (*Violent commotion among the spectators, shouts of approval, many voices shout "Long live Danton, down with the Decemvirs!" The prisoners are led out of the room by force.*)

SCENE 10. *Square in front of the Palace of Justice. A crowd of people.*

SOME VOICES. Down with the Decemvirs! Long live Danton!

FIRST CITIZEN. Yes, that is the truth. Heads instead of bread, blood instead of wine!

SOME WOMEN. The guillotine is a very bad mill, and Samson is a miserable baker. We want bread! We want bread!

SECOND CITIZEN. It's Danton who has eaten your bread. His head will give bread to all of you. He was right.

FIRST CITIZEN. Danton was with us on the tenth of August, Danton was with us in September. Where were those who now accuse him?

SECOND CITIZEN. And Lafayette was with you in Versailles and yet he was a traitor.

FIRST CITIZEN. Who says that Danton is a traitor?

SECOND CITIZEN. Robespierre.

FIRST CITIZEN. And Robespierre is a traitor.

SECOND CITIZEN. Who says so?

FIRST CITIZEN. Danton.

SECOND CITIZEN. Danton wears beautiful clothes, Danton has a beautiful house, Danton has a beautiful wife, he bathes in Burgundy, eats game from silver plates and sleeps with your wives and daughters when he's drunk. Danton used to be as poor as you are. Where did all this come from? The Veto bought it for him, so he would save his crown for him. The Duke of Orléans gave it to him so he would betray all of you. What does Robespierre own? You know him, all of you!

ALL. Long live Robespierre! Down with Danton! Down with the traitor!

ACT IV

SCENE 1. *Julie, a Boy.*

JULIE. This is the end. He makes them tremble. They kill him out of fear. Go! I have seen him for the last time. Tell him that I cannot see him in this condition. (*She gives him a lock of hair.*) There, give him this and tell him that he will not go alone—he'll understand. And then come quickly back, for I want to read his glances in your eyes.

SCENE 2. *A Street. Dumas, a Citizen.*

CITIZEN. How can they sentence all these innocent men to death after such a trial?

DUMAS. It is indeed extraordinary. But those revolutionaries have a sense which other people lack, and that sense never betrays them.

CITIZEN. The instinct of the tiger. You have a wife.

DUMAS. Soon I will have had a wife.

CITIZEN. So it is true?

DUMAS. The Revolutionary Tribunal will pronounce the divorce and the guillotine will separate us from bed and board.

CITIZEN. You are a monster!

DUMAS. Idiot! Do you admire Brutus?

CITIZEN. Deeply.

DUMAS. Must one be a Roman consul and have a toga to cover one's head if one wishes to sacrifice what one holds dearest to the fatherland? I shall dry my eyes with the sleeves of my red coat. That's all the difference there is!

CITIZEN. It is horrible!

DUMAS. Go away, you don't understand me.   (*Both leave.*)

SCENE 3. *The Conciergerie. Lacroix and Hérault sitting on one, Danton and Camille sitting on another bed.*

LACROIX. Hair and nails are growing in such a way one really has to be ashamed of oneself.

HÉRAULT. Be a little careful. You are sneezing sand all over my face.

LACROIX. And don't you step on my toes, my friend. I have corns.

HÉRAULT. You also seem to be suffering from vermin.

LACROIX. Oh, if only I could get completely rid of the worms.

HÉRAULT. Well, sleep well! We'll see how we get along with each other. There isn't much room. Don't scratch me with your nails while you're asleep! There. Don't tug at this shroud so much; it's cold down there!

DANTON. Yes, Camille, tomorrow we'll be like worn-out shoes that are thrown into the lap of that beggarwoman, Earth.

CAMILLE. The cow-hide from which the angels cut themselves the slippers they use to patter around on earth, according to Plato. Looks like it, too. Oh, my Lucile!

DANTON. Calm, now, my boy.

CAMILLE. Can I be calm? Do you think, Danton? Can I? They must not touch her! The light of beauty which radiates from her sweet body is inextinguishable. Even the earth would not dare to fall on top of her; it would form a vault around her, the dampness of the grave would sparkle on her eyelashes like dew, crystals would shoot from her limbs like flowers, and clear springs would sing her lullaby.

DANTON. Sleep now, sleep!

CAMILLE. Listen, Danton. Between the two of us, it is quite miserable, to have to die. It is good for nothing. I want to steal from life's beautiful eyes their last glances; I want to keep my eyes open.

DANTON. You are going to keep them open anyhow, my boy. Samson doesn't close one's eyes. Sleep is more charitable. Sleep now, sleep!

CAMILLE. Lucile, your kisses are dancing on my lips, each kiss turns into a dream, and my eyes close around it to hold it tight.

DANTON. Will the clock not stop ticking? With every tick the walls are closing in on me, until they are as close together as the sides of a coffin. As a child I once read a story like that, and my hair stood on end. Yes, as a child! It really wasn't worth their trouble to feed me and to keep me warm until I was a man! It just made work for the gravedigger.

I feel as if I smelled already. My dear body, I will hold my nose and try to think that you are a woman, sweaty and smelly from dancing, and I will pay you compliments. We used to entertain each other differently in the past.

Tomorrow you'll be like a broken fiddle, and gone the melody you used to play. Tomorrow you will be an empty bottle, the wine drained, but I won't be drunk from it and go to bed sober. Lucky the people who can still get drunk! Tomorrow you will be a pair of seat-worn pants that is thrown into the wardrobe to be eaten by moths, no matter how much you stink.

Oh, there is nothing to be done about it! Yes, it is miserable having to die. Death apes birth: we are as helpless and as naked when we die as new-born babies. Of course, we get a shroud as a diaper. What good is that? We can whimper as much in the grave as we did in the cradle.

Camille!—He is asleep. (*He bends over him.*) A dream plays on his eyelids. I do not want to wipe the golden dew of sleep from his eyes. (*He rises and steps to the window.*) I will not go alone! Thank you, Julie! Yet, I would have liked to die differently, without any effort, as a star shoots across the sky, as a sound of music expires, kissing itself to death with its own lips, as a ray of light buries itself in clear water.

The stars are sprinkled through the night like shimmering tears. The eyes from which they dropped must be full of great sorrow.

CAMILLE. Oh! (*He sits up and feels for the ceiling.*)

DANTON. What is it, Camille?

CAMILLE. Oh, oh!

DANTON (*shakes him*). Do you want to scratch the ceiling down?

CAMILLE. Oh, it is you! You—hold me! Talk to me!

DANTON. Your whole body is trembling, drops of sweat are on your forehead.

CAMILLE. This is you, and I am here—there! This is my hand! Yes, now I remember. It was terrible, Danton!

DANTON. What was terrible?

CAMILLE. I was lying here, between dream and waking, when suddenly the ceiling disappeared and the moon sank down, quite near, very close, so close that I could touch it. The heavens dropped down with all their lights until my head hit against them, I touched the stars and I was suffocated like a drowning man under a sheet of ice. It was terrible, Danton!

DANTON. The lamp throws a round spot of light on the ceiling; that is what you saw.

CAMILLE. Perhaps. At any rate, it does not take much to make us lose the little bit of reason that is left. Madness had gripped me by my hair! (*He rises.*) I don't want to sleep any more, I don't want to go mad. (*He takes a book.*)

DANTON. What are you reading?

CAMILLE. *Night Thoughts.*

DANTON. Do you want to die ahead of time? I shall read *La Pucelle.* I don't want to steal out of life as from a prayer stool but rather as from the bed of one of the Sisters of Mercy. Life is a whore; she sleeps with everybody.

SCENE 4. *Square in front of the Conciergerie. A Jailer, two Draymen with tumbrils, women.*

JAILER. Who called you here?

FIRST DRAYMAN. My name isn't "Here." A silly name that is.

JAILER. Idiot, who gave you the order?

FIRST DRAYMAN. Nobody gave me an order. All I got was ten sous per head.

SECOND DRAYMAN. That scoundrel wants to steal my bread.

FIRST DRAYMAN. You call that bread? (*Pointing to the prisoners' windows.*) That's food for worms.

SECOND DRAYMAN. So are my children worms, and they want their share. Business is bad, and yet we are the best draymen around.

FIRST DRAYMAN. How is that?

SECOND DRAYMAN. Who is the best drayman?

FIRST DRAYMAN. The one who drives farthest the quickest.

SECOND DRAYMAN. Well, you ass, who drives farther than the one who drives out of this world, and who drives quicker than the one who can do it in a quarter of an hour? It's exactly a quarter of an hour from here to the Place de la Révolution.

JAILER. Hurry up, rascals! Closer to the door! Make room there, girls!

FIRST DRAYMAN. Stay where you are! One doesn't drive around a girl but straight into the middle.

SECOND DRAYMAN. That I'll believe. You'll drive in with your tumbril and horses, the tracks are so well-worn. But you'll have to stay in quarantine when you come out. (*They drive up.*)

SECOND DRAYMAN (*to the* WOMEN). What are you staring at?

A WOMAN. We're waiting for old customers.

SECOND DRAYMAN. Do you think my tumbril is a brothel?

This is a decent cart; the King himself and all the gentlemen of Paris have been driven to dinner in it.

(LUCILE *enters. She sits on a stone under the prisoners' windows.*)

LUCILE. Camille! Camille! (CAMILLE *appears at a window.*) Oh, Camille, you make me laugh with your long coat of stone and the iron mask in front of your face. Can't you bend down? Where are your arms?—I'll call you sweetly, my darling bird. (*She sings.*)

> Two little stars gleam in the sky,
> They are brighter than the moon.
> The one glows at my sweetheart's window,
> The other at her bedroom door.

Come, dear friend, come! Quietly up the stairs—they're all asleep. The moon has kept me company in my long wait. But you can't get through the door, in your absurd costume. This is going too far, this is no joke! Now stop it! And you do not move, why don't you speak to me? You frighten me. Listen, the people say that you must die and they are making very serious faces. Die! Their faces make me laugh! Die! What kind of a word is that? Tell me, Camille! To die! I'll think about it. There—there it is! I'll run after it. Come, my sweet friend, help me catch it! Come, come!   (*She runs away.*)

CAMILLE (*shouts*). Lucile! Lucile!

SCENE 5. *The Conciergerie. Danton, at a window which opens into the adjoining room; Camille, Philippeau, Lacroix, Hérault.*

DANTON. Now you are quiet, Fabre.

A VOICE (*from the other room*). I'm dying.

DANTON. And do you know what we are going to do now?

THE VOICE. Well?

DANTON. Something you have been doing all your life— *des vers!* [1]

CAMILLE (*to himself*). Madness gleamed behind her eyes. Many people have gone mad before—that is the way it goes. What can we do about it? We wash our hands of it. And it is best that way.

DANTON. I am leaving everything in terrible confusion. None

[1] The plural *"vers"* has a double meaning: "verses" (poetry) and "worms."

of them knows anything about governing. It might yet work out if I could leave my whores to Robespierre and my legs to Couthon.

LACROIX. We would have made a whore of liberty!

DANTON. What of it! Liberty and whores are the most cosmopolitan things under the sun. Now Liberty will prostitute herself most decently on the marital couch of the advocate from Arras. Yet, I have an idea that she may act the part of Clytemnestra against him. I don't give him more than six months—I shall drag him along!

CAMILLE. Heaven may send her a comfortable fixed idea. The usual fixed ideas, which we call "common sense," are unbearably boring. He would be the most fortunate of men who could imagine himself to be God Father, Son, and Holy Ghost.

LACROIX. Those idiots will shout "Long live the Republic," when we come by.

DANTON. Does it matter? The deluge of the Revolution may deposit our bodies wherever it decides. Our fossilized bones will still be good for bashing in the heads of kings.

HÉRAULT. Yes, if there happens to be a Samson to use our jaw bones.

DANTON. They bear the mask of Cain.

LACROIX. There is no more convincing proof that Robespierre is a Nero than the fact that he was never more friendly toward Camille than two days before his arrest. Isn't that true, Camille?

CAMILLE. Suppose that it is true, what does it matter? (*To himself.*) How lovely is this child of hers, her madness! Why must I leave just now? Together we could have laughed with it and rocked and kissed it.

DANTON. Once History opens her vaults, the aroma of our corpses may still be enough to suffocate the tyrants.

HÉRAULT. We stank enough while we were alive. These are phrases for posterity, Danton. They don't really have anything to do with us.

CAMILLE. He makes a face as if it were to petrify and be dug up by posterity as an antique. It's really not worth the trouble to purse your lips, to put on a little rouge and to talk with a refined accent! We ought to take off our masks for once; then we would see, as in a gallery of mirrors, everywhere the same age-old, toothless and indestructible blockhead—no more and no less. The differences aren't very great. We are all villains and angels, fools and geniuses, all in one. These four are not as huge as we usually think, there's room for all of them in the same body. Sleep, digest, make children, that everybody does. And all the rest is nothing but variations on a theme, played in different keys. There's really no need to walk on tiptoes and make faces, no need to be so bashful in front of each other! We've all been eating more than our fill at the same table, now we have a bellyache. Why do you hold the napkins in front of your faces? Go ahead, scream and moan to express what you feel! Only don't make such virtuous, witty, heroic, and inspired grimaces! After all, we know each other, save yourselves the trouble.

HÉRAULT. Yes, Camille, let us sit next to each other and scream. Nothing is more stupid than to bite your lips when something hurts. The Greeks and their gods used to scream, the Romans and the Stoics grimaced heroically.

DANTON. They were all good Epicureans, one as much as the other. They tailored themselves quite a cozy self-respect. It's not a bad idea to drape the toga and look over your shoulder to see if you cast a long shadow. Why make such a fuss? What does it matter whether we tie laurel leaves, a wreath of roses, or vine leaves in front of our genitals or whether we carry the ugly thing open and let the dogs lick it?

PHILIPPEAU. Friends, one need not stand very high above the surface of the earth to lose sight of all the confusion, the flutter and the glittering; your eyes will be completely filled with the sight of a few great, divine lines. There is an ear which hears all the confused shouting and the cries of distress—which stupefy us—as a stream of perfect harmonies.

DANTON. Yes, but we are the poor musicians and our bodies the instruments. Are those ugly sounds which are amateurishly squeezed out of them destined only to rise higher and higher and, finally fading into silence, to die in heavenly ears like a voluptuous breath?

HÉRAULT. Are we like sucking pigs which are whipped to death for the table of princes so that their meat will be tastier?

DANTON. Are we children, who are roasted in the fiery Moloch arms of this world and tickled with a few rays of light, so the gods may laugh at their laughter?

CAMILLE. Is the ether, with its golden eyes, nothing but a dish with golden carps that stands on the table of the blissful gods, and the blissful gods laugh forever and the fish die forever and the gods delight forever in the play of colors during their death struggle?

DANTON. The world is chaos. Nothingness is the World-God, still unborn.

(*The* JAILER *enters.*)

WARDER. Gentlemen, you may now go. The carriages are at the door.

PHILIPPEAU. Good night, my friends! Let us calmly spread over us the great blanket, under which all hearts cease to beat and all eyes close. (*They embrace each other.*)

HÉRAULT (*taking* CAMILLE'*s arm*). Be glad, Camille. We are going to have a beautiful night. The clouds hang in the still evening sky like a fading Olympus with paling figures of the sinking gods. (*They leave.*)

SCENE 6. *A room. Julie alone.*

JULIE. Crowds were running around in the streets. Now all is quiet. I don't want to let him wait even one moment. (*She takes a vial from her garment.*) Come, you beloved priest, whose Amen sends us to bed. (*She steps to the window.*) It is so pleasant to take leave. All that is left to do now is close the door behind me. (*She drinks.*)

It would be nice to stand like this forever. The sun has gone down. The earth had such sharp features in its light, but now her face is serene and solemn like that of a dying woman. How beautifully the evening light plays around her forehead and cheeks. Paler and paler, like a corpse it floats downstream on the ether's current. Won't any arm reach out to grasp her golden locks, to pull her out of the river and bury her?

I leave quietly. I won't kiss her, so that not one breath, not one sigh may disturb her slumber. Sleep, sleep! (*She dies.*)

SCENE 7. *The Square of the Revolution. The tumbrils drive up and stop in front of the guillotine. Men and Women sing and dance the Carmagnole. The Prisoners intone the Marseillaise.*

A WOMAN WITH CHILDREN. Make room there! Make room! My children are crying from hunger. To keep them quiet I have to let them get a good look. Room there!

A WOMAN. Eh, Danton, now you can seduce the worms!

ANOTHER WOMAN. Hérault, I'll have myself a wig made from your beautiful hair.

HÉRAULT. My forest isn't thick enough to cover a *mons Veneris* that's been deforested as much as yours.

CAMILLE. Damned witches! Before you're through you'll shout "Ye mountains, fall upon us!"

A WOMAN. The mountain has fallen on you, or rather you've fallen off the mountain.

DANTON (to CAMILLE). Never mind them, my boy. You're hoarse from shouting.

CAMILLE (gives the DRAYMAN some money). There, old Charon, your tumbril is a good serving platter! Gentlemen, I will be served as the first course. This is a classical banquet. We lie on our cushions and spill a little blood as libation. Farewell, Danton! (He mounts the steps of the scaffold, followed, one after the other, by the other prisoners, DANTON last.)

LACROIX (to the crowd). You kill us on the day you lost your reason; you will kill them the day you regain it.

SEVERAL VOICES. We've heard that before. What a bore!

LACROIX. The tyrants will break their necks stumbling over our graves.

HÉRAULT (to DANTON). He thinks his corpse will be a hotbed for liberty.

PHILIPPEAU (on top of the scaffold). I forgive you. I hope that your hour of death may not be harsher than mine.

HÉRAULT. I thought so! He simply has to pull out his shirt once more to show the people down there that his linen is clean.

FABRE. Farewell, Danton! I die a double death.

DANTON. Adieu, my friend. The guillotine is the best doctor.

HÉRAULT (trying to embrace DANTON). Oh, Danton, I can't even think of a joke any more. That means the time has come. (A hangman pushes him back.)

DANTON (to the hangman). Do you want to be more cruel than death? You can't prevent our heads from kissing at the bottom of the basket!

SCENE 8. A street.

LUCILE. There is something serious about this, after all. I want to think about it a little. Something is dawning on me.

Dying—dying! Everything is allowed to live, this tiny mosquito there and the bird. Why not he? The whole stream of life would stop if only this one drop were spilled. The blow would open a wound in the earth.

Everything moves, the clocks tick, the bells ring, people run around, the water flows, and so everything goes on until— no! It must not happen. I'll sit down on the ground and scream so that everything is frightened to a standstill, stops dead—that nothing moves. (*She sits down, covers her eyes and lets out a scream. After a pause, she rises again.*) That doesn't work either. Everything is exactly as it always is, the houses, the street, the wind blows, the clouds move. It seems that we must live with it. (SEVERAL WOMEN *come down the street.*)

FIRST WOMAN. A handsome man, that Hérault.

SECOND WOMAN. When he stood by the triumphal arch on Constitution Day, I sort of thought that he would look quite well on the guillotine, I thought. That must have been a premonition.

THIRD WOMAN. Yes, one should be able to see people in all situations. It's a good thing that dying is getting to be such a public affair. (*They pass on.*)

LUCILE. Oh, Camille! Where shall I look for you now?

SCENE 9. *Place de la Révolution. Two executioners working at the guillotine.*

FIRST EXECUTIONER (*stands on the guillotine and sings*).
  And when home I go
  The moon shines so. . . .

SECOND EXECUTIONER. Hey! Are you going to finish soon?

FIRST EXECUTIONER. In a minute! (*He sings.*)
  The moon shines in my father's window,
  Fellow, where have you been so long?
There! Give me my coat! (*Both leave, singing.*)
  And when home I go
  The moon shines so . . .

LUCILE (*entering and sitting down on the steps of the scaffold*). I shall sit on your lap, you silent angel of death. (*She sings.*)
  There is a reaper, he's called Death,
  Has power from Almighty God.
Dear cradle who has rocked my Camille to sleep, who suffocated him with your roses. Bell of Death who sang at his grave with your sweet voice. (*She sings.*)
  Their number is legion, no one knows
  How many his sickle has mown.
(*A patrol enters.*)

CITIZEN. Halt, who goes there?

LUCILE (*lost in thought, suddenly comes to a decision*). Long live the King!

CITIZEN. In the name of the Republic!
                    (*She is surrounded by the guard and taken away.*)
                    CURTAIN

SELECTED BIBLIOGRAPHY

GENERAL

Robertson, J. G., *A History of German Literature*. London, 1959.

DRAMA

Mann, Otto, *Geschichte des deutschen Dramas*. Stuttgart, 1960.

Bruford, W.H., *Theatre, Drama, and Audience in Goethe's Germany*. London, 1950.

Wiese, B.v. (ed.), *Das Deutsche Drama vom Barock zur Gegenwart*, Düsseldorf, 1958.

LESSING

Garland, H.B., *Lessing, the Founder of Modern German Literature*. Cambridge, 1937.

GOETHE

Fairley, B., *A Study of Goethe*. Oxford, 1947.

Vietor, K., *Goethe the Poet*. Cambridge (Mass.), 1949.

Bergstraesser, A., *Goethe's Image of Man and Society*. Chicago, 1949.

Peacock, R., *Goethe's Major Plays*. Manchester, 1959.

Wilkinson, E.M., "The Relation of Form and Meaning in Goethe's Egmont." Publ. Engl. Goethe Society, 1949.

SCHILLER

Garland, H.B., *Schiller*. London, 1949.

Witte, W., *Schiller*. Oxford, 1949.

Stahl, E.L., *Friedrich Schiller's Drama. Theory and Practice*. Oxford, 1954.

Kaufman, F.W., *Schiller, Poet of Philosophical Idealism*. Oberlin, 1942.

Mann, Thomas, "On Schiller," in *Last Essays*. New York, 1959.

KLEIST

Blankenagel, J.C., *The Dramas of Heinrich von Kleist*. Chapel Hill, 1931.

March, R., *Heinrich von Kleist*. New Haven, 1954.

Silz, W., *Heinrich von Kleist*. Philadelphia, 1961.

Stahl, E.L., *Heinrich von Kleist's Dramas*. Oxford, 1948.

BÜCHNER
   Knight, A.H.J., *Georg Büchner*. Oxford, 1951.
   Peacock, R., "A Note on Georg Büchner's Plays," in *The Poet in the Theatre*. New York, 1946.

The woodcuts on the cover of this
Bantam Classic are reproduced through
the courtesy of the picture collection
of the New York Public Library.

BANTAM CLASSICS

are chosen from the whole span of living
literature. They comprise a balanced
selection of the best novels, poems, plays
and stories by writers whose works and
thoughts have made an indelible impact
on Western culture.

BANTAM CLASSICS

NOVELS

(continued on next page)

SEVEN PLAYS BY AUGUST STRINDBERG.......SC70 75¢
  (Introduction by John Gassner)
FIVE PLAYS BY OSCAR WILDE.................FC80 50¢
  (Introduction by Hesketh Pearson)
FIVE PLAYS BY GERHART HAUPTMANN......HC107 60¢
  (Introduction by John Gassner)
HAMLET William Shakespeare (Edited by Oscar Campbell)...FC114 50¢
MACBETH William Shakespeare (Edited by Oscar Campbell).FC115 50¢
JULIUS CAESAR William Shakespeare.................FC116 50¢
  (Edited by Oscar Campbell)
ROMEO AND JULIET William Shakespeare...........FC117 50¢
  (Edited by Oscar Campbell)
FOUR GREAT PLAYS By IBSEN.................HC177 60¢
  (Introduction by John Gassner)
LAST PLAYS OF IBSEN..........................HC94 60¢
  (Translated by Arvid Paulson)

COLLECTIONS

HENRY JAMES: FIFTEEN SHORT STORIES......SC84 75¢
  (Introduction by Morton D. Zabel)
75 SHORT MASTERPIECES: STORIES FROM THE WORLD'S
LITERATURE (Edited by Roger B. Goodman)...........HC106 60¢
FIFTY GREAT POETS...........................NC104 95¢
  (Edited by Milton Crane)
KEATS: POEMS AND SELECTED LETTERS.....SC127 75¢
MILTON: POEMS AND SELECTED PROSE......NC128 95¢
SWIFT: GULLIVER'S TRAVELS AND OTHER
WRITINGS...SC165 75¢
  (Edited by Miriam Starkman)

NON-FICTION

ONLY YESTERDAY Frederick Lewis Allen.............FC15 50¢
THE BIG CHANGE Frederick Lewis Allen.............FC79 50¢
SINCE YESTERDAY Frederick Lewis Allen............HC126 60¢
BEYOND THE PLEASURE PRINCIPLE Sigmund Freud FC49 50¢
  (Translated by James Strachey—Introduction and Notes by
  Dr. Gregory Zilboorg)
GROUP PSYCHOLOGY AND THE ANALYSIS
OF THE EGO Sigmund Freud.........................FC58 50¢
  (Translated by James Strachey—Introduction by Dr. Franz Alexander)
THE PELOPONNESIAN WAR Thucydides...........NC188 95¢
  (Translated by Benjamin Jowett—Introductions by Hanson Baldwin &
  Moses Hadas)
MY LIFE AND HARD TIMES James Thurber........FC88 50¢
  (Introduction by John K. Hutchens)
BUCKSKIN AND BLANKET DAYS..............HC119 60¢
  Thomas Henry Tibbles

SPANISH DRAMA

Lope de Rueda
The Olives

Cervantes
The Vigilant Sentinel

Lope de Vega
Peribañez

Tirso de Molina
The Rogue of Seville

Alarcón
The Truth Suspected

Calderón
Life is a Dream

Moratín
When a Girl Says Yes

Echegaray
The Great Galeoto

Benavente
The Bonds of Interest

Lorca
Blood Wedding

Edited and with an introduction by
Angel Flores

75¢ wherever Bantam Classics are sold